TECHNOLOGICAL CHANGE AND INDUSTRIAL TRANSFORMATION

Industrial transformation is a research and teaching field with a focus on the phenomenon and mechanisms of industrial development and renewal. It concerns changes in economic activities caused by innovation, competition and collaboration, and has a rich heritage of evolutionary economics, institutional economics, industrial dynamics, technology history and innovation studies. It borrows concepts and models from the social sciences (sociology, history, political sciences, business/management, economics, behavioural sciences) and also from technology and engineering studies.

In this book, the authors present the key theories, frameworks and concepts of industrial transformation and use empirical cases to describe and explain the causes, processes and outcomes of transformation in the context of digitalization and sustainability. They stress that industrial transformation consists both of Darwinian "survival of the fittest" selection, and of intentional pursuits of innovation, and of industrial capabilities creation. The work argues that managing the global trends of transformation is not only about new technology and innovation: existing institutional settings and dynamic interactions between technological change, organizational adaptation and economic activities also have a profound impact on future trajectories.

The areas under investigation are of great relevance for strategic management decisions and industrial and technology policies, and understanding the mechanisms underlying transformation and sustainable growth.

Vicky Long is an Assistant Professor at the Centre for Innovation, Entrepreneurship and Learning (CIEL) research, Halmstad University, Sweden, and an Associated Researcher at the Ratio Institute. Her current research centres on the digital transformation of Intellectual Property Rights-related appropriability regimes.

Magnus Holmén is a Professor in Innovation Sciences at Halmstad University, Sweden, where he is the Research Director of the Centre for Innovation, Entrepreneurship and Learning (CIEL) research. His current research interests include innovation processes, business model innovation, industrial transformation and digitalization.

RIOT!

Routledge Studies in Innovation, Organizations and Technology

Developing Capacity for Innovation in Complex Systems
Strategy, Organisation and Leadership
Christer Vindeløv-Lidzélius

How is Digitalization Affecting Agri-food?
New Business Models, Strategies and Organizational Forms
Edited by Maria Carmela Annosi and Federica Brunetta

Social Innovation of New Ventures
Achieving Social Inclusion and Sustainability in Emerging Economies and Developing Countries
Marcela Ramírez-Pasillas, Vanessa Ratten and Hans Lundberg

Sustainable Innovation
Strategy, Process and Impact
Edited by Cosmina L. Voinea, Nadine Roijakkers and Ward Ooms

Management in the Age of Digital Business Complexity
Edited by Bill McKelvey

Citizen Activities in Energy Transition
User Innovation, New Communities, and the Shaping of a Sustainable Future
Sampsa Hyysalo

How Ideas Move
Theories and Models of Translation in Organizations
John Damm Scheuer

Managing IT for Innovation
Dynamic Capabilities and Competitive Advantage
Mitsuru Kodama

Technological Change and Industrial Transformation
Edited by Vicky Long and Magnus Holmén

For more information about this series, please visit: www.routledge.com/Routledge-Studies-in-Innovation-Organizations-and-Technology/book-series/RIOT

TECHNOLOGICAL CHANGE AND INDUSTRIAL TRANSFORMATION

Edited by Vicky Long and Magnus Holmén

Routledge
Taylor & Francis Group
LONDON AND NEW YORK

First published 2022
by Routledge
2 Park Square, Milton Park, Abingdon, Oxon OX14 4RN

and by Routledge
605 Third Avenue, New York, NY 10158

Routledge is an imprint of the Taylor & Francis Group, an informa business

British Library Cataloguing-in-Publication Data
A catalogue record for this book is available from the British Library

Library of Congress Cataloging-in-Publication Data
Names: Long, Vicky, 1971- editor. | Holmén, Magnus, editor.
Title: Technological change and industrial transformation / edited by Vicky Long and Magnus Holmén.
Description: 1 Edition. | New York : Routledge, 2021. | Series: Routledge studies in innovation, organizations and technology | Includes bibliographical references and index.
Identifiers: LCCN 2021006952 (print) | LCCN 2021006953 (ebook)
Subjects: LCSH: Industries--Technological innovations. | Technological innovations--Economic aspects. | Industrial organization (Economic theory) | Evolutionary economics.
Classification: LCC HD2326 .T423 2021 (print) | LCC HD2326 (ebook) | DDC 338/.064--dc23
LC record available at https://lccn.loc.gov/2021006952
LC ebook record available at https://lccn.loc.gov/2021006953

ISBN: 978-1-138-39002-7 (hbk)
ISBN: 978-1-138-39003-4 (pbk)
ISBN: 978-0-429-42355-0 (ebk)

Typeset in Bembo
by Deanta Global Publishing Services, Chennai, India

CONTENTS

CONTRIBUTORS

Steinunn Arnardóttir is Senior Director of Engineering at Native Instruments, Berlin, Germany, where she leads a team of 80+ people. Native Instruments is a leading manufacturer of software and complementary hardware for computer-based music production and DJing. Among Native's product portfolio is Kontakt, which is a widely used software program in film music production. Previously, she was a part of Native's research team as a DSP Developer where she worked on audio effects such as compressors, limiters, reverbs and filters for most of the company's product range, including Maschine, Traktor, GuitarRig and Kontakt. She holds a BSc in Electrical and Computer Engineering from the University of Iceland and an MA in Music Science and Technology and an MSc in Electrical Engineering, both from Stanford University.

Klas A.M. Eriksson is a PhD student at Stockholm University and an Associate Researcher at the Ratio Institute, Stockholm, Sweden. His research interests include institutions, disruptive innovations, cultural economic history, structural transformations and urban history. He also teaches the history of economic ideas at Stockholm University.

Andrea Geissinger is a PhD student in business administration at Örebro University and the Ratio Institute, Stockholm, Sweden. She has a strong interest in societal change processes facilitated by technological drivers. Her main research focuses on the specific societal challenges and opportunities that arise out of the sharing economy for individuals and organizations alike.

Jonas Grafström is an Assistant Professor at Luleå University of Technology and a researcher at Ratio-Näringslivets forskningsinstitut in Stockholm, Sweden. Furthermore, he is a visiting fellow at Oxford Institute for Energy Studies.

His research focus is employment and technological change. He has also published research about energy economics and energy policy.

Magnus Holmén is a Professor in Innovation Sciences with a focus on Industrial Management at Halmstad University in Sweden. He is the Research Director for the Centre for Innovation, Entrepreneurship and Learning (CIEL) research at Halmstad University, and he is a Visiting Professor at Innovation and entrepreneurship at the Department of Economy and Society at the University of Gothenburg. His research interests involve the micro, meso and macro levels with a focus on knowledge and technology creation. During his PhD, he studied the emergence of technological innovations systems within regions. As a research associate at the Australian National University, he studied the emergence and growth of innovation systems. His current research interests include processes of business model innovation, industrial transformation and the evolution of new technologies such as additive manufacturing and AI.

Petter Johansson is a Researcher at the Institute of Innovation and Technology, Göteborg, Sweden. His areas of research interest are in the fields of industrial dynamics, innovation management and business strategy. His fields of study have focused primarily on the energy area and energy-related technological transitions. In recent years, he has focused on structural changes in the electricity sector.

Örn D. Jónsson is a Professor of Innovation and Entrepreneurship at the Faculty of Business Administration at the University of Iceland, Reykjavik, Iceland. Örn was the director of the Fisheries Research Institute at the university and previously a Vice Director of the Technological Institute of Iceland. His field of study has been on the innovative and transient aspects of the user-driven production and consumption of geothermal energy in everyday living. In recent years, his studies have furthermore included diversified aspects of the multifaceted ties emerging from the shift from national to supranational platform-based ties.

Staffan Laestadius is Professor Emeritus of Industrial Dynamics at the Royal Institute of Technology (KTH) in Stockholm, Sweden. He is also a board member and Senior Advisor at the independent think tank Global Utmaning and was a 2015–2016 member of the Swedish Government Commission on Green Transformation. During recent years, Laestadius has analysed the conditions for Swedish and European societies to combine industrial and social transformation with climate change mitigation and adaptation. He is a frequent policy advisor, lecturer and expert contributor to the public and academic discussion on those issues. His most recent books are *Triple Challenge for Europe: Economic Development, Climate Change, and Governance* (ed., 2015, Oxford: Oxford University Press), *Klimatet och omställningen* (2018, Stockholm: Borea) and *En strimma av hopp* (2021, Stockholm: Verbal förlag).

Vicky Long is an Assistant Professor at the Centre for Innovation, Entrepreneurship and Learning (CIEL) research, Halmstad University, and an associated researcher at Ratio-Näringslivets forskningsinstitut in Stockholm, Sweden. Her research is focused on knowledge sourcing, knowledge generation and knowledge appropriation in technology-based firms. Her recent project is about the use of intellectual property rights (IPRs) and other appropriability means in the Swedish video games industry and the digital (transformation) era.

Peter Markowski is a Management Consultant and Researcher, currently residing in Stockholm, Sweden. He obtained his PhD in Operations Management from Stockholm University, Sweden. He also holds an MSc in Industrial engineering and Management from KTH Royal Institute of Technology in Stockholm. Markowski's research interests include organizational capabilities and digitalization. He currently advises organizations on issues of digital transformation and change.

Maria Morgunova is a lecturer at Department of Civil and Industiral Engineering, Uppsala University, Sweden. Maria acquired a PhD degree in International Economics at Gubkin Russian State University of Oil and Gas, and a PhD in Industrial Engineering and Management at KTH Royal Institute of Technology, Sweden. Her key research interests are concentrated around the Arctic region development, energy resources economics and management, and sustainability transitions in energy.

Rasmus Nykvist is a doctoral student at Örebro University and Ratio-Näringslivets forskningsinstitut in Stockholm, and a Research Assistant at the House of Innovation at the Stockholm School of Economics. His current doctoral work is focused on using the privatization and digitalization of the Stockholm Stock Exchange to develop frameworks for understanding the historical relationship between regulation and technology. His general research interest lies in understanding how the interaction between market actors, interest organizations and regulators shape the regulatory responses to major technological transformations.

Rögnvaldur J. Saemundsson is a Professor in Industrial Engineering at the University of Iceland. His research is focused on technology-based innovation and entrepreneurship, especially the dynamics of knowledge and innovation.

Kent Thorén is an accomplished Researcher and Executive Advisor in the fields of strategic foresight, strategy and innovation. He has published many articles that take a wide range of perspectives on the interplay between dynamic industry development and the strategic manoeuvring of firms. Dr Thorén is affiliated with the Department of Industrial Management and Economics at KTH – Royal Institute of Technology in Sweden and the international Strategic Foresight Research Network hosted at Aarhus University, Denmark.

PREFACE

The basic premise of this book is that we want to develop our understanding of industrial transformation by focusing on the role of technology. The idea for this book is hardly new, as many are talking about the need to go back to the early work of Rosenberg, Vincenti and others to highlight the role of technology in shaping how industries emerge, expand, decline and perhaps terminate. Still, we wanted to do this in a modern way by trying to bring in the ongoing and increasingly important phenomena of digitalization and environmental change.

For various reasons, books cannot cover everything. This is certainly the case here. Hard choices have to be made, if nothing else because of format constraints, but more importantly because of limits of time. Indeed, in this book, we have deliberately ignored important phenomena such as the spatial dimensions of industrial transformation, the industrial catching up and technological upgrading dimension, the various forms of innovation systems (and pooled labour markets), the role and changes of formal and informal institutions, such as deregulation and standardization, and the role of higher education institutions or a triple helix setting in industrial transformation.

We wanted a phenomenon-oriented book with empirical chapters addressing industrial transformation in a variety of ways, without too much *ex ante* theorizing or advanced coding or modelling. Basically, the idea was to let the empirical studies speak! This approach nicely fits the style of an edited book.

Moreover, an important part of our intended audience is graduate students in industrial economics and management studies. Many of these so-called *second circle* or *third cycle* students come from a background of engineering training. They need to know and are interested in knowing the cogs and wheels of industrial transformation.

In short, technological knowledge is embedded in industrial activities throughout the process of industrial transformation, and the actors within the sector are the major players. Institutions can act as enablers or constrainers, and sometimes both. Transformation is not an optimization, not a system of general equilibrium. Indeed, Akerlof-ian information asymmetry applies, so do Knightian uncertainty and Simonian bounded rationality. Successful transformation is accompanied by an assimilation process: learning is an active process, rather than a by-product of investment and capital accumulation. Industrial activities vary significantly across industry sectors, not least because the nature of technological knowledge differs across sectors. Without moving down to the meso level, or even to the value-chain level, it is hard to reveal the black box of transformation.

It may be argued that there are many grand challenges – beyond digitalization and environmental changes – that any industry has to deal with in its transformation, say servitization. They are also endogenous elements rather than being contextual. Fundamental structural transformation, namely reallocation of economic activities across broad sectors, has to be in place to ensure a successful one-sector transformation, and the role of technology in that is also to be explored, exemplified not least with Tesla software-based over the air upgrading (OTA). Post-industrial activity is essentially a transcendence of Fordism throughout the economy. The era of the service economy being defined as the residual economy (due to agriculture and industry) is long gone. We may argue that this approach to service activities is embedded in this book (e.g. in service production). It was our intention to cover the *product*, *process* and *service* sectors empirically to probe the post-industrial changes in economic activities.

Moreover, we wanted to include early stage scholars who were working with fresh empirical data, rather than big guns with abstractions that are hard for engineering students to understand.

Many scholars and organizations have contributed to this book. Just to name a few – the Ratio Institute: for providing working and seminar locations and for constructive feedback; Rögnvaldur Saemundsson: apart from being a co-author of two of the chapters, Rögnvaldur helped the editors to sketch the logic and content of the book. We are extremely grateful to him for the time he was able to put in, and for his comments on Chapter 2; Per-Olof Bjuggren: for feedback on Chapter 1; Daniel Ljungberg: for a useful critique of the conclusion chapter; the KTH (The Royal Institute of Technology) Industrial Dynamics research team: for helping with the design and content of the book; Staffan Laestadius, Pär Blomkvist and Petter Johansson: for good discussion about the need for this type of book.

We are grateful to the KK Foundation project "Business model innovation when adapting to digital production – opportunities and problems" (220018), and to the Vinnova project "Appropriability strategies in the Swedish games industry in the digital era" for funding.

Finally, we are grateful to all the chapter authors for stimulating conversations and good work.

It has been a rewarding journey for all who were involved in this process. In our field, we often name-drop Kenneth Arrow's learning-by-doing concept when arguing that continuous practice can lead to productivity. Here we may say the same of learning by editing.

Magnus Holmén and Vicky Long
Halmstad and Stockholm, Sweden
September 2020

1

WHY THIS BOOK?

Vicky Long and Magnus Holmén

Introduction

This book analyses industrial transformation, which broadly refers to changes in the nature of industrial activities: how these activities are organized, what firms and other actors know and do and how they interact with each other. The analysis and explanation of industrial transformation critically depend on the definitions and applied theoretical lenses in use. The terminology *industrial transformation* implies the existence of an industry. What is defined as an industry, however, is changing. Often, an industry refers to a set of competing and collaborating manufacturing and service firms creating, producing and disseminating similar products or services for adjacent markets. While such a view suffices in many cases, the very fact that industries are emerging, converging or diverging and even disappearing (e.g., Kodak film) due to firms' entrepreneurial activities and fundamental changes in technologies, institutions and consumption suggest that the definition of an industry needs to be broader. An industry therefore refers to a set of dynamically changing firms that by interacting are capable of creating, delivering and capturing values.

More precisely, industrial transformation consists of qualitative changes in the types of inter-firm activities as well as in the forms of interactions and relations involved when actors create value and deliver services. Activities include, but are not limited to, those related to innovation, competition and collaboration. Relations and interactions include, but are not limited to, networks and the division of labour between firms.

Industrial transformation as a phenomenon is not new: industries have always changed, arguably at a greater speed during the last few decades. Industrial transformation is also increasingly an international phenomenon, with an even longer tail to its product life cycle, for example. Over time, the main driving forces of the transformation change, and so do the characteristics of the transformation. This book stresses two novel phenomena and challenges: digitalization and sustainability.

Digitalization refers to changes in human and business behaviour enabled by digital technologies. These can be viewed as a result of increased use and diffusion of information and communication technologies (ICT). Recently, digitalization has begun to cover technologies such as digital platforms, cloud computing, the Internet of Things (IoT), autonomous systems, artificial intelligence (AI) and machine learning (ML).

Sustainability covers a balanced development capable of handling challenges in, for example, environmental degradation and (the projected) depletion of natural resources. These challenges are related to the recent labelling of our time as the Anthropocene, in which there is a socio-ecological (im)balance within the environment. The notion of sustainability used here is in line with industrial policy-related transition studies that address how to make the transportation and energy sectors environmentally and economically sustainable, for example. This is distinct from the macro-oriented notion of sustainability used in UN reports, which deals with broad environmental, economic and social challenges, such as overconsumption, social inequalities and ageing populations.

While the two phenomena have been observed and studied for a long time, the novelty in this book is the depth and breadth of interactions between them and industrial activities. Indeed, digitalization and sustainability[1] have hitherto mostly been discussed in a rather separate manner.

The departure of this book is that we argue that if these urgent and prevailing challenges are ever to be met and reconciled, a coherent understanding of industrial transformation is needed. The focus of the book is on the changes in technology that are associated with industrial transformation. Our argument is that an understanding of the cogs and wheels of the changes in technology underlies an understanding of industrial transformation.

Industrial transformation in this book is viewed as a dynamic historical process in the sense that the process incorporates factors that may only be fully manifested over time. Industrial transformation is context specific, with qualitative changes that condition quantitative steps, and vice versa. This means that industrial transformation can be understood as an interaction between technological change, organizational adaptation and economic activities, and endogenous institutional forces.

Given this, it is clear that industrial transformation is a dynamic process, embracing changes in (types of) *actors*, (types of) *activities* (what they do) and (types of) *interactive norms* (e.g., standardization in telecommunication industries). It should be noted that while firms are normally the main actors in a capitalistic regime, this does not exclude other actors, such as universities, non-profit organizations, public organizations and authorities, from playing pervasive, necessary and critical roles in initiating, guiding, shaping, constraining or terminating industrial transformation processes.

The aspirations of actors are crucial because industrial transformation is largely endogenously driven. An endogenous process is a change from within, even when such a process is triggered and affected by responses to external pulls and shocks such as changes in institutions and technologies. For example, industrial entry may at times be necessary for industrial transformation, but the entry of new firms into a sector is insufficient to explain the nature and outcome of the process. However, industrial transformation is not an isolated process, but an open one. Thus, it may involve restructuring and adaptation in, for example, a globalized value chain or a globalized circular economy.

Industrial transformation is not an automatic process. We argue that industrial transformation is the result of intentions, driven by the aspirations of firms and other organizations. These intentions can be seen in proactive behaviours such as an active adoption of Industry 4.0 in manufacturing processes. Intentions can also be seen in problem-solving-based reactive behaviours, exemplified by the reorientation of the pulp-and-paper industry in the era of a dramatic downturn of newspaper demand to produce recyclable plastics. This means that industrial transformation is, to a certain extent, predetermined by changes in (types of) inputs and regulations.

Here we also subscribe to the importance of learning endeavour argued by the assimilation school, which deviated from the arguments put forward by the accumulation school (cf. Nelson and Pack, 1999). While the latter – the accumulation school – argues that learning is a by-product of capital investment, for example, the former – the assimilation school – argues that learning is an intentional behaviour that requires arduous effort. However, this does not imply that the intentions and aspirations of central firms and other actors are sufficient. An accumulation of production factors (capital, labour) is also necessary. Indeed, transformation may be the unintended consequence of the aspirations and activities of competing firms, for example.

This means that industrial transformation involves uncertainty of different kinds: (a) the Knightian (1921) uncertainty, namely that we do not know future outcomes and nor can we assign any measurable probabilities; (b) the Rosenbergian (1996) uncertainty, namely that the rate and direction of technological change are unknowable; and (c) the organizational (learning) uncertainties due to the presence of bounded rationality and tacit knowledge. Industrial transformation therefore needs to move away from equilibrium analysis by treating technology evolution and competition as an open-ended process, along which many actors can have a say (with varied power, though).

Much of the time, industrial transformation is a cumulative process, implying it is path dependent. This implies that organizational capabilities, routines and technological trajectories play key roles in shaping the development. Therefore, industrial transformation needs to be understood as dealing with the creation, survival and death of firms and other types of organizations, and not limited to aspects of growth and success.

Given our stress on uncertainty and the dynamics of changes, this book consists of process-oriented studies of industrial transformation. The empirical chapters embrace historical elaborations on the causes, conditions and pathways of this new wave of transformation, where technologies are deployed, actors are engaged, forms of interactions are adjusted and consumption patterns are derived and/or coevolved.[2]

In the following, we present in detail the objectives of this book and the key contributions of this volume.

The new stylized facts

What has happened in recent years at the *digitalization* front and at the *sustainability* front that calls for the contribution of this book?

Digitalization

The word *digitalization* can be viewed as an umbrella concept that embraces:

- Technological developments in fields like big data, cloud computing, the IoT, ML, AI and Industry 4.0.
- The rapid growth of artefacts, applications, services, processes, standards (protocols) and platforms produced by industry actors, ranging from basic connectivity (switches and grids) to highly interactive and big data analysis-based content services (Facebook, Uber). Some products (smart grid) are relevant to specific industries and customer segments, but increasingly more products and offerings (augmented reality, Swish/Alipay as a mobile payment app) have a platform function, a *generic* enabling function, which is instrumental to the transformations of other industry sectors and the whole of society.
- Observed laws and regularities such as Moore's law[3] and the "second half of the chess board",[4] related to the rate and the direction of technological development.
- Mechanisms such as increasing returns, network effect and externalities. Increasing returns due to the scale and scope of development, production and adoption are frequently observed (e.g., in operating systems); network effects arise on the demand side (e.g. in Facebook, *World of Warcraft*), creating a bandwagon effect. It may be assumed that when some of the mechanisms are in operation, there is an effective tendency towards monopoly (as indicated by Google or Amazon, for example). Such an outcome, however, is not predetermined because these mechanisms may also be counteracted by new technologies, policies or competitive forces. Blockchain, for example, supports peer-based collaboration and a decentralized governance system.

The above lists embrace both ontological and epistemological developments under the umbrella of digitalization. While most of the above-mentioned stylized facts have arguably been observed and discussed quite recently, we should keep in mind that the digitalization process has not occurred overnight. Long (2016, p. 225) argues that digitalization has been an ongoing process for at least five decades, with the first two decades (the 1970s and 1980s) consisting of technological breakthroughs in major sub-ICTs (e.g., integrated circuits, LANs) and the last three decades (1990s–) with a wide range of industrial deployments and transformations throughout the economy (mobile, cloud, big data, analytics, visualization, the IoT, smart machines and AI).

Sustainability

The terminology of sustainability is used in different ways, broadly referring to making human activities environmentally, socially and economically viable. From an environmental perspective, in the field of *sustainability*, there is a huge number of reports that are updated daily (e.g., the UN Environment Emissions Cap Report[5]), presenting alarming figures and projections. In this book, sustainability is an environmentally oriented umbrella concept that has links with industrial transformation at the following points.

- *It causes changes in the relative prices of the factors (land, labour, capital) of production.* There is a growing consensus that the widespread problems of pollution and climate change are caused by humankind's over-utilization of finite (natural) resources. The recent labelling of our time as the *Anthropocene*[6] speaks of the human-influenced atmospheric, geologic, hydrologic and biospheric conditions, which arguably threaten to wipe out other species. This changes the factor endowments of a country in general and the conditions for industrial development and transformation in particular regions. For example, a regional drought can cause the shutdown or relocation of process industries (e.g., Coca-Cola production, paper mills). At the same time, a change in environmental conditions is itself a spur to innovation, in a Hicks-ian (1932) manner, such that innovation can be directed to economizing the use of a factor that has become relatively expensive.
- *It causes changes in the paths and directions in which a firm actually goes exploring for new technologies and development.* Many argue that humankind is rapidly approaching planetary boundaries. A transition towards sustainable alternatives, in both consumption and production, is both necessary and urgent. This change is far from trivial. Production, as well as consumption, is path dependent, causing a so-called carbon lock-in (Unruh, 2000), which is also visible in lifestyles. A planetary boundary is a factor at work that compels firms to look in some directions rather than others. An effectiveness improvement is argued to be insufficient where, say, the increased fuel efficiency of cars is becoming irrelevant because of the increasing numbers of cars. This implies that for a number of industries, path creation rather

than path dependency is warranted. A recent example would be moving away from internal combustion engine vehicles to battery electric vehicles.

- *It calls for changes in the role of public policy.* It may be argued that the increasing changes in atmospheric, geologic, hydrologic and biospheric conditions are slowing down or even putting a stop to the capitalist engine, which is, as argued by Landes (1998), unbounded and driven by continuous technological advancement. Technological advancement is sometimes depicted as S-curves (cf. Foster, 1986), with rapid advances for a while before decreasing returns set in, and where the technology fails to cross a threshold from the perspective of performance or use value. Environmental degradation can set a performance ceiling for the current S-curves as some trajectories are not environmentally viable. One way to reduce the cost is to legitimize the intervention of science, technology and innovation policy. Schot and Steinmueller (2018) argue that this can be done if public policy focuses on the *directionality* of pathways of development and sociocultural lifestyles.
- *It calls for a new assessment on the role of technology.* The so-called technological fix view – the idea that all problems can find solutions in technologies – has somewhat disappeared or at least been toned down when the above-mentioned grand challenges are concerned. It is now recognized that there are limits on how much technologies can solve, at least within the short and medium term. Carbon capture and storage technologies, for example, have hitherto mostly been used close to large point sources (e.g., to treat a cement factory), rather than be operated for large-scale direct air capture. The role of incremental innovations along the existing lines of technological solutions, however, may be recognized. Recently, a surprising (and counterintuitive) trend of dematerialization has been observed. Phrased as "with less we produced more" (McAfee, 2019), dematerialization refers to a statistically shown trend that some (advanced) economies have managed to grow while using fewer (raw) materials (e.g. nickel, gold, fertilizer, water for irrigation and timber). The capitalist engine – including the quest for efficiency – has acted as the driving force in that process. The advancement of (digital) technologies is also part of the explanation. This dematerialization may reduce the severity of the climate change problem.

What do the new stylized facts imply for industrial transformation?

Digitalization embraces the development of many technologies that can be referred to as *General Purpose Technologies* (GPTs) (Bresnahan and Trajtenberg, 1995),[7] such as the IoT and ML. GPTs underlie contemporary transformation into what is labelled *the second machine age* (Brynjolfsson and McAfee, 2012, 2014) with a bounty on the one hand and a spread on the other. *Bounty* refers to the mass opportunities that the exponentially growing digital capacity offers.

Spread refers to the large emerging gaps among people in income, wealth and skills that follow.

GPTs modify the factor prices underlying technical change and industrial transformation and help to shape the trajectory of transformation. To elaborate, a factor price is the unit cost of using a factor (e.g., land, labour, capital) of production. Much technological change allows for attempts to replace the more expensive factor (e.g., labour cost in OECD countries) or to increase the overall efficiency. The demand for digital technologies in monitoring, controlling, optimization and automation (e.g., in driverless cars) may increase even faster to reduce the cost of labour. Network effects may emerge, particularly when a new technological standard is adopted. When the demand responds in a reciprocal manner to the technological supply,[8] increasing returns occur in production and adoption and a new technological trajectory is formed.

The above implications are confined to the established theorizing around factors affecting the rate and direction of industrial transformation, and by treating digital technologies, including autonomous systems and AI, as key enabling technologies that increase productivity. Three less-discussed aspects of digitalization that affect the magnitude and outcome of industrial transformation follow.

First, the deepening of digitalization may decentralize *the governance structure*, also referred to as the "multi-stakeholderization [of Internet governance]" (Brown and Marsden, 2013), for example, via the use of blockchains. Social networks can introduce virtual currencies (e.g., Libra offered by Facebook) since platforms often operate two-sided markets. Words like the sharing economy and apps like TikTok exemplify this trend. This blurs the boundaries between supply and demand and creates different types of interactions central to any industrial transformation. It is difficult to foresee whether this will become the norm of Internet governance or just another structural variety of interactions. Nonetheless, the changes in the governance structure will affect the degree of openness in data management, and in patterns of interactions[9] such as competition or innovative activities among industry actors.

Second, the deepening of digitalization such as the use of AI technologies is claimed to lead towards a virtual economy (Arthur, 2017) that is running at its own pace in part independently of the physical world. There is a system of information (and knowledge) that is external to human beings, and even in the best case is only partly grasped by human beings. How and to which extent does this AI wave and its related innovations differ from, for example, the Fordism (mass production) introduced in the early twentieth century in its transformative power and competition? The debates related to this have hitherto mostly concerned technological unemployment, arguing that machines will replace lots of occupations. This (un)employment problem is not new in the transformation literature: this perspective was covered by John Maynard Keynes (1930).

Technical change, like industrial transformation in the long run, has always been skill-based, implying that technological changes will qualitatively and quantitatively affect the labour market. While the demand for at least some types of skills will increase as new technologies are introduced, what they are will only become clear over time. This can be exemplified by the (semi-skilled) assembly line managers needed for Fordism production. More theoretically, Adam Smith's pin factory case shows that the extension of the division of labour is also an extension of the division of (specialized) skills. If a virtual economy will be running in parallel with our physical economy, there is then a radical element in the often cumulative transformation. It is then perhaps more than a paradigm shift,[10] as there are places that human cognition cannot reach. It is hard to know whether firms and industries will have the capacity to utilize the knowledge generated in the virtual economy, and the impact on industrial transformation is uncertain.

Third, the deepening of digitalization is not only an endogenous mechanism of industrial transformation but also an endogenous factor for societal transformation, which in turn affects industrial transformation. There is therefore a need to look at broader issues to understand industrial transformation. For example, in the case of a cashless society transformation, where emerging economies such as China are rapidly catching up (with Alipay, WeChat Pay, etc.), the technology development per se does not explain that much. The vested interests, the (infrastructural) conditions, the absorptive capacity and perhaps the general evolutionary mechanisms have equally important explanatory powers. For example, the mobile-based payment app *M-pesa* in Kenya took off in 2007, while the Swedish alternative *Swish* did not kick off until 2012. The availability of technology does not explain why Kenya adopted the new services so early. Rather there was a lock-in to a VISA- or MasterCard-based payment system in developed economies that led to a delayed response to the more advanced (mobile) payment system. Digitalization is therefore only part of the story of the societal transformation. The causal arrows can go both ways.

Digitalization is not the only current phenomenon influencing industrial transformation. Environmental degradation, or more precisely, the expectation of firms, markets and politics around environmental degradation, sets a limit for industrial transformation that in turn shapes the rate and the direction of the transformation. This has affected practitioners, customers and academics alike, stressing the concept of *sustainability*, going back to Schumacher's (1973/2011) well-known formulation, small is beautiful. Related concepts such as *inclusive innovation* and *ecosystems* are established under the sustainability umbrella.

To reach sustainability, much of the industrial transformation – and the industrial catching up from late adopting countries – may embrace path creation rather than path following. For example, industries that are based on fossil fuel-based technologies are expected to be downplayed. Explorations of sustainability would then need to progress simultaneously on several fronts: (a) viable alternatives for technological trajectories are needed and (b) the capabilities and routines that can be extracted from past industrial experiences may be limited, but at the same time there is plenty of scientific knowledge related to the new trajectory capable of being industrially prototyped.

If the work of Schumacher[11] (1973/2011) and Schumpeter[12] (1934, 1942) is combined, localization – and local specialization – will gain new importance, as will the visible hand (e.g. in adjusting policy stimuli packages) (cf. Mazzucato, 2011). Recently, customers and users have demanded sustainable products and services, unlike in a not-so-distant past when sustainability was only an exogenous constraint. This is illustrated by the increasing popularity of ecological food and sustainable fashion (e.g., so-called slow fashion). Sophisticated demand can in turn act as an important pull for innovation as the textbooks suggest. This means that sustainability has started to act as an endogenized factor affecting the rate and the direction of industrial transformation by setting the conditions, affecting the factor prices and changing the utility function (i.e., the measures of the consumer's preferences over a set of goods and services).

Objectives of this book

This book is phenomenon oriented, and it is intended to serve academia and postgraduate students including master's students and doctoral students. The goal of this book is to shed light on the causes, processes and outcomes of industry transformation in the context of dealing with digitalization and sustainability by having an empirical focus and stressing the role of technology and technological change in the transformation process.

To be more concrete, the aims of writing the book are:

- to integrate theoretical pillars and empirical cases and to promote understanding of the complexities of the causal mechanisms in industrial transformation. In other words, there is an intentional preference, a mechanism approach[13] (Elster, 1989, 1998) – on the causes, processes and outcomes of this round of transformation – rather than a construct of strict causation;
- to emphasize the changes in technology that are associated with industrial transformation;
- to combine the hitherto rather separate tracks of industrial transformation debates – one related to environmental degradation or more broadly sustainability and the other one related to digitalization, robotization, AI and the platform economy;

Our intention is to address the phenomenon, to describe and lift up some of the stylized facts and to reflect on some of the key mechanisms, rather than to provide comprehensive answers to the fundamental questions exemplified as follows:

- What is industrial transformation?
- What characterizes industrial transformation? What characterizes the system within which the industrial transformation processes have taken place?

- How do we know that one industry has – digitally and/or sustainably – transformed or not? What measurements or proxies are useful and what are their limitations?
- What are the causes, conditions and driving forces of industrial transformation and growth? Which ones are necessary versus sufficient conditions of a successful transformation? Why?
- What determines the rate and the trajectory of the technological change? Is it an independent process or a coevolution with industry structure (actors, competitions) and institution?
- What are the linkages between the transformation processes and their micro-foundations (e.g. resources, organizational structure, business models)?
- What forces determine the direction(s) in which a firm explores new technology (e.g. Facebook's adoption of blockchain) that in turn underlies its transformation?
- Which frameworks or theories are the most useful for analysing industrial transformation, and for what purposes?

A roadmap for this volume

In addition to the introductory and concluding chapters, this book consists of ten empirical chapters. Chapter 2, by Vicky Long and Magnus Holmén, discusses important aspects of industrial transformation by referring to the prior literature. To do so, the chapter first goes through the industrial transformation proper by reviewing key historical accounts and three thematic approaches. Examples of illustrated literature include studies of evolutionary economics, innovation systems, industrial dynamics, disruption and industry life cycles. It then proceeds to the recent literature on the two novel phenomena addressed in this book: digitalization and sustainability. Finally, it develops the positions adopted in this book.

The following six chapters analyse the relationship between digitalization and industrial transformation. The third chapter, "How digital platforms transform industries", by Kent Thorén, outlines the nature of digitalization and how this affects industries and business models. His chapter describes and explains the logic of platforms and how and why they connect actors differently, allowing for increased variety creation while economizing on resources. In addition, by drawing on publicly available documents, he explains how and why the emergence and use of digital online platforms connect actors into a value-creating ecosystem. His chapter argues the importance of addressing the locus of value appropriation in an industry structure, as ultimately this will determine patterns of innovation and the division of (innovative) labour.

Peter Markowski's chapter (Chapter 4), "Digital transformation of the home help service sector through welfare technology", shows how the extended health sector has changed because of the increased use of digital technologies. By drawing on case studies, he shows that despite the relatively low complexity of new technologies, the nature of the services for the elderly and the relations between subcontractors and subservice providers have changed dramatically. This creates tensions for public organizations delivering services, but it allows for new business opportunities to open. Stuck in the middle are family members who are given the opportunity to care for their relatives but may also get stuck with increased responsibilities. This outlines a potential for a coming transformation of the healthcare sector, with new forms of specialization and new entries of firms, for example, IT companies.

Chapter 5, "Doing more by knowing less: The evolution of the division of innovative labour in software creation", by Magnus Holmén and Rögnvaldur Saemundsson, explains improvements in software creation by focusing on the continued development and support of abstraction mechanisms, which explains why new divisions of innovative labour become feasible and realistic. They argue that this explains innovative and productive improvements across most industries as software has become increasingly important. They sketch an innovation-oriented model based on Allyn Young and Nathan Rosenberg's explanations of cumulative causation. This model addresses the role of abstraction and abstraction mechanisms as a means of increasing the division of (innovative) labour and technological convergence, and thus productivity on the one hand, and for increasing the size of the market by allowing for more customer and user-oriented creation, which in turn affects the division of (innovative) labour, on the other hand.

Chapter 6, "Rags to riches: Digitalization and the transformation of the Icelandic film industry", is written by Örn Jónsson, Steinunn Arnardóttir and Rögnvaldur Saemundsson, focusing on the composition, performance and recording of films and film music in Iceland over four decades. The chapter shows that the boundaries of innovative and routine work have changed because of digitalization. The former, serial approach has changed, and some decisions can be postponed to the post-processing stage because digital technologies allow the designer to control more activities than in the past. At the same time, the new technologies allow isolated regions to source technologies and skills internationally, reducing the importance of the local labour market.

Chapter 7, "What prevents machine learning from transforming industries?" by Vicky Long and Jonas Grafström, describes how ML has been deployed in three firms and which forces are at work in supporting or hindering ML to transform businesses. It identifies that while the value of ML in making sense of vast quantities and varieties of data in business terms is commonly recognized, the hindering effect mainly lies in finding sensible collaborative modes of data access and sharing. ML technology thrives on access to big, comprehensive and varied datasets, which come from multiple sources. There is also an institutional uncertainty, namely specifying the ownership of the data (e.g. machines as authors do not receive copyright protection). What is clear, from a transformation perspective, is that firms' boundaries are disappearing in the era of ML and AI, so new forms of collaboration and competition need to be in place to facilitate an unprecedented level of connectivity and allocate the rents. Transaction cost in a networked world needs to be reassessed and so does the appropriability regime pertinent to industrial transformation.

Chapter 8, "'Own it' or 'share it': Sharing and community aspects of the industrial transformation of the Swedish housing market", written by Rasmus Nykvist, Andrea Geissinger and Klas Eriksson, addresses how changes in technology, institutions and norms have affected the nature of shared housing. The chapter compares the rise of the hybrid sharing model, where affordable housing became possible by having residents owning the right to use a flat and to vote for the governance of the building together with other residents, rather than ownership proper. By drawing on public documents and topic modelling, they analyse the transformation of the housing market's evolution and show similarities and identify differences between today's situation since the emergence of Airbnb and similar flexible sharing models and changes over the last century.

Three chapters relate to environmental issues. The ninth chapter "Industrial transformation in the Anthropocene", by Staffan Laestadius, argues that because of environmental pressures, most explicitly the threat of climate change – the Great Acceleration after World War II – industries will need to change faster than ever before. Based on his reading of the literature on structural change, industrial transformation and other evolutionary approaches, he problematizes the nature of three areas of industrial activities and analyses the conditions and potentials for their transformation within the medium term.

Maria Morgunova's chapter, "Is the oil and natural gas industry transforming? Evidence from the offshore Arctic" (Chapter 10), shows and explains the lack of industrial transformation proper in the offshore Arctic oil and gas industry. This needs to be explained not only from an institutional perspective but also in terms of the importance of competing on a commodity market for explorers, producers and distributors alike. Despite huge technological and organizational challenges, explorers, producers and distributors are shifting their focus from mainstream offshore activities to the severe weather of the Arctic region.

In Chapter 11, Petter Johansson analyses the emergence and transformation of the heat pump sector over 50 years by focusing on a Swedish setting. From a development block perspective, he shows that industrial and institutional coevolution took place due to sequences of complementary investments in upstream and downstream industries, but also in industries that because of technological convergence became related. The industry's growth, crash and re-emergence were largely determined by exogenous shocks in terms of oil prices. Importantly, he shows that a main reason the leading actors survived and became world leaders was because of downstream investments in complementary assets, especially service channels, but this lesson was ignored by the same companies during their internationalization phases.

The concluding chapter by Magnus Holmén and Vicky Long synthesizes lessons from the book chapters by analysing how technological changes allow firms to change their business models and their relations with other firms. The chapter analyses how digitalization has led to increased control of industrial activities, which allows for increasing returns on R&D, production and adoption. This means that digitalization and new market demands are transforming industries by cumulatively affecting both supply and demand, creating positive feedback.

Notes

1 The two challenges have different terms in different academic traditions. For example, the UCL Institute for Innovation and Public Purpose (IIPP) in its May 2019 *A Mission-Oriented UK Industrial Strategy*, identified that these challenges include *an Ageing Society*, the *Future of Mobility*, *Clean Growth* and the *AI and Data Economy*.
2 We use the terminology industrial transformation because it is close to the focus of this book: a historical elaboration.
3 Originated by Gordon Moore (cofounder of Intel), who observed that every 12 months the number of transistors in a minimum-cost integrated circuit doubles (Moore, 1965). Moore's law (and variations of it) have been applied to understand the improvements in fields like disk drive capacity, display resolution and bandwidth. To simplify, there is a (memory/storage) capacity doubling every 12 months (Long, 2016, p. 228).
4 The label was coined by Ray Kurzweil (1990), a computer scientist who was director of engineering at Google. It is often referred to as the wheat and chessboard problem: having one grain placed upon the first square of a chessboard and then doubling the number of grains on each subsequent square and continuing that way (i.e. constant doubling). What occurs on the second half of the chessboard (with this exponential growth) is a pile perhaps bigger than Mount Everest.
5 www.unenvironment.org/resources/emissions-gap-report-2018: "to achieve the goal of limiting climate change to 2°C, countries need to triple the level of their commitments made under the Paris Agreement".
6 The *Anthropocene Epoch*, according to the National Geographic Society's definition, "is an unofficial unit of geologic time, used to describe the most recent period in Earth's history when human activity started to have a significant impact on the planet's climate and ecosystems" (www.nationalgeographic.org/encyclopedia/anthropocene/).
7 Bresnahan (2010, p. 764) set out a similar simplified definition where a GPT is: (a) widely used, (b) capable of ongoing technical improvement and (c) enabling innovation in application sectors. The combination of (b) and (c) is also called innovational complementarity.
8 Young (1928).
9 Patterns of interaction are central to the system of innovation literature (cf. concepts like the national system of innovation, the sectoral system of innovation and large technical systems).
10 A paradigm shift properly embraces both an artefactual dimension (a solution) and a heuristic dimension (common cognitions).
11 Representing sustainability thinking.
12 Representing innovation thinking.
13 "Mechanisms are frequently occurring and easily recognizable causal patterns that are triggered under generally unknown conditions or with indeterminate consequences" (Elster, 1998, p. 45).

References

Arthur, B. (2017). Where is technology taking the economy? *McKinsey Quarterly*, October 5, 2017. https://www.mckinsey.com/business-functions/mckinsey-analytics/our-insights/where-is-technology-taking-the-economy#

Bresnahan, T.E. (2010). General purpose technologies. Chapter 18, in Hall, B. and Rosenberg, N. (eds) *Handbooks of the Economics of Innovation*. Amsterdam: North-Holland, pp. 761–791.

Bresnahan, T.E., and Trajtenberg, M. (1995). General purpose technologies: Engines of growth? *Journal of Econometrics*, 65(1): 83–108.

Brown, I., and Marsden, C. (2013). *Regulating Code: Good Governance and Better Regulation in the Information Age*. Cambridge: MIT Press.

Brynjolfsson, E., and McAfee, A. (2012). Race against the machine: How the digital revolution is accelerating innovation, driving productivity, and irreversibly transforming employment and the economy. MIT Sloan School of Management. http://ebusiness.mit.edu/research/Briefs/Brynjolfsson_McAfee_Race_Against_the_Machine.pdf

Brynjolfsson, E., and McAfee, A. (2014). *The Second Machine Age*. New York: W. W. Norton & Company.

Elster, J. (1989). *Nuts and Bolts for the Social Sciences*. Cambridge: Cambridge University Press.

Elster, J. (1998). A plea for mechanisms. In Hedström, P., and Swedberg, R. (eds) *Social Mechanisms*. Cambridge: Cambridge University Press, pp. 45–73.

Foster, R. (1986). *Innovation: The Attackers Advantage*. New York: Summit Books.

Hicks, J.R. (1932). *The Theory of Wages*. New York: Macmillan Co.

Keynes, J.M. (1930). Economic possibilities for our grandchildren. In *Essays in Persuasion*. New York: Harcourt Brace, 1932, pp. 358–373. https://assets.aspeninstitute.org/content/uploads/files/content/upload/Intro_and_Section_I.pdf

Knight, F. (1921). *Risk, Uncertainty, and Profit*. Boston: Houghton Mifflin.

Kurzwei, R. (1990). *The Age of Intelligent Machines*. Cambridge, MA: MIT Press.

Landes, D. (1998). *The Wealth and Poverty of Nations: Why Are Some So Rich and Others So Poor*. New York: W.W. Norton. https://tsu.ge/data/file_db/faculty_humanities/Landes%20-%20The%20Wealth%20and%20the%20Poverty%20of%20Nations.pdf

Long, V. (2016). Dynamics: In the ICT industry. In Blomkvist, P., and Johansson, P. (eds) *A Dynamic Mind: Perspectives on Industrial Dynamics in Honour of Staffan Laestadius*. Stockholm: School of Industrial Engineering and Management (INDEK), KTH, TRITA IEO-R2016:08, pp. 223–247.

Mazzucato, M. (2011). *The Entrepreneurial State*. London: Demos.

McAfee, A. (2019). *More from Less: The Surprising Story of How We Learned to Prosper Using Fewer Resources*. London: Simon & Schuster.

Moore, G. (1965). Cramming more components onto integrated circuits. *Electronics Magazine*, 38(8) (April 19): 114.ff.

Nelson, R., and Pack, H. (1999). The Asian miracle and modern growth theory. *The Economic Journal*, 109(457): 416–436.

Rosenberg, R. (1996). Uncertainty and technological change, Chapter 8, in Rosenberg, R. (eds) *Studies on Science and the Innovation Process: Selected Works of Nathan Rosenberg, 2009*. Singapore: World Scientific Publishing Co. Pte. Ltd., pp. 153–172.

Schot, J., and Steinmueller, E. (2018). Three frames for innovation policy: R&D, systems of innovation and transformative change. *Research Policy*, 47(9): 1554–1567.

Schumacher, E.F. (1973/2011). *Small is Beautiful: A Study of Economics as if People Mattered*. New York: Random House.

Schumpeter, J.A. (1911/1934). *Theorie der Wirtschaftlichen Entwicklung. English Translation: The Theory of Economic Development*. Cambridge, MA: Harvard University Press.

Schumpeter, J.A. (1942). *Capitalism, Socialism and Democracy.* New York: Harper Torchbooks.

UN Environment Emissions Cap Report.2018 United Nations Environment Programme, November 2018 ISBN: 978-92-807-3726-4. https://www.unenvironment.org/resources/emissions-gap-report-2018.

Unruh, G. (2000). Understanding carbon lock-in. *Energy Policy*, 28(12): 817–830.

Young, A. (1928). Increasing returns and economic progress. *The Economic Journal*, 38(152): 527–547.

2

WHAT DO WE KNOW ABOUT INDUSTRIAL TRANSFORMATION?

Vicky Long and Magnus Holmén

Industrial transformation is about changes

This chapter presents the relevant literature on industrial transformation and it has a particular focus on technological development.

Industrial transformation is essentially about changes in economic activities, which, in turn, affect the utility in the market. These changes are related to, affected by or caused by changes at:

(a) *The macro level*: there are changes in institutions (North, 1990), in the relative prices of the factors of production (Hicks, 1932) and the bandwagon effects on demand (see Veblen, 1899: the concept of *conspicuous consumption*).
(b) *The meso level*: there are changes in technological opportunities and in the nature of the cumulativeness of technological knowledge, which, in turn, affects the appropriability regime, namely the likelihood of profit (see the concept of the *technological regime* in Marsili, 1999; Stefano et al., 2000).
(c) *The micro level*: there are changes at firm level such as resources, capabilities and strategies, which affect R&D spending and the choice of technologies (see Penrose, 1959 on the resource-based view of the firms, and the concept of *dynamic capabilities* in Teece et al., 1997).

Regardless of the level, changes can be episodic or sequential, cumulative or discontinuous, but they are often contingent upon the outcome of critical events such as radical innovation, regulatory change, firm entry or business model innovation.

Fundamentally, a change is not an island, but it is connected to antecedent changes, and the new change itself may trigger further changes. "Any study of society shows that every solution creates a new situation which breeds its own new needs and problems" (Bertin, 1991, p. 14). The saying of Heraclitus – "one can never step in the same river twice" – illustrates the same view. Industrial transformation ontology, for example, what constitutes an industry prior to, during and after transformation, may therefore be viewed as constantly on the move, although sometimes only incrementally.

Often, the outcome of the changes is unknown *ex ante*. "The notion of transformation provides the link with evolution and the open-ended, essentially unpredictable, development of capitalism" (Metcalfe, 2014, p. 11). Knightian (1921) uncertainty applies here in the sense that actors cannot have perfect knowledge, either of future events or of the outcomes of those events. However, actors can in most instances assess the odds, at least to some extent, reasonably well. Some dimensions of the changes are:

(a) *The process*: "a story of the growth, and development, of a manufacturing sector, from birth to maturity, and perhaps until death, that seems to fit many cases" (Nelson, 1994, p. 47). Typically, there is a coevolution of technology, industrial structure and supporting institution.
(b) *The causation*: there are history-friendly models that clarify the causal effect on, for example, firms' entries, variety of actors and relationship to the competition (e.g. Malerba and Orsenigo, 2002; Malerba et al., 2008, 2016); there are also causal mechanism approaches on, for example, the determinants and consequences of technological changes in industrial transformation (Rosenberg, 1994).
(c) *Activities*: what firms do relates to the activities they perform to transform inputs (materials, information) into outputs. This is based on what they know, including technology. Technology can be seen as a form of knowledge: "human designed means for achieving a particular end" (Dosi and Nelson, 2009, p. 4). What actors do and know are also embodied in routines, organizational structures and working processes.

The changes are non-trivial. Borrowing the Oslo Manual's way of framing innovation (OECD/Eurostat, 1992/2018), transformation in this book refers to changes in industrial activities that are new to the world, or to a sector, not just to a single firm or a minority of firms. What is non-trivial, however, cannot be determined *ex ante*, and not even the most historical-friendly model can make such predictions reliably.[1] This causes great difficulty in understanding changes in the nature of the ongoing competition, for example. Firms can enter or exit a sector, grow or decline, without there being any major changes in the structure of and interactions within the sector (Spender, 1989). Transformation can also be a process of natural evolution, in which the shakeouts are caused by a mounting dominance by the entry of innovative firms (Klepper and Simons, 1997), which is inherent in any market economy. Transformation is a qualitative change, with not only the creation of new actors and the disappearance of old actors but also new forms of interactions and relations and new types of industrial activities.

Many if not most explanations of industrial transformation are related to the manufacturing sectors. There are classic seminal works studying changes in the automotive sector (e.g. Abernathy and Utterback, 1975, on the product life cycle concept) and in consumer electronics (Vernon, 1966, on the impact of sophistication of demand in innovation and the resulting global shift). The macro context, however, has changed today. In particular, servitization refers to how the proportion of services increases not only in value delivered in manufacturing goods but also throughout the economy. Digitalization refers to how digital technologies have, for example, enabled the platform economy to reach across competition on an unprecedented scale and scope (e.g. Uber), and there is also a sustainability agenda to meet.

What constitutes an industry prior to, during and after the transformation can be very different. For example, what was called a cross-industry competition in the 1990s is now analysed as within-industry competition. Terms like *industry convergence* (between data-com and tele-com) and *killer applications* were frequently used years ago, before terms like *platform economy* got hold in circa 2010. Consequently, the property of industrial knowledge also changes. "New products are appearing, firms are assuming new tasks, and new industries are coming into being", as Young (1928, p. 528) described when discussing changes that are external to an individual firm. "[I]n short, change in this external field is qualitative as well as quantitative" (ibid.). In general, there is a need for a broader and more dynamic view of what should be referred to as industry and industrial transformation.

The complexity of the changes may be viewed as a jigsaw puzzle consisting of various pieces of different shapes that need to fit. The pieces are in very different theoretical fields, of diverse power in explaining industrial transformation and appealing to different audience groups such as policy makers, industrial managers and economists. The hitherto academic explorations of industrial transformation are either following historical timelines, namely explaining factors pertinent to that particular period or engaging in thematical categorization. In this chapter, we briefly discuss both, in "Selected historical accounts of industrial transformation" and "Key thematic approaches to industrial transformation", respectively.

A particular weight in this book goes to the literature that can promote understanding of the operative causal mechanisms related to digital transformation and sustainable transformation, which are the two empirical foci of this book; they relate to the changes in technology (development) that are associated with industrial transformation, which is the niche of the book.

The changes in technology that are associated with industrial transformation can be exemplified as:

(a) *Changes in the nature of technological knowledge.* These include the cumulativeness versus discreteness of technological knowledge (Merges and Nelson, 1990) and the tacitness versus codifiability of technological knowledge (Nelson and Winter, 1982). These changes can be minor, and they mainly occur within particular sectors. To illustrate, Laestadius (1998) and Asheim and Gertler (2005) argue that codified knowledge, embodied heavily in software coding systems or biomedicine sectors, is easier to transfer over distance than tacit knowledge heavily embodied in process industries such as the pulp-and-paper industry and the food beverage industry. These changes can also be dynamic with general impacts throughout industry sectors. One example relates to machine-generated data in the era of the Internet of Things, namely data created by sensors, actuators, robots and machines. Is this kind of data information, knowledge or property? The boundaries between this trilogy – information/knowledge/property – are not always clear, and the shift along positions has important bearings, not least on the technological opportunities and appropriability pertinent to industrial transformation.

(b) *Changes in the Schumpeterian methods of production.* These are changes in how material, energy and information is sourced, processed and consumed by economic actors: the rise of general-purpose technologies (GPTs) like additive manufacturing (sometimes denoted 3D printing) not only provides cost-effective methods of prototyping, but also expands both user and producer pools.

(c) *Changes in the interactions between the actors and technological development.* This is largely discussed in the product development literature in concepts like *Co-creation* (O'Hern and Rindfleisch, 2010), and in the innovation studies literature in concepts like *Democratizing Innovation* (von Hippel, 1998). In computer games development, for example, users' involvement can occur in the alpha phase of the product due to the opportunities offered by online gaming (e.g. early access games). This affects not only the types of value creation/skipping along the digital transformation at the business front but also the direction and rate of technological change at the industrial transformation front.

(d) *Changes in how firms and other actors relate to each other along technological development.* For example, platforms like Airbnb and Uber have not only extended the channel of supplies and the types of services (packages), but also the types of interactions.

Changes in technology can be the main force driving industrial transformation. Changes in technology can also be the part that coevolves with industrial transformation. The role of technological changes in industrial transformation varies depends on the historical context. Thus, an implicit priority of this review goes to so-called "appreciative theorization" (Malerba et al., 2016, p. 23) rather than formal (mathematical) modelling on industrial transformation.[2]

This chapter is organized as follows: in this section, we define the word *change*, the very property of industrial transformation, to which we come back in later sections.

"Selected historical accounts of industrial transformation" and "Key thematic approaches to industrial transformation" briefly review key theories on industrial transformation.

"Selected historical accounts of industrial transformation" presents a few key *historical accounts* of technological change and industrial transformation. In this field, many theoretical abstractions are generated *ex post*, to offer explanations of past events, such as the historically actuated variables of a salient phenomenon. Explanations on the driving forces and the rate and direction of transformations may be found, for example, in the so-called three industrial revolution literature (e.g. Ashton, 1948; Landes, 1969; Mokyr, 1994. It is argued that the First Industrial Revolution occurred circa 1760–1840 and was powered by steam; the Second Industrial Revolution occurred circa 1870–1914 and was based on electricity. "The third industrial revolution, which is unfolding now, is fuelled by computers and networks" (Brynjolfsson and McAfee, 2012, p. 8). It is therefore important to trace developments back to the key events that occurred then. This, in turn, supports theoretical abstraction, which has predictive power in explaining today's digital and sustainable transformations.

"Key thematic approaches to industrial transformation" illustrates three key thematic approaches to industrial transformation: the (evolutionary) economics perspective, the institutional economics-influenced system perspective and management studies. The evolutionary economics school acknowledges the cumulative and path-dependent nature of technological change and industrial transformation. The system approach argues that transformation needs to be understood from a systemic perspective in which actors, institutions and knowledge are largely interlinked nodes coevolving in a dynamic manner. Management studies highlight conjunction points (in transformation) between firm-level elements such as resources, capabilities and strategies and meso-level elements such as product/technology life cycle and appropriability. As will be discussed, there are both key differences and complementarities among these three approaches, in their levels of analysis and in their intended audience groups.

"Digitalization and sustainability: Recent literature" discusses the literature that is directly relevant to digitalization and sustainable transformation. The final section synthesizes the conclusions.

Selected historical accounts of industrial transformation

Industrial transformation has occurred ever since the existence of industry, if industry is broadly defined as organized economic activities beyond craft production. This understanding of industrial transformation is essentially empirically driven, based on observations of major technological and economic changes (e.g. waves of industrial revolutions). Many theories are generated *ex post*, after the historical events have occurred, because transformation stages and causal effects are often inexplicable except in retrospect. Some theories, however, grow abductively in parallel with the ongoing transformation.

Over the years, there have been several important insights into the nature of industrial transformation. We briefly go through a few key historical accounts while focusing on the interactions between technological changes and industrial transformation.

Adam Smith's (1776) *Wealth of Nation* came out at the dawn of the (First) Industrial Revolution (circa 1760–1840) when technological change turned sharply upwards and capitalist enterprise was in its embryonic stage. It was the start of a period of general transformation from hand-based craft production to steam engine-powered industrial machinery (Ashton, 1948; von Tunzelmann, 1978). Adam Smith's famous pin factory case – arguing for the division of labour by suggesting that the pin production process can be broken down into 18 distinct steps – is essentially about change, about ways to improve productivity, about innovation in the organization of production methods. The Smithian account – that the division of labour is limited by the extent of the market – indicates that the industry coevolves with the market, in the sense that the factory can only create a market sized to fit a pre-existing (pin production) technology. A larger market may make it economically meaningful to increase the specialization of labour further. However, there is little account of new technologies being instrumental in creating economies of scale, starkly visible in the Industrial Revolution, except for a brief mention of fire engines (steam engines) in chapter 1.

In Karl Marx's *Das Kapital* in 1894 – written after the First Industrial Revolution – the role of technology in industrial transformation is more explicit than from Smith: technology discloses the interaction between human beings and nature; technology change and capitalism (transformation) are deeply intertwined, in the sense that technology sits in the means of production (controlled by the bourgeoisie), and that in turn changes the conditions for labour. Being active in the age of steam, iron and railways (1840–1890), Marx's thinking addresses key tensions relating to the early Industrial Revolution (1760–1840), a macro condition that has an important bearing on industrial transformation.

Alfred Marshall's (1890/1920) *Principles of Economics* came out in the middle of the Second Industrial Revolution (circa 1870–1914), a period of rapid standardization, of increasing scale economies and large-sized firms being normalized in industrial practices and an emergence of large technological systems, such as electrical power systems (see Hughes, 1987).

Marshall's interest in industrial organization triggered his analyses of the phenomenon of industrial districts. The concept of *industrial district* exemplifies an agglomeration of both industries and industrial activities in certain geographic regions. He used the Lancashire cotton district and the Sheffield Cutlery Trades' Technical Society as examples to illustrate the geographic concentration of specialization of businesses. According to Marshall (1890/1920), three reasons explain this tendency: an infrastructure of specialized supporting industries, the presence of skilled labour available to firms within a region and the presence of non-pecuniary (non-financial) externalities, which he expressed as "[knowledge of the trade is] in the air" (p. 225) (i.e. knowledge creation is a consequence of the interactions). Contemporary terms like clusters, agglomerations, development blocks, innovation systems and competence blocs may be viewed as extensions of Marshall's idea on industrial districts. While geography often functions as a platform to organize innovative activity (Feldman and Choi, 2015), Marshall's industrial district thinking sheds light on the understanding of, for example, why technological spill-overs are more likely to occur in Industrial Region A than in B or C. It triggers further thinking on what types of industrial knowledge are geographically sticky or slippery.

Industrial transformation has always had a regional dimension: some regions, such as Silicon Valley, can transform faster to online working during crises, such as pandemics, due to the IT competencies and infrastructural conditions throughout the region, and not least, the industrial knowledge embedded in the product. This echoes the macro and meso conditions discussed in "Industrial transformation is about changes".

The puzzle on industrial transformation then shifted to the entrepreneurs in the writings of Joseph Schumpeter (1911, 1942). His discussion on the role of entrepreneurship and of entrepreneurs' *creative destruction* ("revolutionizes the economic structure from within", 1942, p. 83) in industrial transformation was built on Say's (1855) seminal definition of entrepreneurship, namely that risk-bearing is a fundamental characteristic of entrepreneurship. The entrepreneur is a hero in Schumpeter's eyes, beyond the managerial function implicitly assumed in earlier writings by authors such as Marshall. The Schumpeterian entrepreneur is the one who is capable of combining factors of production to create new combinations of products, processes, markets, supplies and organizations. This new combination later serves as one of the most commonly used characterizations of innovation, in which innovation is broadly defined, beyond technological invention. Moreover, by continuing the Marxian line of exploration on means/methods of production, Schumpeter's theory sets the very ground of industrial transformation by viewing economics as an organic (evolving) and dynamic process.

Having mentioned these four seminal names associated with a mechanism approach on industrial transformation, we highlight a few more recent examples.

Paul David's (1985) work on the standardization of the QWERTY keyboard design instead of the Dvorak keyboard leads to the conceptualization of *path dependence* and introduces an evolutionary thinking approach. In David's assertion, the QWERTY keyboard is an example of lock-in to technological inferiority. The Dvorak keyboard layout, developed after the QWERTY layout became well established, is arguably technically superior. The historical circumstances and market processes, however, prevented Dvorak's adoption. It was simply too costly to coordinate all users – typists and employers – to make the switch to the new standard. For the industrial economist, this has become a stylized fact: technologies that are selected in the market are often not the most advanced technology at that period; factors like demand play a role (Adner and Levinthal, 2001).

Nathan Rosenberg is another historian to be highlighted here, particularly due to his accounts of the economic forces that shape the direction and speed of technological change (e.g. Rosenberg, 1994), which should also be viewed as a unique process at a historical time (of a particular sequence of events and/or institutions, for example). In his elaboration on the shape of the American system of manufacturing (which arose in the United States in the nineteenth century), both supply- and demand-side forces are observed at work, and factor substitution and the cumulation of technological knowledge coexist[3]: on the supply side, there was a labour-saving (therefore, capital-using) bias due to the abundance of natural resources and the scarcity of labour (Rosenberg, 1969; see also Habakkuk, 1962). On the demand side, there were rapidly growing markets and there was an acceptance of highly standardized products. The transfer of new technology from one industry to another when standardizing products consequently became popular too. In other words, the resource conditions and capabilities conditions are interlinked.

Parallel to Rosenberg's "Exploring the Black Box" (of technology) (1994), there was a rise in the (technological) capability approach in the 1990s. This is sometimes called Sen's capability approach in development studies (cf. Sen, 1987, 1999) and the assimilation school as opposed to the (capital) accumulation school[4] in innovation studies (Nelson and Pack, 1999). The simplified message of this capability approach is that, first, capability accumulation is as important as capital accumulation in growth, and second, both technological capabilities and the accumulation processes are largely specific to individual persons, firms and countries of a locally differentiated nature. Knowledge and capabilities remain important in understanding the nature of the process of industrial transformation.

Erik Dahmén (1950, 1988) is another important researcher, with his historical analysis of industrial transformation and the concepts of *development blocks* and *structural tensions*. While the former – development blocks – stresses the coevolution of different parts of the economy in a complementary manner, the latter – structural tension – refers to "a depressive pressure in stages which are 'premature' as long as the complementary ones are missing" (Dahmén, 1988, p. 5). Dahmén's analyses are mainly at the micro and meso levels.

This is not a place to repeat all the historical accounts that are important for the study of industrial transformation. Irrespective of the empirical evidence – historical cases or statistical analyses – industrial transformation may be viewed as rarely radical and predominantly cumulative.

Key thematic approaches to industrial transformation

Industrial transformation as a field has roots in studies of industrial management at the micro level, industrial dynamics at the meso level and industrial economics at the macro level. It is a topic addressed by scholars in fields like entrepreneurship, history of economics, business and technology, economic geography, and institutional economics and organization studies and its subfields such as organization theory, management strategy and finance.

There are at least two reasons why so much literature is relevant for a broader understanding of industrial transformation. One is the level of analysis and

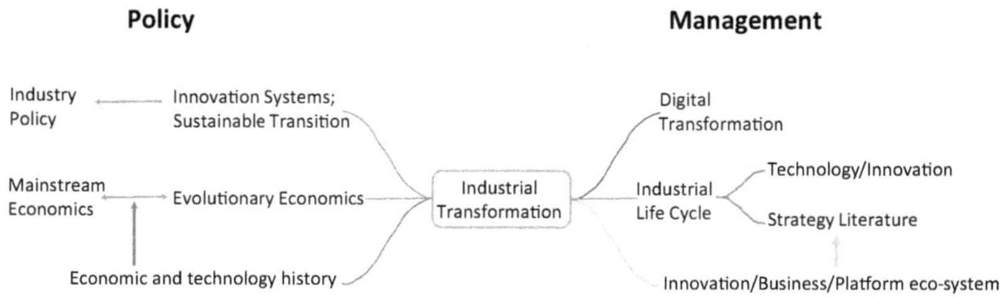

FIGURE 2.1 The recipient perspective of the industrial transformation literature.

explanation, whether the focus is on the firm or management, industry or competition, or the broader economy. The other is related but distinct: who is the intended audience of the research apart from the researchers' peers? A simplified view is given in Figure 2.1.

Figure 2.1 summarizes the key literature explaining industrial transformation but addressing different audience groups: from an academic point of view, economists and historians (left side), and strategy and management scholars (right side) and from a practitioner-oriented perspective policymaker (left side) and managers (right side).

To elaborate, in what follows, we offer a snapshot of the three categories of literature relating to technological change and industrial transformation. It should be noted that the groups are not mutually exclusive. The first group (see "In the eyes of evolutionary economics") views transformation as occurring in a market system, whereas structural transformation goes hand in hand with growth. Elements of the Smithian invisible hand are clearly observable in transformation processes. Causal relations – affecting the outcome of the transformation – can be traced and modelled. Coevolution with institutions (i.e. elements of the visible hand) is acknowledged in evolutionary economics. The primary scholarly recipient group are economists, while policymakers are the relevant practitioner group.

The second group (see "The system perspective") holds that the transformation occurs in a system setting, where actors include not only firms but also public institutions and universities that interact with each other based on common rules. In other words, the transformation of an industry (or a region) does not occur in isolation but is heavily conditioned by the very nature of the interactions in the system. Moreover, the system is dynamically changing and the vectors affecting that change include not least the varied reactions from heterogeneous actors, dynamically changing institutions (e.g. industrial standards, licence agreements, a quasi-market rule) and knowledge bases (affected by technology advancement, for example). The policy makers are the primary recipients here.

The third group (see "The management approaches") views the transformation as primarily a management problem. The carrier of that transformation – often characterized as the incumbent firm or entrant – is embedded in a competitive setting, whereas product life cycle (PLC), new business models (e.g. Airbnb) and the attack of new entrants (e.g. Netflix v. Blockbuster) from peripheral technologies or segments play a role in the final outcome of the transformation. In this strand of literature, actors are analysed in a detailed and nuanced manner with a focus on value creation. Industrial practitioners and management researchers are the primary recipients here.

In the eyes of evolutionary economics

The contemporary industrial transformation study continues to take a longer historical evolutionary perspective and focuses on the causes of changes. The more recent roots may be found in *evolutionary economics*, in which economic theory is inspired by evolutionary theory (and biology). It is argued that mechanisms like *variation, selection, adaptation* and *retention* – largely used in Darwinism analyses of biological evolution – are also applicable to social, technical and economic changes, a position tracing back to terms like *Social Darwinism*, which emerged in the late nineteenth century, and names like Herbert Spencer. On the economic front, evolutionary thinking can be found not least in the classic analyses of Alfred Marshall (on industrial districts), Joseph Schumpeter (on entrepreneurship/innovation theory), Thorstein Veblen (on institutional theory), Erik Dahmén (on development block and structural transformation) and more recently Nelson and Winter (on an evolutionary theory of economics) and Nelson and Dosi (on technological paradigm shift/semiconductors and pharmaceuticals).

This is not the place to give a detailed account and comparison of the evolutionary approaches to biology and economics (cf. Nelson and Winter, 1982; Baum and Singh, 1994). In short, adopting an evolutionary approach to industrial transformation analysis is focusing on the historical conditions rather than on competitive equilibrium. History matters is a fundamental statement, in the sense that history can create inertia, embodied in sunk costs, technology standards (dominant design) and existing infrastructures/systems, for example. History can affect actors' choices of pathways because of cognitive constraints (of the organization) and institutional heritage. This evolutionary line of thinking is mirrored in concepts like learning, coevolution, absorptive capacity, structural tensions, technology and product life cycles.

Unlike orthodox or mainstream economics, the evolutionary approach is in nature appreciative; that is, it often favours establishing salient stylized facts via historical analysis, for example, to explore the underlying driving forces for change, rather than searching for formalized models. While "formal theory is an important source of the ideas invoked in appreciative theory" (Nelson and Winter, 1982, p. 47), the industrial transformation study – often with causal mechanisms in focus – is heavily influenced by evolutionary economics.

Much of the focus is on the mechanisms of changes in this evolutionary track, and this can be illustrated in the seminal contribution of Nelson and Winter (1982). While the Knightian *uncertainty* and purposeful *learning*, arguably, are the two major deviations triggering the evolutionary approach as a departure from the orthodox view of economics, other terms related to mechanisms of changes can be categorized into this school of thoughts. Examples include disequilibrium, increasing returns to scale and scope, network effects, path dependency, lock-in and institutions (North, 1990).[5]

Many of these mechanisms are considered inherent in change today and intuitive in explaining phenomena, not least in the so-called platform economy (e.g. Airbnb, Uber). They were, however, not taken for granted in orthodox economics, where there are strong foci on markets, prices and the perfect conditions for equilibrium (with perfect information and rational actors).

The adoption of the evolutionary approach is visible where industrial catching up (e.g. Hobday, 1995) is concerned. Sometimes it is called the *accumulation school* versus the *assimilation school* (of thoughts) (Nelson and Pack, 1999). The latter (assimilation) may be perceived as a subset of the former (accumulation), on the one hand, and it differs from the former in viewing learning as an intentional act, rather than a by-product of capital investment. In other words, it is a static view to see a state of knowledge incorporated in a firm's production set (see Arrow and Hahn, 1971).[6] Rather, firms' absorptive capacity (Cohen and Levinthal, 1990) is dynamically changing, and intentionally designed R&D conduct does have an impact.

Arguably, this school of thoughts includes transition studies, long waves and the business cycle literature, historical studies of innovation and catch-up studies.

Transition studies may also be referred to as social-technical system studies: this is illustrated by Geels (2002) on multiple level systems, Unruh (2000) on the concept of carbon lock-in and Schot (2016) on Deep Transition (p. 449). The major focus is on how policies (and policy makers) can induce transformations of industrial systems to address grand societal challenges, such as global warming. This track of thinking is also heavily influenced by institutional economics, not least as illustrated by terms like the *techno-institutional complex*. An account of this will follow.

The long waves or business cycle literature includes the upstream R&D and innovation waves, and downstream diffusion waves derived from the effects of generic technologies, later termed GPTs, on the economy. This includes how they make new industries and transform/destroy existing ones. Such studies are attempts to identify historical regularities and theories of dynamics. This may be associated with the names of Schumpeter (business cycles), Christopher Freeman (R&D and innovation waves) and Carlota Perez (GPTs and their diffusion waves)

Historians' contributions to innovations include literature on industrial revolutions. Historians usually focus on the history of technology and the role of technological change in specific industries and periods. Sometimes broader, more long-term changes, such as the origins of the Industrial Revolution, are also incorporated. The classics may be illustrated by Rosenberg (on technological convergence/the machine tool industry), Mokyr and Landes (on the origins of the industrial revolution in the UK and the United States), Hughes (reverse salient concept, the energy industry), David (path dependence, the QWERTY standard/IT industry) and North (the path of institutional change in the United States). The three Industrial Revolutions literature may also be included here (Ashton, 1948; Landes, 1969; Mokyr, 1994, 1998; Perez, 2002). Typically, it is argued that the First Industrial Revolution occurred circa 1760–1840 and was powered by steam. The Second Industrial Revolution occurred circa 1870–1914 and was based on electricity. The Third Industrial Revolution is seen as fuelled by computers and networks (Brynjolfsson and McAfee, 2012).

Developing country centred catch-up studies involves addressing the convergence clubs' study on first-tier tigers and more recent emerging economies (Fagerberg and Srholec, 2007).

The system perspective

Systems approaches or systemic approaches have a bearing on industrial transformation and embrace at least six subconcepts. Most of these approaches are heavily influenced by institutional economics. Systems approaches have emerged since the late 1980s. The innovation process and the associated industrial transformation process is seen as non-linear and having a systemic character:

(a) National system of innovation (e.g. Lundvall, 1992; Freeman, 1987; Johnson et al. 2003).
(b) Sectoral system of innovation (e.g. Malerba and Orsenigo, 1997), arguably a cousin of the concept of *technological regimes* (e.g. Breschi et al., 2000).
(c) Technological innovation systems (e.g. Carlsson and Stankiewicz, 1991; Eliasson, 1997; on competence bloc theory).
(d) Regional systems of innovation (e.g. Cooke, 1992; Asheim, 1996).
(e) Large technological systems (Hughes, 1987; Bijker et al., 1989).
(f) The multilevel perspective (MLP) on sociotechnical transitions (Geels, 2002; Geels and Schot, 2010).

The first five system approaches inspired and targeted research and innovation policies and arose in an era (the late 1980s) in which innovation was increasingly seen as pivotal for economic growth and industrial catching up. This means there was a stress on the need to go beyond the conventional (orthodox) economic theory of viewing innovation merely as a growth-enhancing factor in the aggregate production function (see Romer, 1986, 1990). Innovation was seen not just as the allocation of knowledge, but also as driven by the creation and diffusion of new knowledge from interactions among many actors and institutions. New knowledge is endogenously created (assimilated) through R&D and is not a by-product of capital investment. Moreover, innovative activities are deeply embedded in the competitive processes of the whole economy. For example, the concept of *national innovation systems* offers a framework to discuss innovation from an actor perspective, including the role of heterogeneous actors and their cooperation, framed from the role of national institutions. This conclusion is based on the experience of comparatively small economies, such as Sweden and Denmark (Lundvall and Jonsson, 1994) but also large economies such as Japan (e.g. Freeman, 1995). It sheds light on the role of innovation and technology for economic development in emerging and transition economies (see Malerba and Lee, 2016, on catching up economies).

The last system approach emerged more recently, and it has acted as an important tool in explaining grand challenges related to industrial transformation. Given the focus on grand challenges, it seems to be normative in terms of addressing aspects such as sustainability, for example, climate change. The transition literature, which may also be called the *sociotechnical system* literature, is particularly powerful in addressing the role of institutions, including the role of government and industrial policies, in dealing with grand challenge-related industrial transformations.

The recently popularized MLP on sociotechnical transitions – the *sociotechnical system* literature – addresses the role of the state, the government and industrial policy. The state can act as a driving force, as illustrated in the history of Sweden's industrialization, whereas key infrastructure – canals, railways, the telecommunication system and electricity networks – were created as important conditions for industrial development (Bruland, 1991; Kaijser, 1994). The state can obstruct industrialization, as Mokyr (1992) illustrated by China's fall from being the world's leading nation of scientific and intellectual advancement since the fourteenth century.

MLP is relevant in sustainability-related transformation studies. Transition, rather than transformation, is the term used in that strand of the literature. The explanatory power of the MLP perspective lies in its focus on treating transition as an outcome of the interplay of dynamics at three levels: landscape, regime and niches. The landscape level refers to the (global) broad contexts and factors that open new opportunities (or provide pressure to change), regime is synonymous with institution (including informal institutions shaped in society, e.g. networks) and niches refer to areas where radical novelty exists and experimental conduct can occur.

The main argument of the system literature, especially the *sociotechnical system* literature, on industrial transformation may be characterized as follows: since the desired direction of economic change is set (at an abstract level) due to constraints from expected climate changes and natural resource depletion, for example, the resources committed to actors' innovative efforts need to be coordinated to ensure progress in a sustainable direction. This can also mean that there is a need to change the course of existing activities – radically or cumulatively – that are no longer seen as socially desirable. The transformation is therefore not only about firm growth or survival, but also about solving societal problems, which is bigger than a given firm's or industry's problems per se. Coordination, incentives and capabilities (beyond organizational boundaries) need to be in place. Transformative innovation policy is therefore needed to ensure the pursuit of the desired direction. This brings in the role of institutions in transformation. The role of institutions can be very different in a sustainability transition context from their regulating-focused traditional role. To be concrete, it is in practice very unclear how innovation policies can steer development into certain directions and the extent to which institutions can intervene in firms' operations to steer them into sustainable directions.

To take a step back, the system approaches relate to and have been influenced by *institutional economics*. The role of institutions, in firm dynamics and industrial transformation studies, is arguably rooted in Coase's (1937) "The Nature of the Firm" as developed by Oliver Williamson (1975) and Douglas North (1990). Informal institutions, including social norms, can come into play as well, as illustrated by Thorstein Veblen's (1899) conspicuous consumption concept, which suggests an incorporation of social and cultural dimensions into the analysis of problems related to economic development and transformation. John Rogers Commons's (1931) collective action concept also holds here, namely the interplay between state and other institutions is essential to understand economics.

Like evolutionary economics, new institutional economics also addresses mechanisms like (adaptive) learning, bounded rationality and increasing returns that have always played a central role in industrial transformation. This position is exemplified by North (1990, p. 95): "In a world in which there are no increasing returns to institutions and markets are competitive, institutions do not matter". Such a world fits schoolbooks but does not exist in reality.

In *industrial transformation* studies, the incorporation of the new institutional economics is primarily reflected in the above-mentioned six types of system approaches. Nelson (1995) illustrates a commonly held position with a coevolution statement, namely that technology advancement and industry structure coevolve with supporting institutions.

In the system approaches, firms as a group of agents are only one of the key linkages in the system, together with other network agents (e.g. financial institutions, universities and public labs). The role of the state/institution/policy can be endogenized, but this depends on the empirical actuality. Often, the agents' (including firms') cognitions (e.g. learning effects), actions (e.g. strategies) and interactions (e.g. upstream/downstream integration) are enabled, if not shaped by institutions. For example, the innovation and learning effects for organizations are among the many consequences of a new institutional setting (e.g. R&D lab infrastructure). In short, institutions, industrial policies and the state are dynamic factors incorporated in system approach-related industrial transformation studies. The impact of this is specific to the sector, however.

There are few shortcomings of the system literature in explaining industrial transformation:

(a) The literature says little on the process, particularly at the sectoral level; consequently, the industrial activities involved in the transformation remain unknown (with some exceptions in the technological and sectoral system of innovation literature). The literature does not provide much help to understand the intra- (and inter-)industry actors and the structures (including vertical value chains and horizontal market concentration).

(b) The literature says little on the causality, or by merely presenting the complexity picture in a descriptive way, the causality remains implicit.

(c) The role of technology is not clear: is it a GPT where machine learning or 3D printing, for example, may fit into that description? Or is it a simple form of capital input (in the production function), where machine learning and 3D printing also fit into that description?

(d) We may suggest that the literature can be perceived as having a somewhat limited understanding of politics, given its focus on policy, as if these domains are not interdependent.

To summarize, system approaches are central to understanding the linkages of the interactions and to analysing industrial transformation empirically.

The management approaches

Industrial transformation is operated at the organizational level. In this literature, individual firms, business units or managers carry out the transformation. They operate, manage activities and resources, and their actions, decisions and performance largely determine whether they will prosper, survive or die.

Industrial transformation may therefore be viewed in part as an issue of strategic or organizational behaviour. Firms differ in resources, capabilities and strategies that in turn affect the process, pathway/direction and outcome of industrial transformation. The theoretical roots can be traced back in part to industrial organization, in which well-known concepts such as monopolistic competition (Chamberlin, 1933) and game theory – used in analyses of industrial alliances and patent pooling, for example – are relevant for understanding industrial transformation.

In the wide ocean of management literature, three approaches stand out in explaining industrial transformation.

The first is the life cycle approach, which describes, analyses and explains phases and stages of industrial transformation. Familiar approaches include industry life cycles and product life cycles.[7] Industry life cycles and concepts like technological (life)cycles, dominant designs and S-curves (Utterback and Abernathy, 1975; Foster, 1986; Anderson and Tushman, 1990) primarily address the supply side, although the demand side also plays a major part. From the demand side, there are technology adoption life cycles or adoption chasms to cross in adoption (Roger, 1962; Moore, 1999).

These models contain, on the one hand, descriptions or theorizing on stages in product supply (introduction-growth-maturity-decline), technology advancement (ferment-take off-maturity), innovation (fluid-transitional-specific-phase) and adoption (early adopter-late majority-laggards).

The model provides insights and explanations of industrial transformation in, for example:

(a) The (dis)continuity of technological progress: technology advances sometimes cumulatively and sometimes with major technological breakthroughs.
(b) In the early stage(s), there are great varieties of both small actors/firms and technology searches (trajectories). Reaching a dominant design is therefore a process of shaking out of both actors and alternative technologies. There are rounds of attacks and counterattacks among different technological trajectories (see the S-curve literature).
(c) A combined sequence of innovation and adoption that stabilizes the selection environment. Here, producers and users alike may select a dominant design such as wind turbine architecture or photovoltaic system architecture to the detriment of other designs or technologies after a period of experimentation.
(d) While life cycle approaches often focus on the supply side, such as product or process innovations, they (indirectly) portray how firms, customers and users share expectations of the nature of products and services, indicating a coevolution between supply and demand. The late majority in adoption is often associated with a dominant design and the early adopters are often involved in the fermenting stage of product supply.
(e) From a value-creation perspective, the PLC also implies a process of commodification: appropriability moves from the Schumpeterian temporary monopoly rents (i.e. with high profit) to combinations of price reduction (e.g. by competing for economies of scales) and complementary innovations, which at times consist of feature creep.
(f) From a skills/capability perspective, there is a shift of focus where the upstream innovative capabilities give way to downstream manufacturing (and marketing) capabilities. A detailed analysis is found in the profiting from innovation framework, which discusses the linkage between innovation and complementary assets (Teece, 1986). The latter – often combined with the former – plays a bigger role in appropriability when the PLC gets into the paradigmatic phase.

The second approach is the incumbents *versus* entrants approach, typified in concepts like disruptive innovation or disruption (Christensen, 1997), which describe a common failure of market leaders when facing technological threats or business model innovations. Entrants often come from below the radar via an inferior offer for the incumbents' mainstream customers but offering advantages for niche or fringe customers. Mainstream customers are initially uninterested in the entrants' offer, but over time, as the products and services improve, they may decide to switch. During this time, incumbents fail to grasp or at least act on the emerging threat. Christensen (1997) uses the changes in the disk drive market to illustrate how persistent old modes of practices can eventually lead to a crisis:

among data-storage technologies, the 14-inch hard disk drive was disrupted by the 8-inch floppy disk drive, which in turn was disrupted by the 5.25-inch drive, which in turn was disrupted by the 3.5-inch floppy disk drive. The difficulty of responding in time for incumbents is because managerial cognition, organizational capabilities and resources are path dependent. Fundamental organizational transformation and evolutionary adaptation of the core products need to be in place, to change in time.

The Christensen (1997) inspired disruptive innovation literature is widespread, particularly in business schools, due to its power in explaining why powerful incumbent firms (e.g. Kodak) fail to sustain competitive advantages. Entrants can grow over time and eventually disrupt the market. These entrants were initially inconspicuous because they only served peripheral customers. For industrial dynamics scholars, this view coincides with the product life cycle literature (cf. Abernathy and Utterback, 1975) in explaining the rise and fall of certain technologies. In other words, a dominant design is historical in nature, and what shifts is not only a technology, but also the actors who possess the knowledge of that technology. What stands out in this disruptive innovation group of literature is that dangerous (and innovative) competition can come from below the radar of high margin or mainstream customers and consequently managerial attention, and there can be a dynamic shift between what is core and what is peripheral in certain customer segments. Epistemologically, what is considered as disruptive has evolved from a product (e.g. 14-inch disk drive in Christensen, 1997) to business models (e.g. Airbnb, Uber) (Björkdahl and Holmén, 2013). The reason to position the disruptive innovation literature under the umbrella of digitalization here is because most of the empirical evidence from the hitherto disruptive innovation literature is related to digital technologies and businesses, and it has a supply centred approach.

There is a rich literature analysing how firms may respond to threats. The rise of terms like ambidextrous organization (Duncan, 1976; Raisch and Birkinshaw, 2008) may be viewed as a defence from the incumbents' perspective. An ambidextrous organization is capable of being explorative, searching for new opportunities, and being exploitative, efficiently utilizing its resources, capabilities and mental models. At first, this may sound counterintuitive, but Tushman and O'Reilly (1996, 2002, 2004) argue that it is possible to be both explorative and exploitative by linking senior executive levels while separating business units. The two units often have different processes, structures and cultures, which helps to unify the inherently contradictive operations within the same company. This strategy is sometimes called structural ambidexterity, discussed together with terms like sequential ambidexterity (Duncan, 1976) and contextual ambidexterity (Gibson and Birkinshaw, 2004). Sequential ambidexterity means that organizations can achieve ambidexterity in a *sequential* fashion and shift structures over time. Contextual ambidexterity can be achieved by having a common goal throughout the organization and by empowering individuals to make their own judgments about how to divide their time between the conflicting demands of tasks. Issues such as the importance of routines are further raised in this context in an attempt to pursue both exploration and exploitation in the organization (Adler et al., 1999; Simsek et al., 2009). Existing routines can enable as well as constrain operations (Leonard-Barton, 1992; Gilbert, 2005). Competition derived from disruptive new entrants and powerful incumbents, namely attack and counterattack, is by nature a dynamic process. Technology (dis)continuity also plays a role (e.g. Rosenbloom, 2000), embodied in, for example, the *architectural versus modular* innovation (Henderson and Clark, 1994, on semiconductors) in transformation.

The third approach highlighted here often deals with practical questions of business strategy and economic organization from the perspective of firms and managers. This includes literature on business models and business model innovation, value networks (value webs), complementary assets (Teece, 1986), the extended dynamic capabilities perspective (Teece and Pisano, 1994) and industrial alliances and firm boundaries (e.g. vertical integration). Where the firm positions itself in the value chain, upstream versus downstream or lead versus non-lead, is the departure point in configuring strategies to transform. At times, the above-mentioned literature is perceived as a cousin to the transaction cost literature, but its value in understanding industrial transformation is not sufficiently taken into consideration. For example, the technological regime underlying an industry varies depending on where the firm stands along the value chain. In the video games industry, for example, digitalization, particularly online distribution, connotes very different things for game developers, game publishers, so-called first-party manufacturers (producing game consoles, for example) and retailers.

Several of these approaches, such as industrial architecture, modularity, value streams or value chains, have been combined into the emerging ecosystems literature, which addresses how complementary firms, organized differently from value chains, create value for customers and users. The unit of analysis varies, whether it addresses a business ecosystem in how a firm governs complementary firms, platform ecosystems in terms of platform-orchestrated firm-customer interactions such as multisided markets or innovation ecosystems dealing with how actors coordinate and compete to launch complementary or competing offers (e.g. Baldwin, 2008; Adner, 2017; Parker et al., 2017; Jacobides et al., 2018). The second group of literature – the two-sided market literature (e.g. Rochet and Tirole, 2003; Rysman, 2009) – is often discussed together with the *platform literature* (e.g. Parker and Van Alstyne, 2005, 2017; Parker et al., 2016). Sometimes, the former is treated as a subset of the latter. The two-sided market, also known as the *two-sided network*, is a product of the rise of the (digital) platform economy. A two-sided market refers to the phenomenon that "two sets of agents interact through an intermediary or platform … The decisions of each set of agents affects the outcomes of the other set of agents, typically through an externality" (Rysman, 2009, p. 125). Typical examples include eBay, Facebook and LinkedIn. Interactions tend to be multifarious and occur on both sides of the market. This goes far beyond the linear sequence of supply versus demand. Mechanisms such as network effect, increasing return, economies of scale/scope/speed and even the prisoners' dilemma apply. Consequently, there are implications for industrial transformation, not least in strategies relating to competition, pricing and openness (Rysman, 2009).

Digitalization and sustainability: Recent literature

While many of the chapters collected in this book deal with digital transformation and sustainability, a brief review of recent literature related to them may be needed.

On the *digitalization* study front, they are the disruptive innovation literature (e.g. Christensen, 1997) and the two-sided market literature and its associated platform literature (e.g. Rochet and Tirole, 2003, 2006), and the transformative impact in, for example, social production (Benkler, 2006). The above-mentioned literature is mostly approached from the managerial perspective, as was discussed in "The management approaches".

There are two additional sections of digitalization literature that are primarily approached from an economics perspective.

First, the industrial revolution literature analyses such topics as artificial intelligence (AI) and machine learning (ML) (Varian, 2018; Brynjolfsson and McAfee, 2012, 2014), and it may be viewed as an extension of the GPT approach (cf. Bresnahan and Trajtenberg, 1992; Helpman, 1998; Bresnahan, 2010).

This literature is particularly pertinent to industrial transformation. The second machine age literature (Brynjolfsson and McAfee, 2014), for example, summarizes what computers can and cannot do today, as well as discussing the consequences of that development, namely a bounty on the one hand and a spread on the other. *Bounty* refers to the mass opportunities that the exponential digitization capacity can offer and *spread* refers to the big gaps among people in income, wealth and so on.

Second, the development perspective addresses (a) disparities in digitalization, sometimes phrased as the digital divide (e.g. Hilbert, 2016) and (b) new conditions for industrial catching up: digital convergence (Long, 2014; Long and Laestadius, 2016; Ernst and Kim, 2002; Ernst et al., 2014).

The general ground for the digital divide school is that although accessing the digital world is no longer the privilege of a few, disparities – between those who have access and those who do not have – remain. By the end of 2019, there were still 3.4 billion people who were not online (ITU, 2019).[8] "The bad news is that the digital access divide is here to stay" (Hilbert, 2016, p. 567) if the digital access divide is measured by bandwidth (by treating the access as a moving target), rather than by the number of subscriptions, which shows that the gaps are rapidly closing over time (c.f. Compaine, 2001). The existence of "the bottom of the pyramid" (Prahalad and Hart, 2002, p. 1) in digital access may be attributed to a lack of capital (infrastructural investment), institutions, capabilities (see

Sen, 1999) and transferability of certain digital technologies (e.g. 3D printing technology as described by Woodson et al., 2019). The knowledge/capabilities constraint is also referred to as the "second-level digital divide" (Hargittai, 2002) and "digital literacy" (ITU, 2015).[9] The existence of the digital divide certainly has implications for the transformation of industries, particularly industries that are highly dependent on globalization. Concepts like appropriate technologies and inclusive innovations (cf. Schumacher, 1973/2011) are discussed in this context (e.g. Heeks, et al., 2014).

The other school of thoughts – the digital convergence school – may be traced back to the convergence club's discussion popularized in the 1990s when the second-tier Asian tigers (e.g. Taiwan, Singapore, South Korea) managed to catch up to the advanced economies industrially (Baumol et al., 1989; Abramovitz, 1994). In that process, the information and communication technologies industry has been singled out as one of the leading sectors in learning, imitating and absorbing advanced technological knowledge. That, in turn, builds up grounds for capabilities-based and technology transfer-focused catching up (Linsu, 1997; Hobday, 1995; Linsu and Nelson, 2000), rather than following Latin American countries' experiences in relying on capital (i.e. foreign direct investment) in the 1970–1980s (Amsden, 2001). The potential of information and communications technologies for leading industrial catching up has been explored from a global value chain perspective (Ernst and Kim, 2002; 2020 on the chip industry), a modular knowledge perspective (Long and Laestadius, 2016), and a conditions for leapfrogging in application perspective (e.g. M-pesa mobile payment in Kenya since 2007) (Hughes and Lonie, 2007).

On the *sustainability* study front, the recent sustainability literature includes the triple-bottom-line approach (economic, environmental and social aspects) on sustainability management. In this section, we focus on the recent inclusion of the environmental aspect. Triple-bottom-line is a management approach that departed from the accounting school and later expanded into other subfields such as corporate social responsibility. The phrase "triple bottom line" was coined by John Elkington (1994), as his way of measuring performance in corporate America. A sustainability management system can and should be measured on all three fronts: financial, social and environmental. This approach goes beyond the traditional profit-and-returns-on-investment-focused accounting measures of firm performance, sometimes referred to as the three Ps: profit, people and planet (Savitz, 2006).

Moving up to the meso (industry) level and taking an industrial transformation perspective, this triple-bottom-line thinking has been incorporated into understanding the outcomes of transformation. There is a consensus that a successful transformation is an environmentally or ecologically healthy transformation. In the energy sector, for example, sustainability is a normative goal that guides strategies and actions (Raven, 2006). The transition is treated as an evolutionary process, but with an element of intention that influences the process. Typical approaches may be found in the following strands of the literature.

First, an early approach is the large technical systems literature (Hughes, 1983, 1989) arguing that in an infrastructural system (e.g. an electricity system), any embedded institutional, sociopolitical, technological or cultural element can profoundly affect the change patterns of the whole system. There are many extensions on that, such as Kaijser (2005) describing the urban transport system as "a system of systems", and Blomkvist and Nilsson (2017) on the piped water infrastructure system, where the degree of alignment of upstream activities differs greatly from that of downstream activities, potentially causing the failure of the whole system.

A more recent approach is the so-called transition literature. A larger system – rather than a system component – is the most common unit of analysis (see "The system perspective"). Many studies empirically deal with energy systems and examine the dynamic logic of the larger system in transition. Much of the literature has strong science and technology policy implications. MLP, which is also called sociotechnical transition studies (Geels, 2002, 2004; Geels and Schot, 2010) is also frequently used. It consists of a synthesized and all-embracing type of framework, addressing not only layers of changes in technology, but also regulations, networks, cultures and infrastructure, and process of changes. Derived terms include "energy regime" (van der Vleuten and Högselius, 2012), which can help researchers to understand the dynamics of incumbent energy sectors as well as the interaction and alignment between multiple technical and non-technical elements (e.g. power plants, legislation, company strategies and consumer habits) in transition processes in transnational electricity and natural gas systems.

The transition literature relates to a number of policy-focused terms such as "sustainable innovation policies" (Nill and Kemp, 2009), "Eco-innovation policy" (Kemp, 2011), "transformative innovation policy" (Steward, 2012), "innovation policy 3.0" (Schot and Steinmueller, 2016) and "mission-oriented innovation policy" (Mazzucato, 2018), illustrating a widely debated policy directionality on sustainability.

Second, from a trajectory perspective, there is the well-established avoid-shift-improve (ASI) framework, which was initially used in the German transport sector in the 1990s when structuring policy measures to address environmental impact (Bundestag, 1994), and was later adopted by the International Energy Agency in its 2013 report, "A Tale of Renewed Cities". The ASI approach embraces (a) avoiding travel needs (through viable urban planning or working from a distance), (b) shifting the means of travel (to low/no carbon emission options) and (c) improving the energy efficiency of vehicles. The ASI approach can be used in other sectors too.

From the transformation perspective, enormous effects are being made throughout industry, which is similar to the discussion at the macro level, the so-called *dematerialization* trend, which was coined by McAfee (2019) in his influential book *More from Less: The Surprising Story of How We Learned to Prosper Using Fewer Resources – and What Happens Next*. Based on US statistical data, McAfee explains how the US economy is growing while using less and less material (timber, metals, fertilizer). This dematerialization trend is partly attributed to the use of new technologies, including digital technologies.

While *factor prices* (in production) and *demand* are the two classic elements affecting the choice of technologies, the (degree of) *competition* – between different technological alternatives – is the third element introduced by induced innovation theory, which guides our understanding of the trajectory changes in transformation.

Third, and from an industry sector perspective, industries are crudely divided into brown (sometimes referred to as black) industries and green industries. Thus, any industry can be roughly positioned along the brown-to-green line. Challenges, opportunities and obstacles that occur in transformation are consequently varied along brown-to-green industry lines. Erik Dahmén's (1950, 1988) development blocks concept is sometimes used in analysing such effects as the structural change in the heat pump sector and petroleum industry elsewhere in this book (see Chapter 10 and Chapter 11). Terms like tradable white certificates or emissions trading are used to address the dynamics of the changes occurring in different industry sectors for energy efficiency and energy saving.

Synthesis

Industries transform, at times digitally or sustainably, whether an appropriate analytical tool – with a box of inquiry – is in place or not. There is interest in the scholarly community in identifying both the regularities of and the contingency factors influencing industry transformation. The focus is on empirically analysing the drivers, processes and outcomes of the transformation, and conceptually, the characteristics and properties of the transformation and its causal factors.

What are the regularities hitherto identified? Industries and firms differ greatly in the pathways and trajectories they choose to transform. That, in turn, is derived from changes in the relative prices of the factors of production, which, in turn, spur innovations directed to economizing the use of factors that have become relatively expensive. This is sometimes phrased as a factor-saving bias, put forwards originally by Hicks (1932) in his discussion on labour-saving inventions, and discussed extensively in the economics literature (cf. Fellner, 1962). The message is that technological change is induced by factor substitution. The classic factors introduced in the textbook embrace land, labour and capital, among which mobility varies according to the sequence of the three. While the factor endowment of a country holds constant in certain historical periods, the changes in the factors are subject to today's degree of globalization.

The nature and the reservoir of industrial knowledge affect the nature of economic activities in firms. Technological knowledge involves various degrees of specificity, tacitness, complexity and independence (Winter, 1987). That, in turn, affects the scope of opportunities, the cumulativeness of knowledge and the appropriability of innovations, as shown by the concept of *technological regimes*

(Malerba and Orsenigo, 1997). For example, the transformation of Nordic pulp-and-paper companies (e.g. Stora Enso) to the field of bio-refinery, or bio-composites, is partly driven by the shrinkage of demand for newspapers and partly by the need to replace oil in chemical/plastic products. The new trajectory is problem-solving-biased on the one hand, and path-dependent on new knowledge formation on the other hand. The following factors are important.

The specific stage of the technological life cycle the firm is entering. The competition landscape changes dynamically with the evolution of the key technology within the industry. Technologies can evolve in a *cumulative* manner, exemplified by generations of Telecom technologies, or in a *discrete* manner, exemplified by many chemical technologies. A detailed analysis of the typology of cumulative versus discrete technology is found in Merges and Nelson's (1990) analyses of patents and the connectedness of patents in different industries. For many cumulative technologies, emerging technology and incumbent technology evolve by attack and counterattack from a continuous base, elaborated in, for example, the S-curve literature (e.g. Foster, 1986). The videogame industry, for example, is now re-entering a fluid phase of innovation due to the rise of mobile gaming and other digital platforms for gaming (e.g. Steam). The earlier industry consolidation, evident in the AAA game era,[10] may be disrupted (see Long, 2020).

Complementarities of technologies and technological (sub)systems. There is a kind of interdependence among different technological systems and solutions, illustrated by the Heat Pump Technology chapter. By the same token, while hydropower has traditionally dominated the energy supply in Norway and there is no sign that demand will surpass supply, incentives to develop wind energy systems remain minimal, even though there are good conditions to develop wind energy there.

The Institutional framework, not the least industrial policies. This is illustrated in, for example, the transition literature (e.g. Schot and Steinmueller, 2018). "Even an act of legislation that imposes a constraint may lead to exploratory activities which eventually confer an advantage to those who were constrained" (Rosenberg, 1969, p. 19). This is illustrated by many rapid switches to low-emission technologies. The development and test of electric road-based charging systems by major industry actors such as Renault, Citroen, Peugeot, Fiat, Volvo and Scania organized around a European consortium, FABRIC (feasibility analysis and development of on-road charging solutions for future electric vehicles), may illustrate an escape route from the range constraints of battery technologies.

The above-mentioned factors only serve as illustrations of elements that have a bearing on industrial transformation, factors that are also covered in various theoretical strands introduced in this chapter.

There are also contingency factors to be incorporated when understanding industrial transformation. Transformation occurs in a wide technological, institutional, social and even geographic context. The contingency approach lifts up the changing contextual factors that cause certain processes and practices to apply or not to apply, certain relationships to hold or not to hold, certain methods to work or not to work. The contributions of this approach include identifying important contingency variables that distinguish the varieties of contexts or that group different contexts. The transformation and adoption of waterless toilets, for example, is a response to not only the increasing shortage of water and the unevenness of key infrastructures, but also the varieties of local conditions: developing versus developed countries, cultural and personal preferences, technology acceptance levels and so on. A match, not only between supply and demand but also between the production/installation systems and local priorities, has to be in place to enable the transformation.

Notes

1 "For many important considerations, especially those connected with the manifold influences of the element of time, do not lend themselves to mathematical expression" (Marshall, 1890/1920, p. 850).
2 This chapter is not the result of a detailed bibliometric study, which we might call a supply based approach (on transformation), because it departs from the literature pool to see what is available to explain industrial transformation. Rather, we use a demand-based approach, namely what we consider useful for master's/doctoral students and the general academic community to understand industry transformation cases.
3 Neoclassical theory often argues that factor substitution and the accumulation of technological knowledge are not applicable simultaneously.
4 On the role of learning, the accumulation school argues that learning is a by-product of (capital) investment, while the assimilation school argues that learning is an endogenous (intentional and painstaking) process that involves Knightian uncertainty and economic risk in essential ways.
5 "Institutional change shapes the way societies evolve through time and hence is the key to understanding historical change" (North, 1990, p. 3).
6 Nelson and Winter (1982, p. 60) discuss this issue in depth by quoting Arrow and Hahn (1971, p. 53): "the production possibility set is a description of the state of the firm's knowledge about the possibilities of transforming commodities".
7 The terms industrial life cycle, product life cycle and technology life cycle are used interchangeably throughout the literature. No literature, as far as we know, has provided a standard answer to the actual differences among these concepts in understanding industrial transformation, except an obvious difference in the unit of analyses. In an earlier discussion with Utterback, we asked why a product, rather than a technology, is addressed in PLC theory. It is generally not clear whether a product thinking or a technology thinking approach would provide more value or not in understanding the cycles.
8 www.itu.int/en/ITU-D/Statistics/Pages/stat/default.aspx.
9 http://digitalinclusionnewslog.itu.int/2015/11/16/towards-digital-literacy-of-all/.
10 This refers to console-based video games, often with high budgets, which have been distributed via major publishers since the late 1990s.

References

Abramovitz, M. (1994) The origins of the postwar catch-up and convergence boom. In Fagerberg, J., B. Verspagen, and N. von Tunzelmann (eds) *The Dynamics of Technology, Trade and Growth*. Aldershot: Edward Elgar, 21–52.

Adler, P., Goldoftas, B., and Levine, D. (1999) Flexibility versus efficiency? A case study of model changeovers in the Toyota production system. *Organization Science*, 10: 43–68.

Adner, R. (2017) Ecosystem as structure: An actionable construct for strategy. *Journal of Management*, 43(1): 39–58.
Adner, R., and Levinthal, D. (2001) Demand heterogeneity and technology evolution. Implications for product and process innovation. *Management Science*, 47(5): 611–628.
Amsden, A. (2001) *The Rise of "The Rest": Challenges to the West From Late-Industrializing Economies*. New York, NY: Oxford University Press.
Anderson, P., and Tushman, M. (1990) Technological discontinuities and dominant designs: A cyclical model of technological change. *Administrative Science Quarterly*, 35(4): 604–633. doi: 10.2307/2393511
Arrow, K.J., and Hahn, F.H. (1971) *General Competitive Analysis*. San Francisco: Holden-Day, Inc.
Asheim, B.T. (1996) Industrial districts as 'learning regions': A condition for prosperity. *European Planning Studies*, 4(4): 379–400.
Asheim, B.T., and Gertler, M.S. (2005) The geography of innovation: Regional innovation systems. In Fagerberg, J., Mowery, D., and Nelson, R. (eds) *The Oxford Handbook of Innovation*. Oxford: University Press, 291–317.
Ashton, T.S. (1948) *The Industrial Revolution, 1760–1830*. London; New York: Oxford University Press.
Baldwin, C.Y. (2008) Where do transactions come from? Modularity, transactions, and the boundaries of firms. *Industrial and Corporate Change*, 17(1): 155–195.
Baum, J., and Singh, J.V. (eds) (1994) *Evolutionary Dynamics of Organizations*. Oxford: Oxford University Press.
Baumol, W.J., Blackman, S.A.B., and Wolff, E.N. (1989) *Productivity and American Leadership*. Cambridge, MA: MIT Press.
Benkler, Y. (2006) *The Wealth of Networks: How Social Production Transforms Markets and Freedom*. New Haven and London: Yale University Press. 528 pp.
Berlin, I. (1991) *The Crooked Timber of Humanity*. London: Fontana.
Bijker, W., Hughes, T., and Pinch, T. (1989) *The Social Construction of Technological Systems: New Directions in the Sociology and History of Technology*. Cambridge, MA (United States): MIT Press.
Björkdahl, J., and Holmén, M. (2013) Business model innovation – the challenges ahead. *International Journal of Product Development*, 18(3/4): 213–225.
Blomkvist, P., and Nilsson, D. (2017) On the need for system alignment in large water infrastructure: Understanding infrastructure dynamics in Nairobi, Kenya. *Water Alternatives*, 10(2): 283–302.
Breschi, S., Malerba, F., and Orsenigo, L. (2000) Technological regimes and Schumpeterian patterns of innovation. *Economic Journal, Royal Economic Society*, 110(463): 388–410.
Bresnahan, T.F., and Trajtenberg, M. (1992) General purpose technologies: Engines of growth? *NBER Working Paper Series Working Paper No. 4148* https://www.nber.org/papers/w4148.pdf
Bruland, Kristine (eds) (1991) *Technology Transfer and Scandinavian Industrialisation*. New York: Berg Publishers.
Brynjolfsson, E., and McAfee, A. (2012) Race against the machine: How the digital revolution is accelerating innovation, driving productivity, and irreversibly transforming employment and the economy. MIT Sloan School of Management. http://ebusiness.mit.edu/research/Briefs/Brynjolfsson_McAfee_Race_Against_the_Machine.pdf
Brynjolfsson, E., and McAfee, A. (2014) *The Second Machine Age*. New York: W. W. Norton & Company.

Bundestag (1994) Zweiter Bericht der Enquete-Kommission "Schutz der Erdatmosphaere" zum Thema Mobilitaet und Klima — Wege zu einer klimavertraeglicher Verkehrspolitik. Deutscher Bun- destag Drucksache 12/8300.

Carlsson, B., and Stankiewicz, R. (1991) On the nature, function and composition of technological systems. *Journal of Evolutionary Economics*, 1(2): 93–118.

Chamberlin, E.H. (1933) *The Theory of Monopolistic Competition: A Re-Orientation of the Theory of Value*. Cambridge, MA: Harvard University Press.

Christensen, C.M. (1997) *The Innovator's Dilemma: When New Technologies Cause Great Firms to Fail*. Boston, MA: Harvard Business School Press.

Coase, R.H. (1937) The nature of the firm. *Economica*, 4: 386–405.

Cohen, W.M., and Levinthal, D.A. (1990) Absorptive capacity: A new perspective on learning and innovation. *Administrative Science Quarterly*, 35(1): 128–152. Special Issue: *Technology, Organizations, and Innovation*. (March, 1990).

Compaine, B.M. (2001) *Digital Divide: Facing a Crisis or Creating a Myth?* Cambridge, MA (United States): MIT Press.

Cooke, P. (1992) Regional innovation systems: Competitive regulation in the new Europe. *Geoforum*, 23: 365–382.

Dahmén, E. (1950) *Svensk industriell företagarverksamhet. Kausalanalys av den industriella utvecklingen1919–1939. Del I–II*. Stockholm: Industriens utredningsinstitut.

Dahmén, E. (1988) 'Development blocks' in industrial economics. *Scandinavian Economic History Review*, 36(1): 3–14. doi: 10.1080/03585522.1988.10408102

David, P.A. (1985) Clio and the economics of QWERTY. *American Economic Review*, 75: 332–337.

Dosi, G., and Nelson, R.R. (2009) Technical change and industrial dynamics as evolutionary processes. *LEM Working Paper Series*, No. 2009/07, Scuola Superiore Sant'Anna, Laboratory of Economics and Management (LEM), Pisa. http://hdl.handle.net/10419/89555

Duncan, R. (1976) The ambidextrous organization: Designing dual structures for innovation. In R.H. Killman, L.R. Pondy, and D. Sleven (eds) *The Management of Organization*. New York: North Holland, 167–188.

Eliasson, G. (1997) Competence blocks and industrial policy in the knowledge based economy. *Science Technology and Industry Review*, 22: 209–241.

Elkington, J. (1994) Towards the sustainable corporation: Win-win-win business strategies for sustainable development. *California Management Review*, 36(2): 90–100.

Ernst, D. (2020) Competing in artificial intelligence chips: China's challenge amid technology War. https://www.cigionline.org/publications/competing-artificial-intelligence-chips-chinas-challenge-amid-technology-war

Ernst, D., and Kim, L. (2002) Global production networks, knowledge diffusion, and local capability formation. *Research Policy*, 31(8–9): 1417–1429.

Ernst, D., Lee, H., and Kwak, J. (2014) Standards, innovation, and latecomer economic development: Conceptual issues and policy challenges. *Telecommunications Policy*, 38: 853–862.

Fagerberg, J., and Srholec, M. (2007) The role of "capabilities" in development: Why some countries manage to catch up while others stay poor. Centre for Technology, Innovation and Culture, University of Oslo. *DIME Working Paper Package* 31(2007.08) in the series on "Dynamics of Knowledge Accumulation, Competitiveness, Regional Cohesion and Economic Policies".

Feldman, M., and Choi, J. (2015) Harnessing the geography of innovation: Toward evidence-based economic development policy. In Archibugi, D., and Filippetti, A.

(eds) *The Handbook of Global Science, Technology and Innovation*. Hoboken, New Jersey: Wiley-Blackwell, 269–289.

Fellner, W. (1962) Does the market direct the relative factor-saving effects of technological progress? In *Universities-National Bureau Committee for Economic Research, The Rate and Direction of Inventive Activity*. Princeton, NJ: Princeton University Press.

Foster, R. (1986) Working the S-curve: Assessing technological threats. *Research Management*, 29(4): 17–20.

Freeman, C. (1987) *Technology Policy and Economic Performance: Lessons from Japan*. New York: Pinter Publishers.

Geels, F. (2002) Technological transitions as evolutionary reconfiguration processes: A multi-level perspective and a case-study. *Research Policy*, 31: 1257–1274.

Geels, F.W. (2004) From sectoral systems of innovations to socio-technical systems: Insights about dynamics and change from sociology and institutional theory. *Research Policy*, 33(6–7): 897–920.

Geels, F.W., and Schot, J. (2010) The dynamics of transitions: A socio-technical perspective. In Grin, J., Rotmans, J., and Schot, J. (eds) *Transitions to Sustainable Development: New Directions in the Study of Long-Term Transformative Change*. London: Routledge, 9–101.

Gibson, C.B., and Birkinshaw, J. (2004) The antecedents, consequences, and mediating role of organizational ambidexterity. *Academy of Management Journal*, 47: 209–226.

Gilbert, C. (2005) Unbundling the structure of inertia: Resource versus routine rigidity. *Academy of Management Journal*, 48: 741–763.

Habakkuk, H.J. (1962) *American and British Technology in the Nineteenth Century*. London: Cambridge University Press.

Hargittai, E. (2002) Second-level digital divide: Differences in people's online skills. *First Monday*, 7(4). doi: 10.5210/fm.v7i4.942. https://firstmonday.org/ojs/index.php/fm/issue/view/144

Heeks, R., Foster, C., and Nugroho, Y. (2014) New models of inclusive innovation for development. *Innovation and Development*, 4(2): 175–185. doi: 10.1080/2157930X.2014.928982

Hicks, J.R. (1932) *The Theory of Wages*. New York: Macmillan Co.

Hilbert, M. (2016) The bad news is that the digital access divide is here to stay: Domestically installed bandwidths among 172 countries for 1986–2014. *Telecommunications Policy*, 40(6): 567–581.

Hobday, M. (1995) *Innovation in East Asia: The Challenge to Japan*. Cheltenham: E. Elgar.

Hughes, N., and Lonie, S. (2007) M-PESA: Mobile money for the "unbanked" turning cellphones into 24-hour tellers in Kenya. *Innovations: Technology, Governance, Globalization*, 2(1–2). MIT Press. https://www.mitpressjournals.org/doi/abs/10.1162/itgg.2007.2.1-2.63

Hughes, T. (1989) The evolution of large technological systems. In Bijker, W.E., Hughes, T.P.E., and Pinch, T.J. (eds) *The Social Construction of Technological Systems: New Directions in the Sociology and History of Technology*. Cambridge, MA: MIT Press, 51–82.

Hughes, T.P. (1983) *Networks of Power: Electrification in Western Society, 1880–1930*. Baltimore, MD: Johns Hopkins University Press.

Hughes, T.P. (1987) The evolution of large technical systems. In Bijker, W.E., Hughes, T.P., and Pinch, T. (eds) *The Social Construction of Technological Systems: New Directions in the Sociology and History of Technology*. Cambridge, MA: MIT Press, 51–82.

International Energy Agency (IEA) (2013) Policy pathway: A tale of renewed cities. https://www.iea.org/reports/policy-pathway-a-tale-of-renewed-cities

Jacobides, M.G., Cennamo, C., and Gawer, A. (2018) Towards a theory of ecosystems. *Strategic Management Journal*, 39(8): 2255–2276.

Johnson, B.H., Lundvall, B.-Å., and Edquist, C. (2003) Economic development and the national system of innovation approach. In *The First International Globelics Conference: Innovation systems and Development Strategies for the Third Millenium*, Rio de Janeiro, November 2–6, 2003.

Kaijser, A. (2005) How to describe large technical systems and their changes over time? In Gunilla, J., and Emin, T. (eds) *Urban Transport Development*. Berlin, Heidelberg: Springer, 12–19. https://doi.org/10.1007/3-540-27761-7_3

Kemp, R. (2011) Ten themes for eco-innovation policies in Europé. In Mainguy, G. (éd.). *S.A.P.I.EN.S Surveys and Perspectives Integrating Environment and Society*, 4(2). http://journals.openedition.org/sapiens/116

Klepper, S., and Simons, K.L. (1997) Technological extinctions of industrial firms: An inquiry into their nature and causes. *Industrial and Corporate Change*, 6(2): 379–460.

Knight, F. (1921) *Risk, Uncertainty and Profit*. Boston, MA: Houghton Mifflin Co.

Laestadius, S. (1998) Technology level, knowledge formation and industrial competence in paper manufacturing. In Eliasson, G., Green, C., and McCann, C.R. (eds) *Microfoundations of Economic Growth: A Schumpeterian Perspective*. University of Michigan Press, 212–226.

Landes, David S. (1969) *The Unbound Prometheus: Technological Change and Industrial Development in Western Europe from 1750 to the Present*. Cambridge, UK: Cambridge University Press.

Leonard-Barton, D. (1992) Core capabilities and core rigidities: A paradox in managing new product development. *Strategic Management Journal*, 13: 111–125.

Linsu, K. (1997) *Imitation to Innovation: The Dynamics of Korea's Technological Learning*. Boston: Harvard Business School Press.

Linsu, K., and Nelson, R. (2000) *Technology, Learning, and Innovation: Experiences of Newly Industrializing Economies*. Cambridge: Cambridge University Press.

Long, V. (2014) A Technological Capabilities Perspective on Catching up – the Case of the Chinese ICT Industry. Doctoral thesis at The Royal Institute of Technology.

Long, V. (2020) Profiting from innovation in the digital era: Evidence from the Swedish videogames industry. In Mention, A., and Pierre-Jean, B. (eds) *Managing Digital Open Innovation*. London: Imperial College Press, 139–173.

Long, V., and Laestadius, S. (2016) An indigenous innovation: An example from mobile communication technology. *Oxford Development Studies*, 44(1): 113–133. doi: 10.1080/13600818.2015.1111319

Lundvall, B.-A. (1992) *National Systems of Innovation: Towards a Theory of Innovation and Interactive Learning*. London: Pinter.

Lundvall, B., and Johnson, B. (1994) The learning economy. *Journal of Industry Studies*, 1(2): 23–42.

Malerba, F., and Lee, K. (2016) Theory and empirical evidence of catch-up cycles and changes in industrial leadership. *Research Policy*, 46(2). doi: 10.1016/j.respol.2016.09.008

Malerba, F., and Orsenigo, L. (2002) Innovation and market structure in the dynamics of the pharmaceutical industry and biotechnology: Towards a history-friendly model. *Industrial and Corporate Change*, 11: 4.

Malerba, F., Nelson, R., Orsenigo, L., and Sidney, W. (2016) *Innovation and the Evolution of Industries: History-Friendly Models*. Cambridge: Cambridge University Press.

Malerba, F., Nelson, R.R., Orsenigo, L., and Winter, S. (2008) Vertical integration and disintegration of computer firms: A history-friendly model of the coevolution of the computer and semiconductor industries. *Industrial and Corporate Change*, 17(2): 197–231.

Malerba, F., and Orsenigo, L. (1997) Technological regimes and sectoral patterns of innovative activities. *Industrial and Corporate Change*, 6(1): 83–118.

Marshall, A. (1890/1920) *Principles of Economics*, 8th edition. London: Macmillan.

Marsili, O. (1999) Technological regimes: Theory and evidence. *Working Paper*. http://www.lem.sssup.it/Dynacom/files/D20_0.pdf

Mazzucato, M. (2018) Mission-oriented innovation policies: Challenges and opportunities. *Industrial and Corporate Change*, 27(5): 803–815. doi: 10.1093/icc/dty034

Merges, R., and Nelson, R. (1990) The complex economics of patent scope. *Columbia Law Review*, 90(4): 839–916. doi: 10.2307/1122920

Metcalfe, S. (2014) Capitalism and evolution. *Journal of Evolutionary Economics*, 24: 11–34. doi: 10.1007/s00191-013-0307-7

Mokyr, J. (1992) *The Lever of Riches: Technological Creativity and Economic Progress*. New York: Oxford University Press.

Mokyr, J. (1994) That which we call an industrial revolution. *Contention*, 4: 189–206.

Mokyr, J. (1998) Editor's introduction: The new economic history and the industrial revolution. In J. Mokyr (ed) *The British Industrial Revolution: An Economic Perspective*, 2nd ed. Boulder: Westview Press.

Moore, G. (1999) *Crossing the Chasm, Marketing and Selling High-Tech Products to Mainstream Customer* (revised edition). New York: HarperCollins Publishers.

Nelson, R. (1995) Co-evolution of industry structure, technology and supporting institutions, and the making of comparative advantage. *International Journal of the Economics of Business*, 2(2): 171–184. Taylor & Francis Journals.

Nelson, R., and Pack, H. (1999) The Asian miracle and modern growth theory. *The Economic Journal*, 109(457): 416–436.

Nelson, R.R. (1994) The co-evolution of technology, industrial structure, and supporting institutions. *Industrial and Corporate Change*, 3(1): 47–63.

Nelson, R.R., and Winter, S.G. (1982) *An Evolutionary Theory of Economic Change*. Cambridge, MA: Harvard University Press.

Nill, J., and Kemp, R. (2009) Evolutionary approaches for sustainable innovation policies: From niche to paradigm. *Research Policy*, 38(4): 668–680.

North, D. (1990) *Institutions, Institutional Change and Economic Performance*. Cambridge: Cambridge University Press.

OECD/Eurostat (2018) *Oslo Manual 2018: Guidelines for Collecting, Reporting and Using Data on Innovation*, 4th edition. Paris: The Measurement of Scientific, Technological and Innovation Activities, OECDPublishing/ Luxembourg: Eurostat. https://doi.org/10.1787/9789264304604-en; https://www.oecd.org/science/oslo-manual-2018-9789264304604-en.htm

O'Hern, M.S., and Rindfleisch, A. (2010) Customer co-creation: A typology and research agenda. *Review of Marketing Research*, 6: 84–106.

O'Reilly, C.A., and Tushman, M.L. (2004) The ambidextrous organization. *Harvard Business Review*, 82(4): 74–81, 140.

Parker, G., and Van Alstyne, M. (2005) Two-sided network effects: A theory of information product design. *Management Science*, 51(10): 1494–1504.

Parker, G., and Van Alstyne, M. (2017) Innovation, openness, and platform control. *Management Science*. August: 1–18.

Parker, G., Van Alstyne, M., and Choudary, S.P. (2016) *Platform Revolution: How Networked Markets Are Transforming the Economy – And How to Make Them Work for You*. New York: W.W. Norton & Company.

Parker, G., Van Alstyne, M., and Jiang, X. (2017) Platform ecosystems: How developers invert the firm. *MIS Quarterly*, 41(1): 255–266.

Parker, G.G., and Van Alstyne, M.W. (2000) Internetwork externalities and free information goods. In *Proceedings of the 2nd ACM Conference on Electronic Commerce.* AC Med, pp. 107–116.

Penrose, E. (1959) *The Theory of the Growth of the Firm.* Oxford: Basil Blackwell.

Perez, C. (2002) *Technological Revolutions and Financial Capital: The Dynamics of Bubbles and Golden Ages.* Cheltenham, UK: Edward Elgar. 198 pages, ISBN 1 84064 922 4

Prahalad, C.K., and Hart, S. (2002) *The Fortune at the Bottom of the Pyramid.* Strategy+Business e-Doc (26): 1–16.

Raisch, S., and Birkinshaw, J. (2008) Organizational ambidexterity: Antecedents, outcomes and moderators. *Journal of Management*, 34(3): 375–409.

Raven, R. (2006) Niche accumulation and hybridisation strategies in transition processes towards a sustainable energy system: An assessment of differences and pitfalls. *Energy Policy*, 35, 2390–2400.

Rochet, J.-C., and Tirole, J. (2003) Platform competition in two-sided markets. *Journal of the European Economic Association*, 1(4): 990–1029.

Rochet, J.-C., and Tirole, J. (2006) Two-sided markets: A progress report. *The RAND Journal of Economics*, 37(3): 645–667.

Romer, P. (1986) Increasing returns and economic growth. *American Economic Review*, 94: 1002–1037.

Romer, P. (1990) Endogenous technical change. *Journal of Political Economy*, 98: 71–102.

Rosenberg, N. (1969) The direction of technological change: Inducement mechanisms and focusing devices. *Economic Development and Cultural Change*, 18(1): 1–24.

Rosenberg, N. (1994) *Exploring the Black Box: Technology, Economics, and History.* Cambridge, New York, Port Chester, Melbourne, Sydney: Cambridge University Press.

Rosenbloom, R.S. (2000) Leadership, capabilities, and technological change: The transformation of NCR in the electronic era. *Strategic Management Journal*, 21: 1083–1103.

Rysman, M. (2009) The economics of two-sided markets. *Journal of Economic Perspectives*, 23(3): 125–143.

Savitz, A. (2006) *The Triple Bottom Line.* San Francisco, CA: Jossey-Bass

Say, J.B. (1855) *A Treatise on Political Economy*, trans. Clement Biddle. Philadelphia, PA: Lippincott, Grambo & Co.

Schot, J. (2016) Confronting the second deep transition through the historical imagination. *Technology and Culture*, 57(2 April): 445–456.

Schot, J., and Steinmueller, W.E. (2016) *Framing Innovation Policy for Transformative Change: Innovation Policy 3.0.* Science Policy Research Unit (SPRU). https://foroconsultivo.org.mx/innovacion_transformadora/docs/lecturas/18.-Innovation_policy_3.0.pdf

Schot, J., and Steinmueller, E. (2018) Three frames for innovation policy: R&D, systems of innovation and transformative change. *Research Policy*, 47(9): 1554–1567.

Schumacher, E.F. (1973/2011) *Small is Beautiful: A Study of Economics as if People Mattered.* New York: Random House.

Schumpeter, J.A. (1911/1934) *Theorie der Wirtschaftlichen Entwicklung. English translation: The Theory of Economic Development.* Cambridge, MA: Harvard University Press.

Schumpeter, J.A. (1942) *Capitalism, Socialism and Democracy.* New York: Harper Torchbooks.

Sen, A. (1987/1999) *Commodities and Capabilities.* New Delhi: Oxford University Press.

Sen, A. (1999) *Development as Freedom*. Oxford: Oxford University Press.
Simsek, Z., Heavey, C., Veiga, J.F., and Souder, D. (2009) A typology for aligning organizational ambidexterity's conceptualizations, antecedents, and outcomes. *Journal of Management Studies*, 46: 864–894.
Smith, A. (1776) *The Wealth of Nations*, 2010 edition., North Mankato: Capstone Press.
Spender, J.-C. (1989) *Industry Recipes: An Enquiry into the Nature and Sources of Managerial Judgement*. Oxford: Basil Blackwell.
Stefano, B.S., Malerba, F., and Orsenigo, L. (2000) Technological regimes and Schumpeterian patterns of innovation. *The Economic Journal*, 110: 388–410.
Steward, F. (2012) Transformative innovation policy to meet the challenge of climate change: Sociotechnical networks aligned with consumption and end-use as new transition arenas for a low-carbon society or green economy. *Technology Analysis & Strategic Management*, 24(4): 331–343. doi: 10.1080/09537325.2012.663959
Teece, D.J. (1986) Profiting from technological innovation: Implications for integration, collaboration, licensing and public policy. *Research Policy*, 15: 285–305.
Teece, D., and Pisano, G. (1994) The dynamic capabilities of the firms: An introduction. *Industrial and Corporate Change*, 3(3): 537–556.
Teece, D.J., Pisano, G., and Shuen, A. (1997) Dynamic capabilities and strategic management. *Strategic Management Journal*, 18: 509–533.
Tushman, M.L., and O'Reilly, C.A. (1996) The ambidextrous organization: Managing evolutionary and revolutionary change. *California Management Review*, 38: 1–23.
Tushman, M.L., and O'Reilly, C.A. (2002) *Winning through Innovation: A Practical Guide to Leading Organizational Change and Renewal*. Boston, MA: Harvard University Press.
Unruh, G. (2000) Understanding carbon lock-in. *Energy Policy*, 28(12): 817–830.
Utterback, J.M., and Abernathy, W.J. (1975) A dynamic model of process and product innovation. *Omega*, 3: 639–656. doi: 10.1016/0305-0483(75)90068-7
Van der Vleuten, E., and Högselius, P. (2012) Resisting change? The transnational dynamics of European energy regimes. In Geert Verbong and Derk Loorback (eds) *Governing the Energy Transition: Reality, Illusion, or Necessity?* London: Routledge, 75–100.
Varian, H. (2018) Artificial intelligence, economics, and industrial organization. NBER Working Paper Series. Working Paper 24839 http://www.nber.org/papers/w24839
Veblen, T. (1994) The theory of the leisure class. In *The Collected Works of Thorstein Veblen*, Vol 1 1899, Re-print, London: Routledge, 1–404.
Von Hippel, E. (1998) Economics of product development by users: The impact of "sticky" local information. *Management Science*, 44(5): 629–644.
Von Tunzelmann, G.N. (1978) *Steam Power and British Industrialization to 1860*. Oxford: Oxford University Press.
Williamson, O.E. (1975) *Markets and Hierarchies: Analysis and Antitrust Implications*. New York: Free Press.
Winter, S.G. (1987) Knowledge and competence as strategic assets. In D.J. Teece (ed.) *The Competitive Challenge: Strategies for Industrial Innovation and Renewal*, Cambridge, MA: Ballinger, 159–184.
Woodson, T., Alcantara, J., and Nascimento, M.S. (2019) Is 3D printing an inclusive innovation? An examination of 3D printing in Brazil. *Technovation*, 80–81: 54–62.
Young, A. (1928) Increasing returns and economic progress. *The Economic Journal*, 38(152): 527–547.

3

HOW DIGITAL PLATFORMS TRANSFORM INDUSTRIES

Kent Thorén

Introduction

Industries change and transform all the time. Recently, however, the rate of change appears to have risen, leading to vivid discussion in media and academia about whether and how digitalization is involved. "Digitalization" refers to the process of socioeconomic change triggered by the introduction of digital technology (Hirsch-Kreinsen, 2016). As the currently ongoing "long wave" of technology-based development, digitalization is having massive effects on most socioeconomic systems (Avant, 2014). One of the most noted effects is the widespread transformative impact on pre-existing industries.

Industry transition occurs as start-ups or other companies "invade" a mature industry and replace established ways of doing things with new business models that satisfy customer needs better or at lower cost (Berggren and Bergkvist, 2006). Incumbents, in turn, predictably respond ineffectively and gradually lose their dominant positions (Christensen et al., 2004, 2015). This pattern is typical for industry development. However, when digital technology is involved, it appears that the invaders' value propositions are remarkably insensitive to classic industry entry barriers (c.f. Porter, 1980). In some cases, even single firms have caused dramatic transformation of industries by building innovative business models that organize value creation and capture in untraditional ways. Rather than executing all the core activities themselves, they deliberately seek to become a coordinating focal point for interaction and transactions, thereby including many separate actors in the fulfilment of end customers' needs. As this provision of a coordinating and enabling space for other actors' business activities is the entrants' primary focus, we often refer to them as *platforms*. When successful, these collaborative operations are exceptionally scalable but still so lean that it is nearly impossible for incumbents to compete (Baldwin and Woodward, 2008).

What remains less clear is the nature of industrial transformation and how the competitive dynamics of successful platforms affect the roles and behaviours in industries by changing who interacts with who, how profits are redistributed and why.

The purpose of this chapter is to identify the particularities of digital platforms that are causing industry transformations and explain the mechanisms through which it happens.

This purpose is accomplished by examining several transformed industries, viewing their initial and transformed states as structures that create, deliver and capture value for some end customer – referred to henceforth as *value structures*. This focus on value is motivated by the assumptions that end customers generally aim to maximize value and that their purchasing choices in the marketplace are their primary way of doing so. This implies that they will not make the effort of shifting to a new alternative unless it promises more value. Explaining *how* digitalization causes transformations should, therefore, be possible by empirically tracing how the underlying technologies more precisely lead to increased value and thus new choices. This is done in the case descriptions in "Learning from major industry transitions" and the patterns found are thereafter analysed more deeply in " Overall patterns" and "Conclusions". The sections preceding this aim to clarify the concepts and theories required for structured and effective analysis.

The connections between value, technology, digitalization and digital platforms

Value can be defined in several ways. Kim and Mauborgne (2004), for example, define value as utility minus price minus cost. This definition outputs what is called "added value", which is used in many business decisions. Another definition, the EU standard definition of value (Standard EN: 12973), states that customer value is the *satisfaction of customer needs* in relation to the *use of customer resources*. Both definitions emphasize a judgement of what a customer gets from using a product or service, the *utility*, versus what it must give in order to enjoy it, which includes everything that customers have to sacrifice when buying and using that product. To guide product development, Lindstedt and Burenius (2003) divide these sacrifices into three dimensions, namely monetary cost (again, including both price and other costs), time and effort. They specifically encourage innovators to seek to reduce all three customer sacrifices whenever possible and not only focus on increased utility, as it leads to stronger and more sustainable market positions.

The actual manifestation of customer value happens through the activation of *functions* that satisfy the customer's needs (Lindsted and Burenius, 2003). The functions, in turn, are accomplished by using the (technical) *solutions* of the utility carrier. The usefulness of the function concept lies in it providing a layer of abstraction between product features and need fulfilment. This forces product developers to explicitly state the specific *nature* of fulfilment promised by alternative feature sets, which makes it possible to compare them. Optimal design choices can then be made by relying on the logic of the value definition, as it dictates that the amount of value realized depends on the performance versus costs balance of the functions. To make the design work efficient and avoid misunderstandings between the many professions involved in product development, functions are expressed in very strict syntax, including only the function provider, the function and the function receiver (e.g. the gunpowder – propels – the bullet). Functions that are necessary, but not directly fulfilling a customer need, are called "support functions" (e.g. the shell – protects – the gun powder). Functional thinking and language thereby enable actors from different disciplines to communicate clearly, helping them to co-engineer value for their organizations.

Technology is linked to value through attributes of the solutions. Normann (2001) argued that technology leads to enhanced value primarily by removing boundaries and limitations. This applies to both the numerator in the value model, increasing utility by satisfying more needs or current needs to a higher degree, and the denominator, increasing the efficiency in need satisfaction. When it comes to digitalization, the bulk of its impact has come from applying the technologies of computers and networks in combination. The digital format itself, even with its fluidity and flexibility, was mostly applied by industry actors to perform what they were already doing more efficiently, but it did not seem to change the distribution of industry roles to any large degree. In other words, as business models were maintained, there was little transformation in terms of industry structure even though its overall efficiency was improved.

Networks, on the other hand, allow actors to exploit the dematerialization of information that comes with digitization (first introduced by the telegraph) differently. With ubiquitous networks, both the input and output of computer processing became accessible at virtually any point in time and space. New business models thus become possible when communication is immediate and distance irrelevant, as proximity constraints get eliminated. Such business models tend to focus on organizing information rather than on carrying out the physical flow of products and services. A key difference to traditional ways of providing value is the focus on building an infrastructure with functions enabling services, rather than on ownership of the content that is desired by customers or the means of producing it. Another word for such infrastructures is a *platform*.

What is a business platform?

While far from all platforms are digital, the strategy appears particularly powerful in the digital domain, as the electronic format and available networks make it is relatively easy to create the necessary value-enabling point in time-space that can facilitate a multitude of functions and connect to extremely large audiences.

According to Prof. Mark Meyer, a platform is a set of subsystems and interfaces that form a common structure from which a stream of derivative products can be efficiently developed and produced (Meyer, 1997). Moreover, Baldwin and

Woodward (2008, p 19) argue (from the work of Tushman and Murmann, 1998) that:

> the fundamental architecture behind all platforms is essentially the same: namely the system is partitioned into a set of "core" components with low variety and a complementary set of "peripheral" components with high variety. The low-variety components constitute the platform. They are the long-lived elements of the system and thus implicitly or explicitly establish the system's interfaces, the rules governing interactions among the different parts.

This combination of stable low-variety core system elements and high-variety low-reusability complementary elements gives rise to *modularity*, which grants the platform owner several strategic benefits. Modularity in turn requires specifying appropriate interfaces that establish predictable formats for module boundaries before opening the platform for other actors. Due to their critical role in coordinating the platform, interface specifications must be a part of the platform's stable core and strictly under the platform owner's control.

Once boundaries are standardized, the modules can contain just about anything the platform owner wants to be able to easily change at a low cost without losing continuity of the core or the market identity. For example, some modules provide actors using the platform the key functions they need in order to deliver services. Other modules might organize customers' information and selection activities or provide payment and delivery functions. Through modularity, the platform achieves not only the variation needed to achieve system-level evolvability, but also a reduction of coordination and transaction costs (Baldwin and Woodward, 2008).

A digital platform owner usually seeks to become the focal firm, occupying the nexus of some multi-actor value creation. If successful, it will gain economies of both scope and scale with a minimum of capital expenditure. The optimal goal is to accomplish a stable system of value creation and exchange in which the platform has a central position. However, to describe how this happens and how it interplays with pre-existing value structures we must first give some attention to fundamental industry models.

Industries as value structure configurations

Those who create the core utility of a product or service are often unable to successfully commercialize it at scale on their own. In order to generate substantial profits, an innovation needs to somehow be sold in large volumes in the market. But to get there usually requires the engagement of other actors that perform production, marketing, delivery and so forth. Consequently, all contemporary industries have many actors that interlink their business models into a larger system that connects value creation to utility for customers. The value structure thus mirrors the configuration of those system dependencies that align the efforts towards collective results.

Teece (1986) expresses this phenomenon as innovators relying on access to relevant complementary assets or capabilities in order to profit from their innovations. Traditionally, downstream sets of complementary capabilities channelled the output of upstream value creation activities to the market in chain-like value structures. The distribution of profits among the actors then depends on the imitability of the innovation, including the innovators' possibilities to protect it, versus how critical and specialized these complementary capabilities are (Teece, 1986). This basis for power thus appears compatible with the "resource-based view", which refers to the firm's tangible, intangible and human assets as *resources* while *capabilities* are the firm's abilities to appropriately deploy, coordinate and integrate its resources for productive activities. The resource-based view proposes that resources and capabilities can only generate high rates of return for owners if they are rare, valuable, inimitable and non-substitutable (Wernerfelt, 1984; Grant, 1991). While this theory is traditionally used to explain competitive success among rival firms, the same factors appear to determine the bargaining power among co-dependent firms in industries.

However, as previously explained, value comes directly from someone or something performing a function. A pile of passive resources lying around is not sufficient. Functions are, in contrast to capabilities and resources, active constructs capturing all the actual effects that contribute to satisfying customer needs. Capabilities and resources are constructs at the process level, which are two steps further away from value, according to both Lindsted and Burenius (2003) and the jobs-to-be-done perspective of innovation used in research on industry disruption (Christensen, et al., 2015; Ulwick, 2005).

Applying functional logic in industry-level analysis therefore provides more descriptive precision than the resource-based view. Luckily, it is also rather straightforward. Individual firms organize value creation through a business model – which can be viewed as a micro-level value structure. Analogously, the fact that ecosystems converge their efforts towards a single value-proposition implies that they do the same thing on the meso level. This means that functions, being the only way to create value, could work as an analytical construct also for the study of value creation in ecosystems.

In industries, the set of firms involved in the creation, delivery and capture of value, manifested by some end product or service, are hence connected through dependent functions. Due to historic commonalities in conditions and drivers for industry formation, it appears that such value structures have archetypical configurations. For physical products, the dominant structure is the well-known value chain (Porter, 1980). The value chain appears to occur as activities performed in the provision of physical products by necessity follow a logical sequence; before anything can be built, some raw materials must be available and components need to be finished before they can be put together into a product. The formation of value chain steps is in turn largely dependent on how activities can be effectively bundled within firm boundaries. Over time, the firms involved specialize on performing their activities with regard to the roles and requirements of adjacent actors. They thereby build capabilities that complement each others', but at the expense of making investments that are not fully reversible. Such co-specialization thus increases both integration and dependence within a value structure (Teece, 1986). The result is higher efficiency leading to higher actor profits or lower customer prices, which brings some stability to the overall role set. But this also brings rigidity to industry paradigms and higher entry barriers. General stability is therefore the norm, even to the point that the interest of all actors to preserve the current structure may keep it operational long after more effective ways have become possible (Teece, 1986).

Ecosystems

Looking at alternative configurations, Jacobides et al. (2018) argue that when there is sufficient downstream-actor freedom and upstream-actor independence, value structures should not be classified as hierarchical. Neither can they be seen strictly as markets if the actors are coordinated in some manner that leads to collective value creation. Instead, this independently coordinated form makes up a distinct category that works like a sort of *ecosystem* for business (Teece, 2014).

An ecosystem can be thought of as an economic community of interacting agents that affect each other through their activities (Jacobides et al., 2018). More specifically, Adner (2017) argues that to constitute an ecosystem, these activities need to be coordinated so that the individual firms' offerings get combined into a coherent, customer-facing value proposition.

While coordination can occur through different processes, it is enormously assisted by modularity. Some, therefore, argue that modularity is a key enabler for ecosystem emergence, "as it allows a set of distinct yet interdependent organizations to coordinate without full hierarchical fiat" (Jacobides et al., 2018, p.2255).

The link to platforms should be evident: modularity is a main feature of platforms and a key element in the platform owner's strategy for exponential growth with maintained flexibility. Digital platforms can thus be seen as a class of technologies that handles the coordination of actors – including the platform owner, all complementors and customers – towards a focal value proposition by providing a modular architecture and rules for interaction.

It should be noted that ecosystem participation is not without drawbacks. The higher volumes for complementors tend to come with lower margins due to the value sharing requirements of membership. Complementors may also need to make investments to be able to join, if not in upfront fees then at least in the form of adaptation costs so they comply with rules and interface standards. From this follows the risk that parts of the resources adapted for ecosystem participation may not be easily employed elsewhere at a reasonable cost. So, in addition to being linked by the joint value propositions and co-dependence, actors are also "bound together by nonredeployability of their collective investment" (Jacobides et al., 2018, 2255), and thus their fate is no longer fully separable from that of the platform. If the platform is unsuccessful, it might not generate enough revenues to cover the sunk costs, leading to synergetic loss instead of profit.

Platforms and industry transformation

When business platforms transform industries, it is because they give rise to ecosystems that create more value than the pre-existing value structures. There must therefore exist some difference between the two systems' value creation processes. Building on the observations about platforms, it is possible to infer the cause of an ecosystem's superior value creation through the two basic components of the value definition (Lindsted and Burenius, 2003). (a) On the *cost* side, value advantages come from economies of scale for complementors – who can mass-produce within the given module boundaries and access larger audiences than they could without the platform – in synergy with the low capex and opex required from the platform owner. (b) On the *utility* side, it is often possible for platforms to perform better by adding functions or by improving the performance of functions. However, it should be noted that this is not strictly necessary if the cost advantages are large enough. This means that a transformed industry features an enhanced function that is organized in a new way, manifested by the new roles taken by ecosystem members. The new structure shows the alignment of the ecosystem members' interdependent activities that constitute the overall flow (Adner, 2017).

An ecosystem value structure resulting from a successful platform strategy is thus in effect comprised of all the actors that make the platform more valuable (Jacobides et al., 2018). Digital platforms tend to coordinate functions of many independent actors, often (but not always) in a hub-and-spoke type value structure and rarely in a sequential chain, into an abundance of customer options. A *minimum requirement* for high customer utility is therefore the important functions of sorting, assessing and combining usefully from the offer abundance. This is a function that platform owners tend to reserve for themselves, as it puts them in control of the hub, lets them own customer relationships and bestows them the important dominance position in the market. The platform owner can take this leadership role because of its control over the infrastructure. They hence become the ecosystem architect who decides system-level goals, roles, rules and access criteria for complimentary actors (Adner, 2017).

Learning from major industry transitions

Examining digital platform's ability to uproot established value-producing constellations in detail requires mapping and comparing between old and new systems and identifying reasons for both similarities and differences. The empirical transitions cases below focus on understanding which limitations different platform components remove, the resulting change in the function set and the reconfiguration of the structure of roles performing it. The pre-transformation value structure for each case industry will be illustrated as a map of how the major functions involved were distributed over the traditional business roles. The *roles*, in turn, manifest themselves through firm boundaries around subsets of functions that were bundled due to practical reasons and through historical specialization paths. The method can therefore be summarized as:

- Identify industries that have transformed into ecosystems.
- Backtrack and describe the industries' historical value structure based on journalistic and academic writing, plus interviews with market participants.
- Review of the preliminary value structure descriptions with two senior professors who were personally involved in previous analysis of the same industries.
- Map the new ecosystem's structure in the same way and then compare the two descriptions while asking questions like:
- What limitation was removed by the platform leading to an increase in value?
- What was unbundled from the original value proposition?
- What are the differences in the function set?
- What are the differences in the distribution of functions?
- What are the sources of the advantage of the new ecosystem?

Each industry has a rich history extending over several decades. Their alignment structures also vary to some degree between geographies. Therefore, major abstractions and simplifications were needed to capture the relevant aspects of big-picture patterns without drowning in too many details. Value structures were illustrated following principles outlined in two papers by Andersson et al., in 2011a & b, with some adaptations.

Functions are represented by ovals in the illustrations. They are the key results that each part of the system contributes to the creation and delivery of the joint value proposition.

Roles are the classes of firms performing typical bundles of functions. They are indicated by rectangles around each corresponding function set.

Relationships between functions are also important for understanding the structure of value creation. They are indicated with lines, but only if they span role boundaries.

In the post-transformation descriptions, some functions might be removed or added. Functions and roles that remain are kept in the illustrations but greyed out, while new ones are in full black contour. Roles changed as well but sometimes became irrelevant, in which case they are removed in the post-transformation figure. The new ecosystem can be easily identified at its proper position, marked with grey semi-transparent fill, over the remaining parts of the old value structure.

Transformation of the book retail industry

The book business has been through several transitions during its long history (Giertz and Reitberger, 1987). The original core function for book production was printing. As printing technology gained high-volume capacity and transportation of goods became cheaper, newspapers and book publishers invested in having their own in-house production. Editing, layout and handling illustrations were mostly seen as support functions, preparing the content for typesetting and reproduction. Publishers were early users of specialized hardware and software, with which they started to make digital originals. But as such IT tools became more universally available, business customers started to produce their own originals that enabled them to shop around for printing, causing some price pressure in that market. Printing, the previous core activity was eventually outsourced, turning editing, financing, promotion and distribution into the main activities for publishers (see Figure 3.1).

The pre-platform value structure had a chain configuration with publishing and printing upstream, followed by wholesale actors who in turn distributed books to retailers. The retail business was highly local, with physical stores placed at locations convenient for consumers wherever there was sufficient demand. These stores sold books over the counter and staff provided services such as finding specific books among the shelves, giving recommendations and ordering books not found in the local inventory. Customers main alternative was to buy books from remote suppliers offering mail-order services.

The most distinctive aspect of the modern book industry is the gigantic online retail business. Books were one of the first categories targeted by Internet entrepreneurs, as their enormous range fits well with database organization and because the products are small, non-perishable and thus easy to send by mail (Wiggins, 1997). In the new online ecosystem, book searches became unbundled from catalogues and inventories and thus the purchase disconnected from location. Digitalization thereby effectively removed limitations of proximity and product range from the business model. This in turn made it easy for customers to compare prices and take advantage of bargains from all over the world, which decreased the margins for traditional retailers. The mail-order actors who tried

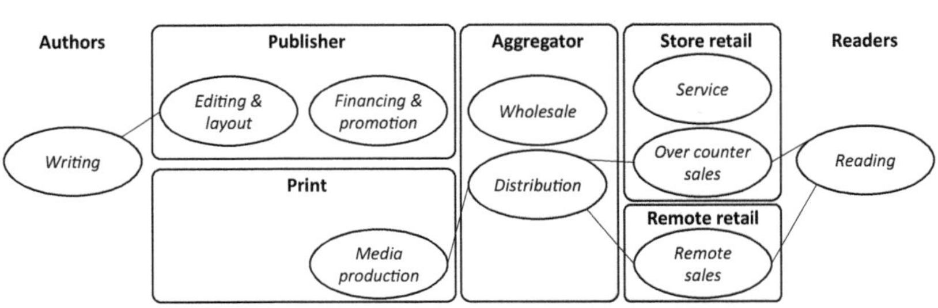

FIGURE 3.1 The historic book industry value structure.

to co-opt online sales did so, quite predictably, without changing their business model and were therefore effectively disrupted by the e-commerce actors (cf. Christensen et al., 2004). However, some physical stores remained, partly by increasing purchase volumes and gaining synergies by forming chains, and partly by diversifying the offering with more accessories, trinkets, gift cards, board games and other adjacent products. The survivors thus managed to stay relevant for customer needs by extending the value proposition beyond book selection, incorporating things like gift-giving, products for children and supplies for school or office work.

Unlike the mail-order actors, surviving bookstores co-opted online sales over time, but not by building competing platforms. Instead, they started to add some of their own inventory to the new externally available platforms, like Amazon, thereby recovering some lost volume by becoming complementors in the ecosystem. This new channel for unsold books also helped their second-hand business, as it benefited from the massively improved customer reach (that someone strolls into your store looking for precisely the used books you happen to hold is far less likely than matching someone online who is actively searching). This co-option by partnering was encouraged by some of the largest platforms.

To some degree, the products themselves have also been digitalized. While many readers still prefer physical books, downloadable audiobooks and e-books are popular alternatives. Among the three, a quick online search suggests that physical books appear to have maintained a slow increase since a drop in 2010 when e-books had their market breakthrough. Since then, audiobook sales have increased, while e-book popularity peaked some time ago. But there are regional differences and large variations between categories.

Figure 3.2 presents the post-transformation state. The new platform-enabled ecosystem exists in parallel with parts of the old value chain. The mail-order business was efficiently replaced by e-commerce and, higher in the value-chain, the wholesale business largely diminished as the new retail chains started to exploit their bargaining power by sourcing directly from publishers. At the upstream end, digital consumer software and abundant availability to online market channels have enabled self-publishing as an alternative to the publisher role. While it has

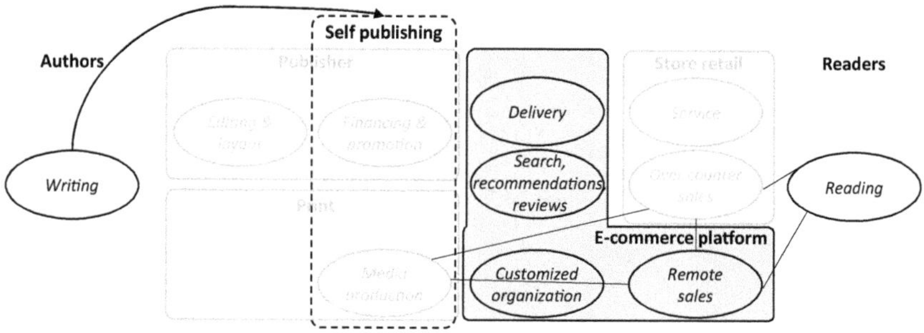

FIGURE 3.2 The transformed book industry value structure.

been difficult to assess the magnitude of such indie- and self-publishing, it seems to have the industry's fastest-growing volumes and highest reliance on digital formats.

The continued development of many of these platforms has been growth by diversification. By repeatedly adding new categories of products and services, they leverage the flexibility of the platform and strengthen their position as a convenient purchasing point. Some, most notably Amazon, even entered B2B markets with quite advanced services.

Transformation of the fashion industry

In the area of clothing and fashion, the traditional value structure's main roles were manufacturers producing clothes designed by brand owners or by larger retail chains. The activity of wholesalers and importers was varied between retail business model categories. For example, an importer of shoes might commission their own manufacture of some models, while also selling for other brands. Larger fashion brands could sometimes have their own representation in a market, while sometimes using agents or selling directly to retail chains. Due to this complexity, the wholesale step is not described in Figure 3.3.

In the retail step, physical stores strongly dominated over a much smaller mail-order activity (which is omitted in Figure 3.3). However, there were, and still are, two business models that dominate in-store sales. On the one hand, large retail chains such as H&M, Zara and the like, design and create their own ranges of clothes and have them manufactured in large volumes in low-cost countries and then shipped to stores across the globe. In addition to design, these chains work very hard with sourcing and logistics to avoid ending up with a cost disadvantage versus rivals, since they all compete in the relatively price-sensitive mass market. The chains also differentiate their product lines by using multiple brands within an overall strategy of availability and price. The products they market are normally not sold to other retailers.

On the other hand, there are independent shops (or small chains) that source from established brands and aggregate their own "collection" by selecting

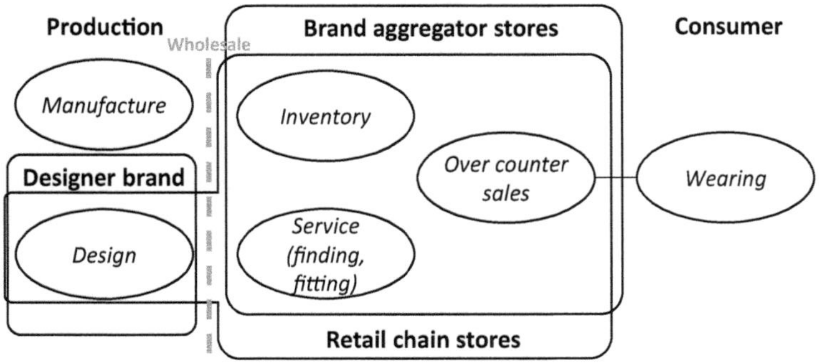

FIGURE 3.3 The historic fashion industry value structure.

products they believe appeal to their particular set of customers. Prices in these boutiques are typically higher than in the chains and they usually make large efforts to provide good service and form relationships with customers to stimulate repeat purchases. Hybrids of the two models, like US chain retailer Nordstrom, sell both their own and international brands.

Like the book industry, the structure of functions and roles in fashion has been transformed by online sales. However, consumer uptake was considerably slower, as clothes (in contrast to books) need to physically fit the individual. Many customers were initially hesitant to buy without trying, but a transformation started as some consumers shifted their behaviour towards trying clothes in a store but then buying them online. This pressured store margins, as they had to cover their fixed costs with decreasing revenues.

Unbundling sales from stores, however, makes two new activities necessary: delivery and billing. The former appears to have been a key to market uptake because convenient and simple delivery and return functions made customers less uneasy about buying untried clothes. For some consumers who dislike store shopping, or who have little time to spare, the online option even turned out to be preferable. Many soon realized that they could buy using a credit card, try the clothes on at home and then return the ones they do not like before the credit is due. This removed most financial risks and lowered the consumption of customers' time. Today, nine out of ten shoes bought online are returned.

Early online actors, like Zappos (founded 1999), went for the brand-aggregator business model. In contrast to the small bookstores, some larger fashion retail chains successfully co-opted e-commerce by launching their own online stores. The unbundling of product range from the physical location has therefore mostly caused problems for the brand-aggregator boutiques, as online retail functions in the same way but with less limitations of range, storage and available display space. To make it worse, they also had to compete directly with online stores put up by some of their brands, like philipp-plein.com.

The new and old ecosystems coexist as no functions were fully removed from the traditional value structure. Instead, e-commerce has become an alternative channel. More recently, the transformation continued as another aggregator business models emerged. Some online fashion retail platforms were launched with the aim of providing a channel for traditional boutiques rather than for selling their own selections. One example is Farfetch, launched in 2007 by José Neves. Farfetch and similar businesses instead enable independent boutiques to compete online, offloading some products to a larger audience, while keeping their stores and independent identities (The Economist, 2013). Taking a role where the inventory is provided and handled by the platform complementors, these meta-aggregators' business model is extremely scalable and mirrors those in both the book industry and in some crowd-sourced ecosystems studied below (Figure 3.4).

The meta-aggregator platforms give the independent stores new channels and removes market reach limitations of the physical store model. As a result, they can compete online without investing in building their own e-commerce solution.

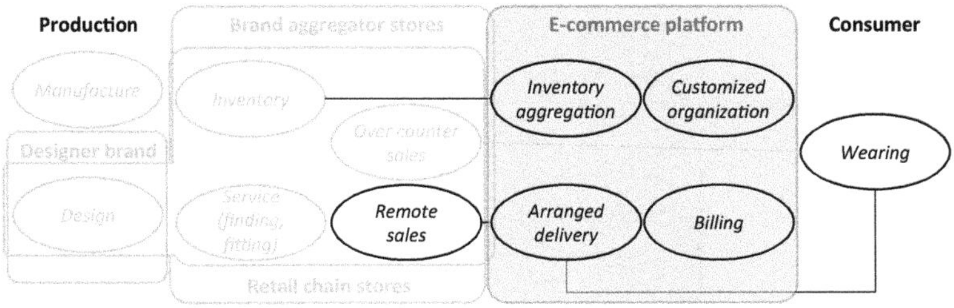

FIGURE 3.4 The transformed fashion industry value structure.

More importantly, however, is that the platform provides them a complete solution in terms of billing, packing material, shipping solutions, returns handling and so on. Most independent retailers would not easily sort all this out by themselves, so such standardized solutions are probably conductive to onboarding the boutiques as complementors. Given the platform's dependence on sourcing from independent merchants, the smooth operation of these standardized modular functions becomes crucial for the platform's scalability.

Broad e-commerce actors diversifying horizontally into fashion (e.g. Amazon) also tend to go for the meta-aggregator role. Access to an audience is a compelling function to offer retailers and manufacturers alike, and with every successful sector entry, the audience grows which strengthens the advantage.

Transformation of the hotel industry

The second half of the twentieth century saw a huge economic boom in industrialized nations that led to larger parts of their populations travelling more. In addition to newly acquired wealth driving this growth in travel, population explosion, urbanization and demographic developments all contributed to increasing the demand. As a result, the hotel industry has boomed and is still growing. Other synergetic trends include the emergence of low-price airlines, travel checks and credit cards, the abundance of car rental and much more.

To find and book accommodation, customers used to turn to travel agents for assistance. These had the knowledge and systems necessary for creating travel and accommodation solutions that matched customers' needs. Larger corporations sometimes had in-house staff for handling travel arrangements, but more often they entered long-term agreements with travel agencies who gave discounts in exchange for being their exclusive service provider. Travel agents thus enjoyed double revenue streams in the form of margins on the sales price and commissions from travel operators and hotels. (As seen in Figure 3.5, hotels could, and still do, book their own rooms as well.)

While the core business of the hotels has not changed significantly, the value structure around it has transformed in two steps. First, it was quick to take advantage of the Internet to make it possible to book, compare and review hotels online. This

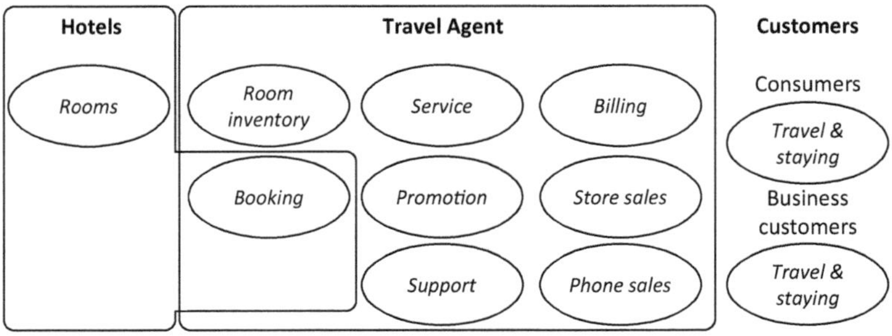

FIGURE 3.5 The historic hotel industry value structure.

made phone and store sales irrelevant for many travellers. However, the underlying unbundling of room information and booking functions also enabled a new ecosystem role: the virtual hotel providers who do not own any rooms themselves. Offer aggregators, like Booking.com (founded in 2000 through the merger of two pre-existing sites) and Expedia.com (founded by Microsoft in 1996 and then spun off, starting with an IPO in 1999), were active early on both enabling and exploiting the digitalization of room inventory and other hotel information. Similarly, many other digital businesses, from online travel agents to map services and event organizers, began integrating unbundled hotel information to strengthen value propositions by making the customer process more effective. Such services also included rating and recommendation functions, which eventually made online reviews a key factor for selling accommodation. In response, many hotels began to engage channel managers specialized in actively optimizing their online presence.

The increase in comparability could have resulted in some price pressure for hotels, but overall, the increasing global demand for travel has neutralized this risk. Both the number of nights sold and the number of rooms available are still rising.

The traditional travel agent role has largely diminished. Today, they mostly work with corporate travel and with consumers who are not yet comfortable making online purchases or want to make advanced trips (many participants, multiple stops and exotic destinations).

More recently, yet another new type of platform business emerged that quickly gained popularity. These are also offer aggregators, but in contrast to hotel booking sites, they source the room inventory dynamically in a customer-to-customer (C2C) model. The archetypical example of such peer-to-peer accommodation is Airbnb, founded in 2008 by three guys trying to make a little extra money by renting out air mattresses in their loft (Aydin, 2016). They started with a simple site, airbedandbreakfast.com, and slowly developed the business. Despite being dismissed by dozens of investors and having to relaunch the company at least three times it was valued at US$31 billion in 2019.

Some thought the peer-to-peer business would pose a major threat to hotels, but so far this seems to not be the case. To the extent hotels have closed down,

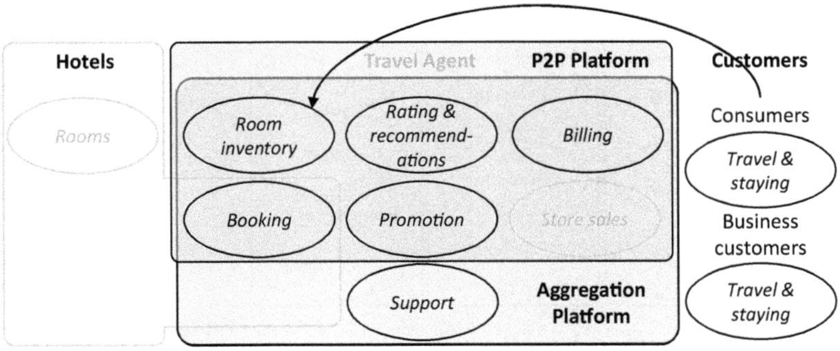

FIGURE 3.6 The transformed hotel industry value structure.

it predominantly occurred in the countryside, while peer-accommodation is mostly a city phenomenon. In addition, the volume of nights offered is still in the single-digit percentage of the hotel business and, conversely, only a few percentage of Airbnb customers say they would have stayed at hotels instead if they could. The offers thus seem to meet different customer needs (Melin, 2017) and can therefore coexist, as seen in Figure 3.6.

In summary, it appears that online aggregation sites have taken over much of travel agents' business. The importance of functions such as store and phone sales have decreased, while rating and recommendations have to some degree replaced travel agents' service by enabling self-service. The exceptions are corporate services and complex consumer trips. Peer accommodation is an add-on to the new ecosystem.

Transformation of the music industry

The music industry used to have much in common with the book industry. Content creators entered contracts with specialized publishing companies, referred to as record labels, who helped finalize songs, produced the physical media (records, tapes and covers) and promoted the artist. The industry lacked a clear pattern for wholesale, as national labels built their own distribution to retailers and the big international players preferred to represent themselves in local and regional markets. The retailers, on the other hand, were similar to their book industry counterparts. Sales occurred through stores and mail order, both having the key functions of organizing an interesting inventory and advising customers. But stores sales also required giving prospective buyers access to equipment so they could pre-listen to albums before buying. Hanging out in record stores and listening to music became something of a lifestyle for some people who socialized around their shared enthusiasm for music genres.

The chain-type value structure in Figure 3.7 was rather stable and did not change with the introduction of new playback technologies, like the CD. While

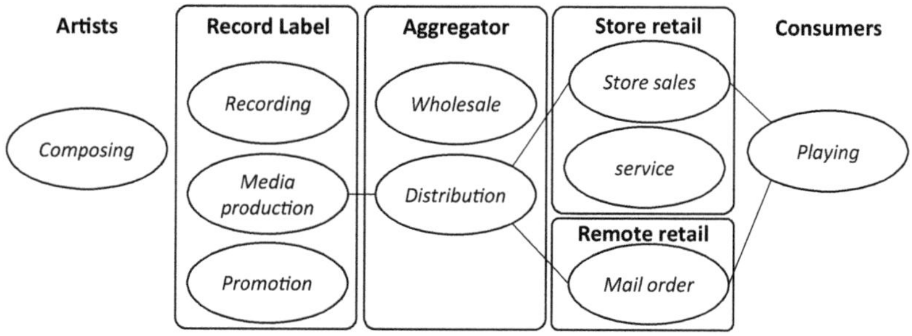

FIGURE 3.7 The historic music industry value structure.

record labels did get concerned about losing sales due to customers recording and sharing music, the tendency was reasonably manageable as long as it had to be stored on physical media. However, with the mass market breakthrough of personal computers, consumers could store music as files and effortless replication became a problem. Sales decreased as customers instead ripped the music from CDs and shared it with each other.

Unbundling the content from its physical media made it transferrable over networks. So as more and more consumers got access to broadband, it removed the remaining limitations of time and space for music acquisition. Unfortunately for the industry, it also removed the constraint of cost for those users who were comfortable with illegal downloading. Online platforms, providing independent peer-to-peer file sharing functions, like Napster (active between 1999 and 2001), soon removed additional constraints such as the need for personal relationships between sharers. Even though almost all music downloading was in compressed formats like MP3, this quality level was sufficient for most consumers and the sales of physical records plummeted. In 2015, the total revenues for the music industry in the United States was half of what it was in 1999 and the revenue share of physical discs dropped to about 20% of the total (Smith, 2016). But in terms of volume, CD and vinyl are insignificant today, as the 80% revenue share of network-enabled sales occurs at a much lower price point.

Piracy was a very serious problem for record companies. Many consumers gave up CDs altogether and MP3 players became the dominant solution for portable music playing and also became common in home-entertainment systems. Network capacity kept growing and music downloading services in virtual stores, most notably Apple iTunes, started to appear for those who wanted a legal alternative. Large content owners like Universal Music Group, EMI, Warner and Sony signed up to make their music available on the iTunes Store. In contrast to the book industry, almost all physical retail stores were gradually put out of business because the physical formats they worked with were unnecessary for the utility of music consumption. In fact, even high-end customers could eventually purchase downloads at specialized sites with higher quality than CDs, although this is still a rather small niche segment.

Despite these legal alternatives, piracy remained high. Not only was it free of charge, but many also felt that it was morally acceptable. In 2006, when Daniel Ek persuaded several reluctant record label executives to allow Spotify to try streaming their content in selected markets, music sales had decreased for five of the six preceding years and a turnaround was nowhere in sight (US market, from Smith, 2016). Streaming quickly became popular, however. In 2010, music industry revenues finally stopped falling, as sales from streaming and downloads started to make up for the lost CD volumes. Since 2015, the industry's revenues have recovered significantly but are still nowhere near pre-Internet levels. In hindsight, it can be observed that downloads only dominated for about four years, which is the shortest format era in the industry (Rosenblatt, 2018). Even in the exotic high-end niche, downloads face new competition from a revival of analogue vinyl and high-quality streaming in the MQA format.

As can be seen in Figure 3.8, both retail and wholesale roles were eventually disrupted as store and post-order sales became a thing of the past. Even though online solutions can only partly provide the service functions around music search and recommendations that were available in stores, the added convenience of app control, personalized content organization through playlists, access to crowd ratings, integration of editorial content, instant home access and superior price more than make up for that loss of utility. To the extent music is still a theme for socializing, these activities have also moved to online solutions. But hanging out in stores is no longer an option.

Transformation of the television industry

TV traditionally meant the broadcast of video content through radio signals or cable networks. Customers exercised choice by selecting between channels, which usually were profiled thematically, for example, sports, movies, music, news and so on. However, they could not influence what to see on a channel at

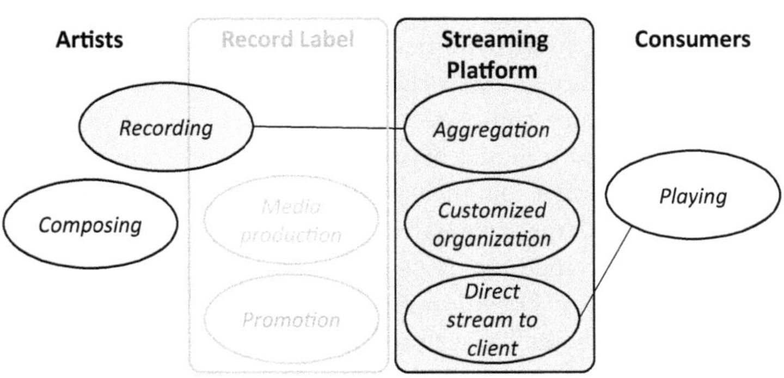

FIGURE 3.8 The transformed music industry value structure.

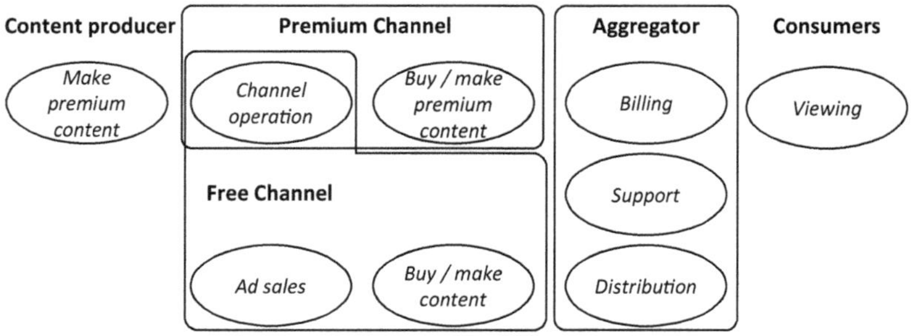

FIGURE 3.9 The historic TV industry value structure.

the time of viewing. The dominating broadcast business models were (a) free-of-charge content financed through advertising, where companies bought time slots for their TV commercials and (b) paid subscription for premium content without advertising. Public service television can be seen as a version of the latter.

In local markets, cable TV companies aggregated channels into subscription packages among which the consumer could choose according to their interest and budget. Value capture occurred through fixed monthly fees and the cable companies were the consumers' point of contact for support. This value structure, shown in Figure 3.9, was stable for a long time. When new technologies entered the industry, it was either through direct support, or reactive co-option, from the established actors. Similarly, when video and movie-box rental services penetrated the mainstream market in the 1980s, they did not disrupt the TV business. Consumers would not replace subscriptions with continuous rental due to the former's obvious advantages in cost and convenience.

When the Internet appeared on the stage, it brought a new way to unbundle video from the traditional utility carriers' unpractical physical media and inflexible broadcasting. This attracted new actors who tried to profit from TV. For example, the telecom operator Telia was pioneering IPTV while also driving the introduction of ADSL broadband, as the two services mutually reinforced the value of each other (Kaulio, et al., 2017). The business model for these services was typically pay-per-view, a set-up referred to as "online video rental", which removed the broadcast models constraints regarding viewing time. The new services were available through web clients, home broadband boxes and later through apps in video game consoles, smartphones and smart TVs. Cable TV companies who controlled a digital network infrastructure responded by offering broadband services, often bundled with video-on-demand offers, as their bandwidth could handle large-scale traffic (Evans, 2017).

But just like in the music industry, it proved to be challenging to compete with the widespread piracy. Downloading from peers occurred primarily through dedicated sites using the BitTorrent protocol, like the Swedish site Pirate Bay (active 2003 to 2014). In attempts to curb the trend, content creators introduced a "piracy – it's a crime" message on DVDs, which ironically only paying viewers had to see. Other anti-piracy measures included lobbying for legislation and pressuring Internet operators to block content.

But with the video streaming platforms, customers finally got the view-on-demand option combined with an affordable fixed cost subscription model. Netflix, which started as an online DVD rental that sent discs back and forth by post in 1997, began to provide video streaming in 2007. The increased convenience and the subscription model's zero marginal cost made mainstream consumers less eager to bother with downloading and its associated risks for malware and getting caught. The geographical spread was surprisingly slow, probably due to property rights concerns, so Netflix was not Europe-wide until 2015. Other online actors followed, for example, Amazon Prime added a video streaming function in 2012.

The on-demand streaming ecosystem gained its popularity at the expense of the cable TV business. Content producers also most likely lost some revenues, but they also gained a more direct market channel and could let old productions be available for streaming indefinitely, thereby extending their viewership. They also benefited from the resulting decrease in piracy. Some producers, most notably the TV production company HBO, co-opted streaming technology and created their own platforms, something that did not happen in the otherwise similar music industry. This co-option is still spreading, as more content producers launch their own streaming services (Figure 3.10). It remains to be seen if they can compete effectively with the bundled value propositions of streaming services that can exploit a meta-aggregator advantage. An opposite upstream diversification trend has also been noticed, as streaming platforms started to create their own premium series and movie content. Hence, the roles and boundaries of the TV industry are still in a formative phase.

Overall patterns

Industry transitions have some interesting commonalities and differences from which conclusions can be drawn. It is therefore useful to start by summarizing some major observations as a few overall patterns.

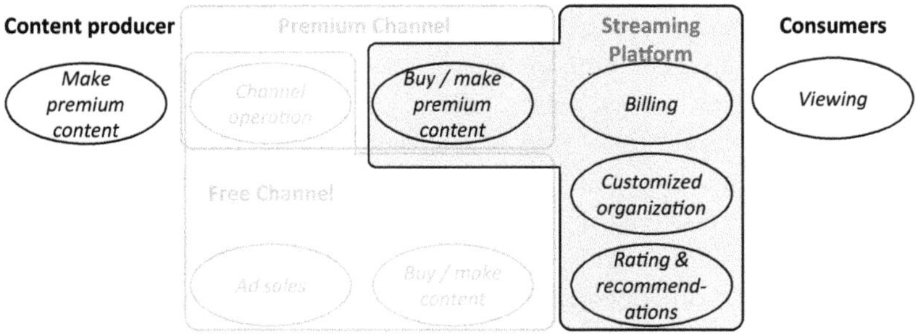

FIGURE 3.10 The transformed TV industry value structure.

Case commonalities in structural development

A value structure connects a point in time and space where end customers can obtain value to the points where it is created. The rest of the roles in a value structure provide support functions to the system. The value chain logic adds to the understanding of dependencies between these intermediary roles. In pre-transformation configurations, the roles in each step were essentially the customers for the preceding step, who performed integrating functions like building a range to pick from, keeping inventory at hand, supporting a search for the right option, ordering, customer service, payment and the handling of returns. In the downstream end of the chain, the traditional retailers owned the end-customer relation and thus controlled both the function of the delivering system's aggregated value proposition and the position that captured value from it. This gave them the power to amass payments from customers and pass the other actors' share of revenues up the chain.

This sequenced creation and delivery of value is fundamentally different from how ecosystems work. In ecosystems, all actors instead serve the end customer through an amalgamated value proposition that is accessible all the time from anywhere. The non-sequentiality has more significance than just the ordering of activities. It also implies that value creation is triggered by the customer, not the producer, who simultaneously activates – through the platform's modules – a whole section of the ecosystem when making a purchase. Moreover, this method for value creation is far more tightly integrated and efficient, for example, having a much smaller need for tying up value as stocks of components, raw materials or finished products in every role.

Case commonalities in the transformation process

The traditional downstream roles in value chains could seize shares of the captured value due to their control over functions needed for reaching the market. This control comes from their possession of important complementary assets needed for function execution. Examples of such assets include import rights, distribution channels or sales networks in the chain's wholesale roles, and ownership of physical outlets with custom-built information systems at the retail end. As these functions provided the only way for upstream actors to reach the market, they, and their underlying complementary assets, could be regarded as both *important* and *tightly held* (cf. Teece, 1986).

But technology weakens this power of intermediate roles by providing alternative ways to carry out their functions, one by one over a long period of time. For example, payment has long since been unbundled from physical money (by actors outside of the studied value chains, like credit card companies and payment plan providers). Consequently, retailers are no longer holding the payment function in their exclusive control tightly enough for it alone to force customers to their channels. In addition, their physical outlets lost some importance as their traditional functions – like being a place to browse a range of offers or pick up products – received competition from alternative solutions. For example, the mail-order business model simply complemented these two functions with an ordering function and a warehouse to successfully unbundle value delivery. The result was a slow but steady reduction of the relevance of the retailer role, although most could still survive due to the lack of dramatically better points of purchase and the prevalence of the general shopping paradigm. So while asset or resource possession can explain how the specific mix of actors in an established system came to emerge under competition, it does not necessarily mean that the same resources have an advantage that guarantees the survival of the role when circumstances change.

It appears that the unbundling of information about products was a real game-changer for role sustainability in many industries. Digital product information, available to everyone through the Internet, relaxed the incumbents' hold on the integrative downstream functions. And platforms, it turned out, can perform these functions much better. Platforms can – in contrast to shops – hold an unlimited range of offerings, available from anywhere at any time while utilizing generated data patterns and customer feedback to create additional value.

Moreover, all the studied platforms entered their markets with an unbundled value proposition at a price lower than the contemporary market level. Incumbents, on the other hand, typically had broad bundled service sets as a result of them countering the price pressure in historic industry internal competition. Faced with the platform threat, their response options were all bad. They could not effectively co-opt the platform business model as their customer reach was too limited, nor could they slash prices as their assets and operations were too costly. Survival required resolute rationalization and restructuring so that volumes increased while costs were at the same time cut through operational synergies. Even then, many were disrupted despite their hard efforts to adapt, as will be explained in the next section.

When platforms achieved volume growth, it often self-reinforced their position, as the growth itself helped attract both more customers and more complementors (cf. Casadesus-Masanell and Ricart, 2011). The transformative effect was a radical, rather than an incremental, establishment of a new dominant value structure. With the incumbents being either replaced by, or repositioned into, the new structure, the second step for many platforms was to bundle additional products and services by engaging new categories of complementors. New offers could be quickly introduced to the market, often on a trial-and-error basis, and then scaled. As additional complementors (or new bespoke capabilities) aggregated services to a platform, the scope widened. Some platforms exploited this heavily, trying to become the go-to place for the broadest possible set of customer needs. Seeking this "first place to go to find something" position resembles the strategy known as "first-mover advantage" (Lieberman and Montgomery, 1988) in that it gives the successful firm a semi-monopoly position. The most well-known strategy for such self-reinforcing effects is probably Amazon's "everything store" (Stone, 2013).

Case differences in transformation end states

All five transformations started by an unbundling of information about products or services rather than unbundling of their utility. This first phase primarily has repercussions for roles in the later steps of the traditional value chain structure, towards the retail end. The upstream actors are involved with the functions of creating the utility carriers, and these are not substituted. Instead, utility carriers were redirected to a new channel towards the market. Downstream actors, however, who operate value delivery and capture, helplessly witnessed how many of their most attractive functions were taken over by the platform.

But in the next step of transformation, some interesting path variations occurred. Whenever customer utility requires interaction with physical objects, like hotel rooms, books and clothes, there is a pattern where retailers can survive even though new ecosystems take over most of the market. When utility relies on a physical format, retailers can sometimes successfully reduce the value gap versus the platform by restructuring to a degree sufficient for remaining relevant. This is typically done by forming chains, broadening the offering and emphasizing a superior service or shopping experience. If surviving, the retailers could sometimes expand their market reach by becoming complementors themselves, using the very same or challenging platforms to increase their sales. So when utility carriers are physical, it is possible for old retailers to survive by piggy-backing on platforms in combination with restructuring.

On the other hand, whenever the physical format is irrelevant for the customer's needs, as in the case of music and video, even the very utility itself tends to get unbundled. Once captured in a digital format, it can be directly transferred to customers, bypassing the downstream functions altogether. In the industries studied, this first occurred through downloads and then later through direct streaming. Apparently, once a non-physical utility carrier emerges, there is little hope for an industry's downstream businesses.

Conclusions

The purpose of this chapter was to identify the particularities of digital platforms that cause industry transformations and explain the mechanisms through which it happens. By relying on the value model – that value is created only through the satisfaction of needs through the performing of functions – the analysis revealed how the studied transitions occurred as changes in the relevance and location of functions in the overall value structures. At least five fundamental effects particular to platforms were involved in this. First, platforms *remove limitations* such as market reach and product scope by exploiting the fact that digitalization unbundles information from physical utility carriers and makes it accessible through networks. Second, by providing a flexible and scalable infrastructure, based on a *modular architecture*, platforms can source contributions to customer value from many ecosystem participants, each able to provide at volume what they do best while the totality of operations becomes order-of-magnitude less costly than before. Third, for customers, a platform coordinates all the necessary functions at a *single convenient access point* regardless of the physical location of its complementors. Its availability at anytime from anywhere is superior to that of any imaginable physical outlet. The only drawbacks seem to be the personal service and instant delivery possible in over-counter sales. However, and fourth, platforms also come with additional benefits of *user customizability and service extension*. For instance, the data resulting from customer behaviour on the site can be collected and exploited for decision making or through additional functions like sorting, searching, matching and recommendations which can compensate for some of the loss in personal service while solving some problems even better. Fifth, platform modularity also makes it comparably simple to make changes in both the range of functions and in the set of participants (Meyer and Lehnerd, 1997). As seen in the case descriptions, this opens strategic options that can give the platform company access to vastly wider roles over time.

The transition mechanisms, on the other hand, can be inferred from the change sequences in the case descriptions. In all of them, the studied platforms entered their respective market by *first securing the functions for delivery and capture of value* interacting with end customers, while either automatizing or disregarding most other retail functions. The platform's domination of the role as the ecosystem's interface to customers then forces upstream actors to adapt, in ways that depend on the nature of the utility carrier and the continued relevance of their traditional roles.

The value structure shift is thus to a large degree explained by the enabling of *functions to be performed in a different manner and by new actors* than before. Complementors can carry out some of these functions, but also exploit platform modularity to help broadening both the product range and function set. Ifthey comply with the rules and standards imposed by the platform they canthereby serve a much larger stream of customers than they could attract on their own. In a sense, they are allowed to perform limited specified functions inside the boundaries of another business. But the platform and its complementary *participants work in parallel* rather than in a value chain sequence. Their activities are automatically coordinated by programming, where each purchase activates a call for specific functions to be performed through the corresponding module set. The value chain is thus replaced by a *systemic value network*.

Transition *end states will vary depending on whether the utility in question can be fully unbundled from physical objects*. When utility requires physical manifestation, the prevalence of a need to transport atoms makes the transformation less disruptive and gives incumbents somewhat larger chances to adapt. But if utility can be fully digitalized, it changes the mechanisms for profiting from value creation and this affects the whole system. First, the digital format allows for limitless replication at zero cost. This poses an enormous challenge for the value structure. Upstream actors are affected as they are no longer able to control the production and usage of their own creations, and thus not able to secure revenues from it. Second, digital utility can be transferred without cost through networks, thereby effectively eliminating the need for a physical supply chain altogether. The previously "valuable" resources and capabilities possessed by downstream role holders are therefore suddenly only drivers of cost. Unfortunately, they are at the same time difficult to divest due to their reduced relevance and low transferability. Failure is therefore the likely fate for businesses that focus narrowly on such products and services. These transformations are therefore more disruptive, and a permanent reduction of industry profits can be expected.

In either case, it appears that *functions are more stable than roles*, as functions mostly remain but perhaps move in the structure, while roles might be disrupted all the way to complete annihilation. When this happens, the complementary capabilities and assets (Teece, 1986; Wernerfeldt, 1984; Grant, 1991) that enabled the incumbent retailers to participate in the value chain in the first place have lost their relevance, not so much due to imitation but rather because alternative solutions (i.e. technologies) were even better at performing key functions that were important for customers.

In the end, the new structure creates value at a higher level and customers can enjoy a larger selection with lower prices.

Discussion

Digitalization drives socioeconomic change by bringing new options for value creation and value delivery. Like any technology, its impact comes from the power of removing old boundaries and limitations (Normann, 2001). But in the case of substantial industry transformations, this boundary removal is always driven by entrepreneurial actors who enter the industry and realize the technology's potential through new business models (Baden-Fuller and Haeflinger, 2013). Conversely, a technical innovation cannot reach diffusion in competitive markets unless some substantial advantage can be harnessed, something that can never come from offering the same value proposition in the same way. Business model innovation is therefore a necessity for unlocking the potential of new technology in existing economic sectors.

Industry transitions, in turn, occur if many functions are either taken over by new players or are rendered irrelevant by the technology these players utilize. The old role structure then gets transformed because historic firm boundaries are normally ineffective for organizing the new function set.

The findings in this chapter came from applying the functional thinking proposed by the value model to the analysis of value creation systems at the meso level. It uncovered that functions are more stable than roles and, in extension, than the relevance of resources. In other words, it does not matter how rare, valuable or inimitable resources are in stable environments – when the customer needs change or an alternative way to satisfy them emerges, they become irrelevant because their effects manifest into (a specific instance at) the solution level, not the function level. Just like a platform like Banggood (solution level) is a set of programmed servers connected to a network (resource level), the nature of technical implementation is irrelevant for customers who only value Banggood for being a plentiful source of cheap gadgets (function level). Functions, compared with resources, are thus more informative constructs for explaining the meso-level value provided by industry actors (and when adhering strictly to the prescribed noun-verb-noun syntax they even explicitly articulate that value). It is hence likely that a resource-based research approach (cf. Barney, 1991; Wernerfeldt, 1984; Grant, 1991) would have made the key patterns much more difficult to identify. It would also probably fail to notice that digital entrants are in essence putting incumbent actors out of play *because* their advantages are based on resource and capabilities, and those eventually turn obsolete.

In practice, focusing on functions could help strategists stay more vigilant by regarding their current solutions merely as temporary best options. Such a mindset would make them more adept to handle changes, inspiring them to proactively monitor how the function set evolves and scout broadly for technologies to use in the future.

References

Adner, R., 2017, 'Ecosystem as structure: an actionable construct for strategy', *Journal of Management*, 43(1), pp. 39–58.

Andersson, P., Markendahl, J., and Mattsson, L.G., 2011a, 'Can mobile eco-systems for technical innovations be standardized? _ The case of mobile wallets and contactless communication', *22nd European Regional ITS Conference*, Budapest, pp. 11–21.

Andersson, P., Markendahl, J., and Mattsson, L.G., 2011b, 'Technical development and the formation of new business ventures–the case of new mobile payment and ticketing services', *The IMP Journal*, 5(1), pp. 23–41.

Avant, R., 2014, 'The third great wave', *The Economist* (4), pp. 775–779.

Aydin, R., 2016, 'How 3 guys turned renting air mattresses in their apartment into a $31 billion company', *Airbnb*. Available at https://www.businessinsider.com/how-airbnb-was-founded-a-visual-history-2016-2?r=US&IR=T Accessed 13/10/2019.

Baden-Fuller, C. and Haefliger, S., 2013, 'Business models and technological innovation', *Long Range Planning*, 46(6), pp. 419–26.

Baldwin, C. and Woodward, C.J., 2008, 'The architecture of platforms: a unified view', *SSRN Electronic Journal*.

Barney, J.B., 1991, 'Firm resources and sustained competitive advantage', *Journal of Management*, 17(1), pp. 99–120.

Berggren, U. and Bergkvist, T., 2006, *Invadörerna*, NUTEK B2006:7.

Casadesus-Masanell, R. and Ricart, J.E., 2011, 'How to design a winning business model', *Harvard Business Review*, 89(1/2), pp. 100–107.

Christensen, C.M., Anthony, S.D., and Roth, E.A., 2004, *Seeing What's Next: Using the Theories of Innovation to Predict Industry Change*, Harvard Business Press, Boston, MA.

Christensen, C.M., Raynor, M.E., and McDonald, R., 2015, 'What is disruptive innovation', *Harvard Business Review*, 93(12), pp. 44–53.

Evans, M., 2017, 'When did video on demand start?', *MSA Focus*. Available at https://www.msafocus.com/news/video-demand-start/ Accessed 29/10/2019.

Giertz, E. and Reitberger, G., 1987, *Från informationssamhälle till kunskapssamhälle – En studie av strukturförändringar relaterade till grafisk industri*, Grafiska Arbetsgivareförbundet, Stockholm.

Grant, R.M., 1991, 'The resource-based theory of competitive advantage: implications for strategy formulation', *California Management Review*, 33(3), pp. 114–135.

Hirsch-Kreinsen, H., 2016, 'Digitization of industrial work: development paths and prospects', *Journal for Labour Market Research*, 49(1), pp. 1–14.

Jacobides, M. G., Cennamo, C., and Gawer, A., 2018, 'Towards a theory of ecosystems', *Strategic Management Journal*, 39(8), pp. 2255–2276.

Kaulio, M., Thorén, K., and Rohrbeck, R., 2017, 'Double ambidexterity: how a telco incumbent used business-model and technology innovations to successfully respond to three major disruptions', *Creativity and Innovation Management*, 26(4), pp. 339–352.

Kim, W.C. and Mauborgne, R., 2004, *Blue Ocean Strategy*, Harvard Business Press, Boston, MA.

Lieberman, M.B. and Montgomery, D.B., 1988, 'First-mover advantages', *Strategic Management Journal*, 9(S1), pp. 41–58.

Lindstedt, P. and Burenius, J., 2003, *The Value Model: How to Master Product Development and Create Unrivalled Customer Value*. Nimba.

Melin, M., 2017, 'Airbnb is facing some growing pains', *ValueWalk*. Available at https://www.businessinsider.com/airbnb-could-be-in-trouble-2017-11?r=US&IR=T Accessed 19/10/2019.

Meyer, M.H., 1997, 'Revitalize your product lines through continuous platform renewal', *Research-Technology Management*, 42(2), pp. 17–28.

Meyer, M.H. and Lehnerd, A.P., 1997, *The Power of Product Platforms*, Free Press, New York, NY.

Normann, R., 2001, *Reframing Business: When the Map Changes the Landscape*, John Wiley & Sons, Chichester, West Sussex.

Porter, M.E., 1980, *Competitive Strategy*, Free Press, New York.

Rosenblatt, B., 2018, 'The short, unhappy life of music downloads', *Forbes*, 7/5/2018. Available at https://www.forbes.com/sites/billrosenblatt/2018/05/07/the-short-unhappy-life-of-music-downloads/#69b274ac7e76, Accessed 14/10/2019.

Smith, A., 2016, 'Vinyl records sales fall in 2016', *What HiFi*. Available at https://www.whathifi.com/news/vinyl-record-sales-drop-in-2016, Accessed 23/11/2019.

Stone, B., 2013, *The Everything Store: Jeff Bezos and the Age of Amazon*, Little, Brown and Company, Bantam, London.

Teece, D.J., 1986, 'Profiting from technological innovation: implications for integration, collaboration, licensing and public policy', *Research Policy*, 15(6), pp. 285–305.

Teece, F.J., 2014, 'Business ecosystems', in Augier, M. and Teece, D.J. (eds) *Palgrave Encylopedia of Strategic Managemnet*. Palgrave Macmillan, London.

The Economist, 2013, 'Fetching far flung couture'. Available at https://www.economist.com/schumpeter/2013/02/28/fetching-far-flung-couture, Accessed 05/11/2019.

Tushman, M.L. and Murmann, J.P., 1998, 'Dominant designs, technology cycles, and organization outcomes', *Academy of Management Proceedings*, 1, pp. A1–A33. Academy of Management, Briarcliff Manor, NY.

Ulwick, A., 2005, *What Customers Want*, McGraw-Hill Professional Publishing.
Wernerfelt, B., 1984, 'A resource-based view of the firm', *Strategic Management Journal*, 5(2), pp. 171–180.
Wiggins, R., 1997, 'Web and internet pioneers: Jeff Besos, Founder of Amazon.c om'. Available at https://www.youtube.com/watch?v=rWRbTnE1PEM. Accessed 05/11/2019.

4

DIGITAL TRANSFORMATION OF THE HOME HELP SERVICE SECTOR THROUGH WELFARE TECHNOLOGY

Peter Markowski

The home help service sector is under pressure to deliver more with fewer resources, which is mainly due to an aging population and longer life expectancy. To be able to provide care to larger volumes of patients, new digital technologies are introduced. As this chapter shows, these new technologies alter the operating models of care providers and ultimately contribute to a transformation of the sector. To unfold how this happens the chapter analyses care delivery to see how digital technologies change care delivery routines as well as interactions between providers, patients and other actors. Essentially, these digital technologies increase providers' monitoring capabilities and provide patients with increased autonomy. As a result, services in the new system are delivered on-demand rather than on-schedule, unbound by institutional and geographical boundaries.

Introduction

Digitalization of home care for the elderly: Relatively simple technology with profound impacts

Much like in most developed economies, healthcare in Sweden is facing a growing elderly population. In the home help service sector, as in much of the larger healthcare sector, technology has the potential of making care more efficient (From, 2015). The home help service delivers routine care to elderly people in their homes.[1] In contrast to healthcare, the home help service is focused on supporting everyday tasks such as shopping or taking walks. The home help service does not depend on the advanced diagnostics or complicated medical procedures of more advanced healthcare (e.g. hospitals). Therefore, technology implemented in this sector, referred to as welfare technology, is not very complex compared with typical healthcare technology. Despite this fact, and as this chapter shows, it can change completely the way care is provided by altering the roles and interconnections of different actors in the sector. This chapter shows how the introduction of new technology fuels and interacts with organizational transformation, where organizations in the sector change and re-combine everyday routines to be able to help more patients without increased resources. New technology spurs relatively minor changes in routines for care provision, which together aggregate to create greater change on the sector level. New players, such as technology providers, are starting to take hands-on responsibility as part of care delivery, and the roles of traditional, state-run, home help service providers are changing. In this way, digital technology is enabling an increase in capacity and flexibility in the sector by supporting new entrants as well as new collaborations among actors.

So how can digital technology be instrumental in shifting an entire sector? To understand the dynamics involved in the digital transformation of the home help service sector, we must scrutinize the "nitty-gritty" of how care is delivered to the patient and the way welfare technology affects daily practices. We must understand how care personnel interact with patients, how home help service providers start to coordinate care delivery in new ways, how new players come in to fill the gaps as sector-level roles change and how these different players interact to deliver care across organizational, geographical and institutional boundaries. Essentially, many small changes on the operational level, taken together, are creating larger, structural changes on the sector level. This chapter attempts to explicate this process by scrutinizing the underlying dynamics, thereby shedding light on how the digital transformation of a sector can take place. As a case study, we use the home help service sector in Sweden, where technology-enabled real-time monitoring provides patients with more autonomy and shifts the work of care providers from strictly time-scheduled routines to more flexible, on-demand care delivery. Technology suppliers assume new roles, helping to deliver services with more precision, by increasing control using these real-time technologies (Björkdahl and Holmén, 2019).

The use of real-time monitoring technologies, such as vital signs monitoring for reduced health service use, have been found to improve the care for frail elderly people and people with chronic conditions (Barlow et al., 2007). However, research also points to organizational challenges in making use of telehealth technologies, such as the need to change the routines of care delivery operations in order to benefit from the technology, as well as achieving cooperation between different stakeholders (Nilsen et al., 2016; Hailey and Crowe, 2003). Research suggests it is organizational factors rather than the technology per se which presents obstacles to implementation. Indeed, as this chapter outlines, many municipal care providers already have access to the necessary technology, yet very few have been able to implement and make use of it. Consequently, the digital transformation of the welfare sector in Sweden is slow and politicians and civil servants are actively seeking to understand and solve the situation.

By studying cases where welfare technology has been implemented, this chapter provides insight into ways of moving past such organizational and institutional obstacles. In doing so, it also provides insight into how digital transformation of the welfare sector may occur. Despite the relatively simple technologies used, their implementation rests on the entrance of new actors, thus creating new inter-actor relationships and activities in the sector. The key to the digital transformation of the welfare sector thus seems to lie in the necessity to bring in new actors, revise roles and set up new routines for care delivery. Instead of "pushing" out care routinely, the transformed sector is geared to deliver tailored services, which implies a completely different operating model and the traversing of geographical and institutional boundaries.

In the following, the chapter describes how the home help service in Sweden is organized, followed by a description of the main technologies being implemented, as well as their functionality and use. Following that, we look at a case study of how welfare technology can create changes in routines of care delivery and the resulting effects. Finally, this chapter analyses and connects these operational changes to the aggregate sector level, thus shedding light on the dynamics underlying sector-level change through digitalization.

Data collection

This chapter builds on interview data and other information collected as part of a project that had the purpose of identifying technologies that bring value to municipalities' home help service practices. The study builds on 24 interviews, primarily conducted over Skype or phone. Respondents were selected based on their involvement in the implementation and use of welfare technology in the respective municipality's home help service. There was no direct contact with patients, but as far as possible, the patients' perspective was captured through the interviews and using secondary data. In this respect, the study takes the perspective of the home help service and does not include a deeper analysis of patients' views on the technologies (in reality, the patients' views could also affect the direction of the transformation). However, this shortcoming is mitigated by the fact that in interviews with home help service personnel the well-being of patients was often at centre stage.

Interview questions were aimed at understanding which technologies are used, how well they support the home help service, how they have been implemented, how they affect the way the service is provided and what are the obstacles to implementation as well as how such obstacles were handled. Municipalities in Sweden, being part of the public sector, have a duty to divulge most of the details about their services and projects. This facilitated the discussion, both regarding successes and barriers associated with the implemented technology. Such discussions enabled further insight into the effects of welfare technologies on staff routines. The personnel taking part in the project were working with the planning, leading and daily delivery of the home help service.

The organization of home help services in Sweden and the new functionality provided by welfare technology

Increasing the degree of digitalization in society is an important objective in Sweden. The government has formulated a digitalization strategy with the overarching goal that "Sweden should be leading the way when it comes to making use of the possibilities of digitalization". As part of this, the government and SKR (formerly SKL, an organization representing all Swedish municipalities) agreed on a strategy for national e-health investments, articulating that "in the year 2025 Sweden should be the best in the world at making use of the possibilities of digitalization to promote equal health and welfare, increase participation and make effective use of available individual resources".[2]

As a result of the national e-health strategy, there is a strong drive to increase the use of welfare technology in the home help service sector (also referred to as the welfare sector). This sector is run by municipalities, which are funded by taxpayers. The municipalities organize home help services for elderly citizens who are still healthy enough to live at home yet need some form of assistance to manage their everyday lives. This puts the welfare sector at the intersection of healthcare and social services. It provides services to the elderly and sometimes physically or mentally ill people who may not be ill enough to be healthcare patients, yet not autonomous enough to handle their own everyday lives.

The services provided range from being closely related to healthcare, such as assuring the right dosage of medication (as prescribed by a physician), to being more mundane, such as doing grocery shopping or cleaning the home. In this way, the welfare sector services are far less complex than healthcare and can therefore be provided by people without medical training. However, much like healthcare, these services rely on direct interaction with individuals in need of different kinds of aid, for example, (simple) medical or practical assistance. The sector therefore faces challenges similar to those of healthcare, in particular, a need to increase capacity and efficiency and at the same time to establish and preserve patient relations. An essential part of the service is to continually monitor patients' health to be able to provide adequate help when needed.

Actors traditionally involved in the Swedish home help service sector include but are not limited to:

- *Municipalities*, which manage and finance the home help service and also decide who is eligible for the service (in accordance with national guidelines).
- *Home help service providers*, which plan and perform daily service delivery (and are either run by the municipality or outsourced to a private company that delivers the service according to certain specifications).

Some municipalities are also responsible for the basic healthcare of their citizens. However, this chapter focuses only on the services that are part of the home help service. Here, welfare technology has become a key tool in driving an increase in the capacity of the home help service to meet the demands of an ageing population.

According to The National Board of Health and Welfare (Swedish: Socialstyrelsen), welfare technology can be defined as "digital technology whose purpose is to sustain or increase the safety, activity, participation or autonomy of a person who has or faces an increased risk of suffering health problems".[3] Technology implementation in the home help service sector is driven by several factors related to the general digitalization of society. For example, modern homes are being digitized using broadband Internet connections to control different parts of the home. This growing infrastructure serves as a platform for new welfare technology and specifically the home help service sector, which is centred on the home. Furthermore, the use of digital technology in the larger healthcare sector (e.g. self-diagnosis and remote care) has put patient autonomy and participation at centre stage, and this approach is diffusing to related areas such as welfare. This is driving the development of the welfare sector towards increased patient autonomy, building on advances in digital tools, which make use of connectedness and mobile communication.

The functions and use of welfare technology

The Research Institute of Sweden (RISE) suggests that elderly care is the municipal area that has the largest potential when it comes to increasing its efficiency. Because the home help service is rather standardized, there is potential to increase efficiency and free time for other value-adding activities. At the same time, welfare technology is considered a complex issue due to its presumed high impact on personal integrity, as technology is installed in patients' homes, combined with high requirements regarding the safety and stability of the technology. Despite such debates, welfare technology is generally considered a viable way of coping with an ageing population, as well as of handling shortages in personnel and resources.

In sum, there is a strong rationale for the implementation of welfare technologies, which can explain why, at least on paper, 80% of all municipalities in Sweden report that they use some form of welfare technology. Figure 4.1 shows the percentage of municipalities that (according to what they report) use different types of welfare technologies.[4]

However, through interviews with representatives of different municipalities it is clear that although many municipalities report that they are using welfare technology, they have in fact only begun to try to implement the technology in their care processes. The implementation takes time because these technologies have impacts that reach far beyond the local care processes. To better understand how and why this is the case, it is necessary to dig deeper into the practical implications of these technologies and to explain how they drive a transformation of the sector.

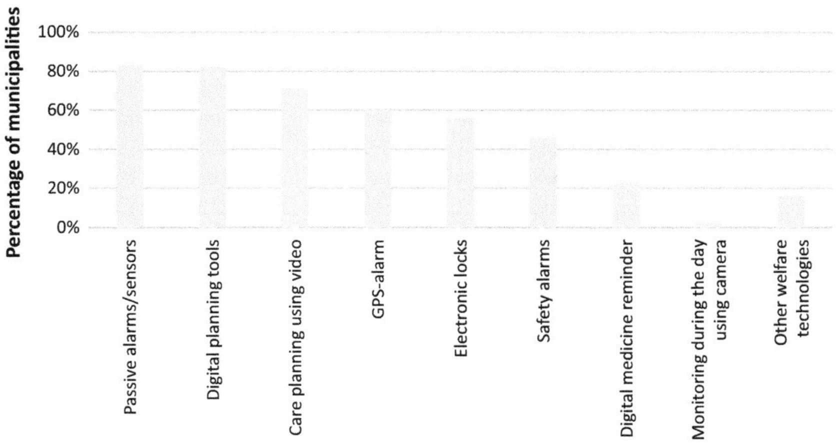

FIGURE 4.1 Percentage of municipalities that report the use of specified welfare technologies.

Table 4.1 describes the most commonly used welfare technologies, as well as their expected potential impact on the home help service. In sum, the potential impact of these technologies is an increase in patient autonomy, since by using the technology patients become more independent of the care provider. For the care provider, these technologies increase coordinative capabilities, both in terms of seamless digital coordination across organizational boundaries and in terms of being able to use resources more flexibly, on demand, based on "who needs help with what", rather than standardizing services for all patients regardless of what is happening in their home. The potential impact of the technologies is large because they shift the relations that are at the core of care delivery – the relation between care provider and patient, as well as between different care providers. However, as described in Table 4.1, the technologies themselves are not especially novel as sensors, GPS alarms and remote cameras are not new inventions. Rather, it is the change in care delivery routines, as well as the new roles of different players involved in care delivery, which provide the large impact of these rather simple technologies.

In the home help service, care delivery routines make up everyday care delivery. Such routines may be, for example, to visit the patient in the night to check whether everything is in order or to help the patient with shopping on a designated day and time.

Such routines, although a mundane concept in everyday parlance, have a significant role in organizations. Routines can be said to embody the way things are done in the organization (Cyert and March, 1963; Nelson and Winter, 1982). To be able to perform tasks as a collective, the organization sets up routines that govern how organizational members should work together to produce output. Routines embody what the organization can do and can thereby be said

TABLE 4.1 Welfare technologies: Function and potential impact on care delivery

Welfare technology	*Description*	*Impact on care delivery*
Passive alarms/ sensors	Different types of sensors are placed in the patient's home, which alert the home help service when something happens (such as if the patient falls) or if something does not happen (such as movement).	Provides information to the care provider when something happens in the home of the patient.
Digital planning tools	Digital tools that allow care providers to perform scheduling, resource planning and problem registration on their mobile phones.	Increases mobility and supports seamless collaboration among care providers.
Care-planning using video	Video tools that enable communication between elderly people who are about to be discharged from hospital, home help service providers and municipal planners.	Serves to connect several actors who are otherwise separated by organizational and institutional boundaries.
GPS alarm	An alarm that tracks the position of a patient outside the home. If the patient presses a button the home help service is alerted. Can also be used to find patients who have disappeared.	Increases autonomy of the patient, while providing the care provider with the possibility of finding the patient on demand.
Electronic locks	Locks that allow the home help service personnel to enter the patient's home using their mobile phone to unlock the door.	Increases efficiency, mobility and flexibility of care providers.
Digital camera	A camera placed in the patient's home, allowing the home help service to perform monitoring at scheduled intervals during the night using the camera, instead of through physical visits.	Provides the care provider with monitoring capabilities.
Digital medicine reminder	Digital aid that reminds the patient to take their medicine at certain hours and provides the right dose.	Reduces the need for physical visits by care providers.
Digital grocery shopping	A service where online grocery shopping is used instead of the home help service personnel physically performing the shopping for the patient.	Increases the autonomy of the patient and reduces the need for visits by the care provider.

to define an organization's current capability. The routines provide stability by governing everyday work in the organization. However, for an organization to learn how to work in new ways, or produce new output, routines need to change (we all know the common response from managers – "we are improving our routines" – when asked about an incident or failure). Such changes can be the result of internal requirements, such as a new strategy, or external requirements, such as new regulations. In both cases, the change in routines embodies the learning of the organization as a collective. Therefore, routines have been suggested by organization scholars to be a source not only of stability, i.e. how things are done in the organization, but also of change, i.e. how new things are learned by the organization (Feldman and Pentland, 2003; Markowski, 2018).

The implementation of new digital technologies often implies new ways of working. This can involve changing both the way work is performed inside organizations and the way different organizations interact within a sector. Thus, to understand how digital technologies can have a transformational effect on the home help service sector, it is helpful to analyse how technology affects routines *within* the home help service provider, while also taking into account how *several actors can combine* their capabilities (i.e. routines governing daily output) to collectively produce a new service to the patient. In this respect, analysing changes to routines allows you to gain insights into the digital transformation of not only the organization but also the sector. Examples of digital technology implementation in practice are presented in the next section.

Cases of implementation of welfare technology in the home help service

Social workers at a municipality starting to implement a digital camera as part of their home help service described how this changed the way care was delivered. In the following, quotations from the informants are not direct, but my paraphrases of their accounts.

> Instead of driving round to patients in the middle of the night to see if they are in bed, we stay at the office and observe them at scheduled times using the camera.

The social workers state that the old routine was to drive to the patient, open the door, look to see if they were in bed and then close the door. The new routine was to instead sit down behind the computer at a certain time, open the system, look through the camera to see if the patient was in bed and then close the system.

> The benefits are that we save time and do not disturb the patient. No interaction is lost since there is none when the patient is asleep anyway.

The social workers said that they saw no drawbacks with using the digital camera for the monitoring of patients during the night. It was laborious to have to drive to patients in the middle of the night and using the camera they could instead stay at the office and still perform the same action – checking to see that the patient was asleep in their bed. The social workers highlighted the apparent efficiency gains of using this technology. Furthermore, since the new routine was to drive to the patient if they should not be seen through the camera, the social workers described that the more laborious task of actually visiting the patient during the night could now be reserved for when it was potentially really needed. Essentially, the digital camera transformed their function as a care provider from "routine visiting" to "routine monitoring". Since monitoring through the camera can be done remotely, they now only perform physical care visits "on demand", triggered by the patient not being in bed. This seemed to make sense to the social workers, mainly because they could spend their energy when it was really needed, triggered by an event that called for action, rather than performing physical visits regardless of need.

However, no matter how clear the rationale behind the camera technology might be, several municipalities report difficulties in extending its use. It seems that the introduction of this function is not so easy. The main problems reported are (a) getting patients to accept having a camera at home and (b) integrating the digital camera in the bureaucracy of the state-funded home help service. First, the new function of the home help service as remote monitoring agents crucially depends on the patient accepting to be monitored in this way. While most patients accept the camera after a while, several representatives from municipalities highlighted the importance of explaining thoroughly how the camera works, as well as providing a positive case for the camera as a way to make it possible for the patient to sleep undisturbed (without someone slamming the door in the middle of the night). The camera must be perceived as care rather than an intrusion into the integrity of the private home. The commonly held view on care as physical and close needs to be replaced by one where physical visits are performed "on demand", triggered by adverse events that only rarely happen. The rest of the time, when there is no pressing need for assistance, visits are replaced with continuous monitoring. Care is still performed routinely, but it is not always observable by the patient as monitoring routines are performed remotely. In exchange, the patient gets more autonomy since no disturbance is caused as long as they are in bed at certain hours. However, this increase in autonomy may come with a long-run increase in isolation for the patient, who may meet caretakers less often once the technology is implemented.

The second problem, namely integrating the digital camera in the bureaucratic routines of the municipal organization, essentially comes from a need to change not only the care delivery routines, but also the administrative routines that govern how and to whom care is provided. The clerks, who follow protocols and make formal decisions on who is eligible for the state-funded home help service, need to understand this new technology. This is difficult because decisions on the home help service are institutionalized parts of the municipal bureaucracy. Changing these requires sponsorship from municipal governance, as these routines are at the heart of the organization's bureaucratic rationale.

In this way, changing the operative routines of care delivery (using digital technology) requires difficult changes of routines further up in the organization.

Municipalities that have succeeded in implementing the digital camera report that they have changed the bureaucratic routines so that the camera is the default care provided.

Furthermore, those who have succeeded in taking on the new role and function using the digital camera report that they have established collaborations with technology providers.

> We have entrusted the technology provider with installing the technology and testing it. They interact with patients in doing this, and report to us regularly.

This shows how an external technology provider is made part of municipal care delivery by becoming a designated technology administrator, in close contact with the municipal workers. This development expands the role of the external provider, which becomes an integrated part of delivering care.

Essentially, succeeding with digitalization in this context seems to require not only changes in internal routines on several levels (both care delivery and bureaucratic routines in the administration), but also establishing collaborations with new actors who can perform installation and maintenance of the technology, thus in effect adding new routines that are necessary but are lacking in the municipality.

In this way, a relatively simple technical artefact such as the digital camera, through its implementation, has effectively driven a transformation of the service provided by forcing a break with established routines (on the governance and bureaucratic levels) and fuelling the entrance of new players (the technology providers) into the daily operations of the home help service.

Another digital technology implemented by the municipalities is the GPS alarm (see Table 4.1). This is also a relatively simple technology, which, when implemented in the home help service, provides new possibilities for the patient and for the care provider. The technology's main function is to enable the patient to leave their home and still be in contact with care providers or the patient's relatives. It is essentially a two-way communication device, which can either be activated by the patient – "find me" – or by the care provider – "where are you?" Much like the digital camera, this device increases the autonomy of the patient, who can move around freely, while providing the care provider with remote capabilities to be able to check on the patient if needed (in this case, checking on the patient is aided by making it possible to locate them). The GPS alarm can be configured using a so-called "geo-fence", which triggers an alarm if the patient leaves a pre-programmed geographical area. Municipalities report that the GPS alarm helps patients to dare go out on their own, not having to worry about falling and not being found, which means that the routine of helping the patient with regular walks in many cases may no longer be needed. This implies efficiency gains for the provider, who can instead deliver help only when needed.

Some municipalities that use the GPS alarm have configured it to first alert the patient's relatives via mobile technology and then to make it possible for them to track the patient's location using their mobile phones. This solution effectively introduces the patient's relatives as an "intermediary" between the patient and the care provider. Although some municipal representatives stress that it is compromising the personal integrity of the patient to allow relatives to track them, the rationale behind this solution points to a key legislative issue raised by the technology: if the patient triggers the alarm outside of the geographical area in which its home help service provider is active – whose responsibility is it then to come to the rescue? Judging by the complexity of this question, introducing the patient's relatives, who can travel anywhere to help them, is potentially a smart move that circumvents the time-consuming legislative problem of setting up required collaboration agreements among municipalities. In a similar fashion, other municipalities report that they have outsourced the alarm-centre function to an external party focused on handling these types of alarms.

Once again, a relatively simple technology disrupts the operating model of geographically organized care provision – while all providers have the routines to handle alarms *within* their geographical area, handling alarms from *anywhere* calls for a very different setup, requiring not only new routines within the municipality but also between different municipalities. To avoid the laborious task of having to bridge organizational and institutional boundaries, municipalities that are successfully using this technology have instead introduced new players (i.e. relatives or firms who specialize in alarm centres) that have taken the role of intermediaries between patient and provider. The care provider only comes into play when really needed (alarms that turn out to require local care assistance), and otherwise remains a more distant actor, albeit with tracking capabilities.

Another digital solution, which is used by municipalities, is digital grocery shopping. In contrast to the GPS alarm and the digital camera, this is not primarily a technology per se, but rather a service integrated with that of the care provider. Instead of physically coming to the home of the patient, collecting a shopping list, going to the grocery store to shop and returning with the groceries, the home help service gives the patient the possibility of grocery shopping online. Being "given the possibility" may sound strange since anyone with a computer and an Internet connection can access this service. Here, however, it is arranged in a way to suit old people who cannot manage this by themselves. The project manager of one of the municipalities actively implementing digital grocery shopping explained their setup:

> We have arranged with the supplier so that it is always the same driver who knows in which order to deliver to the patients, and at what time. This way, the patient gets deliveries according to a schedule, and knows (or can be alerted) that it is time to unpack the groceries, or for those that cannot unpack themselves, we know when we need to be there to help them.

The setup described by the project manager is adapted to be accessible to elderly patients as part of their home help service. Although shopping online is commonplace these days, it requires being able to type into a web interface and deciding on when the delivery should take place, as well as being there to receive the groceries on time. Small errors in this process (pertaining to the buyer, supplier or both) easily result in no groceries received. To make sure that the desired groceries are received every week, the municipality set up a contract with a large web store to become the sole supplier of food to their home help service. Their bargaining power allowed them to negotiate that the food was delivered according to a pre-defined routine, where houses on the same street always received deliveries in the same order, by the same driver. The driver was informed not only about the setup but also about the elderly customers who may need more help than usual and may not even remember the delivery schedule. This way, delivery was managed according to a fixed routine and largely independent of customer dialogue.

To order groceries, the patient needs to be guided through an ordering process on the web. This process can be time-consuming not only because the patient may not be able to see well and use the web, but also because the choice of products is large. For someone who is not used to shopping for his or her own food, this can at first be daunting. The project manager explained:

> I sat down with each patient to explain how the service works, and together go through the choices and choose a shopping basket. This takes time the first time it is done, but after 2–3 times, and when the shopping list is saved in the system from last week, it is swift. Being able to choose for oneself is a great thing for many elderly [people] who are used to just receiving whatever there happened to be available in the store.

The project manager shows that digital grocery shopping increases the autonomy of the patient by allowing them to choose what food they want to buy. Once they are "up and running" with web shopping, they may not even need help with ordering food online. Another municipality described that they had moved past the need to read small letters on a screen by buying tablets with small projectors that can project the screen onto a wall. This made it possible for patients to surf the web on their own. However, in the case of digital grocery shopping, the increased autonomy of being able to order the food of one's choice on the internet, created new problems – the patient needs to have, and use, some form of credit or debit card to pay for the food, alternatively there are invoices that need to be received and paid. In the above-described setup, the municipality paid for transport but arranged with a relative to have the card details of the patient entered into the system and had relatives responsible for taking care of any resulting invoice. For patients who did not have a card of their own, a relative's card was used. If this was not possible, digital grocery shopping could not be offered.

The setup of digital grocery shopping here described is based on the care provider partnering with an external actor to set up and deliver a new service. In this way, the routines of the external service provider are changed to fit the specific needs of the patients – needs that have been understood and articulated by the care provider. Once the patient has been aided in starting the new service (by choosing goods, ordering, saving personal information, etc.), it becomes a matter of routine and replaces the old routine of physically visiting the patient and going to buy food. However, in the new routine, the care provider can remain passive as long as nothing goes wrong and needs to be handled. By bringing in new players, here the web supplier and the relatives who handle invoices and other finances, the care provider introduces a new service that increases efficiency, while also giving the patient more autonomy.

Digital transformation of the home-help service sector

The above-described cases of the implementation of digital technology in the Swedish home help sector show how the introduction of rather simple technologies can drive digital transformation on a system level.

Figure 4.2a illustrates the operating model of the home help service before digital transformation. Here, care is delivered according to routine and a set schedule. Figure 4.2b illustrates the operating model of the home help service after digital transformation. Here, care is delivered on demand, according to signals from the patient. The technology provider supplies the care provider with technical capability on demand and the patient with technologically based services on demand. A specific aspect of what is happening is the role of technology providers as enablers in traversing institutional and geographical boundaries between municipalities.

The origin of "before and after" can be traced to changes in routines and the entrance of new actors. Digital technologies trigger changes to routines of the care provider, and drive collaboration with service providers in the market, thereby transforming the sector.

As illustrated in Figure 4.2a, the home help service was originally based on an operating model where services were defined and agreed upon in advance, and then delivered to the patient on a regular basis (and in pre-defined format). The care provider thus had care delivery routines that were executed regularly more or less regardless of what the patient needed on that specific day.

As illustrated in Figure 4.2b, the transformed home help service is event-driven to a large extent. Thus, digital technology has a transformative effect on the way care is delivered. By means of the new technology, the provider goes from delivering services based on scheduled visits to the patient, to delivering services based on direct demand from the patient. In operational terms, the provider changes its routines from being "time-triggered", i.e. a certain point in time calls for a specific service (regardless of what the patient needs at that specific moment), to "on demand", "just-in-time" care production based

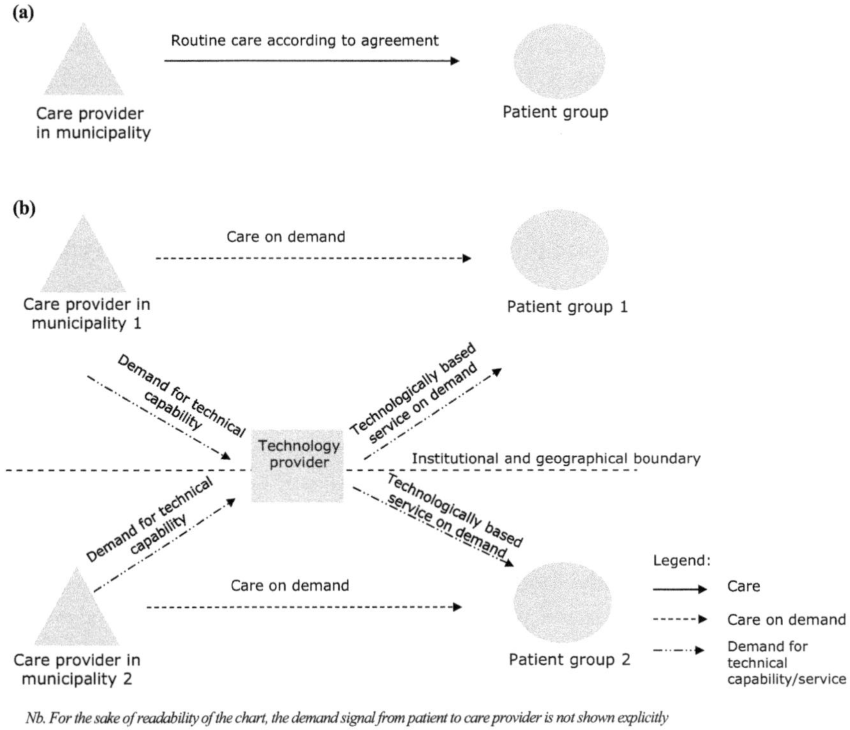

FIGURE 4.2 (a) Operating model of home help service before digital transformation (b) Operating model of home help service after digital transformation.

on care delivery routines that are triggered by an alert from the patient. The old "push" logic of care delivery is now replaced by a "pull" logic, where the patient is autonomous and actively triggers care delivery. This greater autonomy of the patient implies not only an increase in their decision power and freedom but also a new role of the provider, who now needs to be able to deliver the right care to the right patient at the right time – i.e. whenever it is called for. A provider in this digitalized system thus needs to be both an active listener, who can readily respond to alerts from the patient, and a flexible hub of resources that can be deployed to where they are needed. Needless to say, this implies a rather dramatic change in the required capabilities of the care provider (as an organization).

How is this sudden need for new capabilities resolved? Some key capabilities, as the previous cases illustrate, are created through the implementation of new digital technology, for example, being able to monitor the patient from afar. At the same time, in order to be able to use the new technology, new routines and capabilities need to be developed, for example, the technical expertise required to handle configuration and maintenance of the technology itself.

Being able to install and maintain the technology requires capabilities related to technical expertise. Because such capability is not developed overnight, the care provider turns to the market to find partners who can deliver the missing pieces. In the cases presented, this was achieved by partnering with a technology specialist who interacted directly with patients and performed installations in their homes (see Figure 4.2b). Another example is partnering with the firm that took orders via the web and delivered groceries to the home. In both examples, complementary routines and capabilities of other actors are combined with those of the care provider to deliver the new, technology-enabled service to the patient.

Apart from technological expertise, being able to reach the patient is a central dimension of the care services delivered. Traditionally, the home help service is delivered within geographical and institutional boundaries, defined by the geographical area of the municipality within which its institutional mandate is valid. However, the mobility of digital technologies challenges this setup. This is illustrated in the case of the GPS alarm, where the care provider found itself in a situation where the old institutional and legislative structures, which assign responsibilities to different providers based on their geographical location, now directly hindered effective use of this digital technology. The required reach was made available by technology providers who also had call centre capabilities, allowing them to respond to patient alarms regardless of location. In some cases, the relatives of patients could also serve as the first line of contact that was independent of location. In this way, new actors were brought in to overcome the problems caused by these rigid structures and made it possible to use the GPS alarm over geographical and institutional boundaries.

Thus, as new actors are brought in to "fill the gaps" created by the new digital technologies, the home help service sector can be said to become increasingly fragmented and specialized. As services to the patient are digitalized, the number of actors involved in delivering the service increases. As illustrated previously, this can happen when technology providers or external call centres (for receiving alarms) become an integrated part of service delivery, for example. As the number of actors increases, their relative share of service delivery narrows, since they specialize only in a certain part of it. This increase in fragmentation and specialization in turn creates an increased need for cross-organizational coordination. As illustrated in the case of digital grocery shopping, the care provider actively designed the delivery routine to fit their specifications. They also connected the new routine with their own, for example, so that they could schedule visits for the unpacking of food for those patients that needed it. Here, coordination was enabled through the negotiation and setting up of contracts and achieved in practice by creating new "shared" routines across organizational boundaries, tailored to the specific context. These shared routines were combinations of the actors' respective internal routines, which together allowed seamless care delivery, almost as if one organization alone provided the service. It is in this respect that the grocery-delivering actor could "fill a gap" in the capability of the home help service provider. It can be noted that the existence of such specialized actors in the market thus becomes an enabler of, if not a prerequisite for, the digital transformation of the sector. Had there been no specialized actor to partner with, the home help service provider would have had to develop new capabilities de novo.

The cases here presented exemplify how a sector is digitally transformed. The transformation process is characterized by an increase in fragmentation and specialization, but also the creation of new collaborative relations where actors together bring new capabilities to the sector. While the transformation is fuelled by the introduction of new technology, it mainly involves changes to inter-organizational relationships (as well as changes in patient contact), changing and re-combining the routines of different actors to create new capabilities of service delivery. What is shown is how the introduction of new technology sets into motion a dynamic process involving, on the one hand, an influx of new actors, and on the other hand, the development of new contracts and shared routines that bind together different actors in the system. The result is a general increase in flexibility and customization, as care provision gradually moves from being structurally rigid and repetitively delivered according to standardized criteria, to being demand-driven, malleable and tailored to the specific needs of the patient.

A few policy implications can be drawn from the results of this study. Primarily, as indicated by the relatively slow implementation of welfare technology in Sweden, there are several obstacles to its introduction, which should be taken into account in policy design. On an aggregate level, the promotion and use of welfare technologies signify a change in policy towards automation and optimization as guiding principles (From, 2015). This chapter indicates that the governance system needs to be adjusted to accommodate this shift. As the case of the GPS alarm points out, there are legislative restrictions related to the geographic coverage of services. Furthermore, welfare technology requires the development of new administrative capabilities within the sector.

Notes

1 "Home help service" is here used interchangeably with "care provider", and the elderly people who receive the service are also referred to as "patients" for reasons of simplicity (the Swedish word is "brukare" which strictly is not synonymous to "patient").
2 The National Board of Health and Welfare (Socialstyrelsen, 2018) report "E-hälsa och välfärdsteknik i kommunerna 2018 – Redovisning av en uppföljning av utvecklingen inom e-hälsa och välfärdsteknik i kommunerna".
3 Translation to English based on The National Board of Health and Welfare's official translations of terms (Swedish: Socialstyrelsen termbank) - http://termbank.socialstyrelsen.se/.
4 The National Board of Health and Welfare (Socialstyrelsen, 2018) report: "E-hälsa och välfärdsteknik i kommunerna 2018 – Redovisning av en uppföljning av utvecklingen inom e-hälsa och välfärdsteknik i kommunerna".

References

Barlow, J., Singh, D., Bayer, S. and Curry, R., 2007. A systematic review of the benefits of home telecare for frail elderly people and those with long-term conditions. *Journal of Telemedicine and Telecare*, 13(4), pp. 172–179.

Björkdahl, J. and Holmén, M., 2019. Exploiting the control revolution by means of digitalization: value creation, value capture, and downstream movements. *Industrial and Corporate Change*, 28(3), pp. 423–436.

Cyert, R.M. and March, J.G., 1963. *A behavioral theory of the firm*. Englewood Cliffs, NJ: Prentice-Hall.

Feldman, M.S. and Pentland, B.T., 2003. Reconceptualizing organizational routines as a source of flexibility and change. *Administrative Science Quarterly*, 48(1), pp. 94–118.

From, D.M., 2015. With a little help from a... machine. Digital welfare technology and sustainable human welfare. *Journal of Transdisciplinary Environmental Studies*, 14(2), pp. 52–64.

Hailey, D. and Crowe, B., 2003. A profile of success and failure in telehealth—evidence and opinion from the successes and failures in telehealth conferences. *Journal of Telemedicine and Telecare*, 9 (Suppl. 2), pp. 22–24.

Markowski, P., 2018. *Collaboration routines: a study of interdisciplinary healthcare*. Diss. Stockholm Business School, Stockholm University.

Nelson, R. R. and Winter, S. G., 1982. *An evolutionary theory of economic change*. Cambridge, MA: Harvard University Press.

Nilsen, E.R., Dugstad, J., Eide, H., Gullslett, M.K. and Eide, T., 2016. Exploring resistance to implementation of welfare technology in municipal healthcare services–a longitudinal case study. *BMC Health Services Research*, 16(1), p. 657.

Socialstyrelsen, Rapport 2018. "E-hälsa och välfärdsteknik i kommunerna 2018 – Redovisning av en uppföljning av utvecklingen inom e-hälsa och välfärdsteknik i kommunerna".

5

DOING MORE BY KNOWING LESS

The evolution of the division of innovative labour in software creation

Magnus Holmén and Rögnvaldur Saemundsson

Introduction

Much has been written about the transformative and disruptive effects of digitalization on various industries, including its effects on the division of labour across and within firms (e.g. Parker et al., 2016; also see Suarez and Utterback, 1995; Arora et al., 2001; Murmann and Frenken, 2006). For example, multisided markets enable new connections between customers and firms, and supply chain changes shift the locus of production closer to the customer by means of additive manufacturing. Central to the effects that digitalization has on industrial transformation and new divisions of labour is its influence on the growth of knowledge and the division of knowledge. There is a rich literature analysing how technological, industrial and human activities relate to the nature and growth of knowledge (e.g. Vincenti, 1990; Arora and Gambardella, 1994). Despite coevolutionary studies of industries (Murmann, 2003), the subject of knowledge has received relatively little attention in the literature on industrial transformation, such as industry life cycles and industry emergence. This is somewhat surprising as there is a long tradition, and recent resurgence, of considering the growth and division of knowledge as a key driver of economic growth and industrial development (Smith, 1776; Menger, 1871; Pavitt, 1998; Romer, 1990).

In the literature, we can find at least two perspectives on the relationship between knowledge and human activities. The first perspective stresses how humans improve their knowledge of the world and how this improved knowledge increases the ability of humans, firms and other actors to reach desired outcomes. This means that knowledge is improved in the sense that problem-solving is becoming increasingly powerful in reaching desired end results (Arora and Gambardella, 1994). Explanations include the ongoing scientification and codification of knowledge, which allows knowledge to be more easily transferred from the context of its creation to the context of its use, and consequently better suited to market exchanges. However, despite the impressive advances of human knowledge, the puzzle remains of how human beings, with their cognitive limitation, can accomplish so much (Nelson and Winter, 2002). This brings us to the second complementary perspective. This perspective deals with how the total knowledge grows through *increasing differentiation of knowledge*, or what may be referred to as increased decomposition or modularization of knowledge. Here the starting point is the assumption that human cognitive attention span and ability are scarce resources and will always remain so in an uncertain world. Consequently, to be successful, all human beings economize cognition (Loasby, 2001, 2007; Kahneman, 2011). For an individual agent, this is a severe limitation, but humans are able to increase total knowledge in an industry or the economy above the cognitive limitations of each individual through increased specialization (Hayek, 1937; Pavitt, 1998; Loasby, 2000). However, this type of knowledge growth by means of differentiation requires coordination through mechanisms that allow each individual to take advantage of the knowledge of others without sharing that knowledge completely.

A means for this is digitalization, which may be viewed as the pervasive use of digital technologies, i.e. technologies that collect, communicate, transform and present digital information. At the heart of digitalization is software creation, as the functionality of digital technologies is determined by software. The technologies for creating software are themselves digital technologies, which means that the growth of knowledge in software creation is both the source and beneficiary of digitalization.

In software creation, programming languages provide a bundle of mechanisms – termed abstraction mechanisms – to help modularize software and thus assist individual developers to take advantage of the knowledge of others without sharing that knowledge completely (e.g. Guarino, 1978; Shaw, 1984). New abstraction mechanisms are created within the software creation community to aid developers in decomposing software designs in a way that promotes an effective division of developer work and improves software reuse among developers (e.g. Barnes and Bollinger, 1991; Brady et al., 1992; Gamma et al., 1995; Mili et al., 1995; Fichman and Kemerer, 1997). The primary motive of abstractions and abstraction mechanisms is therefore to help developers to economize cognition during development work and allow for the integration of work done by different developers. As we will show, this explains the nature and limitations of the division of innovative labour. The division of innovative labour is a core aspect of innovation as it creates a structure that shapes what and how novelties are invented and produced.

Thus, the purpose of this chapter is to improve our understanding of how digitalization influences the growth of knowledge and the division of innovative labour across and within firms. The chapter analyses the evolution of abstract mechanisms in software creation and conceptualizes how the growth of knowledge coevolves with the division of labour in software creation.

To do this, we extensively review publications in software creation, covering more than 1000 publications from the 1950s until the early 2000s. The search focused on publications in software engineering, computer science and engineering-oriented publications in informatics and information systems. This includes but is not limited to journals and conferences given by the Association for Computing Machinery (ACM), the Institute of Electrical and Electronics Engineers (IEEE) and respected publishers such as Elsevier, Sage, Springer and Wiley. In addition, we have read reflections and books written by researchers that have made seminal contributions, such as Fred Brooks, Edsger Dijkstra and David Parnas, together with historical analyses of the emergence and transformation of software technology and independent software vendors (ISV). We exclude more recent publications, to decrease the number of publications. To the best of our knowledge, this does not limit the chapter's findings.

Abstractions and the evolution of abstraction mechanisms

There are two common definitions of abstractions (Fellbaum, 1998). The first views an abstraction as a representation of a phenomenon in terms of a limited number of elements while leaving out or ignoring others or as the act of creating these simplified representations. An example of such an abstraction is the representation of an employee by his or her title, which removes details. Such titles provide information about the activities that a person is expected to perform without giving any details about that person, such as name, age and education or his or her activities. The second definition views abstraction as a general concept formed by extracting common features from specific instances. Using a similar example as before, the concept of the white-collar worker provides a generalization for workers who do not perform manual labour.

There are distinct differences between these two definitions. The former focuses on the withdrawal or removing of details. The details that are withdrawn depend on the purpose of the abstraction. The latter focuses on creating representations that hold true for a group of instances sharing common characteristics. This provides an opportunity to generalize statements about phenomena that share common characteristics. The two definitions are related in that the former view of abstractions is the superset of the latter as suppression of details sometimes is based on the (successful) identification of common elements among different instances. Increasing generality requires the identification of common elements, and the subsequent suppression of details, which serves the purpose of generalization from specific instances. Increasing generality is thus one of the purposes that may guide how phenomena are represented in terms of a limited number of elements and what details are left out or ignored.[1]

Representations have an important role in problem solving (Newell, 1969; Simon, 1996). Every problem-solving effort starts with the creation of a representation for the problem which is suitable for the problem-solving method used to provide a solution. This amounts to creating an abstraction, i.e. represents the problem in terms of a limited number of elements, which provides a suitable input for the problem-solving method being used to find a solution.

For most of our daily life problems, we are able to retrieve an abstraction from memory, adapt it to the situation at hand and apply a known procedure that may include the use of an artefact (Simon, 1996). Technical development work differs as it is concerned with the invention of an artefact or a procedure that may either be isolated or belong to a larger system, and the sources of the problems being solved may be related to the "contextual needs of society" (Vincenti, 1990, p. 203) or the characteristics of the technologies being used (Laudan, 1984; Vincenti, 1990, pp. 200–207). When developers create new artefacts or procedures, they are often faced with problems that they do not know how to solve and may therefore need to invent and develop new abstractions that allow them to solve problems using known problem-solving methods, extend or renew the problem-solving methods in order to reach a feasible solution using a known abstraction of the problem or create both new abstractions and new problem-solving methods.

The abstractions that can be used by developers depend upon available abstraction mechanisms. These are procedures that enable the developer to specify, implement and use a certain type of abstraction. An example of abstraction mechanisms is modular product architectures, which consist of specific representations of how to construct different products (Ulrich, 1995).

The specification, implementation and use of naming abstractions in software is another example of an abstraction mechanism. Naming allows the programmer to abstract away from the memory addresses of the hardware (Guarino, 1978), which solves the problem of bookkeeping when instructions or data are shifted to a different memory location.

Abstraction mechanisms are a specific class of problem-solving methods that aim at solving problems related to the specification, implementation and use of abstractions. As these problems are at the heart of development work, abstraction mechanisms are a part of the technology of development work. When development work is technical, this technology has been termed the "technology of technical change" (Arora and Gambardella, 1994; Dosi, 1988).

But what affects how abstraction mechanisms evolve? Within the software creation community, there has been an ongoing search for new abstraction mechanisms to promote a more effective division of developer work and improve software reuse. Arora and Gambardella (1994) and Arora et al. (2001) provide some evidence that suggests that improvements in the technology of technical change depend on complementary advances in theoretical understanding of problems, instrumentation and computational capacity. Notably, these three areas have been much discussed in the literature (e.g. Moore, 1965; Rosenberg, 1976; Nelson, 1992; Nightingale, 1998) but there is not any material available that can help us understand how the complementarity of the three areas work.

Fortunately, this can be overcome by referring to studies of the development of science and technology.

The argument for an improved theoretical understanding of problems is related to the claim that there is an increased scientification of technological change and thus that advances in scientific disciplines have an important influence on technological change (Meyer-Krahmer and Schmoch, 1998). Through the use of science, there are improved attempts to identify and understand the principles that govern physical phenomena. In particular, analysis of patent citations shows that inventors increasingly refer to scientific advances in their patent applications (Narin and Noma, 1985; Narin and Olivastro, 1992).

While admitting the relevance of the increased scientification of technological change, other scholars stress that new technological advancements are prime engines of scientific progress (Gazis, 1979; de Solla Price, 1984; Meyer, 2000; Rosenberg, 1992). de Solla Price (1984) argues that advances in instrumentation and experimental techniques have driven and stimulated theoretical advances in fundamental science and innovations. The argument is that advances in physical artefacts or tools such as instruments may generate new opportunities for knowledge creation, regardless of whether these consist of "technological knowledge" or "scientific knowledge". Instruments can be understood as the capital goods of research and development (R&D), meaning that their economic significance comes from allowing researchers or engineers to reduce the cost of solving increasingly complex technical problems (Rosenberg, 1976; Nightingale, 2000).

An important aspect in the development of instrumentation is an improvement in computational capacity (Moore, 1965; Bell and Gray, 2002; Bader, 2004). This improvement refers to the dramatic advancement in the "number crunching" abilities of information technologies that reduce the time it takes to perform a complex calculation. This not only improves the efficiency of existing instruments but opens up for the use of new types of instruments that were not feasible to implement before.

Taken together, complementary improvements in theoretical understanding, instrumentation and computational capacity improve the power of problem-solving methods, i.e. they increase the likelihood of a solution, improve the quality of the solution or reduce the time needed to reach an acceptable solution. On the one hand, these improvements increase the power of existing problem-solving methods, i.e. they move closer to, or reach, their theoretical upper limits. On the other hand, they make it feasible to use new methods, whose power did not fulfil some minimum requirements before.

Evolution of abstraction mechanisms for software creation

In this section, we specifically analyse the evolution of abstraction mechanisms in software creation. We start by describing how abstractions are used in software creation and then show how complementary advances in theoretical knowledge, instrumentation and computational capacity have affected the abstraction mechanisms being created and used. Additionally, we show that the introduction of new abstraction mechanisms that are applied at a higher level of abstraction does not lead to the elimination of older mechanisms, but rather they are used in combination with the new ones to create an evolving galaxy of abstractions that influence what developers need to know and are able to do.

Use of abstraction in software creation

Software creation consists of activities to create programming code to run on a computer system. These activities include the capturing of application and customer requirements, system design, programming, testing and software maintenance (Prieto-Dìaz, 1990; Bellinzona et al., 1995; Glass and Vessey, 1998; Weyuker, 1998). The computer systems may range from single microprocessors to parallel computers and large systems of interconnected personal computers or mainframes. Accordingly, the topics and knowledge involved in software creation consist of a range of factors, where the relative importance of these factors varies greatly according to the application and the targeted computer system (Basili and Musa, 1991; Glass and Vessey, 1998).

The importance of abstractions was discussed by programmers in the 1950s (Jones, 2003). At that time, software played a supplementary role to hardware and software creation was thus viewed as a subfield of existing engineering disciplines. As the design of hardware was analysed in terms of abstraction, it was thus hardly surprising that commentators thought the same ideas should be applied to software (Shapiro, 1997). Despite this early recognition, seminal scientific papers about how to characterize and use abstractions in *software* were not published until around 1970, especially Dijkstra (1968) and Parnas (1972, 1975).

These and other papers were crucial, not just for the explicit identification of abstraction as a fundamental principle of software creation, but also for the rise of modular programming, which is based on abstraction (Parnas, 1972; Brooks, 1995). Importantly, in his 1972 ACM Turing lecture, Edward Dijkstra argued that:

> We all know that the only mental tool by means of which a very finite piece of reasoning can cover a myriad of cases is called "abstraction"; as a result the effective exploitation of his powers of abstraction must be regarded as one of the most vital activities of a competent programmer.
>
> *(Dijkstra, 1972, p. 864)*

At the time, there was little explicit recognition that abstraction meant two different things. This is reflected in the extensive conceptual and semantic confusion in scientific journals and textbooks (e.g. IEEE, 1983; Zimmer, 1985; Booch, 1993). One view of abstraction in software was that abstractions could be created as finite pieces of reasoning by keeping essential details but suppressing irrelevant details from the perspective of some purpose. An argument was made that such formulations could be made more powerful and general, ultimately allowing a programmer full control of the software in line with the role of abstraction in other engineering disciplines.[2]

A more pragmatic approach, and the dominant one during the last few decades, was outlined by Parnas (1972), who argued that abstraction should be viewed as information hiding, where "clean interfaces" among chunks of code allowed for a division of knowledge in software creation. Abstractions permit the representation of phenomena in terms of a limited number of elements while irrelevant details are left out or ignored. What details are included and what are left out depends on the properties or attributes judged to be important for a given purpose (Smith and Smith, 1977; Guarino, 1978; Object Management Group, 2001).[3]

The purposes of software creation vary greatly, and this influences the nature of the abstractions being created or used. Some, such as academics dealing with formal verification or fault tolerance, tend to have quite a strict and mathematically based view of abstractions. This is in line with the view of Dijkstra outlined previously. While such attempts have a long history in computer science and are successfully used in some applications, these approaches have failed to diffuse widely as they are costly to develop and difficult to understand. Others, notably practitioners working in commercial environments may view abstractions more in the way of suppression of details or information hiding following the approach outlined by Parnas (1972). The latter is a more inclusive characterization that is widely disseminated among software developers. This characterization covers all aspects of software creation and is thus a better conceptualization of what abstractions are and how they are commonly used in software creation.

Hence, the fundamental importance of abstractions as information hiding is that by abstracting, software developers are able to conceptualize a phenomenon in a simplified way and ignore, avoid or simply be unaware of a number of "messy" details. In software creation, these details may include the concrete working of a specific software module or application, the operating system or the computer hardware. The use of abstractions is therefore the key means by which software developers decompose a given system specification into modules that can be implemented, analysed and verified independently of each other (Kiczales, 1996; Shapiro, 1997; Booch, 2001; Jones, 2003).[4] Such modularity helps developers to cognitively understand the system, enables different groups of developers to work on different modules and opens up the possibility of reusing existing modules (Booch, 1986; Prieto-Díaz, 1990; Shapiro, 1997).

When abstractions are implemented in software, they include both the presentation of a simplistic view (often denoted interface) of what functionality a software module provides and the details of how that functionality is implemented. The user of an implemented abstraction can be the end-user of the software system, the software developer himself at a later stage or other software developers (McClellan et al., 1998). In this way, abstractions are a way to create a division of inventive labour among developers in time and space.

The programming code or modules may be related in a hierarchical manner leading to multiple levels of abstraction. At a given level of abstraction, the intention is that the developer need only to be concerned with *what* functionality is provided by the lower levels, not *how* the functionality is implemented. Additionally, the programmer can abstract from other aspects of code on the same level, meaning that programmers abstract (hide information) in the horizontal as well as the vertical domain in relation to the hardware. Vertical abstraction means that a programmer working at a given level of abstraction needs only to write a few statements to invoke a functionality that is implemented in a large number of statements at the lower levels. In fact, as the level of abstraction is increased, the ratio between the statements written by the programmer and the statements (instructions) performed at the machine level gets lower. In this way, if the programmer can maintain the same speed in terms of the number of written commands per unit of time, his or her productivity is greatly increased by working on a higher level of abstraction. Empirical observations confirm this by showing that programmer productivity is improved by using higher-level programming languages as compared with the use of lower-level languages (e.g. Boehm, 1981; Jones, 1996; Prechelt, 2000).[5]

The use of abstraction in software creation is not limited to invoking lower-level functionality. Abstractions are also used to delineate modules at the same level of abstraction. Using abstractions is thus a general way of dealing with complexity by allowing selective attention rather than mastering the "whole" (Simon, 1962; Dijkstra, 1972; Parnas, 1972) and the principle of abstraction can be seen as a meta-paradigm underpinning all software creation paradigms. Indeed, the distinction between different programming languages, software architectures or software design paradigms are related to different ideas of how software should be structured (Appleby and Vandekopple, 1997), i.e. what mechanisms are provided that enable the software developer to specify, implement and use abstractions. In the next three sections, we will analyse how complementary changes in theoretical knowledge of problems, instrumentation and computational capacity have changed what abstraction mechanisms are available to software developers. We will then analyse what effects these changes have had on the type of abstractions developers are able to create and use.

Theoretical understanding of problems related to abstraction

A key theoretical problem related to the development of mechanisms and tools to aid programmers to create useful abstractions is the creation and verification of representation in software.[6] This is the problem of specifying an internal representation of programming code that is appropriate for the purpose and expected functionality of the software being created and verifying that the implemented representation is correct. For example, how should a given specification be translated into programming code and how can it be verified that the resulting software works as intended?

This problem is non-trivial for three reasons. First, the users of the software are seldom able to express their specification in a formal language that is consistent with the programming language being used to create the code (Broadfoot and Broadfoot, 2003). Second, it has been mathematically proved that it is impossible to create a general computational routine (algorithm) that can verify if an algorithm completes (successfully terminates) its computation for all possible inputs (Gödel, 1931; Turing, 1936).[7] Third, testing all possible states that a program can enter is infeasible even for relatively simple programs (Jones, 2003).[8] Thus, it is not possible to create general methods that provide a complete validation of representations in software. Instead, methods have to be adapted specifically to each case or a set of related cases. The quest has therefore been to develop tractable ways to deal with the problem rather than being able to provide a formal method for dealing with all possible contingencies (Jones, 2003). This non-triviality has led to ongoing experimentation to support abstraction with the use of abstraction mechanisms (Embley et al. 1995; Monroe et al. 1997; Gil and Lorenz, 1998).[9]

Without loss of generality, we discuss four major events in the development of programming languages to illustrate how theoretical knowledge of abstractions and abstraction mechanisms have evolved (Guarino, 1978). The first step resulted in the development of programming language mechanisms in the 1950s and the early 1960s, which helped to abstract away the specific workings of hardware. Languages such as Fortran included abstraction mechanisms such as naming, which is the ability to use mnemonic names for memory addresses; primitive control abstractions, which include while do loops; basic data abstractions, which include integer and real variables; and basic abstractions for creating modules, such as subroutines. The importance of these abstraction mechanisms was that they helped programmers to automate many simple, but time consuming and error-prone, "book keeping" tasks of programming, many of which related to hardware-specific problems.

The second step was the recognition of the importance of *user*-defined abstractions for the structured decomposition of specification. Here, a user is a programmer who draws on the development work of others, indicating there is a division of *inventive* labour within the task of programming, consisting of at least two specialized developers. The advantage with this new type of abstraction mechanisms was that any software developer and not just the original creator of the software language could modify the abstractions. This meant that the division of labour was not just limited to having a program language developer and an application developer but that there is the *possibility of an arbitrary division of inventive labour* based on user-defined abstractions. Structured languages such as ALGOL 68, SIMULA 67 and PASCAL provided mechanisms for user-defined data object types and in the early 1970s languages were introduced to enforce the correct usage of abstract data types. The introduction of abstraction mechanisms that supported user-defined abstractions greatly increased the ability of programmers for expressing abstractions that were more closely oriented to the application. For many applications, the nature of the actual hardware could now be ignored as new abstractions above the hardware could be supported. However, as programmers created their own supported abstractions, the heterogeneity and unpredictability of the abstractions increased greatly. Even though new techniques for checking the use of abstract data types helped to reduce the problem, they did not eliminate it. Thus, it became more difficult to verify the correctness of abstractions.

The third step was the recognition of the importance of abstractions that could mirror real-life objects and processes (Friedman, 1989). This understanding led to the development of object-oriented languages such as Smalltalk in the 1980s and C++ and Java in the 1990s. In addition to the ability to mirror real-life objects, object-oriented languages provided more powerful abstraction mechanisms to ensure and enforce the independence of different modules (objects), such as information hiding, inheritance and isomorphism. Object-oriented languages provided both better assistance for raising the level of abstraction closer to the specification provided by the user and more powerful abstraction mechanisms at given levels of generality.

The fourth step is the recent dramatically increased use of scripting languages. These have been around since the 1960s, but they require more processing power during runtime compared with other types of programming languages. Thus, they have not been considered practically useful until hardware became much more powerful during the 1990s. These languages have much less emphasis on verification of data abstractions and consequently are much more flexible to use (Ousterhout, 1998). Specifically, scripting languages are more useful for integrating ("glueing") existing components or code than traditional compiled languages. Therefore, their main usefulness comes in terms of reusing (and abstracting) code, written, for example, in some object-oriented programming language.

While the theoretical understanding of the importance of abstraction for program design was established early, it has taken considerable time to develop and implement better means for expressing and verifying abstractions. In part, the reason for this is the time it has taken to develop appropriate development tools. We now turn to the development of these instruments and how in turn it has influenced theoretical understanding of problems.

Instruments and abstraction

A number of different classes of development tools have been created to help the creation and use of abstractions and abstraction mechanisms, for example, compilers that transform human-written code into machine-readable instructions. The compiler supports certain types of abstractions through the implementation of appropriate abstraction mechanisms. Most of the development tools (instruments) are software based, meaning the tools consists of software that is created specifically for the creation of software. We will discuss some important types of instruments.

In order to express abstractions an *editor* is needed. The first editors were mechanical punch card machines where each card represented one line of program code.[10] A code for a program consisted of a stack of cards that were read into the computer and each statement translated into machine instructions by an *interpreter* or a *compiler*. The interpreter or compiler checked if the syntax of the statements fitted the grammar of the programming language. If there were errors these were printed on a printer.

In the late 1960s, the use of console screens for computer output became increasingly popular. The use of consoles made the expression and verification of abstraction much easier and the time between the input of the program and generating an observable output also became much faster than before because of the ability to see the code and the software output on the screen and not just on a printer. The use of the console also enabled the creation of the *debugger*, a program for monitoring and influencing the state of a program while it is being executed. By using a debugger, the developer is able to discover errors ("bugs") in the program that have to do with the logic of the program, including the implementation of its abstractions, in addition to the syntax errors captured by the interpreter/compiler.

Editors, compilers/interpreters and debuggers remain the main development tools for programmers, but their nature has changed dramatically. First, there has been a change in the programming languages they support in line with the development described in this section. Not only do compilers support more complex abstraction mechanisms, which enable abstractions that are closer to the conceptualization of the user's problem rather than the operating of the computer, but the number of utilities to help developers create and manage these higher-level abstractions has also increased. An example of such utilities is graphical diagramming tools enabling developers to visually create and maintain a design in a high-level design language, such as the Unified Modelling Language (UML), which can automatically generate programming language statements based on these designs.

Second, development tools have been created in the form of Integrated Development Environments (IDEs), which makes it easier to relate debugging information to the source code. Additional tools for managing a larger code base have also become a standard feature of an IDE, for example, object browsers and source control systems. The latter is extremely important for managing large software projects involving a large number of developers as it provides various means of version control including mechanisms to mark which part of the code is under revision and monitor interdependencies between different modules.

The implementation of complex high-level abstraction mechanisms, integration of developing tools using graphical interfaces and the management of a large code-base makes imposing demands on processing power and data storage. While the use of existing code may speed up the development process, it is likely to further increase the demands on computational capacity as it is unlikely to be optimally adapted to the problem at hand, both in terms of size and execution speed. Thus, the changes in instrumentation for software creation are very much dependent on increased computational capacity available to programmers.

Computational capacity and abstractions

In the early days of computing, the constraints on the usability of computer systems were related to the cost and capacity of the computer hardware (Friedman, 1989). These constraints included the processing power of the computer hardware, the size of the internal memory used to store programs and for intermediate results, and external data storage.

Improvements in computer technology moving from valves used in the first computers, through using transistors in the 1950s and to using integrated circuits in the 1960s led to remarkable improvements in computer speed as well as memory capacity. Between 1953 and 1965, the average improvement in the performance of processing units and memory were 80% per year while the reductions in costs were 55% for a given performance level (Friedman, 1989). In 1965, Gordon E. Moore estimated that the number of components per integrated circuit would double every 12–18 months, leading to a dramatic decrease in cost per component at least to 1975 (Moore, 1965). Moore based his prediction, later to be termed Moore's law, on empirical observation in the early 1960s but this development has been remarkably stable since. Hence, processing speed and memory capacity have increased exponentially for over 50 years.

Increased computational capacity has made software developers less sensitive to various speed and storage penalties related to the use of certain abstraction mechanisms. A case in point is the use of automatic verification. One approach that is used industrially is assertions (Hoare, 2003). For most types of software, the speed penalty has become relatively less important compared with other considerations in programming.

The increase in computational capacity of individual chips has further been enhanced by increased parallelism (Bell and Gray, 2002; Bader, 2004). Parallelism has been implemented through vector supercomputers or through the clustering of the scalar processor. In the former case, the performance increase is related to the structuring of the computer hardware, whereas in the latter case, it is highly dependent on the software used to distribute and synchronize work across different computers in the cluster (Bader, 2004). This software is based on many years of research on parallel computing and the creation of abstractions that abstract away the details of parallelism for application developers. The creation of these abstractions is based on abstraction mechanisms that enable developers to make a distinction between the specification of functionality and the implementation of the functionality through parallel processing.[11]

Changes in the creation and use of abstractions

The changes in the abstraction mechanisms made possible by complementary advances in theoretical knowledge, instrumentation and computational capacity have influenced what abstractions software developers are able to create and use. These changes have transformed the nature of software creation during the last five decades and expanded the scope of its application.

In its early days, software creation was focused on scientific calculations as the first computer systems were created by researchers or military personnel interested in performing complex calculations with great accuracy (Friedman, 1989, p. 70). The functionality of these programs was almost entirely governed by mathematical equations used to model physical laws. Thus, the created programming code was relatively short and user interaction with the program during program execution was minimal. The focus was on abstracting away the computer hardware to be able to concentrate on the computation itself. Most of these abstractions were provided by the programming language.

Today, software systems are often used to manage very complex processes, such as work processes in large multinational firms or air traffic. Consequently, they have become larger and more complex with extensive user intervention (Friedman, 1989). This has been made possible by the creation of user-defined abstractions that have been increasingly able to mirror real-life processes.

The development of mechanisms and tools to aid programmers to create useful abstractions and help raise the level of abstraction has been central in addressing the issue of complexity and the corresponding "software crisis" (Appleby and Vandekopple, 1997; Booch, 2001).[12] Specifically, programming at a higher level of abstraction improves the ability to focus on the application or problem domain, while ignoring all or parts of the detailed working of the lower levels. This is made possible by "galaxies of abstractions" that hold together "societies of collaborating objects" (Booch, 2001). The galaxies are a network of user-defined representations of the components of a software application. Some of them may be more general than others, for example, components provided by object-oriented frameworks, but many of them are specific to the application being created or to general-purpose tasks at the lower levels of abstractions.

Discussion and conclusion

This chapter aimed to improve our understanding of how digitalization influences the growth of knowledge and the division of innovative labour across and within firms by studying the evolution of mechanisms for economizing cognition in software creation. Specifically, we focused on the evolution of abstraction mechanisms in software creation and how this evolution has influenced the abstractions being created and used by individual software developers when they create new software. Software creation is a crucial context for our analysis as software is a digital technology and developers are very explicit in their analysis of the creation and use of abstractions, but the implications of the analysis are likely to be applicable to other contexts of technical development. This section summarizes the findings of the paper before discussing the similarities and differences with prior research and outlines some areas for further research.

We showed that software creation has been transformed during the last five decades when the scope of its application has expanded from scientific calculation to large-scale collective intelligence systems. During this time, the software creation community has continually searched for and introduced new mechanisms to better manage the increased complexity of software systems and software development processes. This has led to a surge in the number and types of available abstraction mechanisms supporting larger "galaxies of abstraction", i.e. software code that consists of networks of linked representations. This allows developers to specialize their work at different (often higher) levels of abstraction while ignoring the implementation of large parts of the network (such as lower levels of abstractions dealing with hardware-specific issues) while creating new software programs (Booch, 2001). While the number of abstractions in use has increased exponentially, they cannot be connected together in an arbitrary fashion because they need to be built to fit into the structure of existing abstractions.

Second, we described how complementary advances in increased theoretical understanding, improvements in instrumentation and increased computational capacity have shaped the evolution of abstraction mechanisms. Improvements, primarily in instrumentation and computational capacity, have made it economically and technically feasible to use new abstraction mechanisms because of combined improvements in generality and power. While higher-level mechanisms are being introduced due to their higher generality, mechanisms providing lower generality maintain their relative power advantage and are still dominant in software creation. Over time, as the network structure expands and becomes more compact (fine-grained) opportunities are created for the ratio between developers' knowledge and the total knowledge they are able to draw upon in their development work to become lower. In this manner, developers are able to do more by knowing less, which has opened the potential for an increased division of innovative labour between and within firms. In essence, this is in line with what Young (1928) argued when he stated that the size of the market, unfolding over time, not just increases the division of labour, but more importantly, improves productivity because the new specializations increase the affordability of roundabout methods of production. Higher productivity, in turn, lowers costs and generates financial resources that can be invested to further expand the market, which creates a positive feedback circle between demand and supply. An important type of investments and innovative labour leads to technological convergence (Rosenberg, 1976). Technological convergence is when problem-solving skills (knowledge and technology) are transferred from their original context into another context, typically from one industry to another. To exploit the new opportunities, spin-offs or new entry may create a new division of labour in such a way that a new upstream industry serves the old and new downstream industries. In this manner, the size of the market is increased.

We argued that industrial transformations can be understood as changes in the Youngian division of labour describe previously, underpinned by changes in activities, resources and knowledge work. However, what role does the rise of galaxies of abstraction play in these changes? Abstractions are necessary for technological convergence as they are representations that can be reused (infinitely) many times. In addition, abstractions are means of roundaboutness. They allow longer development chains, which economizes work by lowering the demands on developers to understand, master or even know of the whole creative and productive process. Thus, the use of supported abstractions is a fundamental aspect of technological convergence and increased productivity of innovative work. Abstractions do not just lead to higher productivity but can enable variety creation because once they exist, they can be combined in new ways, thus potentially expanding the size (and the nature) of the market.

In this manner, we have sketched out a new model of industrial transformation, where the size of the market limits the division of labour, but where new abstractions and means of abstractions allow for new specializations among firms, individuals and other actors, and increased roundaboutness that extends the length of creative development and opens up new potential for innovative combinations of abstractions, potentially increasing the size and scope of the market.

The results of the chapter have implications for understanding the division of inventive labour and the location of exchange transactions in inventive activities, such as markets for knowledge. We argue that a functioning network of abstractions is *necessary* for having a division of inventive labour among individual developers as each abstraction can be seen as a common ground providing opportunities for specialization between implementation and use. However, this is not a *sufficient* criterion for generating a division of inventive labour as the choice of who should do what is determined by a range of psychological, organizational and economic factors.

Notes

1 In fact, abstractions that are created with the objective to be general, may in use only turn out to suppress details. When used outside its intended domain (population of use instances), the abstraction only provides a suppression of detail, which may lead to an erroneous result when invoking or using the abstraction. We will come back to this important point in the discussion and conclusion.

2 Indeed, problems that computer scientists can successfully solve by a rigorous approach are often dismissed as "toy problems" by industrialists who argue that these problems lack industrial significance (Shapiro, 1997).

3 At the time, the importance of hiding details was not undisputed. Many industrialists and researchers thought that software developers must have full knowledge and understanding of the entire programming code (Mills, 1970, Brooks, 1995). However, 20 years later, such views were rejected, even by its earlier defenders (Brooks, 1995, pp. 271–272).

4 While developers strive for complete independence, it is difficult to achieve in practice. The degree of independence is inversely proportional to the information needed about the inner workings of the module in order for it to be used properly. The information needed in each case is dependent on what abstractions are used as well as the abstraction mechanisms. For example, the abstraction mechanisms provided by object-oriented programming languages provide more powerful means for ensuring independence as compared with older types of languages.
5 In a similar way, when implementing the details at the lower levels closer to the hardware, programmers need only be concerned with how a certain functionality is implemented and may largely ignore the more application-oriented issues, such as to what purpose the functionality is used. They are therefore concerned with developing code that can be used in a large number of different application contexts.
6 There are other problems central to computer science and software engineering that are indirectly related. These problems include computation, which is the problem of determining the computational feasibility and creating and analysing computational routines (algorithms). Another set of problems relates to project management, which is related to the managing of software development projects involving a group of people. Important advances have been made within these fields that have helped to raise the level of abstraction, for example, by standardizing behaviour. However, these issues are outside the scope of this chapter.
7 This is commonly referred to as the undecidability of the halting problem and was first proved by Turing in 1936. The issues raised by the halting problem are similar to those raised by Gödel's incompleteness theorems, which states that it is impossible to create a complete and consistent axiomatization of all statements about natural numbers (Gödel, 1931).
8 A program with n two-way decision points (n >0 and integer) has 2^n possible paths or states.
9 The concept of abstraction mechanisms varies in its scope in the literature. How the concept is used in this chapter is in line with Gil and Lorenz (1998). Their definition has a relatively narrow scope focusing on the technique of abstracting and does not include the tools/artefacts implementing these techniques. Common examples of abstraction mechanisms are the techniques of inheritance and encapsulation used in object-oriented programming.
10 See Jones (2005) for a historical account of the use of punch cards.
11 While improvements in computational capacity have been crucial for the development of instrumentation (development tools) that are able to implement more complex abstraction mechanisms, further increase in computational capacity through networked processors is dependent on increased theoretical understanding of parallel processing and how it can be represented in software. This theoretical understanding provides the foundation for the creation of abstraction mechanisms that developers are able to use to program at a level of abstraction that needs not be concerned with parallelism. These interdependencies between a theoretical understanding of problems, instrumentation and computational capacity provide a good example of how the software community addresses the increasing and arbitrary complexity through raising the level of abstractions with the help of more powerful (and complex) abstraction mechanisms.
12 Following a couple of seminal NATO conferences in 1968 and 1969 in Germany, the IT community at large considered software creation to be a huge problem (e.g. Naur and Randell, eds. 1969). In fact, the situation was deemed to be so bad that the concept "software crisis" was coined, highlighting the widely diffused (but largely erroneous) perception that hardware costs were dropping while software was increasingly expensive. Large software projects in particular have been shown to consistently be over budget, error-prone ("buggy") or delayed. In this sense, software seemed to be very difficult or even impossible to evolve or maintain.

References

Appleby, D. and Vandekopple, J. (1997) *Programming Languages: Paradigm and Practice*, Second edition, Singapore: McGraw-Hill.

Arora, A., Fosfuri, A., and Gambardella, A. (2001) *Markets for Technology: Economics of Innovation and Corporate Strategy*, Cambridge, MA: MIT Press.

Arora, A. and Gambardella, A. (1994) The Changing Technology of Technological Change: General and Abstract Knowledge and the Division of Innovative Labour, *Research Policy*, 23, pp. 523–532.

Bader, D.A. (2004) Computational Biology and High-Performance Computing, *Communications of the ACM*, 47(11), pp. 35-32-42.

Barnes, B.H. and Bollinger, T.B. (1991) Making Reuse Cost-Effective, *IEEE Software*, January, pp. 13–24.

Basili, V.R. and Musa, J.D. (1991) The Future Engineering of Software: A Management Perspective, *Computer*, 24(9), pp. 90–96.

Bell, G. and Gray, J. (2002) What's Next in High-Performance Computing, *Communications of the ACM*, 45(2), pp. 91–95.

Bellinzona, R., Fugini, M.G., and Pernici, B. (1995) Reusing Specifications in O-O Applications, *IEEE Software*, 12(2), pp. 65–75.

Boehm, B. (1981) *Software Engineering Economics*, Englewood Cliffs, NJ: Prentice-Hall.

Booch, G. (1986) Object-Oriented Development, *IEEE Transactions on Software Engineering*, 12(2), pp. 211–221.

Booch, G. (1993) *Object-Oriented Analysis and Design with Applications*, Redwood City: Benjamin-Cummings Publishing.

Booch, G. (2001) Through the Looking Glass, Dr Dobbs Portal, http://www.ddj.com, July.

Brady, T., Tierney, M., and Williams, R. (1992) The Commodification of Application Software, *Industrial & Corporate Change*, 1(3), pp. 48–514.

Broadfoot, G.H. and Broadfoot, P.J. (2003) Academia and Industry Meets: Some Experiences of Formal Methods in Practice, *Proceedings of the Tenth Asia-Pacific Software Engineering Conference (APSEC'03)*, Chiang Mai, Thailand, Dec. 10–12.

Brooks, F.P. (1995) *The Mythical Man-Month – Essays on Software Engineering Anniversary Edition*, Reading, MA: Addison-Wesley.

de Solla Price, D. (1984) The Science-Technology Relationship, the Craft of Experimental Science, and Policy for the Improvement of High Technology Innovation, *Research Policy*, 13, pp. 3–20.

Dijkstra, E.W. (1968) The Structure of the "THE"-Multiprogramming System, *Communications of the ACM*, 11(5), pp. 341–346.

Dijkstra, E.W. (1972) The Humble Programmer, ACM Turing Lecture, *Communications of the ACM*, 15(10), pp. 859–866.

Dosi, G. (1988) Sources, Procedures and the Micro-Economic Effects on Innovation, *Journal of Economic Literature*, 26(3), pp. 1120–1171.

Embley, D.W., Jackson, R.B., and Woodfield, S.N. (1995) OO Systems Analysis: Is It or Isn't It?, *IEEE Software*, July, pp. 19–33.

Fellbaum, C., ed. (1998) *Wordnet: An Electronic Lexical Database*, Cambridge, MA: MIT Press.

Fichman, R.G. and Kemerer, C.F. (1997) Object Technology and Reuse: Lessons from Early Adopters, *Computer*, October, pp. 47–59.

Friedman, A.L. (1989) *Computer Systems Development*, Chichester, UK: John Wiley & Sons.

Gamma, E., Helm, R., Johnson, R., and Vlissides, J. (1995) *Design Patterns. Elements of Reusable Object-Oriented Software*, Reading, MA: Addison-Wesley Publishing Company.

Gazis, D.C. (1979) Influence of Technology on Science: A Comment on Some Experiences at IBM Research, *Research Policy*, 8(3), pp. 244–259.

Gil, J. and Lorenz, D.H. (1998) Design Patterns and Language Design, *Computer*, March, pp. 118–120.

Glass R.L. and Vessey, I. (1998) Focusing on the Application Domain: Everyone Agrees It's Vital, but Who's Doing Anything about It? *HICSS*, 3, pp. 187–196.

Guarino, L.R. (1978) *The Evolution of Abstraction in Programming Languages* (No. CMU-CS-78-128). Pittsburgh, PA: Computer Science Department, Carnegie-Mellon University.

Gödel, K. (1931) Über formal unentscheidbare Sätze der *Principia Mathematica* und verwandter Systeme I, *Monatshefte für Mathematik und Physik*, 38, pp. 173–198. Translated 1962, *On formally undecidable propositions of Principia Mathematica and related systems*, New York: Basic Books.

Hayek, F.A. (1937) Economics and Knowledge, *Economica*, 4(13), pp. 33–54.

Hoare, C.A.R. (2003) Assertions: A Personal Perspective, *IEEE Annals of the History of Computing*, April–June, pp. 14–25.

IEEE (1983) *IEEE Standard Glossary of Software Engineering Terminology*, New York: Institute of Electrical and Electronic Engineers.

Jones, C. (1996) Programming Languages Table, Release 8.2, Software Productivity Research, Inc., http://www.theadvisors.com/langcomparison.htm

Jones, C.B. (2003) The Early Search for Tractable Ways of Reasoning about Programs, *IEEE Annals of the History of Computing*, April–June, pp. 26–49.

Jones, D.W. (2005) *Punched Cards*. Accessed at http://www.cs.uiowa.edu/~jones/cards/ on September 25, 2005.

Kahneman, D. (2011) *Thinking, Fast and Slow*, New York: Farrar, Strauss and Giroux.

Kiczales, G. (1996) Beyond the Black Box: Open Implementation, *IEEE Software*, January, pp. 8–10.

Laudan, R. (1984) Cognitive Change in Technology and Science, in Laudan, R. (ed.) *The Nature of Technological Knowledge. Are Models of Scientific Change Relevant?* Dordrecht: D. Reidel, pp. 83–104.

Loasby, B.J. (2000) Decision Premises, Decision Cycles and Decomposition, *Industrial and Corporate Change*, 9(4), pp. 709–731.

Loasby, B.J. (2001) Time, Knowledge and Evolutionary Dynamics: Why Connections Matter, *Journal of Evolutionary Economics*, 11, pp. 393–412.

Loasby, B.J. (2007) A Cognitive Perspective on Entrepreneurship and the Firm, *Journal of Management Studies*, 44(7), pp. 1078–1106.

McClellan, S.G., Roesler, A.W., and Tempest, J.T. (1998) Building More Usable APIs, *IEEE Software*, May/June, pp. 78–86.

Menger, C. (1981 [1871]) *Principles of Economics*, New York: New York University Press. Original title *Grundsätze der Volkswirtschaftslehre*.

Meyer, M. (2000) Does Science Push Technology? Patents Citing Scientific Literature, *Research Policy*, 29, pp. 409–434.

Meyer-Krahmer, F. and Schmoch, U. (1998) Science-Based Technologies: University-Industry Interactions in Four Fields, *Research Policy*, 27(8), pp. 835–851.

Mili, H., Mili, F., and Mili, A. (1995) Reusing Software: Issues and Research Directions, *IEEE Transactions on Software Engineering*, 21(6), pp. 528–562.

Mills, H.D. (1970) Top-Down Programming in Large Systems, in R. Rustin (ed) *Debugging Techniques in Large Systems*, Englewood Cliffs, NJ: Prentice-Hall, pp. 41–55.

Monroe, R.T., Kompanek, A., Melton, R., and Garlan, D. (1997) Architectural Styles, Design Patterns, and Objects, *IEEE Software*, January, pp. 43–52.

Moore, G.E. (1965) Cramming More Components onto Integrated Circuits, *Electronics*, 38, 8.

Murmann, J.P. (2003) *Knowledge and Competitive Advantage. The Coevolution of Firms, Technology, and National Institutions*, Cambridge: Cambridge University Press.

Murmann, J.P. and Frenken, K. (2006) Toward a Systematic Framework for Research on Dominant Designs, Technological Innovations, and Industrial Change, *Research Policy*, 35, pp. 925–952.

Narin, F. and Noma, E. (1985) Is Technology becoming Science?, *Scientometrics*, 7(3–6), pp. 369–381.

Narin, F. and Olivastro, D. (1992) Status Report: Linkage between Technology and Science, *Research Policy*, 21(3), pp. 237–249.

Naur, P. and Randell, B. (eds) (1969) Software Engineering: Report on a Conference Sponsored by the NATO Science Committee, Garmisch, Germany, Oct. 7–11, 1968. Brussels: Scientific Affairs Division, North Atlantic Treaty Organization (NATO).

Nelson, R.R. (1992) What is 'Commercial' and What is 'Public' about Technology, and What Should Be?, in Rosenberg, N., Landau, R., and Mowery, D.C. (eds) *Technology and the Wealth of Nations*, Stanford, CA: Stanford University Press, pp. 57–71.

Nelson, R.R. and Winter, S.G. (2002) Evolutionary Theorizing in Economics, *Journal of Economic Perspectives*, 16(2), pp. 23–46.

Newell, A. (1969) Heuristic Programming: Ill-Structured Problems, in J. Aronofsky (ed) *Progress in Operations Research, III*, New York: John Wiley & Sons, pp. 361–414.

Nightingale, P. (1998) A Cognitive Model of Innovation, *Research Policy*, 27, pp. 689–709.

Nightingale, P. (2000) Economies of Scale in Experimentation: Knowledge and Technology in Pharmaceutical R&D, *Industrial and Corporate Change*, 9, pp. 315–359.

Object Management Group (2001) *Model Driven Architecture. A Technical Perspective*, Milford, MA: Object Management Group.

Ousterhout, J.K. (1998) Scripting: Higher Level Programming for the 21st Century, *IEEE Computer*, March, pp. 23–30.

Parker, G.G., Van Alstyne, M.W., and Choudary, S.P. (2016) *Platform Revolution: How Networked Markets Are Transforming the Economy and How to Make Them Work for You*, New York: W. W. Norton.

Parnas, D.L. (1972) On the Criteria to be Used in Decomposing Systems into Modules, *Communications of the ACM*, 15(12), pp. 1053–1058.

Parnas, D.L. (1975) Use of the Concept Transparency in the Design of Hierarchically Structured Systems, *Communications of the ACM*, 18(7), pp.401–408.

Pavitt, K. (1998) Technologies, Products and Organization in the Innovating Firm: What Adam Smith Tells Us and Joseph Schumpeter Doesn't, *Industrial and Corporate Change*, 7(3), pp. 433–452.

Prechelt, L. (2000) An Empirical Comparison of Seven Programming Languages, *IEEE Computer*, October, pp. 23–29

Prieto-Díaz, R. (1990) Domain Analysis: An Introduction, Software Engineering Notes, *ACM Sigsoft*, 15(2), pp. 47–54.

Romer, P.M. (1990) Endogenous Technological Change, *Journal of Political Economy*, 98(5, pt. 2), S71–S102.

Rosenberg, N. (1976) *Perspectives on Technology*, Cambridge: Cambridge University Press.

Rosenberg, N. (1992) Scientific Instrumentation and University Research, *Research Policy*, 21, pp. 381–390.

Shapiro, S. (1997) Splitting the Difference: The Historical Necessity of Synthesis in Software Engineering, *IEEE Annals of the History of Computing*, 19(1), pp. 20–54.

Shaw, M. (1984) The Impact of Modelling and Abstraction Concerns on Modern Programming Languages, in Brodie, M.L., Mylopoulos, J. and Schmidt, J.W. (eds) *On Conceptual Modelling. Perspectives from Artificial Intelligence, Databases, and Programming Languages*, Berlin: Springer-Verlag, pp. 49–83.

Simon, H.A. (1962) The Architecture of Complexity. In *Proceedings of the American Philosophical Society*, 106, pp. 467–487.

Simon, H.A. (1996) *The Science of the Artificial*, 3rd edition, Cambridge, MA: MIT Press.

Smith, A. (1776) *The Wealth of Nations*, London: Dent.

Smith, J.M. and Smith, D.C.P. (1977) Database Abstractions: Aggregation and Generalization, *ACM Transactions on Database Systems*, 2, pp. 105–133.

Suarez, F.F. and Utterback, J.M. (1995) Dominant Designs and the Survival of Firms, *Strategic Management Journal*, 16, pp. 415–430.

Turing, A.M. (1936) On Computable Numbers, with an Application to the Entscheidungs Problem, in *Proceedings of the London Mathematical Society*, 2d series, 42, pp. 230–40.

Ulrich, K. (1995) The Role of Product Architecture in the Manufacturing Firm, *Research Policy*, 24, pp. 419–440.

Vincenti, W.G. (1990) *What Engineers Know and How They Know It. Analytical Studies from Aeronautical History*, Baltimore, MD: Johns Hopkins University Press.

Weyuker, E.J. (1998) Testing Component-Based Software: A Cautionary Tale, *IEEE Software*, September/October, pp. 54–59.

Young, A.A. (1928) Increasing Returns and Economic Progress, *The Economic Journal*, 38(152), pp. 527–542.

Zimmer, J.A. (1985) *Abstraction for Programmers*, New York: McGraw-Hill.

6

RAGS TO RICHES

Digitalization and the transformation of the Icelandic film industry

Örn D. Jónsson, Steinunn Arnardóttir and Rögnvaldur J. Saemundsson

Introduction

The film industry in Iceland took off in the early 1980s with 20 full-length movies produced in the period 1980–1985, mainly for the local market. In the period 2013–2018, production had increased to 52 full-length movies and, moreover, Iceland had been used as a shooting location in more than 60 foreign film projects. During this same period, Icelandic films received 378 prizes at international film festivals, including Cannes, San Sebastian and Tokyo. In a period of 40 years, the Icelandic film industry has transformed from a geographically isolated micro-industry creating films for the local market into an international network of virtual craft production with outcomes that receive global acclaim. At the same time, the geographical boundaries of the industry have become less clear. Parts of the network – providing specialized inputs such as creative direction, editing, visual effects or music – are also involved in films not produced by Icelandic producers and may live outside Iceland. An example is the music composer Hildur Guðnadóttir who currently lives in Berlin and has composed the music for the Icelandic series *Trapped* (Ófærð), the US/UK series *Chernobyl* and the US film *Joker*.

The transformation of the Icelandic film industry has coincided with the transformation of the production, distribution and consumption of audio-visual entertainment through the use of digital technologies. This transformation is part of the evolution of a techno-economic paradigm (Perez 2010) that is associated with digital signal processing, the Internet, the World Wide Web, mobile devices, multisided platform business models championed by companies such as Alphabet, Amazon, Apple and Facebook and machine learning for increased automation. During this evolution, activities that for several decades were concentrated on regional clusters, such as the relatively complex craft process of film making, have become more distributed and the market dominance of a few large companies is being challenged. Thus, studying the Icelandic film industry allows us to investigate how activities and relationships change during the process of digitalization, which increases our understanding of the interaction between digitalization and industrial transformation.

In this chapter we will focus on film music. Composing, performing and recording music is a subset of the activities required to produce a film and most of the activities are performed after actual filming has been finished. However, composing, performing and recording music is not unique to the film industry; it is a general set of activities for producing and storing music for later playback. Depending on the level of specialization, the composing, performing and recording of music for films could be seen as an integrated part of the film industry, constituting a separate film music industry, or a set of services provided by the music industry. Today, we do not have a clear understanding of how the relationship between a particular set of generic activities (making music) and the overall set of specific activities (film making) of which the generic activities are but one part, is affected by digitalization and industrial transformation. The purpose of this chapter is to further this understanding by empirically studying the digitalization and transformation of the Icelandic film industry with a focus on film music.

The chapter is structured as follows. First, we provide a selected review of the literature on the transformation of the film industry and the music industry with a special focus on the role of digitalization. Second, we briefly describe the methodology of the study and the collection of empirical data. Finally, we describe our results followed by discussion and conclusions.

Literature review

The film making process consists of three major phases – pre-production, production and post-production (Palmer 2001). Pre-production consists of activities before the actual filming starts, such as funding and the selection of script, cast, crew and locations. Production includes the filming, both on location and in the studio. Post-production concerns the compilation and editing of the filmed material as well as the addition of other media elements, such as visual effects, music and, in recent years, computer-generated visual material.

A number of studies have documented the evolution of the US film industry and its transformation from a localized industrial system to an international project-based organization. Starting out as a regional agglomeration in Hollywood California at the beginning of the 20th century, the US film industry was organized according to mass production principles. This organization changed in the post-World War II period with the introduction of independent producers, which induced vertical disintegration and project-based organization of the film making process at the national level. In the 1990s, runaway productions outside the US took off and as the locations grew stronger with more experience, the project-based organization of film making became more international (Manning 2017; Scott and Pope 2007; Storper 1989).

While digitalization started to influence the film making process in the 1980s, it had little effect on the structure of the industry until around the millennium. In the 1980s, digitization of both sound and images started to affect the production stages. The first steps were taken with sound and soon also included digital cameras and computer-generated special effects. In the late 1990s, the use of specialized software for digital editing took off. Despite these changes in production activities, they had little effect on the industry. Existing systems for distribution were upgraded, i.e. digital surround sound systems were installed in theatres, DVDs replaced VHS and digital broadcasting replaced analogue broadcasting, but the same actors in the industry maintained their dominance. The advent of the Internet and the diffusion of mobile devices, however, have led to significant changes in the distribution and consumption of audio-visual material, not only through peer-to-peer piracy distribution but also through the introduction of new types of actors, such as streaming services, which have reduced the dominance of incumbents (De Vink and Lindmark 2012).

Three recurrent benefits have been associated with increasing digitalization in the film making process: increased cost-efficiency, increased flexibility in the film making process and enhanced quality. Increased cost-efficiency and enhanced quality have reduced barriers to entry for independent producers and increased flexibility allows for more dispersed and non-linear working processes involving a higher number of actors – providing specialized inputs such as music – that collaborate over larger geographical distances (De Vink and Lindmark 2012; Palmer 2001; Scott and Pope 2007).

The effect of digitalization on the music industry mirrors the development of the film industry. At the advent of digitalization and the early development of digital recording and distribution, the music industry was highly concentrated. The transition from LP records to CDs did not lead to significant changes in industry structure. However, the introduction of the Internet as a distribution medium was much more significant for the distribution of music, just like the film industry. The use of standard software formats, such as MP3, spawned the peer-to-peer distribution of music files followed by streaming services, such as Spotify, and the facilitation by social media of a direct connection between artists and their fans (Leyshon 2001, 2009; Hirsch and Gruber 2015; Sigurdardottir 2010). Furthermore, digitalization has also affected the recording side of the industry. Since the late 1990s, digital recording and processing equipment have been available at affordable prices for individuals, making available a process that previously could only be accessed in recording studios. As a consequence, musical creativity has become more distributed, former musical agglomerations built around recording studios have been in decline, new agglomerations focusing on linking ICT and music have emerged and a transnational freelancing economy has emerged (Leyshon 2009; Power and Jansson 2004; Watson and Beaverstock 2016).

Being at the intersection of the film industry and the music industry, the above-mentioned effects of digitalization have shaped the processes of composing, performing and recording film music. The digitization of music and picture, the introduction of sampling and virtual instruments and the use of software for editing and post-processing reduced the dependence on expensive and sophisticated facilities and a large group of skilled musicians, thus lowering the skill barrier of entry for composers without symphonic background and reducing the budget required for high-quality music. Furthermore, extensive sampling of sounds from physical instruments – an approach pioneered by the composer Hans Zimmer (Lehman 2017) – made it possible for composers to make low-cost prototypes of orchestral music early in the film production process to express and discuss ideas with the film director and sound editor. Depending on the budget, the scores of these prototypes would be – partly or in full – played by musicians in the final version of the soundtrack used in the film (Kompanek 2004; Maddocks 2011).

Digitalization of music has not only changed the work process of composing, performing and recording but also its artistic content. On the one hand, composers and artists have reacted to the algorithmic precision and homogeneity of the digital world by developing post-digital aesthetics in order to escape the fascination with digital technology in and of itself (Cascone 2000; Ferguson and Brown 2016). On the other hand, the new technology allows composers to combine the classical with the digital, creating contemporary sound worlds that break down artistic barriers between films, streaming platforms, clubs and concert halls, thus representing digitalization as a post-classical experience (Jackson 2019).

Method

This chapter is based on an empirical study of the Icelandic film industry in the time period of 1980–2019, focusing on activities related to the composing, performance and recording of film music and its relationship to the overall process of film making. Data has been collected through interviews with individuals working in the industry and through secondary data sources.

The interviewees include both people directing the film making process, such as directors, and people involved in the music production process, such as composers and sound engineers. They also include both people who are currently working in Iceland and abroad. The interviews were semi-structured, focusing on the technology used during composition, performance and recording music, the work processes and actors involved and the artistic content. Care was taken to select interviewees who together could cover the whole period under study. Each interview lasted for about 60–90 minutes and in most cases was followed up by shorter communication by email, Facebook Messenger or phone. In total, eight people were interviewed, some of whom had played more than one role in the production process. For example, one of the interviewees was a creative director, music composer and music performer in the same production.

The secondary sources include the database of the Iceland Film Centre (containing information about all Icelandic films), articles from the popular press and interview material from unpublished student projects (e.g. master's theses).

During the analysis, we combined the different sources of data through a process of triangulation. First, we reconstructed an outline of the development of the film industry in terms of the main focus of its activities and sources of funding. Second, we reconstructed the steps of digitalization and selected specific film projects to provide examples of how composition, performance and recording of music took place and the artistic approaches involved. Third, we compared the activities and set of relations for each step in the digitalization process looking for similarities and differences and continuities and discontinuities.

Early on in our analysis, it became evident that our respondents referred to individuals rather than organizations when recollecting the history of the industry. This is likely to reflect the small size of the population of Iceland (fewer than 300,000 inhabitants), the close personal networks involved and the project-based nature of the industry. Even if firms were involved, they were small entities built around individuals (e.g. directors, producers, composers) and used as vehicles for external funding of projects. Being true to our empirical data we refer mostly to individuals when describing the actors in the case, but in most cases, they can be seen as representing the firm or the industry level of analysis rather than the personal level.

Results

For analytical purposes, we divided the history of the Icelandic film industry in general, and Icelandic film music activities in particular, into three periods, each with its distinctive characteristics: 1) building the basic capabilities (1980–1989); 2) internationalization and digitization (1990–2008); and 3) digitalization through virtual networks of craft production (2008–2018).

Building the basic capabilities (1980–1989)

During this period, the basic capabilities for film making were built. This included both the artistic capabilities of telling a story using films as a medium and the capabilities to produce full-length films, including scripting and casting, recording picture and sound and post-production. These capabilities were built in two ways. First, capabilities were built through education, as an increasing number of people went abroad to study at some of the prestigious film schools in Europe and the US. Second, capabilities were built through co-production with leading artists and professionals in the Nordic countries. The establishment of Kvikmyndasjóður Íslands (the Icelandic Film Fund, later the Icelandic Film Centre) in 1979 played a key role in this development as it provided both the incentives and the means for film making, providing grants for screenwriting, production, post-production and promotion. The Film Centre also paved the way for Nordic co-production enabling co-funding by similar agencies in the other Nordic countries. Before the establishment of the centre, only a handful of films had been produced since the production of the first film in 1921.

During this period, and despite new opportunities for funding, most projects were low budget and lacked appropriate funding. This had a strong impact on the music, which was added late in the analogue post-production process once visual editing was completed, at which point most projects had run out of funds. Furthermore, there was limited infrastructure in Iceland for studio recording and audio processing which meant that many of those activities were done in studios abroad.

A landmark film that characterizes the film music process during the emergence of the Icelandic film industry is *Rock in Reykjavík* (*Rokk í Reykjavík*) directed by Friðrik Þór Friðriksson and released in 1982. In this film – which is a documentary of the rock/punk scene in Reykjavík – live recordings of 19 bands, including Björk as the vocalist in the band Tappi Tíkarrass, are mixed with interviews with the musicians on various aspects of life. The recordings were made on portable 8-channel analogue recording equipment and the audio processing and syncing for the film were done in London.

Since the 1970s, London had been the place Icelandic music producers and pop bands looked to for recordings and post-processing. Here they made several attempts to succeed outside Iceland, but with limited success. However, in 1983, the song "Garden Party" by the instrumental jazz-funk group Mezzoforte peaked at number 17 on the UK Singles Chart. At about the same time, several individuals from the rock/punk scene in Reykjavík featured in Friðriksson's documentary were connected into the post-punk and experimental music scene in London, where musicians experimented with electronic instruments and novel production techniques. One of those individuals was the music composer Hilmar Örn Hilmarsson – a long-time collaborator of Friðriksson – who collaborated with the experimental video art and music group Psychic TV. Others included members of the post-punk group KUKL who were also connected to Hilmarsson. KUKL was established in 1983 and developed into the Sugarcubes, whose single "Birthday" became *Melody Maker*'s single of the week in August 1987. Sugarcubes's fame not only paved the way for Björk's solo career, but also generated resources and international networks that promoted independent Icelandic music and experimentation in the Icelandic music scene. The network of people around Smekkleysa (Bad Taste) – the Icelandic production company of the Sugarcubes – later became highly influential for Icelandic film music.

Internationalization and digitization (1990–2008)

During this period, the focus of the industry shifted to the international scene and the digitization of audio-visual content and its post-processing. In 1992, the Icelandic film *Children of Nature* (*Börn náttúrunnar*) – directed by Friðrik Þór

Friðriksson – was nominated for the Best Foreign Language Film Oscar. The nomination increased the attention given to Icelandic films abroad and created an important role model for others to follow. Subsequently, a number of Icelandic film makers, both artistic directors and film production professionals, established themselves in some of the well-known film clusters around the world. At the same time, digital technologies transformed the production process, reducing cost and increasing flexibility, which benefitted the young and growing industry. As in the previous period, improved access to funding and co-production opportunities played a key role in the development of the industry, as Iceland became one of the member states of the Euroimages fund, obtaining access to large European programmes supporting the film industry. Furthermore, starting in 2001, the Icelandic government offered a 25% reimbursement for film and TV production costs incurred in Iceland, which created new opportunities for the industry.

The music production for *Children of Nature* reflects the resource constraints facing composers at the time, but at the same time, it represents the earliest use of digital technologies. The music for the film was recorded on tape but mixed digitally in Norway using Digital Audio Tape (DAT) technology. Because of the lack of resources, the composer – Hilmar Örn Hilmarsson – had to develop workarounds for performing and recording the music. First, he did not have local access to facilities where he could use click-track guidance to coordinate an ensemble of musicians and synchronize sound and picture. Second, even if he had access to these facilities, he did not have the means to hire an ensemble of musicians. Thus, he had to rely on himself and a handful of friends who were willing to work under severe resource constraints. Therefore, the presence of an ensemble needed to be faked through repeated overdubbing (record on top of existing recordings) of the performance of a handful of musicians, which required careful calculations and timings. This resulted in a particular sonic character for which Hilmarsson received the European Film Composer of the Year award in 1991 and soon became a signature sound for Icelandic film music.

In 1992, the producers of *Children of Nature* – The Icelandic Film Corporation (Íslenska kvikmyndasamsteypan) – established a company for sound processing in films – Cinema Sound (Bíóhljóð) – which purchased equipment for completing the process of syncing film and music. The equipment included an AMS Audiofile, a hard disk-based recording system dedicated to post-production, and a Logic Digital Mixer, thus enabling computer processing and digital mixing of sound and music. It was not until the end of the 1990s that picture editing was done on a computer; until then digital sound needed to be synchronized to the picture using a VHS system which created awkwardness in the workflow and required workarounds for syncing to be successful.

Working at Cinema Sound and helping to select the equipment was a young sound engineer, Kjartan Kjartansson, who had graduated from the Danish Film School in Copenhagen in 1988. During his studies, he had requested the first computer for sound recording and processing to be purchased for the Danish Film School and had obtained experience in using it.

In 1992, the film *Remote Control* (*Sódóma Reykjavík*), directed by Óskar Jónasson, was released. The music composer for that film was Sigurjón Kjartansson, who played in the rock band Ham, which was a part of the network of musicians around Bad Taste. Playing with Sigurjón in Ham was Jóhann Jóhannsson, who later became an internationally accomplished composer of film music blending orchestral and contemporary electronic music in a minimalistic way, resembling and extending the signature sound of Icelandic films originated by Hilmar Örn Hilmarsson.

During the second part of this period, the recording of both sound and picture had become digital and editing of both sound and picture was done on computers. Lacking access to facilities for, and experience of, recording orchestral music, Icelandic composers occasionally recorded orchestral performances abroad, more specifically in Eastern Europe with many symphonic orchestras offering reasonably priced services to the filming industry. One film produced in the second part of the period was *Astropia* directed by Gunnar Guðmundsson and released in 2007. The composer was the guitarist and studio engineer Þorvaldur Bjarni Þorvaldsson. Orchestral recordings were made in Eastern Europe, which required Þorvaldur to travel there to oversee the recordings and to return with several hard disks storing the recordings that were later processed and synced with the picture using computer software in Iceland.

As digital technologies started to dominate the post-production of films, including the recording and editing of music, concerns were raised about their limitations and lack of character. The director Dagur Kári Pétursson, who also composes and performs music for many of his films, argues that music performed and recorded digitally does not have its own character in the same way as physical musical instruments and electronic hardware, such as guitar amplifiers and analogue recording equipment. Furthermore, performing and recording the music in bits and pieces and then mixing it together afterwards loses the human character and feeling that is generated by a group of musicians playing together. Thus, in his film *Nói albínói*, released in 2003, Dagur Kári and his friends used analogue amplifiers and analogue tape recorders, watching the moving picture while they played the music together, recording each scene as a whole. At this point, the decision to perform and record the music this way was artistic rather than technical. It is worth noting that recording in bits and pieces was commonly done using analogue technologies and is therefore not specific to digital technologies. Furthermore, the music technology industry has since the end of the 1990s been preoccupied with providing virtual instruments that emulate the character of analogue studio instruments and equipment.

Digitalization through virtual networks of craft production (2008–2019)

In this period, the industry developed into an international network of craft production, connecting Iceland with the major film-related agglomerations around the world, such as Hollywood and Berlin. People from Iceland lived and worked in the film agglomerations but did specialized work for films produced in Iceland. Others – who previously lived and worked in film agglomerations – moved back to Iceland, but still did work on projects originating in the film clusters. Thus, the industry was not only transformed in terms of size, volume of output and international recognition, but it was also transformed in terms of its structure evolving from a geographically isolated micro-industry with limited experience of creating film for the local market into an international network of virtual craft production serving both local and international markets.

Two composers who lived and worked in Berlin during the period were Jóhann Jóhannsson and Hildur Guðnadóttir. Jóhann and Hildur composed the music for the TV series *Trapped* (*Ófærð*) created by Baltasar Kormákur and released in 2015. The starting point in the process was a physical instrument that was digitally recorded. To that were added sampled instruments from a sample bank in order to prepare demos. Communication was mostly through online platforms and cloud services were used for sharing files. Finally, sampled instruments from sample banks were replaced by their own recording of instruments played by trusted collaborators, some of whom were located in Berlin and some of whom were located elsewhere.

Jóhann and Hildur were well known by the people involved in the production of the *Trapped* series, e.g. Sigurjón Kjartansson, who played together with Jóhann in the band Ham in the late 1980s and early 1990s, was one of the scriptwriters. Knowing each other created trust and made it easier to rely on online communication during the project.

In 2015, the composer Atli Örvarsson moved back to his hometown Akureyri in the northern part of the country after studying composition at Berklee College of Music and the North Carolina School of the Arts and having a successful career in Los Angeles working with Mike Post and later Hans Zimmer. Both Post and Zimmer were pioneers in using digital technologies for film music. Mike Post composed, performed and recorded the music digitally, working much faster than was possible earlier and at a lower cost because he reduced the need for performers. As a consequence, he and his team could work on a high number of TV shows at the same time. Hans Zimmer developed a particular method by extended sampling of physical instruments, by which he could digitally create realistic orchestral music that he used as demos. However, in full-featured films, these demos were replaced by traditional recordings of performance by an orchestra in the final soundtrack.

The Internet and online communication technologies made it possible for Atli to move to Iceland and still work for producers in Hollywood. In fact, the process has not changed much by moving to Iceland, because he was already using the same technologies to communicate with collaborators located in Hollywood to avoid spending time in heavy traffic. Furthermore, the ability to move audio files between different workstations on the same internal network can be extended to the Internet, which means that there is little difference between working in Akureyri or Los Angeles.

At the same time that Atli moved to Akureyri his old friend Þorvaldur Bjarni Þorvaldsson was taking over as the director of the symphonic orchestra in Akureyri. Together they decided to start the SinfoniaNord project aimed at offering world-class orchestral services for film, games and television. Almost five years later, SinfoniaNord has been involved in 20 productions, mostly based on Atli's connections and his own projects. In some cases, composers or music directors travel to Akureyri to oversee the recordings, but in others, they follow the recordings through online communication technologies, receive the recordings in full resolution for review after a slight delay and are able to decide if further recordings are required or not.

Atli's operations in Akureyri are on a different scale from any other actor in Iceland. He manages teams in Akureyri and Los Angeles who jointly work on a number of projects at the same time. For a TV series, Atli designs themes and digital components that are combined and recombined by his assistants to create all the scenes that are needed. Instead of a division of labour between a composer, performer and recording engineer, the same person performs all these functions with the help of specialized software. For featured films, the same methods are used to make demos, but usually, real-life recordings are added in the final version using performers that are available around the world. Most of the projects Atli and his teams work on are international, but he has also been involved in films produced in Iceland, most notably *Rams* (*Hrútar*) directed by Grímur Hákonarson and released in 2015.

Conclusion and discussion

The purpose of this chapter was to better understand how the relationship between a particular set of generic activities (making music) and the overall set of specific activities (film making), of which the generic activities are but one part, is affected by digitalization and industrial transformation. Empirically, we studied the Icelandic film industry in the period 1980–2019, focusing on the composition, performance and recording of music, which is a subset of the activities required to produce a film. During this period, whose start coincided with the early start of the digitalization of the film industry, the Icelandic film industry was transformed from a geographically isolated micro-industry into an international network of virtual craft production.

We find that the use of digital technologies has supported an approach to composing, performing and recording film music that was already established using analogue technologies. This approach was developed due to a lack of access to the infrastructure and performers of the traditional musical agglomerations normally required to perform and record at that time. The success of the approach established it as a signature for Icelandic film music and generated resources that were used to build a digital infrastructure for sound recording and processing. Later on, digital technologies would reduce the dependencies on music agglomerations (Leyshon 2009), dependencies that, among other things, had constrained film making in Iceland before the 1990s.

We also find that composers and sound engineers from Iceland were exposed to digital technologies relatively early in the development of these technologies. Through their studies and work abroad they gained access to digital technologies not available in Iceland and participated in communities that were experimenting with their use. The diffusion of these technologies to Iceland was assisted by close personal networks within the Icelandic music industry, most notably the network around the band Sugarcubes, whose international success and later the success of its lead singer Björk, generated resources for experimentation, both musically and technologically.

Finally, we find that advances in communication technologies have played a more important role than digital music technology in transforming the composition, performance and recording of music in the Icelandic film industry. The development of these generic technologies has enabled composers to live in one place, while at the same time working with music editors, film directors, performers and other specialists living in different places around the world. This has materialized in two ways in the Icelandic film industry. On the one hand, Icelandic composers are now living abroad being part of a film music agglomeration but producing music for both Icelandic films and foreign films. On the other hand, Icelandic composers who have lived in a film music agglomeration have moved back to Iceland, continuing to work with actors outside Iceland. As they move back to Iceland, they bring with them knowledge, connections and projects that strengthen the local community as well as new work procedures.

Based on our findings we make the following conclusions. First, we come to the obvious but important conclusion that if digital technologies support existing sets of activities and relations, e.g. both increase quality and reduce cost, they are unlikely to transform these activities and relations. This has historically also been the case for the film and music industry in general (De Vinck and Lindmark 2012; Sigurdardottir 2010) where digitalization of production and post-processing techniques provide an extension of a development that started as early as the 1960s and 1970s when film shooting and sound recording moved out of the studio through the use of more portable cameras and audio recording equipment. However, due to their low cost and flexibility, digital technologies enable the experimentation and scaling up of production and post-production activities almost everywhere in the world, which transforms the local industry that depends on those activities.

Second, we conclude that the emergence of the Internet as a high-speed global communication medium has enabled international networks of craftspeople who base their craft on digital tools. By using the Internet, work processes become more individual in the sense that the people that participate in the film making process, such as directors, composers, artists and sound engineers, can work on their own at their location of choice and independent of the location of their collaborators. Thus, they can continue to work with people they have worked with previously even if they do not share the same location and they can work with them in real time, e.g. observe and guide the recording of performance artists. However, the use of the Internet in this way to support a network of individual craftspeople rather than an industrial supply chain would not have been possible without the extensive digitalization of music technology, i.e. the creation of digital tools.

Third, we conclude that social networks that provide and diffuse access to knowledge and resources for experimentation, both artistically and technically, are important determinants of how activities and relations change due to digitalization. While links between the Iceland film industry and the outside world depend on few successful and well-connected individuals, the dense connections within the Icelandic network ensure that resources are shared and knowledge and expertise are quickly diffused. Initially, networks within the music industry played an important role in building basic capabilities, but with time and the increasing scale of operations, the connections into networks within the film industry itself, as well as specific networks around film music, played a larger role. We see a clear path dependency between generations of composers that have created, shaped and maintained a signature sound of Icelandic films that can be traced to successes in the early 1990s. However, digital technologies make it easier for new actors living at another location and rooted in different technical and artistic traditions to move to Iceland. While they are able to continue working with the same people they have worked with before, in much the same way as before, they can gradually influence, and be influenced, by the local industry.

Two issues identified within this study provide opportunities for further research beyond the film industry. First, digital technologies have not yet led to significant changes in the traditional production and post-production process in film making, but there are interesting and subtle differences in the specialization and division of labour within the process of composing, performing and recording music. Digital tools have enabled less specialization by composers because they can more easily complete the whole process for scores involving multiple instruments, i.e. compose, perform and record the music, instead of being dependent on multiple performers and specialized staff and infrastructure for recording. However, to follow this less specialized process at a higher scale requires a new type of specialization, one in which the composer acts as a designer of themes and sound modules that are reused through recombination by assistants. Thus, digitalization both provides an individual, low volume and craft-based mode of production as well as a new model of high-volume production, but apparently without changing the overall process of film making.

Second, the interaction between digital communication technologies and digital production technologies have changed the nature of roundabout production. Because of increasing post-processing capabilities and ease of communication across distances, it is possible to delay important decisions until multiple alternatives have been explored during the post-processing stage. Thus, the user is less concerned about making the right decisions early in the process because she is confident that most of them can be changed later. Further research is needed to better understand how this interaction affects the relationship between the user (e.g. the film director or the music editor) and the producer (e.g. the composer, sound engineer or film editor) and the overall economics of the production process.

References

Cascone, K., 2000, 'The Aesthetics of Failure: "Post-Digital" Tendencies in Contemporary Computer Music', *Computer Music Journal*, 24(4), pp. 12–18.

De Vinck, S. and Lindmark, S., 2012, *Statistical, Ecosystems and Competitiveness Analysis of the Media and Content Industries: The Film Sector*, JRC Technical Reports EUR 25277 EN/2, Luxemburg: Publications Office of the European Union.

Ferguson, J.R. and Brown, A.R., 2016, 'Fostering a Post-Digital Avant-Garde: Research-Led Teaching of Music Technology', *Organized Sound*, 21(2), pp. 127–137.

Hirsch, P.M. and Gruber, D.A., 2015, 'Digitizing Fads and Fashions: Disintermediation and Glocalized Markets in Creative Industries', in C. Jones, M. Lorenzen, and J. Sapsed, ed., *The Oxford Handbook of Creative Industries*, Oxford: Oxford University Press.

Jackson, C., 2019, 'What is Post-Classical Music?' Available at http://www.classical-music.com/article/what-post-classical-music. Accessed 7.12.2019.

Kompanek, S., 2004, *From Score to Screen: Sequencers, Scores, & Second Thoughts. The New Film Scoring Process*, London: Schirmer Trade Books.

Lehman, F., 2017, 'Manufacturing the Epic Score: Hans Zimmer and the Sounds of Significance', in S.C. Meyer, ed., *Music in Epic Film*, New York: Routledge.

Leyshon, A., 2001, 'Time–Space (and Digital) Compression: Software Formats, Musical Networks, and the Reorganisation of the Music Industry', *Environment and Planning. Part A*, 33, pp. 49–77.

Leyshon, A., 2009, 'The Software Slump?: Digital Music, Democratization of Technology, and the Decline of the Recording Studio Sector within the Musical Economy', *Environment and Planning A*, 41, pp. 1309–1331.

Maddocks, R., 2011, 'Writing Music for Film: MIDI Mockups'. Available at https://intensemusic.wordpress.com/2011/01/23/writing-music-for-film-midi-mockups/. Accessed 5.12.2019.

Manning, S., 2017, 'The Rise of Project Network Organizations: Building Core Teams and Flexible Partner Pools for Interorganizational Projects', *Research Policy*, 46, pp. 1399–1415.

Palmer, I., 2001, 'Changing Forms of Organizing: Dualities in Using Remote Collaboration Technologies in Film Production', *Journal of Organizational Change Management*, 14(2), pp. 190–212.

Perez, C., 2010, 'Technological Revolutions and Techno-Economic Paradigms', *Cambridge Journal of Economics*, 34, pp. 185–202.

Power, D. and Jansson, J., 2004, 'The Emergence of a Post-industrial Music Economy? Music and ICT Synergies in Stockholm, Sweden', *Geoforum*, 35, pp. 245–439.

Scott, A.J. and Pope, N.E., 2007, 'Hollywood, Vancouver, and the World: Employment Relocation and the Emergence of Satellite Production Centers in the Motion- Picture Industry', *Environment and Planning. Part A*, 39, pp. 1364–1381.

Sigurdardottir, M.S., 2010, *Dependently Independent. Co-existence of Institutional Logics in the Recorded Music Industry*, PhD thesis, Copenhagen: Copenhagen Business School.

Storper, M., 1989, 'The Transition to Flexible Specialisation in the US Film Industry: External Economies, the Division of Labour, and the Crossing of Industrial Divides', *Cambridge Journal of Economics*, 13, pp. 273–305.

Watson, A. and Beaverstock, J.V., 2016, 'Transnational Freelancing: Ephemeral Creative Projects and Mobility in the Music Recording Industry', *Environment and Planning. Part A*, 48, pp. 1428–1446.

7

WHAT PREVENTS MACHINE LEARNING FROM TRANSFORMING INDUSTRIES?

Vicky Long and Jonas Grafström

Introduction

Machine learning (ML) may be defined as a set of statistical tools that enabling learning from data and consequently the creation of predictors. Therefore, ML is relevant for industries where data analysis is concerned. The industrial exploitation of ML is, however, still in its infancy; so are studies on ML.

As a subfield of computer science, ML dates back to the 1950s. In 1959, Arthur Samuel explicitly defined ML as a "field of study that gives computers the ability to learn without being explicitly programmed" (Simon, 2013, p. 89). ML's transformative power – for industries and economies – has, however, been hotly debated until very recently (e.g. Varian, 2018; Brynjolfsson and Mitchell, 2017; Chui, 2017).

It is widely understood that ML is capable of mining data for patterns that can be used to make predictions. What is actually learned from the data (e.g. characteristics or relations among the data) and how that learning process takes place remain largely unknown, not least from an industrial activity perspective. This explorative chapter therefore sets out to answer:

- How has ML been deployed in (case) firms, has the deployment of ML transformed current business practices and what are the observed obstacles in this transformation?

This study combines three case studies and a bibliometric study. The selection criteria for the cases are very rudimentary: they were aimed to cover (a) the most common ML-related application areas and (b) both business-to-business (B2B) and business-to-consumer (B2C) cases.[1] For the bibliometric study part, a keyword-based search was used. Both "Three illustrative cases" and "Illustrations from a set of sectors" serve as illustrations of the industrial activities involved in this transformation.

While the evolution of ML from a technical point of view is briefly presented in "The historical evolution of three necessary but not sufficient conditions", in "Three illustrative cases" and "Illustrations from a set of sectors", we focus on the actors and industrial activities involved in this transformation, respectively. In "Analysis and conclusion: The transformative barriers", we summarize the obstacles to transformation and conclude the chapter.

The historical evolution of three necessary but not sufficient conditions

The industrial exploitation of ML technology is conditioned by the technological advancement on the following three key fronts, and much of the development has been going on for more than half a century (Heller, 2017, 2019):

- *algorithms* (methods);
- *computing capacity* (enabling the implementation of large computational models, including developments of such things as transistors and microprocessors since the 1970s and developments fitting the description of Moore's Law or Metcalfe's Law);
- *(big) data* (a system for gathering, transferring and sharing data generated by human beings/sensors/actuators/robots).

To elaborate, first on the evolution of the *algorithm*, a programming algorithm tells the computer what to do in a straightforward way (e.g. sorting data in numeric or alphabetical order). The two major categories of problems that ML solves are regression and classification (Mehta et al., 2019). Regression works on numerical data (e.g. what is the likely wage for someone with a given occupation and skill level?) and classification works on non-numerical data (e.g. will the convict considered for release commit another crime?). An example of such an algorithm is AlphaGo, which managed to beat the champion human Go player (Moyer, 2018).

Second and at the evolution of *computing capacity*, ML builds on the realization that computers are well suited to calculate (statistical) probabilities (Russell and Norvig, 2016), and consequently, to reason and to make logical predictions (Meserole, 2018). ML is therefore firmly tied to the question of how to build computers that improve automatically, by themselves and through experience. Since World War II, there have been tremendous increases in computational power. Stylized facts and radical improvements in microprocessor cost-performance ratios and movements from traditional business computing to ubiquitous computing are well known. "General-purpose computing capacity grew at an annual rate of 58% (from 1986 to 2007)" (Hilbert and López, 2011, p. 60). Moore's law illustrates this observed regularity.

Third, the evolution of *big data* refers to a development of the *volume* (trillions of zettabytes of data), *variety* (structured and unstructured, machine/human-generated) and *velocity* (real time) of data, the so-called three Vs (which have emerged as a common framework for describing big data) (Gandomi and Haider, 2015; Drexl, 2016). Gartner Group gives a typical definition: "Big data is high-volume, high-velocity and high-variety information assets that demand cost-effective, innovative forms of information processing for enhanced insight and decision making" (Gartner IT Glossary, n.d.). Generally, the data have to be big enough – sufficiently large and comprehensive – to be used for training ML algorithms.

The development of the first two – *algorithms* and *computing capacity* – are cumulative, taking place over more than half a century in fields like computer science. The evolution of the third one – *big data* – and particularly the access to and sharing of large volumes of data, is more recent. Today, ML is increasingly used in practical software for computer vision, speech recognition, natural language processing, robot control and additional applications.

These three key technological advancements are, however, *necessary* but not *sufficient* conditions for ML to take off industrially. Other factors are into play, such as a pro-trial-and-error attitude and supporting policies. It is argued that technology coevolves with industry structure and its supporting institutions (cf. Nelson, 1995). In "Three illustrative cases" and "Illustrations from a set of sectors", we focus on these other factors, including firm-level capabilities, resources, routines and meso (industry) activities and institutional obstacles.

Three illustrative cases

No examination of an industrial transformation is complete without describing how the actors interact. No examination of the actors is complete without moving down to the meso level and sometimes even to the value chain and the micro (firm) levels. In the following, we present three cases. The cases cover (a) three common ML-related application areas: image recognition, chatbots and predictive analytics (including demand prediction) and (b) both B2B and B2C cases. The presentation is based on firm-level interview data.

Case 1: 2Park

2Park[2] is an Oslo-based car parking solution provider, with a focus on payment (software and hardware) solutions. The basic idea is that a driver can park anywhere, anytime, at any frequency of entry and exit (e.g. a garage) without the hassle of thinking about payment: an automatic number plate recognition system will handle that.

The ML technology used here mainly involves *image recognition* and *object detection* (in the field of computer vision). The aimed transformation is progressive: currently, as many parking-related steps and interactions as possible should be taken away, and the customer should simply drive in, do his or her thing and drive out again. The next stage is to introduce *dynamic pricing* – different prices for different circumstances and customers (as airlines do) – in which ML can tackle the prediction problem. With 1.2 billion vehicles in mind, 2Park aims to provide a pan-European parking solution named "Autopay" (currently covering eight countries and over 100 locations; it had handled 27 million parking sessions by 2018).

Who are the actors? What do they know and do? Figure 7.1 illustrates the chains of actors involved before the *Autopay* solution takes place and Figure 7.2 illustrates the functional changes after the transformation (which is ongoing), as well as the emergence of new actors in this transformation:

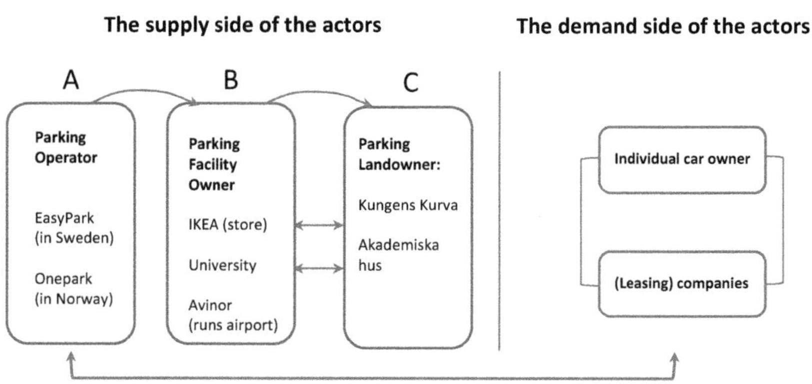

FIGURE 7.1 Chain of actors involved in parking before Autopay (based on interview data).

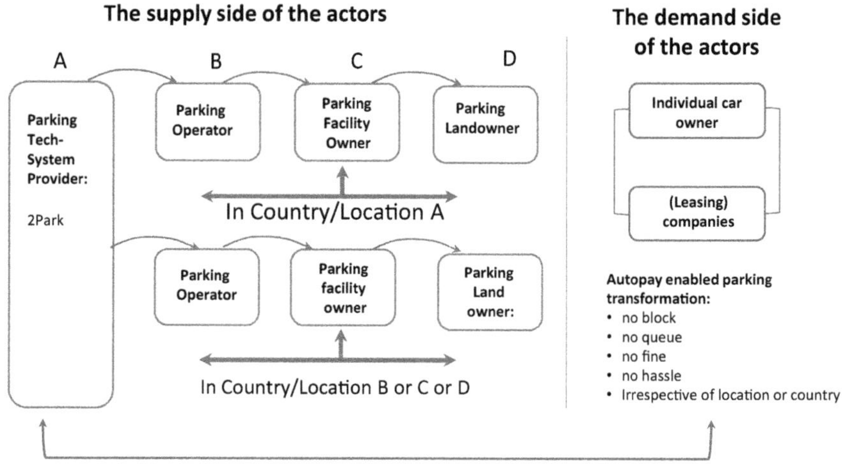

FIGURE 7.2 Chain of actors involved in parking with Autopay (based on interview data).

To elaborate these figures, the major transformation on the supply side is connectivity: more kinds and numbers of actors across more geographic regions (and countries) are connected, which in turn brings a seamless platform service – a high degree of convenience – to the demand side. The whole process requires feeding of the following data:

- Car owner data (number plate inventory);
- Parking action data (time, location);
- Congestion data (parking concentration, availability);
- Parking price data;
- Payment solution data (e.g. some would like to pay within 30 days).

To find a workable way of implementing dynamic pricing, the above data need to be structured according to (a) customer segment (e.g. parking habit data including price-sensitivity data) and (b) parking choices data (on parking availability, price level etc.).

The transformative opportunities are numerous. On the supply side, providers can collect revenues they previously lost, and it helps to open and expand the market. On the demand side, as Figure 7.2 indicates, there is a greater degree of convenience: parking without any hassle.

There are many existing ML-based parking solutions throughout the world. Some focus on map services such as detecting and updating departing cars (by sensor) and recommending empty parking spaces. 2Park's focus is on the payment (which EasyPark also does with a different solution).

Typical barriers for 2Park include:

- *The registration system*: it is not only difficult but (sometimes) impossible to access the (car) registration data, due to the existence of different legislation systems across (European) countries. For example, some countries (e.g. Sweden) are open, while others are not open to the public. Some countries permit access at a small cost, which is affordable for private actors like 2Park, but other countries (e.g. Germany) charge high prices, making the current business model not viable (simply no profit).
- *The complexity of the ownership structure of the parking facilities*: as illustrated in Figures 7.1 and 7.2, actors such as the parking landowner, parking facility owner and parking operator can have different priorities, which in turn can complicate contracts. For example, the 2Park system requires continuity of contracts to build up a (big) database in the first place, while (parking) landowners often can only negotiate contracts for two to five years. Sometimes, according to the law, they must change subcontractors. Again, there are issues such as the cost of installing (or removing) cameras and other facilities.

So, the obstacles primarily involve datasets: some data (e.g. congestion, prices) need to be built up or sorted in a particular format, and some data are not accessible (or expensive to obtain). The company therefore perceives that there is still a long way to go to reach the theoretical potential enabled by ML.

Case 2: Furhat Robotics

This is a chatbots case, where ML is used in user interaction. *Furhat Robotics*[3] is a Stockholm-based start-up founded in 2014, a spinoff from a Swedish university (The Royal Institute of Technology). The firm developed a life-sized robotic face – originally with a fur hat – capable of social interactions, namely speaking more than 40 languages with humanoid expressions. ML here is mainly used for speech recognition. The goal, from a technology standpoint, is to build machines that can communicate with humans on human terms.

From an industrial activity perspective, what has this chatbots service managed to change? Who are the actors and what do they know and do in this robo-advisor-based transformation? While Furhat has been test-used in malls, hospitals and offices, Figures 7.3 and 7.4 illustrate the changes that occurred at Frankfurt Airport,[4] where Furhat serves as a multilingual traffic host. Figure 7.3 illustrates what frontline airport customer services can do, and Figure 7.4 illustrates Furhat-assisted services (after the transformation).

Traditional frontline airport host

The supply side – the air host	The demand side – passengers
Can answer/do: • Airport info (e.g., departure gate); • Flight info (updated but with time lag); • Luggage info (updated but with time lag) • In local language and English • Ticket/flight change (with time lag in coordination)	Basic capabilities required: • Can speak/read airport country language or English; • Basic orientation skills

FIGURE 7.3 Traditional frontline airport host illustration.

Furhat robot-assisted frontline airport host

The supply side – Furhat	The demand side – passengers
Can answer/do: • In 40+ languages • Airport info (e.g., departure gate); • Flight info (real - time updated); • Luggage info (real time updated) • Ticket/flight change (customised, fast) • Personalized maps • Other coordinated info (real-time updated)	Basic capabilities required: • Can speak

FIGURE 7.4 Furhat-assisted frontline airport host illustration.

To elaborate, this robot traffic host changes the very nature of the service offered: multilingual (virtually no human airhost can understand and respond in 40+ languages) and personalized.

What is transformed here is therefore not only the effectiveness (a single robot host can do tasks originally conducted by many human beings), but also the provision of new functions (the robot's answer is not only in the customer's native language, but it is also based on updated and synchronized traffic information). It is:

(a) an issue of *labour replacement* (or reduction of workload), as many technological breakthroughs (e.g. automation) have done;
(b) an issue of *productivity enhancement*, exemplified by real-time information updates and coordination;
(c) an issue of *economies of scope*: the value of ML based on a joint dataset (traffic, luggage, language) is higher than the sum of values of ML based on each database separately. The Furhat robot here is a data aggregator that combines data on traffic, physical infrastructure (departure gate, luggage location) and languages (recognition) into a single consistent dataset. No human air host could provide traffic info instantly in 40+ languages. Here there is an economy of scope in datasets that is new in this potential transformation. There is a functional aggregation in the form of combining speech recognition and response (in 40+ languages) that is beyond human capabilities.

From a technical standpoint, the datasets required for Furhat to work include speech (converted from sound waves to letters and then to sentences), facial expressions, attention (gaze, head pose) and lip movements. Rapid technological progress in speech signal processing (compression, coding and transmission), along with spelling and linguistic error reduction, has enabled this development according to its founder Gabriel Skantze (an error rate reduction from 80% in the 1990s to circa 5% in 2015). Room for improvement also remains, not the least in reducing latency and increasing accuracy.

A full-scale customer experience and engagement of this type in chatbot services (in e-commerce, healthcare, retail), however, is still not there. Obstacles remain:

- It is generally difficult to obtain datasets that are sufficiently large and comprehensive for training. There is either too much data out there or too little: customers (e.g. malls, airports) often do not keep systematic data and it takes time to collect and build up the datasets.
- The data need to be integrated, processed, tagged and *controlled for errors*, but the types (and forms) of errors are dynamically changing. That in turn, sets a high requirement for intra-organizational collaboration, which must occur dynamically.

- When two or more organizations are involved, the interoperability of the data is often an issue. Business processes are different and consequently there are differences in the logics of labelling data.
- The collaboration difficulties also lie in (the degree of) *data monitoring*, namely, the issue of data *security*. There is a dilemma in the degree of openness of data here among collaboration partners.
- There is a general lack of understanding related to the end markets. The functionality of the chatbot services also needs to be validated.

To summarize, much work in data creation and sorting needs to be done and that requires an in-depth understanding of the business logics involved. Collaboration modes play a role as well.

The data collaboration in the Furhat case so far is mostly along the vertical line, as the number of actors involved at this stage is limited. Data access is therefore not a big problem (yet).

Case 3: Paradox Interactive

The ML used in this case is mainly on-demand prediction (customer behaviour analyses). *Paradox Interactive* is a Sweden-based company engaged in the development and publishing of strategy games, primarily for personal computers and console platforms (e.g. PlayStation).

The historical patterns of game consumption are used to derive the possible demand: through building a probabilistic model, *Paradox Interactive* learns the behaviour of gamers and then infers what their next actions will be. Gamers' behaviour – how they interact with the game – is analysed. *Churn customers*, namely customers at high risk to leave the game, are identified by sorting the data in numerical order (0,1) of engagement, or by allocating churn rates to groups (in alphabetical order). Churn customers are given particular attention and consequent retention strategies in the form of (weekend) event invitations or gifts (extra power/weapon free of charge) based on the predictions generated from ML to make the players more engaged and reduce the churn rate (see Table 7.1).

What has been transformed? ML here enables autonomous marketing. This is also commonly used in many B2C sectors, where data analyses of consumers' behaviour are concerned.

Difficulties and obstacles remain, however: *data interpretability* and *data generalizability* are the two highlights here in a typical B2C case.

Typically, difficulties remain in explaining the results from large and complex models in human terms. In other words, the "what" question is easy to answer, but not the "why" question.

It is clear that if a gamer today makes a purchase (e.g. a new weapon), his or her probability of remaining in the game is high (pattern recognition and prediction). Less is known, however, on why this gamer is leaving the game,

TABLE 7.1 The division of labour between machines and humans in gamer behaviour analyses

	What the machines do	*What the staff do*
	• Collect data on gamers' behaviour and what they buy • Create a profile of each user and categorize users • Predict buying/leaving behaviour • Recommend: suggest content to users	Clean, label and train the data.
Exceptions	Machines cannot collect data on gender or age (of gamers) because of privacy regulations and concerns	

for example, and/or why he or she is buying A but not B. Some personal data such as age and gender cannot be collected, which gives no information on the "why" answer. The (purchase) choice criteria cannot be observed and explained. Therefore, the results cannot be used to provide long-term strategic support.

Moreover, the generalizability of the learning result is limited: the remain/leave behaviour in Game A says nothing about that in Game B. This means that each game's dataset is unique, necessitating labelling, cleaning the data and training the algorithm, which is very time consuming.

However, it should be noted that *data access* and *data volume* are not problematic, as there are sufficiently large and comprehensive datasets on gamers' behaviour for training. While ML methods do not often perform well with small data sample sizes, it seems that B2C sectors do not have the data volume and data access problems to the same extent as the B2B sectors.[5]

Illustrations from a set of sectors

ML fits into the description of a general-purpose technology (GPT), namely having the capacity to transform many industry sectors that rely on data analyses (Bresnahan and Trajtenberg, 1995). In this section, we therefore look at a set of sectors to see whether some general patterns of the transformation can be observed or not. This section is based on a bibliometrics study.

The industrial exploitations of ML are many. To exemplify:

- In the *agriculture sector*, ML is used to analyse data collected by sensors and robots, detect crops and weeds, monitor soil and diagnose plant (animal) diseases, an area often described as "smart farming" and/or "precision farming" (EU, 2018, p. 27).
- In the *healthcare sector*, the use of ML ranges from administrative tasks (documentation) to more advanced tasks like image recognition (e.g.

electrocardiogram) and risk prediction (e.g. the Framingham Risk Score in estimating coronary heart disease) (Rahul, 2015).

- In the *bank sector*, data mining and supervised learning are used to track transactions and predict possible frauds (Carneiro et al., 2017).
- In the *telecom sector*, ML is used in customer relationship management to understand consumers' behaviour patterns and then to adjust promotions to ensure a high retention rate (Ullah et al., 2019).
- In the *public sector*, ML is used to monitor foodborne illnesses (and to decide whether further investigation is needed). This can be done by analysing customer reviews using algorithm-based Web scraping (to break down unstructured data from web pages such as Twitter, Yelp and Google) and conducting text analyses and prediction (Maharana et al., 2019).
- Even in one of the most creative sectors – *art creation* – machines can learn to mimic images, music, speech and even prose (Gervais, 2019; implying that a portrait by van Gogh or by a machine general adversarial network may soon be hard to detect).

It is sometimes argued that ML is likely to take off faster in B2C sectors than in B2B sectors, as the vast amount of consumer data – which is as precious as oil[6] – can be exploited (the demand-pull argument). The *Facebook-Cambridge Analytica scandal* may illustrate the value of consumer data. The unrestricted availability of data is also the reason China – rather than the United States – may lead the world in implementing AI (while the United States may be leading discoveries in AI) because China's enormous market size will generate huge amounts of data that in turn will provide a testbed for ML and its AI extension (Lee, 2019).[7]

It is important to clarify that this is not only a *population size* argument but also an argument on *real activities*, namely, that sizable data also come from more intense use of (mobile) Internet (and consequently more data is available for training). Besides the *data volume* argument, *data interpretability* and *data transparency* are important for the success of ML (Bratko, 1997), and this is harder to achieve in B2B sectors (where the data-labelling criteria vary across organizations) than it is in B2C sectors.

It is also, often implicitly, argued that the B2B sectors are by no means lagging behind the B2C sectors in the deployment of ML. This is illustrated by the Internet of Things, where billions of devices – sensors, robots, actuators and drones – are connected, creating oceans of data on which business, engineering and financial processes can draw. Proponents of this argument may be found in *Industry 4.0*-related studies. No legal scheme (yet) provides exclusive rights on machine-generated B2B data (Wiebe, 2017). Viable business models, in conjunction with technical means, arguably can provide remedies to the problems in data access and data interpretability (Martens, 2018).

While ML has kicked off industrially, the obstacles to the exploitation of ML are many. Conventional obstacles, extensively discussed in technology diffusion textbooks (e.g. Roger, 1995), exist: some are technical (e.g. data-labelling methods), some are organizational (capabilities, skills), some are at the system level (infrastructural) and some are institutional (regulations on data access). There are also ML-specific obstacles, and most of them are related to the problem of data, which is the premise of training the ML algorithms. Typically, there are data-quality problems and data-access problems.

On the data quality front, the problems include:

(a) *Bad data and fragmented data.* Junk data, often phrased as "garbage in, garbage out" ("rubbish in, rubbish out" in the UK variation), prevails. Moreover, the incoming data are often fragmented into data islands across databases and legacy archival systems, with an excessive amount of inefficient data duplication and sometimes manifold, separated repositories of data with varying structures (Alharthi et al., 2017).
(b) *Data structuring or labelling problems.* Some 95% of big data is constituted as unstructured data (Gandomi and Haider, 2015). To train ML algorithms and coordinate with other firms, data in a structured and labelled form is a must. As Bodenbender and Kurzrock (2019) described in the property industry, the documentation needs to be transferable when changing to another life cycle phase or participant. The information needs to be clearly identified and structured to ensure protection, access and administration throughout. We must also expect that documents will endure several rounds of restructuring over time, which adds costs and increases the danger of data loss.
(c) *Data-infrastructure incompatibility.* Old infrastructure, which cannot easily be replaced, creates inefficiencies and latencies in performance, as these systems were not constructed to manage the growing demands of today's computing- and data-intensive workload. To tackle the amount of data that sometimes consists of billions of interacting points in an inadequate system, simplifications in the analysis must be made if one wants an analysis in a short time. Aggregates, or reports based on extracts of the data, can be generated more quickly, but at the same time, they lose explanatory value (Schwenk et al., 2019).

On the data access front, there are also problems:

(a) *Institutions are lagging behind in regulating machine-generated data.* In the case of consumer data (B2C data), the European General Data Protection Regulation came into force on May 25, 2018, to modernize laws that protect the personal information of individuals. The first legal verdicts on the new regulation have been handed down. In the case of industrial data (B2B data), "no legal scheme yet provides generally for exclusive rights in data" (Wiebe, 2017). Establishing a new exclusive right to industrial data is a controversial issue, with pros in bringing efficiency and transparency into the market and cons in impeding innovation primarily in the form of limiting access to data (detrimental, for example, in the Internet of Things). Existing institutional frameworks have not yet caught up with this technological development. Existing copyright protection is limited to the information created by human beings, not by sensors and machines (e.g. bitcoins). It is argued that productions that do not result from human creativity should belong to the public domain (Gervais, 2019). In general, there is uncertainty about data ownership.

(b) *Industrial practices on data access remain essentially a black box, with very limited empirical studies.* While data sharing and re-use are generally expected to grow significantly in the near future, there is no consensus on what data sharing means and which collaborative modes exist (EU, 2018). This is a market that now looks more like the Wild West, although contractual practice already treats data like property (Wiebe, 2017). The heterogeneity of the data – structured/unstructured, dynamic/static, open/closed – suggests very different values for data. While "data are defined in their relation to information and knowledge" (Stepanov, 2020, p. 67), this heterogeneity adds another layer of complexity to industrial collaborations.

ML is conditioned by the existence of and access to big data. The obstacles mentioned previously present a major challenge to transformation. Sometimes there is a vicious cycle caused by the magnitude of the problem, as the use of computer-generated data increases these problems. Thus, they can grow exponentially since the use and development of problematic data can also grow exponentially. Over time, an originally small error may have a ripple effect if made to interact with other data points several times.

Analysis and conclusion: The transformative barriers

ML fits into the description of a GPT and it has the capacity to transform many industry sectors. There are, however, obstacles, traditional as well as emerging, that take time to dismantle. ML technology thrives on access to big, comprehensive and varied datasets. The key obstacles observed in this study also relate to data: quality and access. While the value of data often hinges on access to others' data, fundamental questions such as whether the data are big and good enough, who owns them, who has access to them and whether data can be owned in the first place are yet to be settled. There is a high degree of organizational interdependence in data cocreation and value appropriation.

In the case of 2Park, the problems primarily lie in data access and data integration across organizations and institutional boundaries. A pan-European hassle-free parking system requires sharing and cocreation of data across chain actors irrespective of locations and countries. Regulatory obstacles (misaligned or closed data) in data access need to be dismantled. In the Paradox Interactive case, a typical B2C case, we see problems of data insufficiency, or to be more concrete, data interpretability and data generalizability. In other words, there is still a limit on what can be derived from available data under the existing institutional framework. This will probably remain true. This situation may be common in ML-enabled consumer behaviour analyses. In the case of Furhat, the major problems lie in data integration across different business logics. This is visible in data compatibility, data interoperability and different degrees of openness of data. An improved understanding of the end markets among the chain actors needs to in place.

Looking at the pattern through a set of sectors, the problems are similar. First, there are bad (rubbish, biased) data, fragmented data and incompatible data that need cleaning, labelling and restructuring by human beings and through intensive collaborations among organizations. While ML is designed to help human beings by reducing their workload and improving efficiency, it sets a higher standard for manual data processing, at least at this stage. In other words, human beings need to work *harder* and more collaboratively today to get the machines to work for us.

Second, the value of data used in ML often depends on access to others' data, which will require greater interdependence among organizations and increasing blurring of the boundaries of firms. However, access to data is currently not regulated.[8] There is a Wild West in collaborative practices, in which technical means and mutual contractual relationships are the dominant modes, which leads to problems in scalability. Finding sensible collaborative modes is important. This says that the more we automate things, the harder and the more cooperatively we must work to enable the transformation of activities and industries. It also says that knowledge creation, technology advancement and organizational (business) logics are inherently interrelated.

The development of and access to big data is therefore a *reverse salient* in the deployment of ML and ML-enabled transformation. A *reverse salient*, originally used in military battles, refers to a backwards line alongside other continuous and forward lines. It was applied by Thomas Hughes (1983) in his work *Networks of Power: Electrification in Western Society, 1880–1930*. Treating the electrical system as a large technological system, reverse salient was used to describe the subsystem that lags the advancing frontiers of the system due to its lack of performance. Concepts with family resemblances include Dahmén's *structural tension* concepts in his elaboration of the *development blocks* of industry sectors, in which complementarities of each necessary transformative power must be in place (see e.g. Dahmén, 1970, 1988).

To conclude, while ML has a large potential to transform several industries, several barriers need to fall. A single barrier can stop a whole industry transformation. We observed that the institutions of today might not be suitable for tomorrow. It will take time to change this. In some cases, data exist but are restricted due to cost or regulation. A country that wants to promote the utilization of ML must open its data and modernize its regulations.

Notes

1 One Norwegian and two Swedish firms were selected due to convenience of access, as the two researchers are based in Scandinavia.
2 https://2park.no/.
3 www.furhatrobotics.com/.
4 In collaboration with Deutsche Bahn.
5 The data volume problem in B2B is often a consequence of a lack of data access.
6 "Data is the new oil" is a quote credited to UK Mathematician Clive Humby (also an architect of Tesco's Clubcard) that dates from 2006. This quote was recently picked up widely after a 2017 report in *The Economist* entitled "The world's most valuable resource is no longer oil, but data".
7 China's data edge is larger than the US: three times on mobile user ratio, ten times in food delivery, 50 times in mobile payment and 300 times in shared bicycle rides (ibid).
8 There are also contradictions between copyright and *sui generis* rights protection in the EU Database Directive of 1996, for example.

References

Alharthi, A., Krotov, V., & Bowman, M., 2017, 'Addressing barriers to big data', *Business Horizons*, 60(3), p.285–292.

Bodenbender, Mario, and Kurzrock, Björn-Martin, 2019, 'Challenges in machine learning for document classification in the real estate industry." In *26th Annual European Real Estate Society Conference*. ERES: Conference. Cergy-Pontoise, France.

Bratko, I., 1997, 'ML: Between accuracy and interpretability', *Learning, Networks and Statistics*, 382, p.163–177.

Bresnahan, T. F., & Trajtenberg, M., 1995, 'General purpose technologies 'Engines of growth'?', *Journal of Econometrics*, 65(1), p.83–108.

Brynjolfsson, E., & Mitchell, T., 2017, 'What can ML do? Workforce implications', *Science*, 358(6370), p.1530–1534.

Carneiro, N., Figueira, G., & Costa, M., 2017, 'A data mining-based system for credit-card fraud detection in e-tail', *Decision Support Systems*, 95, p.91–101.

China's AI development report 2018, China Institute for Science and Technology Policy at Tsinghua University. By China Institute for Science and Technology Policy at Tsinghua UniversityJuly 2018. http://www.sppm.tsinghua.edu.cn/eWebEditor/UploadFile/China_AI_development_report_2018.pdf

Chui, M., 2017, *Artificial Intelligence the Next Digital Frontier?* McKinsey and Company Global Institute, 47. https://www.mckinsey.com/~/media/mckinsey/industries/advanced%20electronics/our%20insights/how%20artificial%20intelligence%20can%20deliver%20real%20value%20to%20companies/mgi-artificial-intelligence-discussion-paper.ashx

Dahmén, E., 1970, *Entrepreneurial Activity and the Development of Swedish Industry, 1919–1939*. Homewood, IL: American Economic Association.

Dahmén, E., 1988, 'Development blocks in industrial economics', *Scandinavian Economic History Review*, 36(1), p.3–14.

Drexl, J., 2016, *Designing Competitive Markets for Industrial Data - Between Propertisation and Access (October 31, 2016)*. Max Planck Institute for Innovation & Competition Research Paper No. 16-13. Available at SSRN. https://ssrn.com/abstract=2862975 or doi: 10.2139/ssrn.2862975

EU Report, 2018, 'Study on data sharing between companies in Europe', by Everis Benelux commissioned by the European Commission, Directorate-General of Communications Networks, Content & Technology. doi: 10.2759/354943

Gandomi, A., & Haider M., 2015, 'Beyond the hype: Big data concepts, methods, and analytics', *International Journal of Information Management*, 35, p.137–144.

Gartner IT Glossary, n.d., 'On Big data'. http://www.gartner.com/ it-glossary/ big-data/

Gervais, D. J., 2019, 'The machine as author', *Iowa Law Review*, 105.

Heller, M., 2017, 'What deep learning really means', *Infoworld*, February 6, 2017. https://www.infoworld.com/article/3163130/what-deep-learning-really-means.html

Heller, M., 2019, 'ML algorithms explained', *Infoworld*, May 9, 2019. https://www.infoworld.com/article/3394399/machine-learning-algorithms-explained.html

Hilbert, M., & López, P., 2011, 'The world's technological capacity to store, communicate, and compute information', *Science*, 332(6025), p.60–65.

Hughes, T. P., 1983, *Networks of Power: Electrification in Western Society, 1880–1930*. Baltimore: Johns Hopkins University Press.

Lee, K.-F., 2019, *AI Superpowers: China, Silicon Valley, and the New World Order*. Boston: Houghton Mifflin Harcourt Publishing Company.

Maharana, A., Cai, K., Hellerstein, J., Hswen, Y., Munsell, M., Staneva, V., Verma, M., Vint, C., Wijaya, D. M., & Nsoesie, E., 2019, 'Detecting reports of unsafe foods in consumer product', *Journal of the American Medical Informatics Association JAMIA (JAMIA) Open*, 2(3), p.330–338. Also see a review. https://www.bu.edu/sph/2019/08/05/ai-can-predict-product-recalls-from-customer-reviews/

Martens, B., 2018, 'The importance of data access regimes for artificial intelligence and machine learning', *JRC Digital Economy Working Paper*, 2018–09, EU.

Mehta, P., Bukov, M., Wang, C. H., Day, A. G., Richardson, C., Fisher, C. K., & Schwab, D. J., 2019, 'A high-bias, low-variance introduction to ML for physicists', *Physics Reports*, 810(2019), p.1–124.

Meserole, C., 2018, 'What is ML? Part of A Blueprint for the Future of AI,' Report from the Brookings Institution.

Moyer, C., 2018, 'How Google's AlphaGo beat a go world champion'. https://www.theatlantic.com/technology/archive/2016/03/the-invisible-opponent/475611/

Nelson, R. R., 1995, 'Co-evolution of industry structure, technology and supporting institutions, and the making of comparative advantage', *International Journal of the Economics of Business*, 2(2), p.171–184.

Rahul, C. D., 2015, 'ML in medicine', *Circulation*, 132(20), p.1920–1930. https://www.ahajournals.org/doi/10.1161/CIRCULATIONAHA.115.001593

Russell, S. J., & Norvig, P., 2016, *Artificial Intelligence: A Modern Approach*. Harlow: Pearson Education Limited.

Schwenk, G., Pabst, R., & Müller, K. R., 2019, 'Classification of structured validation data using stateless and stateful features', *Computer Communications*, 138, p.54–66.

Simon, P., 2013, *Too Big to Ignore: The Business Case for Big Data* (Vol. 72). New Jersey: John Wiley & Sons.

Stepanov, I., 2020, 'Introducing a property right over data in the EU: The data producer's right – An evaluation', *International Review of Law, Computers and Technology*, 34(1), p.65–86.

Ullah, I., Raza, B., Malik, A. K., Imran, M., Islam, S. U., & Kim, S. W., 2019, 'A churn prediction model using random forest: Analysis of ML techniques for churn prediction and factor identification in telecom sector', *IEEE Access*, 7, p.60134–60149.

Varian, H., 2018, 'Artificial intelligence, economics, and industrial organization', *NBER Working Paper* No. 24839. https://www.nber.org/papers/w24839

Wiebe, A., 2017, 'Protection of industrial data – A new property right for the digital economy?', *Journal of Intellectual Property Law & Practice*, 12(1), p.62–71.

8

"OWN IT" OR "SHARE IT"

Transformations of regulatory and community norms in the Swedish housing market

Rasmus Nykvist, Andrea Geissinger and Klas A.M. Eriksson

Introduction: The role of community norms and sharing ideas on regulating the industrial transformation of the Swedish housing market

The impact of the term *sharing economy* as a socioeconomic ecosystem based on information technology is often discussed in the same way as the agrarian or industrial revolutions.[1] As a phenomenon, the peer-to-peer notion of digital sharing platforms quite literally puts community norms and sharing practices at the core of an ongoing industrial transformation. But is such sharing really a new phenomenon?

In this chapter, we argue that in the setting of Sweden, community and sharing norms as drivers for industrial transformation have deep roots in the history of the country. Williamson (2000) claims that the informal institutions of a society – such as culture, norms and code of conduct – are the most consistent and stable of all institutions, with an average lifespan of a century to a millennium. Formal institutions, however – like constitutions, laws, charters – are of a shorter lifespan, on average, a decade to a century. Many descriptions of formal and informal institutions are in line with this lifespan. For instance, economic historian Hans Sjögren, when describing different phases of Swedish capitalism from 1850 to 2005, claims that:

> The chronological description starts here, but we should keep in mind that the business system, and even the welfare capitalism of Sweden, has roots back to the medieval age.
>
> *(Sjögren, 2008, p. 24)*

During the late nineteenth and early twentieth centuries, experiments with new business models and new organizational forms instilled and moved these informal institutions further into the core of the Swedish model of welfare capitalism. Also,

German cooperative capitalism significantly influenced the formal institutions that would come to characterize Swedish welfare capitalism in the twentieth century (Carlson, 2002). However, from the end of World War II to today, our analysis indicates the model of German cooperative capitalism arguably has been gradually complemented by the model of American competitive capitalism in Sweden.

With the global success of sharing economy platforms, which often have come from the cradle of American technology innovation, Silicon Valley, changes in community norms and sharing practices as a new way of consuming goods and services are now seen as revolutionary events causing major disruption in several industries, such as in housing markets.

Surprisingly, however, something very similar has happened in Sweden in the past. With the emergence of the Swedish model of cooperative housing in the 1920s,[2] community norms took centre stage in the way Sweden related to the transformation of its cities. Consequently, in this chapter, we explore if the sharing economy of today is really built on novel grounds by comparing the historical emergence of Swedish cooperative housing with the main digital accommodation sharing platform in the world, Airbnb. Arguably, cooperatives represent a form of the sharing economy, which is and has been a prominent part of Swedish welfare capitalism during a long historical period. Aiming to understand and find common denominators for these changes, we ask, "How, in times of – and between – large industrial transformations, does the role of community norms and sharing ideas change? Furthermore, who are the actors during such transformations?"

To answer these questions, we use in-depth historical analysis based on secondary sources combined with a topic model of relevant regulatory documents from the 1920s up until the emergence of the platform-mediated sharing economy. The historical analysis uncovers how the transformational power of the contemporary sharing economy and its respective regulation is illuminated by practices from the past.

This chapter is organized as follows: first, we explain our empirical case and then briefly explain our methodological approach. We then focus on the change process of the communal housing cooperatives as well as the digital sharing platforms. Subsequently, we combine the historical analysis with a semantic analysis of official reports from government official investigations (SOUs) to shed light on the interplay between state, market and community norms. Finally, we compare the two *sharing economies of the past and the present* and offer some concluding remarks about the role of community norms in times of industrial transformation.

Historical background

Cooperatives and the sharing economy in the Swedish model

Informal institutions only change every 100–1000 years (Williamson, 2000). Despite the given cultural influence of the United States over the last 100 years, Sweden portrays an interesting version of capitalism, often referred to as the Swedish model or Swedish welfare capitalism.

During the late nineteenth and early twentieth centuries, German informal and formal institutions had a large impact on Swedish society (Sjögren, 2008; Carlson, 2002). At the time, several of the most prominent and influential social science scholars in Swedish civil society were deeply influenced by representatives of the German historical school.[3] The German historical school can be seen as proponents of community and cooperative capitalism under a conservative and nationalist political order (Carlson, 2002).[4] It is this cooperative character that takes centre stage in the Swedish model of welfare capitalism in the middle of the twentieth century and is illustrated vividly in collective agreements of almost all labour relations to large cooperative food chains, insurance cooperatives, pensions funds and, not least, housing cooperatives. Combined with the undeniable impact of the United States, it is reasonable to see the Swedish welfare capitalism of today as a mixture of American competitive capitalism and German cooperative capitalism (Sjögren, 2008).[5] During the last 100 years, the Swedish housing sector, in general, and its cooperative housing sector, in particular, exemplify this development.

The history of Swedish housing cooperatives and their connection to the sharing economy of today

The first housing cooperative was formed by a small group of workers in 1850 (Jacobsson, 2000). Still, housing cooperatives had only a minor share of the Swedish housing stock up until the 1920s. Reasons can be pinpointed to relatively functional rental markets and ownership markets in combination with weak formal legislation for housing cooperatives. This changed during World War I, however, as Sweden implemented its first rent control law in 1917. This law, which was in place until 1923, led to shortages in rental housing. Since owner apartments – a form of tenure where one buys and owns your apartment, similar to buying and owning a house – required large investments, and for many was not a feasible option. The solution of sharing the investment risk with a small group of individuals became more popular, and the housing cooperative tenure form increasingly became a relevant choice (Jörnmark, 2005). With the new housing cooperative law in 1930 (preceded by SOU 1928:16), which is still in place today, the formal legal support for housing cooperatives was strengthened.

Today, the issues of shortages of rental housing and soaring prices of housing cooperatives[6] are on every political agenda. On the one hand, issues like rent control are claimed to be causing enormous welfare losses (Boverket, 2013). On the other hand, soaring prices of housing cooperatives have led to high private debt, which is sometimes taken as a sign of a housing "bubble" (Andersson and Jonung, 2015). This development has paved the way for new sharing solutions in the housing sector through digital platforms where both the problem of accommodation shortages and increasingly unbearable prices can be avoided for many people. Hence, industrial transformation through digital technology and the sharing platform might be called upon to dampen the housing crises of today.

This is particularly interesting as there are many similarities in terms of the institutional solutions during the industrial transformation in the 1920s and today. Both situations were largely the result of a lack of rental apartments, followed by the policy of rent control and unbearable prices on another big tenure form.[7] The solutions to such issues were similar in the 1920s as they are today, namely, to adopt forms of sharing practices to solve institutional tensions that occurred after technological transformations.

The evolution of the housing market, in particular, is also similar: housing cooperatives started as a small-scale solution for communities, which gained a larger share of the housing market over time due to institutional factors and eventually led to marketization in the 1970s (Jörnmark, 2005). A similar process occurred with the platform-mediated sharing economy in the accommodation industry. First, community-oriented solutions such as Couchsurfing filled the need for individuals to find households that offered a place to stay for free. However, first, with the entrance of the global player Airbnb, did the platform-solution scale up into a widespread marketized solution for renting out living space for money. A striking difference is the absence of state management today compared with the early and middle twentieth century. These similarities – and differences – will be examined in greater detail in the next section.

Method: In-depth historical analysis and topic mapping of regulatory documents

When studying the impact of platform technologies, the recent literature provides empirical evidence of the difference in the adoption of the same platform over diverse national contexts. For example, a cross-country comparison found that sharing economy firms shape their institutional environment to gain legitimacy. In addition, the degree to which the local community needs are taken into account by international platform companies, such as Airbnb, highly depends on the regulation put in place by the national government (Uzunca et al, 2018). Meanwhile, inquiries using comparative-historical methodologies looking at the same context during different eras have provided ample descriptions of earlier technological revolutions (Mokyr, 2003; Larsen, 2010). Fewer studies researching this emerging phenomenon, however, are utilizing comparative-historical analysis to track changes and similarities over greater periods of time. Similar to other areas of the economy, the regulation of the communal housing solution, as in our case, did not happen overnight, and neither did its emergence.

By using in-depth historical analysis, we identified in a *first step* five different phases leading up to the current situation, starting and ending in regulatory proposals that with some changes were all put into law. When the Swedish government aims to change a law significantly, it appoints a government official investigation (SOU) as a prelude to the actual law proposal. These can be regarded as traceable outcomes of the specifics from each phase in the history of housing cooperatives in Sweden. Each investigation has its own purpose, but the long timescale makes the language and references used change significantly, in addition to the changes in their general view on housing cooperatives picked up by our topic mapping. In the *second step*, we use a topic modelling approach in Python with a Natural Language Tool Kit (Bird, Klein and Loper, 2009) and Gensim (Rehurek and Sojka, 2010) for each investigation for the years 1928, 1969, 1986 and two separate investigations in 2017. Following a machine learning with python approach (Li, 2018), four topics for each phase were considered as most suitable to specify and explain the corpus.[8] As a *third analytical step*, we combined insights from the two previous analyses to compare the two "sharing economies" in the Swedish housing market and draw conclusions about the role of community norms.

Development of community norms and practices over time

In the case of the establishment of the Swedish housing cooperatives, we can distinguish five chronological phases. Each phase is dominated by specific events and regulatory processes leading to the transformation of the housing sector. The focus is on how these material events affected and were affected by underlying (community) norms and practices.

Throughout the different phases, state intervention in the general housing market in the form of rent control played a pivotal part in pushing the demand for "owning" one's apartment through housing cooperatives. Over time, we looked at the causes and impact of five big government investigations (SOUs) with subsequent regulation: one in 1928, one in 1969, one in 1986 and two in 2017.[9]

Phase 1, 1917–1930: Introduction of market-driven housing cooperatives driven by rent control initiatives

World War I had created a huge boom for Swedish iron exports. By the end of the war, Sweden's economy had experienced a significant increase in exports, and all its pre-war debt had been fully repaid (Sjögren, 2008). The war can be seen as a technical, social and economic *critical juncture* – a point in time where windows of opportunity for change open up. In the case of Sweden's economy, this meant an industrial transformation through institutional and technological shifts. Partly as a result of the war and rent control system, the large-scale housing cooperative foundation HSB (Hyresgästernas sparkasse- och byggnadsförening) was formed in 1923 when rent control was abolished. On the one hand, the creation of HSB was partly due to the risk of rent becoming unbearably higher for many tenants in the short term directly after deregulation (Bengtsson, 1992). On the other hand, the greater demand for housing cooperatives was due to a shortage of rental housing under rent control (Jörnmark, 2005). HSB, which had strong ties to the social democratic party, was the first housing cooperative organization with considerable economic resources and would become a huge actor in building, saving and housing cooperative tenure during the twentieth century.

Another turning point was a new law on housing cooperatives launched in 1930, which was preceded by SOU 1928:16. The law has, in its foundations, been intact ever since, and actually, forbid other housing forms other than a tenant-owner cooperative (TOC) – the form of housing cooperative where a tenant organization owns the estate, and the individual tenants are members of the organization. As a result, rental cooperatives were not terminated, but new ones were not allowed to be built. Since the law regulated the owner structure between the cooperative and the tenant in such a way that the owner's right as a tenant was strong at the same time as the investment of real estate was able to be divided among the cooperative, it became a rather attractive alternative to both the more expensive owner-apartment and the rental housing market, which was, in short, unprofitable from 1917–1923. HSB specialized in TOC, and its dominant position strengthened during the coming years after the cooperative housing law of 1930 (Bengtsson, 1992).

Phase 2, 1940–1960s: Regulation of both rental housing and housing cooperatives

The government neither wanted to take away rent control nor wanted the rental apartment tenure to disappear. Rent control law was thus complemented with a housing cooperative control law, *BoKol*, which hindered the transformation from rental apartments to housing cooperatives. The pressing housing shortage during the 1950s and 1960s was a recurrent issue for the government. Two situations emerged: first, in his role as Sweden's minister of finance, Gunnar Sträng shifted investment from housing to foreign trade, although there was an obvious housing shortage:

> It is, of course, problematic for a socialist government to make this type of intervention, but desperate times call for desperate measures.
>
> *Gunnar Sträng*

This renegotiation of norms had a direct effect on the organization of the market as the leading policymakers and academics, including Gunnar Sträng, wanted to abolish rent control to solve the housing shortage. The Swedish tenant organization *Hyresgästföreningen* frantically opposed any attempt to deregulate the rents. Following several debates and propositions, the extensive public housing project of the "Million Program" was launched instead of deregulating the rents (Lindbeck, 2012). The institutions had then, rather than to deregulate rents, moved towards public ownership, not least in the housing corporation HSB, whose leader commented on the housing policy in this way:

> But, in principle, I do not think it is right to play with housing. It has been my ideal since the 1920s. Houses and homes should be owned, but they shall not be speculation objects.
>
> *Sven Wallander*

Without changing the core regulation of the housing association form, the structure of the market and norms surrounding the housing market had moved through a fundamental shift. Competition thus became hampered through extensive regulations, and with the publicly subsidized million programme, the state formed a coalition with the cooperative builders of HSB, SKB and Riksbyggen, which naturally gave them a strong position in the housing market working together as a producer oligopoly. For ten years, from 1965–1975, the cooperative builders of HBS, Stockholms kooperativa bostadsförening (SKB) and Riksbyggen had a leading role in the building of nearly one million apartments and small houses together with state-owned companies like Svenska bostäder (Ramberg, 2000).

Phase 3, 1970s–1990s: Deregulation of the housing market inspires the re-activation of interest in housing cooperatives

In 1967, an official government investigation (SOU 1966:14) led to a proposition that, when passed in practice, would deregulate the housing cooperatives sector and reform – but not deregulate – the price control on rental apartments. Part of the institutional pressures re-emerged as incentives for transformations from rental apartments to housing corporations became strong. This showed striking resemblances to 1917–1923 when price control was in place at a time when the market for housing solutions was still free. In Stockholm's inner city, the share of housing cooperatives increased from 12% in 1975 to 18% in 1980 and reached 25% in 1990 (Jörnmark, 2005). This shows that some of the pressures would play out in a similar way even 50 years later, albeit in an incremental way due to the lack of truly transformative pressures. As part of a gradual movement away from its community roots, the transformations from rental to housing corporations also changed the public perception of house ownership and became a lucrative business to buy rental apartments and sell them to tenants.[10] The growth of housing cooperatives was extensive during the whole period, and for the first time since the 1940s, the inner city of Stockholm actually grew, largely because of better conditions for cooperative housing development (Jörnmark, 2005; 2007). The market was overheated in the wake of the credit deregulation of 1985, which, together with other factors, produced a financial crisis in the early 1990s (Larsson and Lönnborg, 2014).

Phase 4, 1990s–2010s: Clearance of public housing stock and abolishment of subsidized housing introduces a dramatic rise in prices

The market has been favoured by the large clearance of public housing stock in the 1990s and the abolishment of subsidized public housing projects during the same time (Grabacke and Jörnmark, 2010; Meyerson, Ståhl, and Wickman, 1990). However, resistance to transformations still occurred as a political issue, and rent control has not been abolished. Nevertheless, the share of housing cooperatives in Stockholm inner city went from 25% in 1990 to 55% in 2005 (Jörnmark, 2005). Also, an oligopoly structure in the housing construction sector emerged. According to Psilander (2007), 90% of construction work was done by four large companies (NCC, Peab, Skanska, JM), even though they had higher production costs and were less flexible than small building contractors.

The prices for housing corporation apartments have gone radically up ever since the real estate bubble burst in the early 1990s, creating several debates about a possible new bubble. This is explained both by credit deregulation and excessive demand because of the shortage of rental housing partly due to rent control. A consequence of the continuation of the politically supported rent control policy on both higher prices of housing cooperatives and rental apartment shortage was the deregulation of the second-hand rental market in 2013. This allows housing cooperatives to rent out apartments at the price of the housing corporation cost, which is closer to the market price than the ordinary price-controlled rental apartments (SFS 2012:978). This institutional shift was crucial for the new sharing economy of housing that has developed since.

Phase 5, 2010s onwards: Sharing spaces digitally; rent control and deregulated second-hand market encourages digital sharing initiatives, such as the platform Airbnb[11]

On the Swedish housing market, the sharing economy was first represented by sharing platforms such as Hospitality Club and Couchsurfing that allowed individual homeowners to let other people stay in their apartments for free. Representing a small shift in the way in which short-term accommodation was organized, it was not until the platform Airbnb made it into a scalable global business model that the phenomenon of sharing economy in housing took off. As one of the first truly transformative platforms, it has consequently led to a dramatic shift in business practices by placing agency onto the individual consumer-citizen.

A defining factor of the final phase is how – unlike in the earlier phases – there were signs of the *direct* impact of technology on the regulation of the housing cooperatives. This claim of disruption coming from the platforms mainly hit the short-term accommodation industry in a small but statistically significant way (Zervas et al., 2017). The income for an apartment owner affects how much they can spend on amortization, fees and interest each month, thus compensating for part of the steep increase in living costs. Given the fact that the agency of individual owners (and the state) had already been transferred to the housing cooperative in 1930, the institutional complexity caused by Airbnb grew even more in the Swedish rental market.

From when Airbnb was first launched in Sweden, the national government and the supervision agencies have targeted the emerging sharing economy with particular oversight measures and regulation. In many countries (including

Sweden), sharing economy services are in conflict with current laws and regulations in terms of competition laws, labour market rights and legal rental and housing permits (Sundararajan, 2014; Cohen and Zehngebot, 2014; Aloisi, 2015). Even though it had been even easier to rent out apartments second hand since the new law of 2013 (SFS 2012:978), Airbnb still faces several institutional difficulties. Between 2015 and 2016, there was widespread uncertainty on how to make sure that (a) Airbnb users paid taxes and (b) that renting out short-term did not have an adverse effect on the extremely strained housing markets, specifically in the three biggest cities in Sweden of Stockholm, Gothenburg and Malmö (SOU 2017:26). On a global level, Airbnb increasingly engages in policy debates in the "home-sharing" sector to change "the very fabric of city life" with what has been coined "platform urbanism" (van Doorn, 2019).

Simultaneously, normative issues with new ways of organizing the sharing of apartments started to emerge. For example, several cases of prostitution occurred in the rented-out apartments, creating heated discussions on both social and traditional media (Geissinger et al., 2018). Especially within a setting of restricted access to housing, this tension between novel digital businesses and traditional historical institutional arrangements highlights the spark of a cultural shift. Before the emergence of digital peer-to-peer sharing, only a few individuals would allow strangers into the privacy of their own homes. Today, this has become the "new normal" in cities facing a housing shortage and soaring real estate prices.

As a summary, Table 8.1 highlights the different phases of housing cooperatives starting in the 1850s with the emergence of housing cooperatives and ending with contemporary peer-to-peer platform-mediated sharing solutions.

Gradual change of regulatory norms: From communal to individual solutions

Over 100 years, informal institutions often change only marginally and gradually (Williamson, 2000). Therefore, analysing how language is used in the regulatory considerations of the housing market highlights interesting changes led by the industrial transformations of the time. Table 8.2 shows the outcome of a topic modelling approach for the relevant governmental investigations (SOU) and highlights major shifts based on the regulatory impact of each SOU. Notably, the narrative that emerges from the analysis of topics prevalent in the respective SOU for each given period mirrors the historical narrative presented in the previous sections of this chapter. Just as at the turn of the twentieth century, new technological drivers creating critical junctures for formal institutional shifts are now once again one of the prime facilitators for disruption in the housing market.

The first (*SOU:1928*) deals with *specifying housing cooperatives* focusing on issues about ownership and boundary conditions of what constitutes a housing cooperative as well as financial statistics of housing cooperatives and communal housing as a viable option for cities.

TABLE 8.1 The different phases of housing cooperatives

	Phase 1 *1850–1930 (SOU:1928)*	*Phase 2* *1930–1970 (SOU:1969)*	*Phase 3* *1970–1990 (SOU:1986)*	*Phase 4* *1990–2010 (SOU:2017a)*	*Phase 5* *2010 onwards (SOU:2017b)*
Technology	Steam engine → Industrialization	Combustion engine → Fordism	Computer → Efficiency paradigm and neoliberalism	Digitalization → Information Society	Peer-to-peer → Marketization
Application – Impact of technology	Urbanization – People move into the cities to work in the new cities	Standardization – Houses are mass-produced in a standardized way	Deregulation – Housing cooperative prices are set by markets	Privatization – Public housing are sold off to private actors	Glocalization – Local actors use global solutions to rent out spare living space
Actor	Owners + tenants + early housing association	Oligo-cooperatives + state	Market cooperatives + real estate profiteers	Global market	Global MNC + owners
Impact	Housing shortage leads to the creation and proliferation of housing cooperatives	State legitimization of the housing cooperative leads to a massive expansion	Deregulation and state investments lead to continued expansion but open up for profiteers	Housing shortage due to massive supply/demand misfit leads to the search for new solutions	Global platforms are used to barter housing spaces of tenant-owners
Regulatory goal	Regulate the emergence of communal housing cooperatives	Facilitate apartment ownership on a large scale	Further facilitate apartment ownership at a large scale	Regulate housing cooperatives as a market	Utilize existing housing space

TABLE 8.2 Topic modelling outcome for government official investigations 1928–2017

Topics	*SOU:1928*	*SOU:1969*	*SOU:1986*	*SOU:2017a*	*SOU:2017b*
Definitions and comparisons to other organizational forms	Ownership of apartment	Specifics of housing cooperatives	Conversion process from rental to housing association	How to comply and react to changes to housing coop vs. rental apartments	Digital sharing economy as a viable option to getting your own piece of land
	Example keywords: proprietary rights, apartments, rule, housing census, statistics	*Example keywords: Comparative number, congregation, correspond*	*Example keywords: tenancy, housing community, housing applicant, land code, company, tasks*	*Example keywords: investigation, funds, proposal, rental apartment, considerations, share*	*Example keywords: Sharing Economy, scenario, estate, lawnmower*
Legal and regulatory issues	Delineation of housing cooperative	Legal situation	Legal situation during conversion from rental to housing association	How to protect yourself as an owner within a housing cooperative	Swedish politics to regulate the market in the protection of consumers
	Example keywords: general, mines, lumber mill, conditions	*Example keywords: rules, liquidation, limited company*	*Example keywords: conversion, the law, change*	*Example keywords: rules, build, association law, pledge, protection*	*Example keywords: Sweden, guidance, consumers*
Actor responsibilities and disputes	Defining and assessing the number of housing cooperatives	Specifics of coop owners	Tenants in conflict with their cooperative	Planning when moving to a new housing coop	Platform approaches to housing (user perspective)
	Example keywords: Stockholm, admittance fee	*Example keywords: Permit, value, concession, tenant-owner*	*Example keywords: tenant-owner, invalid, tenants, decision*	*Example keywords: plan, first-hand decision, rules, economic*	*Example keywords: users, platform, tourism, competition*

(*Continued*)

TABLE 8.2 (Continued)

Topics	*SOU:1928*	*SOU:1969*	*SOU:1986*	*SOU:2017a*	*SOU:2017b*
Business and market	Housing cooperative's economy	Termination of contract	Conflicts within the transformation of rental apartments to housing coops	Responsibilities towards housing coop and general market	Peer-to-peer sharing as the new collective ideal
	Example keywords: rules, ready, year	*Example keywords: prohibit, estate, sales*	*Example keywords: apartment, tenant-owner, tenant, keep, members*	*Example keywords: sales law, market impact, neglect*	*Example keywords: user, platform, individual, each other*
Overall trajectory	Focus on specifying housing cooperatives	Focus on communal aspects of cooperative housing	Focus on conflicts between rental and housing coops	Focus on protection, responsibilities and finances	Focus on consumers and markets

The second (*SOU:1969*), of which the main motivation was the removal of a price cap that had existed in the communal housing cooperatives since 1930, focuses more in-depth on the *communal aspect of cooperative housing* with specifics on the housing collective, its owners and the juridical aspects for the entry and exit of cooperatives.

The third (*SOU:1986*), however, seems to indicate a pivotal period in the history of housing cooperatives. The focal area of identified topics centres around aspects of *conflicts between the rental market and housing cooperatives*: how can rental apartments be re-classified as housing cooperatives, and how can potential conflicts of these transformations be dealt with? These tensions mark a shift in the underlying assumption of what communal housing can do for the individual. In the first half of the existence of communal housing (Phase 1 and 2), the societal baseline argument is that of an "own your house" mentality. Housing cooperatives were seen as communal options to facilitate ownership for as many people in cities as possible while staying risk-averse in the aggregate.

After the 1990s, however, topics in official investigations have undergone a shift, and the underlying societal baseline arguments have changed. The most recent (*SOU:2017a*) emphasizes more thoroughly certain *aspects of protection and responsibilities* towards both the housing cooperative and the market by safeguarding finances in both accounts.

A gradual shift from giving the communal aspects of housing cooperatives the most attention to catering to both community and market simultaneously occurred. Indeed, the investigation dealing solely with all aspects of digital sharing platforms across the whole economy *(SOU:2017b*) now focuses almost entirely on *consumers and markets*. Even though Swedish politics are specifically mentioned as a means to regulate the market and protect consumers, peer-to-peer sharing seems to be sublimely accepted as a new collective ideal that focuses rather on a "rent out your home" mentality. By drawing on the community and "sharing" with strangers, an individual orientation for personal utility becomes evident, which seems inherently different from the first sharing economy that emerged in the 1920s and 1930s.

When the topics uncovered in each SOU from 1928 up to 2017 are taken together, a gradual change in norms emerges. The historical sharing economy used a communal orientation to solve a housing shortage in Swedish cities, as indicated by the constant rise of individuals owning their apartments. In return, the contemporary sharing economy is more in line with American competitive capitalism, based on an individualistic regulatory approach that enables renting out spare space on a short-term basis.

Interestingly, as housing cooperatives have such an important stance in the set-up of Swedish society and remain a key building block for arranging housing, there is currently a large discrepancy in power dynamics. The housing cooperatives are one of the main organizing forms of housing solutions today. Similar to secondary literature on the developments, our analysis shows that during the emergence of housing cooperatives as a first sharing economy, the state itself became interested in opting for a communal solution. Compared with the contemporary situation, where the market seems to have more pull, it is the individual users of the peer-to-peer platform that engage in digital sharing activities.

In terms of norms mirroring the general development in Sweden, we find traces of the shift away from those inspired by German cooperative capitalism. The sharing platform that is beginning to transform part of the Swedish housing market – the accommodation sharing company Airbnb – rather taps into ideas from the United States, where it was founded at the heart of contemporary digital capitalism. We find that the role of competition and market considerations play an increasing part across the investigations. Hence, in light of the framework of Hans Sjögren (2008),[12] we would claim that American competitive capitalism has gradually been taking larger shares of the sharing economy of today in relation to German cooperative capitalism back in the 1920s. Here, arguments can be made that the changing industry norms identified in the documents followed a similar trajectory as they did in Norway, in line with an earlier analysis:

> Notably, cooperative housing changed gradually in both countries between the 1950s and the 1990s, when cooperative companies went from being civil society organizations espousing the ideals of self-help, democracy, non-profit and solidarity, towards becoming more market-oriented and profit-seeking.
> *(Sørvoll and Bengtson, 2018, p 124)*

One way of illustrating this transformation of issues and norms around the sharing economy of the late 1900s and early 2000s would be by saying that Sweden went from asking "You live in your apartment, so why don't you own it collectively?" in the early 1900s, to ideas of individuals helping out the collective, asking, "You own your apartment, so why don't you share it for money?" in the early 2000s.

The role of state, market and community in the two sharing economies

In this section, we explore the enabling factors of the industrial transformation processes and their impact on specific aspects of the Swedish housing market. We contrast the emergence of what we refer to as a first sharing economy in the 1920s – namely the housing cooperatives – and the contemporary (new) sharing economy after the 2010s – namely the digital platform intermediaries.

As the historical and regulatory analyses illustrate, norms gradually shifted over time. Yet, several factors were still similar between the two main periods of industrial transformation. For the analysis of these two major industrial transformations, it is crucial to understand that underlying community norms (i.e. informal institutions) have to a large extent persevered over time, while others have developed with the socioeconomic and regulatory conditions. We are interested in how individuals come together to solve problems collectively and share solutions as a community to contrast the two transformations. In other words, we focus on *how* communal sharing solutions are similar, not *what* individual practices look like in detail. In Table 8.3, we give an overview of the main differentiating dimensions between the two industrial transformations in the Swedish housing market.

The environment of the industrial transformation of the housing sector, both in the 1920s and from the 2010s onwards, shows similar *societal push factors*. In both phases, a technological revolution (the second industrial revolution in the

TABLE 8.3 A comparison of the two sharing economies

	1920s: Sharing of the burden of risk	*2010s: Sharing the burden of ownership*
Societal push	Urbanization due to industrialization; expanding cities; underutilization of living space.	Urbanization due to information society (similar to industrialization); expanding cities; underutilization of living space.
Regulatory pull	Liberal market and industrial organization spreading from the UK and continental Europe. Low entry cost and liberal market created an environment for experimentation.	Extensive neoliberal reforms partly spilling over from the UK and the United States. Low entry cost and neoliberal market created good conditions for experimentation and opportunities for private companies, e.g. so-called "regulatory entrepreneurs".
Resulting problem	High risk-taking among home buyers. Insufficient capital to buy your own home. Lack of rental housing.	Surging living prices and high demand for temporary living arrangements and lack of rental housing.
Community solution	Housing co-ownership spreading risks and demand for capital among many individual home buyers. For emerging working class.	Peer-to-peer platforms allowing individual homeowners to share their apartments for profit. Mainly for the established middle class.
Technology	Indirect impact from technology leading to industrialization and new abilities to produce houses, in turn, changing institutional conditions.	Direct technological disruption through the innovation of digital peer-to-peer platforms, in turn, leading to sharing practices and the temporal sharing of housing space.
Local regulation	Introduction of rent control leading to increased demand for people to own their apartments.	Housing market regulation behind as peer-to-peer disruption enters the market. As the new regulation is developed, the market has already outpaced the new regulatory interventions.

early twentieth century and the third industrial revolution now) sparked massive urbanization processes in cities unable to house the increase in demand, partly due to institutions like rent control holding supply back. Whereas in the 1920s the underutilization of living spaces consisted of the inability to build enough living space in time, today, the opposite situation has occurred due to the many years of rent control: the underutilization of the current housing stock in terms of many people not using their square metres/spare rooms[13] in an efficient manner (Boverket, 2013).

In terms of *regulatory pull*, the industrial revolution brought an "industrial logic" of organizing and regulating from the UK, the United States and continental Europe to Sweden. Preceding the rise of the workers' movement in Sweden, there was an opening for anyone to create a company. This affected the housing market but mainly led to the rise of many large Swedish industrial companies (Ahlström, 2013). The housing associations were proliferating as part of the workers' movement. During this quite liberal time, different organizational solutions for resolving the housing problem were tested. Today, years of partial deregulation of the housing market, in combination with only partial regulation of the emerging platform technologies, have, in turn, created ample space for experimentation by private actors. This shift towards distributed governance (Jessop, 2016, van Doorn, 2019) allows for new actors such as Airbnb, who are utilizing new technologies, to engage in "regulatory entrepreneurship", which means that part of the business is engaging in changing laws accordingly (Pollman and Barry, 2016; van Doorn, 2019).

Although the issue of limited living spaces in cities remains up to this day, there are identifiable differences over time. In the 1920s, the *resulting problem* centred around low living standards and overcrowded apartments (Nylander, 2013). The people who needed housing could not afford to own it or did not have access to the rental market because of rent control (Jörnmark, 2005). Even today, rent control still has a regulatory pull. But instead of overcrowding and low living standards, the opposite, *resulting problem* has emerged: today, rent control has led to a waste of living space (Boverket, 2013) because of weak incentives for people with large rental apartments to change to a smaller one, as these are either hard to get or more expensive. Platforms like Airbnb thus offer a mechanism that turns citizens into micro-entrepreneurs by offering monetary incentives to individuals to rent out their spare rooms to high demand.

While the *solution* to formalize and regulate the emerging communal housing was a key issue already from the start, the scalable solutions were following the logic of equipping workers with a place to live, meaning that the new communal housing projects provided very small apartments to a lot of people (who would otherwise not be able to afford it). Today, an emerging solution is formed by digital platforms acting as an intermediary between those who cannot afford housing and others who need to rent a room or apartment short-term. In terms of new formal institutions being part of the solution, the development of this "sharing economy" is still in an emerging phase. While adequate regulation and regulatory interventions take time to develop, the current digital innovation shows no signs of slowing down. In particular, Swedish regulators have often not been able to keep up with the pace of technological advancement, especially not under conditions where political majorities and special interest organizations gain from the *status quo*.

In the 1920s, *discontinuous technology* was indirectly affecting the housing market as industrialization changed the institutional conditions at play. In addition, World War I created a setting where the housing stock was tested to its limit, leading to a real sense of urgency; incentives for new housing construction during wartime is a classical problem, leading to rent souring and thus a demand for rent control. The rent control launched in 1917 through the "rent increase law" (SFS, 1917:219) has ever since acted as an enduring institution affecting the housing market throughout the different phases up until today. In light of current developments, it can be argued that an "information age" revolution (Castells, 1997; Venkatraman, 2014) may start to proliferate into collaborative practices and digital platforms, enabling a new type of social and economic activity (Laamanen et al., 2018).

Overall, it was a combination of societal push factors as well as regulatory and technological pull factors that sparked the increasing amount of novel housing communities, and, in turn, created the need for (further) *local regulation*. Eventually, the Swedish state aided the housing cooperative to really take off in terms of adoption rate, due to the high level of state support in favour of new housing projects throughout the 1900s and leading to the possibility for individuals to share the *burden of risk* of owning their (expensive) apartment. Today, the combination of discontinuous technology and slowly moving regulatory frameworks has created an abundance of sharing or renting parts of houses or apartments, allowing for individuals to share the *burden of ownership* (Moeller and Wittkowski, 2010; Schaefers, Lawson and Kukar-Kinney, 2016) by abiding by inherent rules of community and belonging of the contemporary Zeitgeist.

While seeing completely different answers to a similar housing shortage problem, both the past as well as the present have collective *sharing practices as the common denominator* in their respective contexts. As we can see in both phases, solutions from the periphery often stem from a community orientation, which forms as a result of experimentations at the edge of the field. Such solutions, in turn, are often characterized by institutional lock-ins, when the state and the market move in synchronicity to adopt those communal practices into their respective domains. Hence, community norms and sharing practices seem to function as a solution to uncertainty stemming from industrial transformations and technological revolutions, which become visible in our analysis of the housing market in Sweden for almost a century. This process for Swedish housing is illustrated in detail in Figure 8.1 following the framework by Venkatraman (2014), in which periods of experimentation at the edge are followed by a period of the collision of norms at the core, and finally, reinvention at the root.

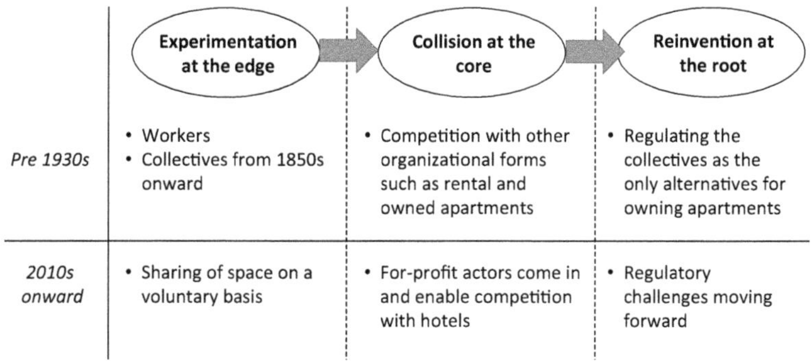

FIGURE 8.1 Process of industrial transformation and regulation in the Swedish housing market (illustrated in the two main analytical periods) using the taxonomy ofVenkatraman (2014).

"Sharing risk" versus "sharing ownership": An interaction between formal and informal factors

In this chapter, we have investigated how the community norms of the industrial transformation of the Swedish housing market instigated sharing practices throughout history. Analysing the transformation in the Swedish housing market by shining light on contemporary phenomena through the lens of in-depth historical contexts, our analyses create awareness about the necessity to reflect upon the core values and norms upon which key informal and formal institutions of any civil society are built upon. We show that similar institutional solutions have emerged as an outcome of different industrial transformations. While housing cooperatives emerged to collectively share the *burden of risk* involved with owning apartments in the city in the 1930s, the current informal institutions of today's sharing economy focus on access-over-ownership (Bardhi and Eckhardt, 2012) and are aimed to collectively share the *burden of ownership* (Moeller and Wittkowski, 2010; Schaefers, Lawson and Kukar-Kinney, 2016). By comparing these two, albeit quite different, versions of sharing economies in the housing sector with each other, we summarized our findings in the following four points.

First, whereas solutions from the socioeconomic system from the past were largely based on German cooperative capitalism, the sharing economy practices of today are to a larger extent based on American competitive capitalism. Even though the Swedish model is considered unique in many regards, the combination of strong cooperative norms with competitive norms, are, of course, not idiosyncratic of only Sweden.

Second, we show that the gradual change of formal and informal institutions induced by sharing practices in cooperatives of the 1920s as well as the platform-mediated sharing practices of today have both transformed the housing and accommodation markets in their respective time. It is paramount to understand the evolution of formal and informal institutions to understand the direction of industrial transformation, both today and in our history.

Third, the strength of the digital sharing economy lies in rediscovering certain informal institutions, for example, community norms, while at the same time offering the individual the freedom to choose community-based solutions. However, oftentimes, platform-mediated sharing actors in Sweden and elsewhere follow global trends by engaging in this particular type of "platform urbanism" (van Doorn, 2019) by using the market to solve problems mainly for the middle class; however, this somewhat neglects low-income citizens and other vulnerable groups in society who might benefit most from cooperative and community-based solutions (Cansoy and Schor, 2016).

Fourth, in the debate about the future of city life, we need to keep in mind that just as at the turn of the twentieth century, new technological drivers and institutional shifts are once again one of the prime facilitators for disruption, creating critical junctures for formal institutional shifts (Mokyr, 2003). We have given an overview of how formal and informal institutions have developed since the first industrial transformation. If new formal institutions are in line with the current state of the informal institutions, they are more likely to be successful – whether they are based on German cooperative capitalism, American competitive capitalism or something else.

Notes

1 For an overview of related concepts, see Acquier et al., 2017. In this chapter, we define the sharing economy as *"a socioeconomic ecosystem that commonly uses information technology to connect different stakeholders – individuals, companies, governments, and others – to share or access different products and services to enable collaborative consumption"* (Laamanen et al., 2018, 213, italics in original).
2 Housing cooperatives as a tenant form have been in place since 1850 (Jacobsson, 2000) but did not gain traction until the 1920s.
3 Some of them, like Gustav Cassel, Knut Wicksell, Gustav Steffen and Otto Järte, had studied directly under one of their most prominent leaders, Adolf Wagner (Carlsson p. 167).
4 Two of the most famous proponents of the German Historical Schools in Sweden were the political scientist and nationalist Rudolf Kjellén as well as sociologist and social democrat Gustav Steffen. Both Steffen and Kjellén are claimed to have had a significant influence on the "four architects" of the Swedish model: Per-Albin Hansson, Gustav Möller, Ernst Wigforss and Gunnar Mydal. Gunnar Myrdal's son, Jan Myrdal, even claimed that Kjellén had more influence on his father's development than Marx and Keynes (Carlsson, 2002).
5 Besides German cooperative capitalism and American competitive capitalism, Sjögren (2008) also adds British private capitalism as a part of Swedish capitalism today.
6 Hence, the same tenure solution for avoiding the souring prices on owner apartments in the 1920s.
7 At that time, *owner apartments* had the same legal structure as owning a single-family house.
8 After processing and clearing the data (e.g. lemmatizing, tokenizing, stemming, deleting stop words), we connected the data into a by-of words corpus and asked LDA to

find four, five and seven topics. We visualized each topic with pyLDAvis to get an understanding of how the topic spread and with the least amount of overlap. In the end, four topics were chosen, and the descriptive title for each topic emerged iteratively.

9 SOU:2017a deals with a continuation of governmental investigations about housing cooperatives, while SOU:2017b focuses on the digitally enabled sharing economy in Sweden.

10 This was the time when the word "real estate wolf", or "fastighetsklippare", became a common word in the Swedish language. A major actor in this transformation process was Adam Backström, a real estate trader, who with exceptional entrepreneurial ability, took advantage of the transformation from rental apartments to housing cooperatives, which took place during the regulatory shift of 1969. In 1973, only four years after deregulation, he had managed to create one of Sweden's biggest stock of inner-city apartments and had become the major owner of Skaraborgsbanken and one of the biggest real estate companies on the Stockholm stock exchange, Credo.

11 We focus on Airbnb as the prime example of a platform-mediated sharing economy solution for sharing accommodation and living space because of its scalability. This particular platform opened up the market for solutions revolving around the community. In addition, in the description and analysis in this chapter, we will also focus solely on the Airbnb hosts that rent out part of their actual living space, i.e. we deliberately ignore hosts that are renting apartments as a part of a larger investment strategy.

12 Sjögren (2008) distinguishes between German cooperative capitalism, American competitive capitalism and British private capitalism.

13 Square metres per person increased when HSB started to build for the masses during the twentieth century (Nylander, 2013, p 43–47). The issue of overcrowding was alleviated during the twentieth century, partly because of a sharing economy solution both in line with technological transformations and overcoming insufficient formal institutions. Today, we have the opposite problem, with too many square metres per person, leading to inefficient utilization of the current housing stock due to the price control of rental housing (Boverket, 2013). The sharing economy of today is thus able to solve the opposite problem; again, solving insufficient formal institutions through technological transformations, hence the digital sharing economy.

References

Acquier, A., Daudigeos, T., and Pinkse, J., 2017, 'Promises and Paradoxes of the Sharing Economy: An Organizing Framework', *Technological Forecasting and Social Change*, 125(December), 1–10.

Ahlström, G., 2013, 'Världsutställningarna, teknologin och den industriella utvecklingen - Sverige under 1800-talet i ett internationellt perspektiv', *Centrum för näringslivshistoria*, 7, 43–59.

Aloisi, A., 2015, 'Commoditized Workers: Case Study Research on Labor Law Issues Arising from a Set of on-Demand/gig Economy Platforms', *Comparative Labor Law & Policy Journal*, 37, 653.

Andersson, F., and Jonung, L., 2015, 'Krasch, boom, krasch? Den svenska kreditcykeln', *Ekonomisk debatt*, 8(43), 17–31.

Bardhi, F., and Eckhardt, G. M., 2012, 'Access-Based Consumption: The Case of Car Sharing', *Journal of Consumer Research*, 39(4), 881–898.

Bengtsson, B., 1992, *Not the Middle Way but Both Ways: Cooperative Housing in Sweden*. Gävle: National Swedish Institute for Building Research.

Bird, S., Klein, E., and Loper, E., 2009, Natural *Language Processing with Python: Analyzing Text with the Natural Language Toolkit*. Sebastopol, CA: O'Reilly Media, Inc.

Boverket, 2013, *Bostadsbristen och hyressättningssystemet: ett kunskapsunderlag: marknadsrapport.* Karlskrona: Boverket.

Cansoy, M., and Schor, J., 2016, 'Who Gets to Share in the "Sharing Economy": Understanding the Patterns of Participation and Exchange in Airbnb.' Unpublished Paper, Boston College.

Carlson, B., 2002, *Ouvertyr till folkhemmet: Wagnerska tongångar i förra sekelskiftets Sverige.* Lund: Nordic Academic Press.

Castells, M., 1997, *End of Millennium: The Information Age: Economy, Society and Culture.* Cambridge, MA: Blackwell Publishing, Inc.

Cohen, M., and Zehngebot, C., 2014, What's Old Becomes New: Regulating the Sharing Economy', *Boston Bar Journal*, 58(2), 69.

van Doorn, N., 2019, 'A New Institution on the Block: On Platform Urbanism and Airbnb Citizenship', *New Media & Society,* 22(10), 1808–1826.

Geissinger, A., Nykvist, R., and Laurell, C., 2018, 'Institutional Orders in the Sharing Economy: Community as an Answer to the State-Market-Interlock', in *Academy of Management Proceedings*, p. 17365. Briarcliff Manor, NY: Academy of Management.

Grabacke, C., and Jörnmark, J., 2010, 'The Political Construction of the 'Million Housing Programme': The State and the Swedish Building Industry', in Lundin, P., Stenlås, N., & Gribbe, J. (eds.), *Science for Welfare and Warfare: Technology and State Initiative in Cold War Sweden*, pp. 233–249. Sagamore Beach, MA: Science History Publications.

Jacobsson, E., 2000, *Till eget gagn-till andras nytta: en komparativ studie av allmännyttigt byggande i Stockholm fram till år 1940.* Dissertation, Stockholm University.

Jessop, B, 2016, *The State: Past, Present, Future.* Cambridge: Polity Press.

Jörnmark, J., 2005, 'Bostadsrätterna, allmännyttan och lagarna', *Ratio Working Papers*, 75, Ratio Institute.

Jörnmark, J., 2007, *Bostadsrättens segertåg - en uppsats om bostadsrätten och dess betydelse för Stockholms utveckling.* Fastighetsägarna.

Laamanen, T., Pfeffer, J., Rong, K., and Van de Ven, A., 2018, 'Editors' Introduction: Business Models, Ecosystems, and Society in the Sharing Economy', *Academy of Management Discoveries*, 4(3), 213–219.

Larsen, E., 2010, *Creating Nordic Capitalism: The Business History of a Competitive Periphery.* Susanna Fellman, Martin Jes Iversen, Hans Sjögren, and Lars Thue, eds. New York: Palgrave Macmillan.

Larsson, M., and Lönnborg, M., 2014, *Finanskriser i Sverige.* Lund: Studentlitteratur.

Li, S., 2018, *Topic Modelling in Python with NLTK and Gensim.* https://towardsdatascience.com/topic-modelling-in-python-with-nltk-and-gensim-4ef03213cd21.

Lindbeck, A., 2012, *Ekonomi är att välja: memoarer,* 121–131. Stockholm: Bonnier.

Meyerson, P.-M., Ståhl, I., and Wickman, K., 1990, *Makten över Bostaden.* Stockholm: SNS Förlag.

Moeller, S., and Wittkowski, K., 2010, 'The Burdens of Ownership: Reasons for Preferring Renting', *Managing Service Quality: An International Journal*, 20(2), 176–191.

Mokyr, J., 2003, 'Thinking about Technology and Institutions', *Macalester International*, 13(1), 8.

Nylander, O., 2013, *Svensk Bostad 1850–2000.* Lund: Studentlitteratur.

Psilander, K., 2007, 'Why Are Small Developers More Efficient than Large Developers?', *Journal of Real Estate Portfolio Management*, 13(3), 257–267.

Pollman, E., and Barry, J. M., 2016, 'Regulatory Entrepreneurship', *Southern Californian Law Review*, 90, 383–448.

Ramberg, K., 2000, *Allmännyttan: välfärdsbygge 1850–2000.* Stockholm: Byggförl. i samarbete med Sveriges allmännyttiga bostadsföretag (SABO).

Rehurek, R., and Sojka, P., 2010, 'Software Framework for Topic Modelling with Large Corpora', in *Proceedings of the LREC 2010 Workshop on New Challenges for NLP Frameworks*. Valetta: University of Malta, 46–50.

SCB – Statistiska centralbyrån, 2019, *Bostadsbestånd efter hustyp, upplåtelseform och region (omräknad) 1990–2018*.

Schaefers, T., Lawson, S. J., and Kukar-Kinney, M., 2016, 'How the Burdens of Ownership Promote Consumer Usage of Access-Based Services', *Marketing Letters*, 27(3), 569–577.

SFS - Svensk författningssamling, 1917, *Lag om oskälig hyresstegring*, 1917:219.

SFS - Svensk författningssamling, 2012, *Lag om uthyrning av egen bostad*, 2012:978.

Sjögren, H., 2008, 'Welfare Capitalism: The Swedish Economy, 1850–2005', in Fellman, Susanna (ed.), *Creating Nordic Capitalism: The Business History of a Competitive Periphery*. Basingstoke: Palgrave Macmillan.

Sørvoll, J., and Bengtsson, B., 2018, 'The Pyrrhic Victory of Civil Society Housing? Co-Operative Housing in Sweden and Norway', *International Journal of Housing Policy*, 18(1), 124–142.

Sundararajan, A., 2014, *Peer-to-Peer Businesses and the Sharing (Collaborative) Economy: Overview, Economic Effects and Regulatory Issues*. Written testimony for the hearing titled The Power of Connection: Peer to Peer Businesses.

Uzunca, B., Coen Rigtering, J. P., and Ozcan, P., 2018, 'Sharing and Shaping: A Cross-Country Comparison of How Sharing Economy Firms Shape Their Institutional Environment to Gain Legitimacy', *Academy of Management Discoveries*, 4(3), 248–272.

Venkatraman, V., 2014, *The Digital Matrix: New Rules for Business Transformation through Technology*. Vancouver: Greystone Books.

Williamson, O., 2000, 'The New Institutional Economics: Taking Stock, Looking Ahead', *Journal of Economic Literature*, 38(3), 595–613.

Zervas, G., Proserpio, D., and Byers, J. W., 2017, 'The Rise of the Sharing Economy: Estimating the Impact of Airbnb on the Hotel Industry', *Journal of Marketing Research*, 54(5), 687–705.

9

INDUSTRIAL TRANSFORMATION IN THE ANTHROPOCENE

Staffan Laestadius

Introduction

The industrial world and the epoch in human society that may be labelled modernity is based on activities that emit greenhouse gases, primarily carbon dioxide (CO_2) and methane (CH_4). After more than two centuries of growing addiction to carbon, humankind is now approaching the limits of the carrying capacity of the planet to absorb further emissions and still maintain reasonable conditions for human life as we are used to.

We are thus, whether we like it or not, facing a great transformation of our way to organize life and activities. This transformation may be *reactive*, i.e. responding to the growing amount, magnitude and consequences of extreme events in the atmosphere, the biosphere and the hydrosphere that already can be observed around us. But it may also be *proactive*, i.e. based on mitigation activities which by intention are introduced to reduce the climate change caused by our impact on the planet.

This chapter is about the magnitude and speed of adaptation and mitigation activities and processes necessary to maintain a Planet for Humans. The focus is on industrial transformation and the role of technical change although it should be reminded that the transformation ahead must, and will, include much more than industry and technology. These other aspects will be present indirectly and analysed through an industrial and technical lens. This chapter, thus, contains only parts of the story. The ambitious reader is advised to consult the reference list for a broader perspective.

The ambition of this chapter is twofold. On the one hand, to put the attention among young scholars to the largest and most urgent transformation in human history, something most academics will have to work with during their future careers, whether they have planned for that or not. This may be labelled the *industrial ambition*. On the other hand, the ambition is to illustrate and analyse the usefulness and shortcomings of the industrial dynamics toolbox. This may be called the *pedagogic ambition*.

The chapter is structured as follows. In "Analysing industrial and technical change", we focus on the theoretical points of departure as regards analysing industrial and technical change, i.e. what we label *industrial dynamics*. This is our methodological section. The third section contains the core concepts and definitions used as regards our analytical focus. "The speed and magnitude of planetary change" summarizes the magnitude and speed of the anthropogenic planetary processes that here are assumed to be of relevance for the industrial analysis. The aggregate consequences for industry and policy of the rapid planetary change are summarized in the fifth section: if the climate crisis is taken seriously – what is outlined there is roughly what has to be done. That section may be looked upon as providing the conditions for the industrial transformation and technical change discussed in the subsequent sections.

"Core industrial issues in the transformation ahead: Three cases" contains three cases illustrating the core industrial issues related to the climate crisis. The final section summarizes and concludes.

The chapter, which has the character of a forward-looking essay, is to a large extent based on my research on the conditions and potential for structural change in the Anthropocene, as reported primarily in my earlier publications, which also contain more detailed references to primary sources than are delivered here (Laestadius, 2013; 2015, 2018, 2021). There are many phenomena challenging the dominant industrial regime. Here, I focus on those related to the Anthropocene – leaving the other challenges to my co-authors in the rest of the book.

Analysing industrial and technical change

In this chapter, we are interested in systems that change, have changed and/or must be transformed. We can identify global systems as well as national and regional ones. We can identify economies, technologies, industries and even firms as systems and focus on certain aspects like innovation, capabilities or competitiveness. Detailed typologies can be found in most basic texts on innovation theory and industrial and technical change (Fagerberg, Mowery & Nelson, 2005). Here, we restrict ourselves to a few comments on the fundamentals, bearing in mind that the transformation ahead is huge.

Although the cross-disciplinary research tradition of industrial dynamics has strong connections with disciplines like economic history, history of science/technology, economic geography, business and industrial economics and sociology, its strong relations with economic theory should be emphasized. Not least, the consequence of the Schumpeterian origin of innovation theory and economic development.

The main heritage from Schumpeterian economics is its strong focus on those economic processes – which Schumpeter labels innovations – that are destabilizing the economy, which distort the strong equilibrium processes and thus contribute to processes of *creative destruction*, i.e. destroys parts of the old and creates new structures on their ruins (Schumpeter, 1934/1968; 1942/2000). Schumpeter's innovation concept was broad, rather a concept for *intentional change* of all aspects in the economy; technology was only one aspect among many. Schumpeter was not alone. Already Alfred Marshall, one of the early synthesizers of modern economics, was worried about how to combine the dynamics of industrial creativity with equilibrium theory (Marshall, 1890/1990; Laestadius, 1992).

Although orthodox economics – with its significant potential for strict mathematical modelling – has retained a strong position in many areas of economic analyses; scholars focusing on innovation and change have to a large extent abandoned equilibrium analyses in favour of *evolutionary economics*, which primarily is inspired by Schumpeter but also by general evolutionary theory (Nelson & Winter, 1982; Nelson, 2018).

Evolutionary theory has an obvious role in our understanding of how societies, economies, industries and technologies transform – and have transformed and developed since the industrial revolution in general and after World War II in particular. This transformation is analysed below from an anthropogenic lens. Here, we shortly discuss what evolutionary theory is about – and not.

Although the differences between evolution in the biosphere and the economic system/technosphere should not be neglected, economists and biologists agree on the *variety – selection – retention* sequence in the evolutionary process (Nelson & Winter, 1982; Mayr, 2001). In short, as selection, in general, takes place within the variety which is or has been created through breeding (in the biosphere) or innovation (in the techno-economic system) this evolution is basically a process of *adaptation* to what is at hand – or, for intentional actors, perceived to be the best strategy for action – and *not necessarily a process of progress.*

In short, the intentional improvements behind the evolutionary processes in society – the economy, the industry, the technosphere, etc. – are conditioned by the dominating thought worlds, our fundamental beliefs on humankind and nature. This is what the extensive literature on *paradigms* in general – but also in relation to technology – is about (cf. e.g. Kuhn, 1962; Dosi, 1982; Nelson & Winter, 1977; Perez, 2010). The *Great Acceleration*, discussed in "Concepts and definitions", may thus be argued to have contributed to, as well as have been fuelled by, fundamental beliefs that this process of exponential growth on all fronts was a natural phenomenon – and forever.

This also means that some scholarly statements that evolutionary economics/theory is the tool for understanding the successive mastering of nature by humankind, and that technological change is similar to "advance" or "progress", is only part of the story (cf. e.g. Dosi & Nelson, 2018). As is the case in the biosphere, processes also controlled by human societies – large-scale systems as well as individual technologies – may, for decades and even centuries, get locked in and develop ("advance") along self-propelling paths towards *cul-de-sacs* (Arthur,

1994; David, 1985; Unruh, 2000). A classic example is the closure in the early twentieth century of automotive technology on gasoline-driven combustion engines rather than on electricity or biofuels (Anderson & Anderson, 2010).

Analyses of transformation and change must handle the distinction between the system as a whole and its parts/sectors. The challenge ahead for humankind is to reduce and ultimately eliminate all climate-destroying human activities and industrial sectors. All the others may flourish. This may, or may not, be compatible on an aggregate level with what we traditionally label "economic growth". Growth, thus, may be looked upon as a secondary and *dependent variable* and not a primary target for policy.

The Italian economist Luigi Pasinetti has developed a tool to handle this kind of analytical problem (Pasinetti, 1981/2009). Basically, he expands a traditional Keynesian one sector model to several sectors to make it possible to *grasp the interplay between declining and expanding sectors*. It may be argued that Pasinetti thus incorporates a Schumpeterian perspective of creative destruction in the Keynesian world. For our purposes here we adopt the structure of the Pasinetti model, but instead of sectors, we identify *activities*. By that, we recognize that most sectors may contain activities that are more or less dirty and that a structural transformation may take place *within* sectors/industries/firms as well as *between* them. In addition, we make no explicit distinction between whether these activities take place on the demand side or the supply side in the economy. The distinction between demand and supply used by economists is of no importance in the analysis of greenhouse gas (GHG) emissions. The details of this reformulation of the Keynes/Pasinetti models are left to another paper.

Our modified and simple model – earlier presented in Laestadius (2013, 2015, 2018) – can be written like this:

$$Y = D_s + D_{se} + D_c$$

Where

Y = total activity level

D_s = green activities (goods) = all non-climate-destroying activities

D_{se} = sustainability enabling activities = activities that may be climate disturbing in themselves but intend to enable sustainability

D_c = black activities (bads) = all climate-destroying activities

Using this simple framework, the transformation, which we will discuss in more depth ahead, is a question of reducing and ultimately eliminating all black activities and sectors. At best, this transformation can be combined with the creation and development of green activities to maintain or even increase the total activity level of the economy. As this transformation will necessitate significant investments in infrastructure, here labelled sustainability enabling (D_{se}) – like railroads – that may, in the short run, increase GHG emissions. As a consequence, the black activities have to be reduced still faster depending on what climate targets are formulated. As investment activities normally emit twice as much CO_2 for each euro spent as consumption, it may be concluded that an ambitious green investment programme on, for example, €50 billion, must be compensated for with a reduction of "black consumption" with twice that amount (Alfredsson & Malmeus, 2019, 2020).

The challenge is to obtain incentives and "drivers" for the transformation to come. Market forces will not be enough to steer away from the present path of fossil dependence. Present prices do not reflect the threat to the planet from industrial activity or the use of its output. Neither do those market actors who set the prices have well-founded visions of the externalities they are causing the planet: the deeper dependence on fossil fuel for an actor the stronger resistance, normally, to expect towards change. And we may expect – and will have to enforce – significant destruction of old structures and systems. At best we can – in line with Schumpeterian reasoning – also stimulate the creation of new, and sustainable, ones. There is no guarantee that this creative destruction will take place in equilibrium, i.e. that new activities will balance those that are closed down.

This process will necessitate a *strong policy aiming for structural change and transformation*. Market signals have to be changed using taxation, fees and regulation, as well as contributing to a new mindset in relation to nature among economic actors. Subsidies are often a more popular tool among politicians than taxes – they do not explicitly create losers – but the transformation ahead is probably the largest in the history of humankind and cannot be driven by subsidies. Decades of neoliberal economic thinking and policy have contributed to a neglect of the fact that governments historically and also in our time have played a significant role not only in infrastructure and technical change but also in the conditions for industrial and entrepreneurial dynamics (Magnusson, 2005; Mazzucato, 2011 & 2016; Zamagni, 2017). The present strong neoliberal position among economists and policy makers has also been based on the – often implicit – assumption of no or negligible externalities distorting price mechanisms. The climate crisis, the decline of populations and species in the biosphere and the rapid accumulation of plastics in nature illustrate the consequences of this neglect.

Whereas the Pasinetti approach may be a variety of Keynesian macroeconomic theory, the *Development Block* (DB) approach introduced by Erik Dahmén may be labelled a *meso-economic* formulation inspired by Joseph Schumpeter as well by two Swedish structural economists, Johan Åkerman and Ingvar Svennilson (Dahmén, 1950; Laestadius, 2016). There is a family resemblance between the Pasinetti and Dahmén approaches: they both analyse the interplay between mechanisms behind the expansion and contraction of sectors (Pasinetti) and blocks (Dahmén). Here we choose to translate their analyses to activities.

A DB is a segment, or subsystem, of the economy with strong connections/relations as regards markets, deliveries and supply/value chains as well as technological and institutional interdependencies. This is not the same as an industry. As the logic of identification of industries is different from DBs, the latter may be related to segments of several different but related industries. The drivers – incentive structures – in the DB are the *tensions* created by the uneven development primarily on an industrial and technological level within a DB. Dahmén identifies these tensions as *necessities* and *opportunities* to which old, as well as new, actors in the DB respond, and often overreact, thus creating new tensions. His study may be looked upon as one of the first empirically based studies on Schumpeterian dynamics. The tensions may be related to expanding as well as contracting markets/sectors and these in their turn may be more or less related to new innovations that may be technological as well as non-technological in kind. And there is also room for policy in this model. Governments may, for example, favour technology shifts and/or expansion of certain markets (Laestadius, 2016). The DB approach has a family resemblance with the *salient/reverse salient* model introduced by Thomas Hughes (1983). Both approaches have their point of departure in the fact that disequilibrium, not equilibrium, is the normal state – and also the driver – in industrial and technological change. This is a core notion in Schumpeterian economics.

Large-scale transformations are normally credited to the development and diffusion of *general purpose technologies* (GPT); and here we may give "technology" a broad definition, close to "knowledge" (Lipsey, Carlaw & Bekar, 2005). The first industrial revolution was based on the enlightened introduction of science, industrial organization and coal, primarily around the steam engine. The second added electricity, oil and advanced steel manufacturing. The discourse on whether it makes sense to talk about a third – or even fourth – industrial revolution or not can be left to another paper (cf. Rifkin, 2011/2013; Brynjolfsson & McAfee, 2016) but it may, however, be argued that the post-World War II development of IC technology – in combination with the upscaling of the oil-based economy – created the conditions for a globalized industrial transformation; not least for emerging economies.

Although bio-based technologies may play a significant role as another and new general purpose – and potentially sustainable – technology, the transformation in the decades ahead will differ from those we have experienced since the industrial revolution, and in particular since World War II. The main difference is that the exponential growth of industrial metabolism has changed the conditions of human activities from being small in an almost unlimited space to becoming large scale on a finite planet.

Concepts and definitions

The expression *Anthropocene* is normally assumed to have been introduced in 2002 by Paul Crutzen and further developed in later publications by him and others (Crutzen, 2002; Steffen et al., 2007; Steffen et al., 2018). Although geologists still discuss the stratigraphic definition of the concept, there seems to be a *de facto* convergence among scholars around two different starting points for this recently identified (or suggested) epoch for the planet, both of which have relevance for the analysis in this chapter:

1. *The first half of the nineteenth century*, when the steam engine became common, not only in stationary use but also in mobile solutions like ships and, not least, in railways. This is also a period characterized by population increase, increased production of food (not least, rice) and a transformation of the American continent, activities all of which had an impact on climate.
2. *The Great Acceleration,* which is the name given by Steffen et al. (2004) on the period starting after World War II and continuing into our century. Not only is this a period of exceptional economic growth in the history of humankind but also a period when human exploitation of nature increased exceptionally and exponentially. The extraction of minerals as well as fossil fuels has doubled every 25 years between 1940 and 2015 (Laestadius, 2018).

Following the OECD based economic historian Angus Maddison, the early nineteenth century is also the origin of *modernity* (Maddison, 2005). The introduction of the steam engine favoured the rapid expansion of world trade as well as long-distance travelling. Rapidly growing railway networks made continents smaller and steamships facilitated the migration between them. Millions of Europeans travelled between European capitals or left the continent for the Americas. This early phase of globalization also contributed to a feeling, or rather culture, of progress and humanity mastering nature (Laestadius, 2018).

Superficially, the Great Acceleration after World War II is a quantitative rather than qualitative jump in the same direction; enforced by the rapid expansion of telecommunications, air travel and large-scale sea transport. But an in-depth analysis of human activities and their impact on the planet reveals that humankind during this period, from a resource perspective, entered the second half of the chessboard. If the consequences of human activity could be neglected when human societies were small on a large planet this is no longer the case when humankind is large, and its activity level is approaching the boundaries of the planet. The exponential growth of resource exploitation has been the norm for more than seven decades in almost every sphere entered by humankind.

The impact of the intensified exploitation of planetary resources could be neglected for a long time due to technical change. Global reserves have often, paradoxically, been *growing*: new and often energy-intensive means to excavate, mine and harvest the resource base have for a long time more than compensated for its extraction (cf. Zimmerman, 1933/1951; Barnet & Morse, 1963). This is also the case with oil. The global reserves are, after 20 years of all-time high production, 36% higher in 2019 than in 1999 (BP, 2020).

This way of looking upon natural resources more or less as social constructs, and the results of engineering progress, may have been relevant for decades. However, sooner or later that day comes when the finiteness of the planet becomes visible also for those who initially neglected it. The irony is that the planetary boundaries have not revealed themselves primarily in a growing shortage of classical "non-renewable" resources like iron ore, copper or fossil fuels – not even oil or gas – but in a shortage of planetary space to store the rest of the products, primarily greenhouse gases (GHGs) like carbon dioxide (CO_2) and methane (CH_4) in the atmosphere and plastics in the oceans. Humankind is now also running short of "renewable systems" like bees, biodiversity, vertebrates, fresh water and rainforests rather than bauxite – or coal.

The speed and magnitude of planetary change

The speed and magnitude of human impact on the planet will – unless we rapidly change present habits – create conditions for human life of which humanity has no experience. Large parts of the globe will be uninhabitable either because of heatwaves and drought or of a much higher sea level. Some places may also be uninhabitable due to higher frequencies and magnitudes of storms, rains and floods. In a presentation of a WMO report recently, the WMO general secretary Petteri Talas summarized the situation as follows:

> The last time the Earth experienced a comparable concentration of CO_2 was 3–5 million years ago when the temperature was 2–3°C warmer and sea level was 10–20 meters higher than now.
>
> *(WMO, 2018)*

In addition, there are indications that during the Eemian period (approx. 125,000 years ago), when the temperature was roughly similar to the present one, the sea level was 6–9 m higher than the present. This was probably due to the melting of parts of the West Antarctic (Voosen, 2018).

Although the discourse on planetary boundaries relates to more than a dozen critical and related topics and the UN 2030 agenda includes 17 areas, we will focus on three interrelated topics: climate change, loss of biodiversity and plastic pollution (Rockström et al. 2009; UN, 2015). With no intention to neglect other items, like, for example, water shortage and the abuse of antibiotics, the development of the three mentioned areas is more than enough to illustrate the relation between man and nature and the consequences for conventional wisdom as regards how we organize industrial activities as well as our welfare societies in the decades to come.

The global mean temperature in the atmosphere is steadily increasing and is now roughly 1.2°C higher than during the nineteenth century. This increase, which also spills over to the sea (where most of the energy is stored), is basically caused by anthropogenic emissions of GHGs of which CO_2 and CH_4 are the most important. These emissions – in particular, long-lived CO_2 molecules – accumulate in the atmosphere. The average CO_2 content in the atmosphere is now 414 ppm, which is 48% above the preindustrial level. The level of CO_2 presently increases with a speed of 2.6 ppm/year, which is three times the speed registered in the 1960s (NOAA, 2020).

CO_2 emissions had – like many other resource-related activities – a take-off immediately after World War II. The doubling time for the magnitude of fossil fuel-related emissions has been approximately 25 years since then (Kelly & Matos, 2017). Although the rate of emissions increase has slowed down recently, there is still no significant indication that emissions are declining. Data for 2018 reveal an increase of 1.9% or even 2.0% to an all-time high level (BP, 2020; IEA, 2019a). Data for 2019 still indicate a global growth of CO_2 emissions of around 0.5% (GCP, 2019; BP, 2020).

Even if emissions were to be immediately interrupted, the CO_2 content in, as well as the temperature of, the atmosphere would, due to system inertia, continue to increase during the years ahead. As a consequence, the 1.5°C target discussed in Paris is probably very difficult, although not impossible, to reach (IPCC, 2018; IPCC, 2019b; Smith et al., 2019).

There seems to be a convergence among international climate institutions and researchers that – unless unlikely (but not impossible) global actions take place – the mean global temperature will increase by more than 3°C during this century (in comparison to the late nineteenth century) and will not necessarily be stabilized at that level (IPCC, 2018; UNEP, 2020). Although there may be surprise effects related to changes in the Northern Oscillation (the Gulf Stream), it may be assumed that the temperature increase on northern latitudes will, as hitherto, be twice the global average (IPCC, 2018).

A higher temperature in the atmosphere and the seas will increase the melting of the cryosphere, which (for land-based and grounded ice shelves) will cause sea level to rise. Sea levels also rise as a consequence of more intense molecular volatility due to the higher temperature in the water. Under certain circumstances, the ice melting process may pass a tipping point, making the melting process self-reinforcing, thus making it impossible to stop for centuries ahead (Steffen, et al. 2018). Recent estimates indicate that mean sea level rise (MSLR) may be as high as 1.5–2.5 m during this century or even higher (NOAA, 2017; Gornitz, 2019).

Towards a rapid and great transformation

All this contributes to a new agenda for humankind, nations, companies, political and sociotechnical systems, socioeconomic classes and individuals. Or, to state it briefly, "This changes everything" (cf. Klein, 2014). Not only is there a need to reformulate policies and industrial strategies for the future, worse, probably, is that actors are locked in into fossil dependent development paths, *trajectories*, along which they have been moving for a long time and which have conditioned their mindsets as well as their artefacts, i.e. their culture. The transformation ahead thus is not only a question of walking in a new direction starting from what has been achieved but to retreat from where we are and identify and make a new beginning.

As discussed below, this U-turn is not only necessary on a local or national level but also a must on the global level. How to – hopefully – obtain the necessary global momentum in a world that hitherto reveals very limited progress in international climate mitigation activities is discussed further below.

Climatologists may never in time agree on exactly how much GHGs can be stored in the atmosphere to stabilize global temperature within 2°C. There is, however, a convergence around the conclusion that the atmosphere can accommodate approximately 2900 Gt CO_2 although that level may fluctuate depending on the interchange with the hydrosphere (the oceans) and the biosphere; 2200 Gt are already emitted by humankind. Left for us, for our children and for all future is thus approximately 700 Gt (Figueres et al., 2017; IPCC, 2018; Lenton et al., 2019). Given our present rate of emissions – if stabilized on today's levels – we have another 20 years until we are on new waters for humankind. Following the historical trend of increasing emissions, and the risks connected with the recent speed of permafrost thawing, we have less time (IPCC, 2019b). Starting a radical transformation now we have a chance to reduce the probability of the worst scenarios.

The necessary rate of decarbonization is in the magnitude of at least 7% annually, starting from the present level of global GHG emissions. The target must be a total phase out between 2040 and 2050, at the latest! This needs some explication:

- This figure is a global mean. It may be argued that some countries, some people and some highly polluting actors should reduce their emissions faster than the average: rich people in rich countries have more polluting activities than poor people in poor countries (Oxfam, 2015; Chancel & Piketty, 2015). There are also historical arguments for variety among countries as regards the speed of the reduction ahead: what is left of the "emission space" should probably be given to the late entrants on the development ladder.
- The reduction path must have *a high upfront profile* to reduce the total amount of accumulated emissions. This is not only a question of calculus but also of political horizons. Formulating annual strategies rather than unprecise decadal targets reduces the implicit tendencies in the political system to put the burden of transformation to a later election period or on later generations of politicians, managers and citizens.
- After a quarter of a century of international climate meetings (since 1992) during which CO_2 emissions have increased by 56% to an all-time high in 2019 (GCP, 2019), there is no empirical evidence that global agreements will significantly contribute to a solution. During 2019, the increase of fossil fuels in the world economy was still in the same magnitude as renewables. In 2018, it was four times as large (BP, 2020). And fossil energy still contributes to 84% of global energy transformation.
- "Plan A", i.e. global agreements on rapid and forceful CO_2 taxes and trading systems, has failed; putting the eggs in such a basket only or primarily is similar to losing them.
- The most recent current policy scenario from the IEA envisions growth of global energy demand to 2040 of 1.3% annually, most of which is based

on fossil fuels. And this scenario, still, is just a little more than half of the increase in 2018 (IEA, 2019b).

- The remaining policy alternatives to change this course must thus, presumably, be based on national bottom-up actions, strategies and policies. Mobilizing people and stimulating actors to take local initiatives in a well-informed globalized network society may create role models and serve as catalysts for local as well as worldwide actions in transforming human activities in a direction that is in line with planetary boundaries. The recent impact of the Swedish 18-year-old schoolgirl Greta Thunberg illustrates the fact that global connectivity is not restricted to the big players and that climate action and mobilization may accelerate rapidly.
- There is also a growing window of opportunity for low carbon business strategies. Even in the absence of policy interventions, there is a growing number of fossil-free technologies and solutions competing on the world market. Not least, this is the case within the electricity sector. Greenfield solar plants and wind power plants now offer cheaper electricity than greenfield coal-based systems (IEA, 2020).
- The necessary transformation ahead is of a magnitude and character where the implication is that standardized programmes of energy efficiency and the substitution of renewables for fossil fuels are not enough. In many cases, there has to be a system transformation where the activity levels of old fossil-based sociotechnical systems – like aviation and automotive systems, not to talk of coal-based power plants – have to be reduced absolutely, rapidly and strongly (see e.g. Laestadius, 2018).
- The need for an upfront profile in the structural transformation ahead necessitates an in-depth analysis of what kinds of innovation are necessary or can contribute to the process. Technologies and solutions that deliver on a large scale after 2030 cannot be dominant in the toolbox. Radical technologies and solutions may be important – but only as complements. Innovative activities and new business models must be focused on promoting a rapid expansion and industrialization of solutions that are already available and/or could benefit from marginal improvements. The innovations of yesterday contain the solutions for rapid upscaling to solve the immediate problems of today.

Core industrial issues in the transformation ahead: Three cases

In line with what was discussed earlier, our analysis is related to *activities* that contribute to human fossil dependence. The activities analysed are carried out by intention to fulfil *functions* deemed necessary or worth striving for by actors. To fulfil these functions, human activities do exploit planetary resources in a more or less sustainable way. Although many functions are necessary for survival – directly or indirectly – most of the functions performed in our advanced and modern political-economic system are social and cultural constructs developed over a long period. Many "black", non-sustainable, activities in the economy can be substituted by "green" ones to provide (almost) the same functions, and – at least some – functions can be substituted and/or eliminated over time. In short, we have options on how to transform in order to economize with planetary resources.

Our aim here is to use the three cases to provide a cognitive platform for thinking outside the box. The main criterium for this selection is the importance of all human activities parallel to their actual and potential role in the climate crisis. The first case, mobility, illustrates that *the mobility function* pervades the entire society and has implications for almost all human activities and industries. The two other cases – on biomass/biotechnology and hydrogen – illustrate the broad functions served by *the general purpose technologies* as introduced earlier. Both these technologies will be important in searching for new solutions and activities in the post-carbon society. All cases illustrate the usefulness of the development block approach. The cases are by necessity connected: development and transformation in one of the spheres have implications for others.

The necessary innovations for climate mitigation (and adaptation) must not only or even primarily be technological: we know a lot already after decades of research and development work. Human, and industrial, creativity in this giant transformation is to a large extent a question of changing mindset and leaving the paradigms of humankind as mastering the nature behind (cf. e.g. White, 1967; Mokyr, 2016). So, although we still need to develop new technologies and improve the old ones, we have to reconsider and reorganize how we do things and why.

Mobility

The unit of analysis in this section is the mobility of people and goods, i.e. all activities related to travel and trade. This set of activities is probably the most important for human welfare and well-being, survival and joy. Roughly 29% of all energy consumption and 25% of all CO_2 emissions originate in transport, although the exact figure depends on how we define the borders of the system (IEA, 2018 & 2019b). For many people, the freedom to travel and trade are fundamental aspects of human life. The coming and necessary transformation is thus potentially a delicate issue: how to transform the technical systems and their usage and substitute other solutions and/or other systems so they may deliver comparable wealth and functions, although in a different and more sustainable form? For practical reasons, the structure in the analysis below follows the classical division of the technical systems.

Automotive transport of people – car travel – is the most frequent way of human transport in all developed countries. In the EU about 83% of personal travel is performed by cars (EU, 2018). This human mobility has at least two functions: transport of goods, more or less necessary for our survival and/or our lifestyle, and transport of ourselves for work and/or for networking or recreation. Although car driving may be a satisfying activity in itself for *homo ludens*, our daily use of cars may be explained as a path-dependent lock-in process where most aspects of our lives have become dependent on cars – and in particular by cars fuelled by fossil fuels. Car dominance – even if we exclude its direct climate impact – has become a giant problem in urban and social planning.

Due to strong car dependence, there is a tendency among actors involved in car transport, from car owners and travellers to industries within what may be labelled the automotive transport block, to look upon the coming transformation primarily as a giant substitution from gasoline-driven cars to cars fuelled by biofuels and/or electricity.

As regards *biofuels*, this is by many stakeholders in the automotive regime assumed to be the simplest solution: for a large part of the existing fleet, it is just to switch to *new fuel in old tanks*; using the same cars, maybe slightly modified. But this technology shift within the existing regime is far from enough. First, because the global supply of biomass will not be enough to meet the demand for fuel from the present, or a growing, car fleet; still less if the demand for biomass from other transforming sectors, like aviation or construction, is considered. Second, because the combustion of biofuels causes CO_2 emissions in the short run. The assumed compensatory CO_2 absorption of growing biomass relates to a different decision process as well as other actors and occurs much later and slower – if ever, in the case of deforestation (Schulze et al., 2012).

As regards substitution to *electricity* this will, third, necessitate a giant substitution of the present car fleet, which in itself will increase CO_2 emissions for the decades ahead. The manufacturing of e-cars, with present technologies, causes 20–50% higher CO_2 emissions than internal combustion engine (ICE) cars. Fourth, it is not, with present known technologies, obvious whether there will be enough metals/materials available in a sustainable and politically acceptable way for all batteries required for the growing electric car fleet (cf. e.g. Berggren & Kågeson (2017) and Wood MacKenzie (2019) for different views). This is an area where innovations in battery technology may contribute to problem solving. The need for new battery technologies is urgent, however, if there is to be momentum in e-car transformation.

But the functions hitherto delivered by cars must not necessarily be fulfilled so in the future. The coming transformation of the present mobility system has to be *more fundamental than business as usual with new fuel*. This transformation can take many forms, including new forms of (light) vehicles, differences between countries and significant policy measures as has historically been the case when our modern transport systems developed from the mid-nineteenth century. Connectivity must not be based on the physical transport of people or material at the same magnitude as the present.

This transformation can, following the IEA (2013) among others, be formulated in a three-leg strategy: avoid, shift and improve. A combined rapid and strong reduction of the activity level within mobility – *avoid* – followed by a *shift* to other means for connectivity/mobility in combination with efforts to increase efficiency – *improve* – is a prerequisite for success. Actors – incumbents as well as newcomers – may profit or lose from these strategies depending on how they can adapt and move between them.

Once the necessity of the giant transformation in personal mobility gains acceptance – which may necessitate strong policy interventions – there will be large-scale creative destructions among actors related to the present automotive regime: a rapid shift to plug-in cars and other light vehicles will cause a giant expansion of the innovative and advanced segment of the – declining – car industry. Electricity may serve as a generic fuel for the automotive system as future vehicles may be powered from various combinations of electric roads, batteries and fuel cells and/with backup functions from biofuel and/or hydrogen. Although the fundamental technological innovations have already been introduced there will be a need for incremental and engineering innovations as well as innovations in business models (Berggren & Kågeson, 2017).

Global aviation has grown rapidly during half a century and is now the origin of a fast-growing and significant part of global emissions. During the recent decade (2009–2019) annual growth was 6.3% and more than 4.5 billion aviation passengers are now carried annually (Statista, 2019). The main problem with aviation from a climate perspective is its lock-in, for decades ahead, to high energy containing fuels for combustion. Sustainable technologies based on electricity and/or hydrogen may have potential, but not in time to play a role in the climate mitigation ahead. The global growth of aviation must thus be halted, and for high emission countries rapidly reduced, as a part of climate crisis mitigation. The remaining aviation activities can preferably within a short time be switched to biofuels. This shift can be rapid and will demand incremental innovations and engineering activities. Many functions today delivered by aviation must, although difficult to accept for dedicated stakeholders and frequent flyers, be delivered in a new way and some at a lower speed. This will have implications on activities and industries.

Railway transport of goods as well as people is, in general, the most energy-efficient and climate-friendly solution and has a large potential for short as well as long-distance mobility. Railway systems in general – and high-speed systems in particular – necessitate, however, a certain density of freight and passengers to become economically and ecologically feasible. The necessary transformation to more railway travel and transport may preferably be based on significant creative logistical solutions, including policy measures rather than radical new technologies. This may in several cases include upscaling investments and more efficient use of medium-speed systems (< 250 km/h) or even slower systems rather than the construction of new high-speed systems (<320 km/h). A 600–700 km long distance can be covered within three hours by a "normal" medium-speed train in a well-functioning railway system. Such a shift must include significant government infrastructure policies as well as rules to change taxes and relative prices in favour of railway-based solutions.

Road transport other than cars includes trucks and buses. As regards *trucks*, there is a potential for e-trucks of all sizes although heavy trucks are not suitable for batteries as the only source of energy but must be fed by electric roads in combination with additional energy – biofuel or hydrogen – for driving off e-roads. Electric roads rolled out on existing road systems are a potentially rapid and cost-efficient alternative to railway investments in some regions that lack a railway network. These e-roads can also feed all forms of road vehicles with energy.

Bus transport has, in many countries, become squeezed between railways and car travel. In a post-fossil logistics system, buses have a large potential as an energy-efficient, climate friendly, comfortable and flexible means for travel in a large segment of travel distances in regions with less frequent travelling. E-buses can run on batteries as well as on biofuel or hydrogen when driving off e-roads. And they can run on dedicated roads – in the form of Bus Rapid Transit (BRT) systems – to increase their speed and comfort. Investment in innovative bus solutions is probably the fastest and most efficient means to transform large parts of the mobility system towards sustainability. Basically, the innovations needed are incremental and even non-technological in nature. The complex and innovative fitting between the electrical and internal combustion systems components for buses is already a known technology (Berggren et al., 2015).

Sea transport is, similar to railways, a potentially climate friendly means of transport and travel on inland waterways as well as in coastal and intercontinental traffic. This potential is in reality far from often realized as shipping, similar to the case with other means of transport, has developed within a paradigm that neglects the externalities connected to the use of fossil inputs. A large-scale transformation in shipping for people and goods, thus, will necessitate a significant transformation of shipping habits as well as be combined with higher prices on fossil fuels in general, which will favour sea transport alternatives. Not least is a need, as well as potential, for slow steaming and a more ecological ratio between ship transport capacity and deadweight in passenger traffic (OECD/ITF, 2018). The slow and climate friendly means of sea transport in the future will challenge our present paradigms on just-in-time processes and world trade as well as our beliefs on what a normal travel and transport time is over the seas.

Biomass and biotechnology

Turning to *biomass*, our overall focus is on how activities and functions can be more strongly related to the *biosphere*. The challenge for humankind is to transform the human use, exploitation and transformation of the biosphere to sustainable activities – i.e. to keep them within the *Planetary Boundaries* – and at the same time, fulfil a growing set of functions for human society. The global growth of biomass on land, and in water, is conditioned by the inflow of solar energy and *must directly and/or indirectly be allocated so it becomes enough to satisfy a large part of all human functions*. This is the consequence of the finite character of the planet.

Bio-based activities have to substitute for all our use of coal, oil and natural gas as well as much of the material metabolism related to cement, steel and other materials. In addition, biomass in various forms is what we eat – and have to eat.

Biomass will, in the post-fossil society, serve as *the most important and renewable generic resource or material*; more or less useful for everything. Potentially, our knowledge and capabilities to utilize and transform biomass represent *our ultimate generic technology.*

An important difference between our use of digital technology – also a typical general purpose technology – and bio-based technologies is that the former does not necessarily challenge the planetary boundaries in the same magnitude as the latter. The fact that the services from biomass potentially can substitute for (almost) everything else is not only a promise for the transformation ahead. The large-scale need – and potential struggle – for biomass is also a threat.

The usefulness of biomass for the transformation to a post-fossil economy/society makes it attractive for all actors and activities. Although the quantitative production of biomass can still be increased significantly (Searle & Malins, 2015; Smith et al., 2012), it should be reminded that declining biodiversity – of zoomass as well as phytomass – on a global level indicates that we are approaching planetary boundaries unless we learn to combine larger harvesting/production with saving the variety of biosphere. This double strategy of more biodiversity and more biomass harvesting is not only a problem for a science-based and sustainable planetary household. It is primarily a policy problem to stop deforestation, overfishing and the depletion of water resources – just to mention some of the threats.

Within this finite character of the planet, the innovation potential of large-scale biotechnology is, however, significant. We are not talking of radical innovations here as much as modular or incremental innovations within the same regimes (cf. Henderson & Clark, 1990). The development, for example, of efficiently produced biofuels with a close to identical molecular structure and performance as the present fossil-based fuels will dramatically reduce the need for adaptation and new investments within the declining fleets of cars and aeroplanes still in use. Much of the innovative work is already done, although there is a need for competence in the upscaling and engineering development of bio-based *electrofuels*. The upgrading of biomass with hydrogen, produced with the help of renewable energy, is not only a means to double the energy output from a certain amount of biomass that is becoming a scarce resource. It is also, as discussed below, a tool to upgrade biofuels to sustainable fuel. The fact that we are still waiting for their upscaling is primarily political: biofuels are more expensive and need policy measures for their development.

The development of new models for urban planning, design habits and new models for wood-based construction may radically transform industries and technologies as well as contribute to carbon sinks. Innovations here will probably be architectural – in their true sense – rather than radical (Henderson & Clark, 1990).

The rapid growth of *plastics production and consumption* during the Great Acceleration has been a neglected phenomenon for a long time. During the period 1950 to 2017, annual plastics production increased from almost zero to approximately 350 Mton (Plastics Europe, 2018). Plastics products are primarily produced from fossil material and are not degraded by nature. Only 9% are recycled and reused. The best material to substitute for fossil-based plastics is bio-based degradable plastics. This is a large and urgent field for technical innovation as well as new business models for consumption, logistics and packaging (Ellen McArthur, 2015). The transformation away from plastics must not necessarily be based on new plastic bags in the old format. There may be other solutions to the rapidly growing functions performed by plastics after World War II.

The questions related to land use, food chains, agriculture and fishing need a chapter or more of their own and will not be analysed in depth here (cf. IPCC, 2019a). However, the core issue as regards this aspect of the human abuse of the biosphere is the unsustainable magnitude on a global level of beef production and related activities (cf. Nijdam et al., 2012; Poore & Nemecek, 2018; Searchinger et al., 2018). The transformation needed in habits and for industries in this part of the bio-based economy is primarily cultural and political rather than based on fundamental innovations. The potential for synthetic meat produced sustainably should not be neglected due to the strong meat culture in our society. And not least, a fundamental transformation of the global food chain will release a giant potential for new and sustainable activities based on biomass.

Timing is a core issue as regards the human sustainable use of the biosphere and also an area of conflict. On the one hand, the urgent need for an upfront profile in bio-based climate change mitigation activities is an argument for leaving existing forests to grow as well as planting new trees and not burning the biomass that has alternative uses for energy and transport, thus causing CO_2 emissions in the short run. On the other hand, biofuels are an attractive short-term solution – close to business as usual – for many actors now burning oil and coal and locked into technologies that are tough to change. Here, electricity, and hydrogen, can deliver alternatives.

Hydrogen and steel

This chapter is characterized by a general *scepticism towards technology fix* solutions to reduce the climate crisis. On the one hand, it is argued that the transformation ahead has to be a U-turn away from the dominant paradigm viewing humans as the master of nature. On the other hand, it is argued that we, after approximately three decades of climate and energy-related innovations, know a lot already; more than enough to enter a new path to a post-fossil economy and society. The immediate and radical innovations and solutions needed are thus primarily non-technical.

Hydrogen is an exception to this statement. Here, I argue that *hydrogen technology has potential to become a general purpose techno*logy that can penetrate many human activities, contributing to the creative destruction of many industries and also new solutions for functions of importance for humankind. The development of hydrogen solutions on a large scale will necessitate and facilitate radical innovations as well as more modest ones – architectural, modular and incremental in the vocabulary of Henderson and Clark (1990). Hydrogen will pervade many human activities.

The core issue – *and the first leg in this emerging development block* – is the potential to use hydrogen for the production of steel. Steel is by far the largest material in use by humankind (Smil, 2016). Global production is 1800 Mt (2018) and increasing rapidly – approximately 3% annually (WSA, 2018; 2019). The steel industry is responsible for about 4–7% of global CO_2 emissions and there are no realistic means to radically reduce steel consumption. On the contrary, many of the infrastructure investments towards a post-fossil economy – for example, railways – are based on large inputs of steel. And so are many other infrastructure investments to increase human welfare (Smil, 2016). We need sustainably produced steel to transform into a post-fossil society.

There is a necessity to increase the recycling of steel. This will, however, not be enough for transformation in the decades ahead. In fact, the recycling of steel is already a giant global industry (Eurofer, 2013) and steel is already the most recycled material on the planet. Recycled steel is also the main input to electro steel ovens (EAF), which, depending on how the electricity is produced, in principle can be a sustainable process; 80% of world stainless steel is produced in EAF processes (ISSF, 2015).

To transform iron ore (Fe_2O_3) to iron (Fe), the oxygen (O_2) has to be removed. Normally, this is done in large blast furnaces where ore and coke are mixed and heated. The oxygen moves from the iron ore to the coke and leaves the top of the blast furnace as CO_2. Melted iron stays at the bottom of the furnace. Even if parts of the energy input to the process can come from renewable energy sources, the chemistry of the present steel process makes large-scale CO_2 emissions inevitable. A typical steel plant produces 1.8–1.9 times more CO_2 than steel (Kundak et al., 2009).

But iron ore can be reduced with other technologies. Of primary interest here is hydrogen, which potentially is the most sustainable. Mixing iron ore with hydrogen in a heat process may result in iron – with water (H_2O) as the only emission. It is also, potentially, possible to reduce iron ore directly with electrolysis (cf. Fischedick, et al., 2014).

The fundamental challenges of this transformation of steel production will not only be related to basic science or technology but to policy and economy, and that from three closely integrated aspects: speed, size and cost. The engineering transformation of this industry needs immediate and large-scale government support as regards the education of engineers and researchers as well as RD&D funding to speed up the process of technological development. In addition, the global scale of this industry, and the fact that the existing steel plants face the same challenges wherever they are located, is an argument for strong international cooperation in the early stages of development. It is time for a reawakening of the origin of the EU, this time in the name of the *European Hydrogen and Steel Union*. Finally, the next generation of sustainable steel will be more costly compared with the steel produced with present technology. This necessitates new international trade agreements. To launch this huge global project there is a need for industrial creativity and large-scale efforts among governments and industry that has a resemblance with the Apollo Project from the 1960s (cf. Kennedy, 1961).

Furthermore, in steel production, there is, at least in principle, a potential for biomass. In short, charcoal and biomass in other forms can substitute for coke in the blast furnaces. Not even, in this case, is basic science the main problem, the carbon atoms are the same in charcoal and coke. The problems occur in the industrialization process, the giant need for biomass, its transport and the new price relations needed (Fick et al., 2014; Mandova et al., 2018). Large-scale introduction of this technology will also add to the global scramble for biomass.

The second leg in this development block is the *sustainable production of hydrogen*. This can preferably be achieved with wind power that is used for the electrolysis of water. This process is normally not assumed to be energy efficient but in situations when there is surplus production of electricity and the marginal cost of extra production in a wind power mill is zero, this is a small problem. "Over investments" in wind power can thus be balanced with hydrogen production when there is a low demand for power. This will create incentives for some technological innovations. Wind power is a mature technology but there is a potential for technology development of various forms of hydrogen systems. The first, and most important, customer of hydrogen is the steel industry. A variety of logistic solutions is possible for connecting wind power sites, hydrogen plants and steel mills.

Once this development process is on track, several *cascade effects* of other activities reveal themselves. Hydrogen-based turbines can be developed from existing gas turbines. Large new turbines, for example, can be co-located with the hydrogen plants and deliver balance power when the wind is not blowing. Not least is this co-location a potential for offshore windmills (GWEC, 2020) But once the scale of hydrogen production increases, several other options emerge. Hydrogen may become a good complement to electricity primarily in buses, trucks and heavy equipment when they have to leave electric roads, either through fuel cells or through small-scale hydrogen turbines. If technology development follows traditional learning curves, hydrogen may also play a role in future electro-hydrogen hybrid cars. Again, there will be a need for policy measures as regards taxation.

In addition, there is, as mentioned, a vast potential to combine hydrogen with biomass to significantly improve the energy content in various forms of biofuels. In short, instead of "spoiling" bioenergy to produce heat and power, this is a means to use power to produce gas and other energy-efficient fuels.

These sustainable electrofuels can more than double the energy output of biomass (Ahlström, 2018; Hannula & Kurkela, 2015).

Hydrogen is also an obvious candidate for the transformation of long-distance aviation, either directly as an energy carrier for aeroplanes or indirectly through its enhancement of biofuels. This also takes us back to mining. Open pit, as well as underground mining activities, are energy consuming, not least as open pit equipment is highly fossil-based. In the future, this equipment has to run on electricity and hydrogen-based fuels if the life cycle of our most important metals – not least, iron – will become sustainable from a life cycle perspective.

Finally, but not least, hydrogen can be mixed with CO_2, for example, emissions from industrial processes like cement that by their nature cannot fully avoid CO_2 emissions. This is a way to produce methane or methanol. It is not energy efficient nor fully sustainable, but it is a means to close the carbon cycle using wind power-based hydrogen produced when the wind is blowing more than needed in the economy. This may, on the margin, turn out to be an acceptable form of carbon capture and sequestration (ICCT, 2018).

Concluding discussion on the transformation of human activities

Whether the transformation ahead will commence and diffuse around the world in time to significantly reduce the climate crisis is an open question. CO_2 emissions and the burning of fossil fuels are larger than ever. More than two decades of international negotiations, with only limited success, indicate that the international agreement strategies may fail. The alternatives to this failed top-down process may well be a set of various entrepreneurial bottom-up strategies: local and national market interactions between demand and supply of sustainable activities and solutions; strong national policy interventions in sustainable infrastructure development and creation of markets for sustainable activities; and policy clubs between like-minded countries (e.g. within the EU) to promote large enough "take-off markets" for sustainable solutions.

The Covid-19 pandemic commencing in early 2020 does not necessarily change the fundamental conditions for the transformation ahead. The reduction of activity levels in many of the fossil-based sectors discussed in this chapter could be looked upon as an opportunity in line with the famous expression "never waste a crisis" often connected to Winston Churchill. But at the time of writing this chapter, we know that this opportunity has not been fully grasped, although many industrial analysts argue for structural transformation rather than the restoration of old activities as business as usual.

So, in the post-Covid-19 economy, the three and related activity segments discussed previously – mobility and the upgraded transformation of biomass and hydrogen/steel-based activities – may still serve as cornerstones in a set of integrated development blocks that can constitute the core of new sustainable industrial dynamics. Together, they can lead the transformation towards a new technological and fossil-free regime. And they may well connect to other activities not analysed directly in this chapter, like, for example, wind power, photovoltaics and AI/advanced digital technology. And, as mentioned, degradable biomass-based products are probably the main substitute for present plastics products. This may also be one of the most urgent needs for innovation – in technology as well as in policy – in the transformation away from fossil-based society.

A fundamental challenge facing all transformation strategies will be the *activity levels* in the future economy. Presently, GHG emitting activities are increasing globally to all-time high levels and also contribute to indirect GHG emissions in service activities. Efforts to increase energy efficiency and general productivity increases will never be enough to provide the necessary overall reductions of the necessary magnitude of 7% annually to obtain a reasonable chance to limit temperature increases below 2°C or more.

Combination strategies, as formulated, for example, in the ASI model (avoid, shift, improve) used by the IEA (2013) and focused directly on fossil-based activities and systems may be useful here. Reducing the activity level to half in a sociotechnical system, followed by a shift of half the activities to another solution, which in itself is improved, is a means to obtain a rapid and radical transformation on a systems level. And that has to be performed in parallel in all fossil-based systems. Many stakeholders will react, arguing that "their" activities or systems are responsible for just a fraction of all emissions. There may, of course, be a need for variety between activities and how to reorganize functions and obtain their necessary speeds of reduction. But that can – in fact, must – be negotiated and will result in significant as well as incremental innovations. The important thing is to get a quick start rather than get stuck in the details. Under all circumstances, there will be a need for policy: technology policy as well as policies for prices, taxes and rules to regulate competitiveness. The steel of tomorrow will by necessity be more expensive than the steel of today. And mobility will be more expensive, and less frequent, than today. That is what the transformation is about.

What is ahead may be characterized as a new industrial revolution, differing from the former two (or three depending on how we define them) in that the present revolution is not primarily technology-driven but made necessary due to the human neglect of the finite character of our planet. Instead of expansion and growth drawing on the planetary capital, we have to transform within the limits given by the daily inflow of solar energy and what it delivers. This is not a small base for the new industrial revolution. In fact, the sun delivers as much energy per hour as humankind presently manages to capture in a whole year (Sandén, 2008).

The industrial dynamics today thus opens for a new role for human creativity, innovation activities, entrepreneurial spirit and engineering ideology; more in line with what science teaches us and what has been neglected, by many and for a long time. This will be a process in disequilibrium, i.e. characterized by tensions. There will be bottlenecks – as well as rapidly growing opportunities. Established activities, habits and industries will decline and will be substituted by growing and sustainable ones in this process that – hopefully – will be a good illustration of what Schumepeterian creative destruction is, at best.

References

Ahlström, J., 2018, *Cost Effective Pathways for Large-Scale Gasification-Based Production of Biofuels*, Licentiate Thesis, Gothenburg: Chalmers University of Technology.

Alfredsson, E. & Malmaeus, M., 2019, "Real Capital Investments and Sustainability – The Case of Sweden", *Ecological Economics*, 161, p. 216–224.

Alfredsson, E. & Malmaeus, M., 2020, *Hållbara investeringar – hur mycket grön omställning har vi(inte) råd med?*, Stockholm: Arena Idé.

Anderson, C.D. & Anderson, J., 2010, *Electric and Hybrid Cars – A History*, 2nd ed., Jefferson, NC: McFarland & Company.

Arthur, B., 1994, *Increasing Returns and Path Dependence in the Economy*, Ann Arbor, MI: UMP.

Barnett, H. & Morse, C., 1963, *Scarcity and Growth – The Economics of Natural Resource Availability*, Baltimore, MD: Johns Hopkins University Press.

Berggren, C. & Kågeson, P., 2017, *Speeding Up European Electro-Mobility – How to Electrify Half of Car Sales to 2030*, A Report to Transport and Environment (EU), https://www.transportenvironment.org.

Berggren, C., Magnusson, T. & Sushandoyo, D., 2015, "Transition Pathways Revisited: Established Firms as Multilevel Actors in the Heavy Vehicle Industry", *Research Policy*, 44(5), pp. 1017–1028.

BP, 2020, *BP Statistical Review of World Energy*, June 2020.

Brynjolfsson, E. & McAfee, A., 2016, *The Second Machine Age*, New York: Norton & Co.

Chancel, L. & Piketty, T., 2015, *Carbon Inequality: From Kyoto to Paris – Trends in the Global Inequality of Carbon Emissions (1998–2013) & Prospects for an Equitable Adaption Fund*, Paris: Paris School of Economics.

Crutzen, P., 2002, "Geology of Mankind", *Science*, 415, p. 23.

Dahmén, E., 1950, *Svensk industriell företagarverksamhet, band 1, (IUI)*, Uppsala: Almqvist and Wiksell.

David, P., 1985, "Clio and the Economics of QWERTY", *American Economic Review*, 754(2), pp. 332–337.

Dosi, G., 1982, "Technological Paradigms and Technological Trajectories – A Suggested Interpretation of the Determinants and Direction of Technical Change", *Research Policy*, 11, pp. 147–162.

Dosi, G. & Nelson, R., 2018, "Technological Advance as an Evolutionary Process", in Nelson, R., et al., eds. *Modern Evolutionary Economics*, Cambridge: Cambridge University Press.

Ellen MacArthur, 2015, *The New Plastics Economy – Rethinking the Future of Plastics*, Ellen MacArthur Foundation, https://www.ellenmacarthurfoundation.org.

EU, 2018, *Energy, Transport and Environment Indicators*, 2018 ed., Luxembourg: Eurostat.

Eurofer, 2013, *A Steel Roadmap for a Low Carbon Europe 2050*, European Steel Association, Eurofer. https://www.eurofer.eu.

Fagerberg, J., Laestadius, S. & Martin, B., eds., 2015, *The Triple Challenge for Europe – Economic Development, Climate Change and Governance*, Oxford: Oxford University Press.

Fagerberg, J., Mowery, D. & Nelson, R., eds., 2005, *The Oxford Handbook of Innovation*, Oxford: Oxford University Press.

Fick, G., et al., 2014, "Using Biomass for Pig Iron Production: A Technical, Environmental and Economical Assessment", *Waste Biomass Valor*, 5, pp. 43–55.

Figueres, C., et al., 2017, "Three Years to Safeguard Our Climate", *Nature*, 546(29), June, 593–595.

Fischedick, M., et al., 2014, "Techno-economic Evaluation of Innovative Steel Production Technologies", *Journal of Cleaner Production*, 84, pp. 563–580.

GCP, 2019, "Global Carbon Budget 2019, Global Carbon Project, Acq. 20191215", https://www.globalcarbonproject.org/carbonbudget/

Gornitz, V., 2019, "New York City Panel on Climate Change 2019 Report, Chapter 3: Sea Level Rise", *Annals of the New York Academy of Sciences*, 1439, pp. 71–94.

GWEC, 2020, *Global Offshore Wind Report 2020*, Brussels: Global Wind Energy Council.

Hannula, I. & Kurkela, E., 2015, *Doubling of Synthetic Biofuel Production with Hydrogen from Renewable Energy*, ppt. presentation, VTT Technical Research Centre of Finland.

Henderson, R. & Clark, K., 1990, "Architectural Innovation: The Reconfiguration of Existing Product Technologies and the Failure of Established Firms", *Administrative Science Quarterly*, 35(1), pp. 9–30.

Hughes, T.P., 1983, *Networks of Power: Electrification in Western Society, 1880–1930*, Baltimore, MD: Johns Hopkins University Press.

ICCT, 2018, *Economic and Environmental Performance of Electrofuels in Europe*, The International Council of Clean Transportation, Fact sheet, 20181005, www.theicct.org.

IEA, 2013, *A Tale of Renewed Cities*, International Energy Agency, Paris: OECD/IEA.

IEA, 2018, *CO2 Emissions From Fuel Combustion, Overview, International Energy Agency*, Paris: OECD/IEA.

IEA, 2019a, *Global Energy and CO_2 Status Report – The Latest Trends in Energy and Emissions in 2018*, Paris: OECD/IEA. https://www.iea.org/reports/global-energy-and-co2-status-report-2019

IEA, 2019b, *World Energy Outlook 2019*, International Energy Agency, Paris: OECD/IEA.

IEA, 2020, *Sustainable Recovery, World Energy Outlook Special Report*, Paris: IEA.

IPCC, 2018, *Global Warming of 1.5°C, IPCC Special Report*, Intergovernmental Panel on Climate Change, October.

IPCC, 2019a, *Climate Change and Land – An IPCC Special Report on Climate Change, Desertification, Land Degradation, Sustainable Land Management, Food Security, and Greenhouse Gas Fluxes in Terrestrial Ecosystems*, Intergovernmental Panel on Climate Change, August, IPCC, WMO & UNEP.

IPCC, 2019b, *The Ocean and the Cryosphere in a Changing Climate*, Final Draft, IPCC, WMO & UNEP.

ISSF, 2015, *Stainless Steel and CO_2: Facts and Scientific Observations*, International Stainless Steel Forum.

Jacobs, M. & Mazzucato, M., eds., 2016, *Rethinking Capitalism – Economics and Policy for Sustainable and Inclusive Growth*, Chichester: Wile & Blackwell.

Kelly, T. & Matos, G., 2017, *Historical Statistics for Mineral and Material Commodities in the United States* (2016 version), United States Geological Services, https://minerals.usgs.gov/minerals/pubs/historical-statistics/.

Kennedy, J.F., 1961, *Urgent National Needs*, speech to a Joint Session of Congress, 25 May, Boston, MA: J. F. Kennedy Library.

Klein, N., 2014, *This Changes Everything – Capitalism vs. the Climate*, London: Allen Lane/ Penguin.
Kuhn, T., 1962/1970, *The Structure of Scientific Revolutions*, Chicago, IL: University of Chicago Press.
Kundak, M., et al., 2009, "CO_2 Emissions in The Steel Industry", *Metallurgija*, 48(209), pp. 193–197.
Laestadius, S., 1992, *Arbetsdelningens dynamik*, Lund: Arkiv förlag.
Laestadius, S., 2013, *Klimatet och välfärden*, Umeå: Borea bokförlag.
Laestadius, S., 2015, "Transition Paths – Assessing Conditions and Alternatives", in Fagerberg, J., Laestadius, S., & Martin, B., eds., *Triple Challenge for Europe – Economic Development, Climate Change, and Governance*, Oxford: Oxford University Press.
Laestadius, S., 2016, *Erik Dahmén and Industrial Dynamics*, I Blomkvist och Johansson, red, 2016, *A Dynamic Mind – Perspectives on Industrial Dynamics in Honour of Staffan Laestadius*, Stockholm: Royal Institute of Technology, KTH.
Laestadius, S., 2018, *Klimatet och omställningen*, Umeå: Borea bokförlag.
Laestadius, S., 2021, *En strimma av hopp*, Stockholm: Verbal förlag.
Lenton, T., et al., 2019, "Climate Tipping Points – Too Risky to Bet Against", *Nature*, 575, pp. 592–595.
Lipsey, R., Carlaw, K. & Bekar, C., 2005, *Economic Transformations – General Purpose Technologies and Long Term Economic Growth*, Oxford: Oxford University Press.
Maddison, A., 2005, *Growth and Interaction in the World Economy – The Roots of Modernity*, Washington, DC: AEI Press.
Magnusson, L., 2005, *Den synliga handen*, Stockholm: SNS Förlag.
Mandova, H., et al., 2018, "Possibilities for CO_2 Emission Reduction Using Biomass in European Integrated Steel Plants", *Biomass and Bioenergy*, 115, pp. 231–243.
Marshall, A., 1890/1990, *Principles of Economics: An Introductory Volume*, 8th ed., London: Macmillan.
Mayr, E., 2001, *What Evolution Is*, New York: Basic Books, Perseus.
Mazzucato, M., 2011, *The Entrepreneurial State*, London: Demos.
Mazzucato, M., 2016, Innovation, the State and Patient Capital, in Jacobs, M. & Mazzucato, M., eds., *Rethinking Capitalism – Economics and Policy for Sustainable and Jnclusive Growth*, Chichester: Wile & Blackwell.
Mokyr, J., 2016, "Progress Isn't Natural: Humans Invented It – And not the Long Ago", *Atlantic*, November 17.
Nelson, R., ed., 2018, *Modern Evolutionary Economics*, Cambridge: Cambridge University Press.
Nelson, R. & Winter, S.G., 1977, "In Search of a Useful Theory of Innovation", *Research Policy*, 6(1), pp. 36–76.
Nelson, R.R. & Winter, S.G., 1982, *An Evolutionary Theory of Economic Change*, Cambridge, MA: Belknap Press of Harvard University Press.
Nijdam, D., Rood, T. & Westhoek, H., 2012, "The Price of Protein: Review of Land Use and Carbon Footprints from Life Cycle Assessments of Animal Food Products and Their Substitutes", *Food Policy*, 37, pp. 760–770.
NOAA, 2017, *Global and Regional Sea Level Rise Scenarios for the United States*, Silver Spring, MD: National Oceanic and Atmospheric Administration.
NOAA, 2020, *Earth System Laboratory, Global Monitoring Division, Acq. 20200113*, https:/ /www.esrl.noaa.gov/gmd/ccgg/trends/
OECD/ITF, 2018, *Decarbonizing Maritime Transport – Pathways to Zero-Carbon Shipping by 2035*, OECD, International Transport Forum.

Oxfam, 2015, *Extreme Carbon Inequality*, Oxfam Media Briefing, December 2, 2015, www.oxfam.org

Pasinetti, L., 1981/2009, *Structural Change and Economic Growth*, Cambridge: CUP.

Perez, C., 2010, "Technological Revolutions and Techno-Economic Paradigms", *Cambridge Journal of Economics*, 34(1), pp. 185–202.

Plastics Europe, 2018, https://www.plasticseurope.org/application/files/6315/4510/9658/ Plastics_the_facts_2018_AF_web.pdf

Poore, J. & Nemecek, T., 2018, "Reducing Food's Environmental Impacts through Producers and Consumers", *Science*, 360, pp. 987–992.

Rifkin, J., 2011/2013, *The Third Industrial Revolution*, London: Palgrave/Macmillan.

Rockström, J., et al., 2009, "Planetary Boundaries: Exploring the Safe Operating Space for Humanity", *Ecology and Society*, 14(2), September, Art 32.

Sandén, B., 2008, "Solar Solution: The Next Industrial Revolution", *Materials Today*, 11(2), pp. 22–24.

Schumpeter, J., 1934/62, *The Theory of Economic Development*, Cambridge, MA: Harvard University Press.

Schumpeter, J., 1942/2000, *Capitalism, Socialism and Democracy*, London and New York: Routledge.

Searchinger, T.D., et al., 2018, "Assessing the Efficiency of Changes in Land Use for Mitigating Climate Change", *Nature*, 564, pp. 249–253.

Searle, S. & Malins, C., 2015, "A Reassessment of Global Bioenergy Potential in 2050", *GCB Bioenergy*, 7, pp. 328–336.

Schulze, E.-D., et al., 2012, "Large-Scale Bioenergy from Additional Harvest of Forest Biomass is Neither Sustainable nor Greenhouse Gas Neutral", *GCB Bioenergy*, 4(6), pp. 611–616.

Smil, V., 2016, *Still the Iron Age*, Amsterdam: Elsevier.

Smith, C.J., et al., 2019, "Current Fossil Fuel Infrastructure Does not Yet Commit Us to 1.5°C Warming", *Nature Communications*, 10(101), pp. 1–10.

Smith, K., Zhao, M. & Running, S., 2012, "Global Bioenergy Capacity as Constrained by Observed Biospheric Productivity Rates", *Journal of Bioscience*, 62, pp. 911–922.

Statista, 2019, https://www.statista.com/statistics/564717/airline-industry-passenger-traffic-globally/

Steffen, W., Crutzen, P.J., and McNeill, J.R., 2004, *Global Change and the Earth System: A Planet under Pressure*, Berlin: Springer Verlag.

Steffen, W., Crutzen, P.J., and McNeill, J.R., 2007, "The Anthropocene: Are Humans Now Overwhelming the Great Forces of Nature?", *Ambio*, 36(8), pp. 614–621.

Steffen, W., et al., 2018, "Trajectories of the Earth System in the Anthropocene", *Proceedings of the National Academy of Sciences of the United States of America (PNAS)*, 115(3), pp. 8252–8259.

UN, 2015, *Transforming Our World: The 2030 Agenda for Sustainable Development*, United Nations: Resolution adopted by the General Assembly on 25 September 2015 (70/1).

UNEP, 2020, *Emissions Gap Report 2020*, Nairobi: United Nations Environmental Programme.

Unruh, G.C., 2000, "Understanding Carbon Lock-In", *Energy Policy*, 28(12), pp. 817–830.

Voosen, P., 2018, "Antarctic Ice Melt 125000 Years Ago Offers Warning", *Science* 362(6421), December 21, pp. 1339.

White, Lynn Jr., 1967, "The Historical Roots of Our Ecological Crisis", *Science*, 155(3767), 10 March.

WMO, 2018, *Greenhouse Gas Levels in Atmosphere Reach New Records*, WMO Press Release 22112018, Geneva: World Meteorological Organization.
Wood MacKenzie, 2019, *Can Metals Supply Keep Up with Electric Vehicle Demand? – Battery Raw Materials Could Face Supply Crunch by Mid-2020s*, Edinburgh: Wood MacKenzie Resource Consultancy Company.
WSA, 2018, *Steel Statistical Yearbook 2018*, Brussels: World Steel Association.
WSA, 2019, *World Steel in Figures 2019*, Brussels: World Steel Association.
Zamagni, V., 2017, *An Economic History of Europe Since 1700*, Newcastle upon Tyne: Agenda Publishing.
Zimmerman, E., 1933/1951, *World Resources and Industries*, New York: Harper & Brothers.

10

IS THE OIL AND NATURAL GAS INDUSTRY TRANSFORMING?

Evidence from the offshore Arctic

Maria Morgunova

Introduction

The global energy system is seeing powerful change. Sustainability, climate issues, sanctions against Russia and Iran, a crisis in North African countries and political and security challenges in the Middle East are only some of the major concerns faced by the global energy system today. The shale gas revolution and the changing architectonics of the natural gas trade (BP, 2019a, 2019b) have caused additional turbulence in the global energy system. Meanwhile, long-term challenges, such as energy demand growth, depletion of traditional oil and natural gas resources and other challenges urge governments and companies to secure their oil and natural gas production and supply (International Energy Agency, 2018). The above-mentioned short- and long-term issues spur energy companies to search for new energy resources and technological solutions. Today, the geography of oil and gas production has broadened significantly from easy-to-develop conventional resources to unconventional resources and unexplored frontiers such as the Arctic (Morgunova, 2015).

The offshore Arctic is one of the "edges" of the global oil and gas industry. In recent years, the awareness of Arctic offshore oil and natural gas development has risen considerably due to its huge potential for undiscovered oil and natural gas resources (USGS, 2008). These resources may bring significant economic opportunities, but their exploitation also involves environmental, technological and industrial challenges. Corporate and governmental interests in the oil and gas activities in the Arctic have also grown as the region becomes of geopolitical, economic and social importance (Larsen and Huskey, 2015).

The natural vulnerability of the Arctic, harsh weather, cold, darkness and especially sea ice conditions challenge traditional operation principles that require new technological and organizational solutions. However, the nature and pace of the industrial activities related to the exploitation of offshore oil and natural gas in the Arctic have not been fully understood. While the Arctic presents a variety of both opportunities and challenges to the current oil and natural gas industry, this chapter examines the extent to which industrial transformation is occurring in Arctic offshore oil and natural gas resource exploitation through investigating the scope of activities, technological innovations and the actors involved.

What is the Arctic?

The Arctic region within the Arctic Circle constitutes as much as 11% of the world's surface area. However, there are multiple definitions of the Arctic and a broad understanding of oil and gas activities in the Arctic. Arctic borders may vary depending on governance, average temperature, vegetation, permafrost, etc. (Bjørnbom, 2013). Arctic oil and gas activities imply a broad variability of geographical and physical parameters: deposits located offshore, onshore or partly onshore, explored from on- or offshore installations, located in Northern or Arctic seas, seasonal ice-covered seas or ice-free water. Many studies on the offshore Arctic oil and natural gas resources apply the geographical parameter (cf. Budzik, 2009; Gautier et al., 2009; USGS, 2008).

The Arctic usually incorporates the northern territories of eight countries: Canada, Finland, Greenland (Denmark), Iceland, Norway, Russia, Sweden and the United States (Figure 10.1). Five of those countries have sea outlets

FIGURE 10.1 Arctic map (adapted by the author from Botev, 2008) (Wikimedia Commons CC BY-SA 2.5).

to the Arctic Ocean. The main Arctic offshore areas are the Barents, Pechora and Kara Seas, Ob and Taz Bays, the Beaufort Sea, the waters of the Canadian Arctic Archipelago, Prudhoe Bay, the Chukchi and Norwegian Seas and the waters of Greenland (Baffin Bay, the waters south and east of Greenland and the Greenland Sea).

The total population of the Arctic reached seven million inhabitants in 2017 (Jungsberg et al., 2019, p. 13). This is approximately 0.1% of the global population, which generates near 0.5% of the global gross domestic product (Glomsrød et al., 2015, p. 28).

Today, the Arctic is a region in which national economies are built on natural resources. These resources are used both for internal consumption and for exports. Some of the Arctic regions are fully oriented towards large-scale extraction of non-renewable resources such as fossil fuels and minerals (i.e. oil and natural gas on the North Slope of Alaska in the United States, the Khanty-Mansi Autonomous Area in Russia, nickel in Norilsk and the Kola Peninsula in Russia, diamonds in the Northwest Territories of Canada and gold in Chukotka in Russia); others are more oriented towards natural renewable resources such as fish and wood (Duhaime et al., 2008). Among those, the Russian Arctic economy is the largest. It generates more than 10% of Russia's GDP (approximately 70% of the Arctic's total GDP) and more than 20% of its exports (oil, natural gas, minerals and fish). Canada and Denmark (Greenland and the Faroe Islands) take second and third place after Russia by Arctic territory size, but both their populations and their economic activities are much lower. In other Arctic countries – Finland, Iceland, Norway and Sweden – populations and industries are relatively large compared with national levels. In Canada and the United States, the Arctic population is approximately 1% of the country's population. Economic growth in the Arctic regions is double that of non-Arctic regions. Growth rates are very high in regions that have relatively recently started to produce oil and natural gas (e.g. Russia's Evenk Autonomous Area). At the same time, the spread between regions' economic development and industrial distribution is substantial. Four Arctic regions generate more than 60% of the Arctic's total GDP (the Khanty-Mansi and Yamal-Nenets Autonomous Areas in Russia's Republic of Sakha and Alaska in the United States). In addition to the Arctic's substantial economic opportunities, the socio-ecological impact of extractive industries is significant and hydrocarbon resources play a substantial role in it.

Oil and gas activities in the Arctic

Oil and gas activities have been taking place in the Northwest Territories of Canada and also in northern Russia and Alaska since the 1920s, followed by extensive exploration during World War II (AMAP, 2007). This period was followed by large discoveries and constructions throughout the Arctic (North Slope fields, Yamal, the Mackenzie Delta and the Beaufort Sea, the Trans-Alaska

Pipeline System, pipeline systems in Russia, etc.). When oil prices increased significantly in the 1970s and 1980s, Arctic oil and gas seemed an attractive investment option for many governments and companies. By the 1980s and 1990s, oil and gas activities extended further along the Arctic frontiers towards the Arctic Ocean and offshore areas (Morgunova, 2015). In Canada, a small deposit, Bent Horn, was developed in the islands of the High Arctic. Norway started operations in the Barents Sea in 1981, and the Norwegian oil company Statoil discovered a huge Snøhvit gas field. Offshore exploration in Russia also opened up a large resource potential, such as in the Shtokman and Prirazlomnoe fields. In the 1990s, a new period of exploration started in northern Alaska. Since the 1970s, billions of dollars worth of both oil and gas have been produced in the Arctic regions of Canada, Norway, Russia and the United States (AMAP, 2007), and oil and gas production in the Arctic region are a substantial part of the total hydrocarbon production of some of the Arctic countries.

To date, approximately 550 oil and natural gas fields have been found in the Arctic basins (Budzik, 2009), including approximately 61 large oil and natural gas fields, 43 of which are located in Russia. The share of Arctic oil production (not only offshore) represents approximately 10% of the global production, and this figure is approximately 21% for natural gas (Lindholt and Glomsrød, 2008). The cumulative production of oil and natural gas in the Arctic region reached 20.8 billion tonnes of oil equivalent (toe) by 2017, of which 85.9% was produced in the Russian Arctic and 13.6% in Alaska (Bogojavlenskij and Bogojavlenskij, 2017).

A great hydrocarbon resource potential is considered to be one of the strongest incentives in striving towards the Arctic frontiers (Johnston, 2012; Koivurova, 2015; Morgunova and Westphal, 2016). Arctic waters may hold up to 22% of the world's undiscovered oil and natural gas resources (USGS, 2008), including almost 4% of conventionally recoverable oil resources and 30% of natural gas resources (Gautier et al., 2009, p. 1178). The total oil and natural gas resource potential could be as high as 60 billion tonnes of oil equivalent (Budzik, 2009, p. 6) and exceeds developed onshore Arctic oil and natural gas reserves.

Comparatively high oil prices, political instability in major oil and gas exporting countries, government incentives and new technological approaches stimulated interest towards oil and gas exploitation in the offshore Arctic in the 2000s, conditions that were repeated during the 2010s. During the times of high activity in the Arctic, an exploration process was unfolding in Alaska (US), offshore Greenland, the Norwegian Sea and the Barents (both Russia and Norway) Sea (Morgunova, 2015). At that time, the first oil from the Beaufort and the Chukchi Seas – highly challenging locations for exploration from the environmental and technical perspective – was expected to come as early as 2020 and 2022 respectively, while the total number of planned Arctic offshore oil and natural gas fields in production by 2030 reached 22. By that time, the number of already producing fields was ten from the total of 55 identified fields in the offshore Arctic (three in Canada, 14 in Norway, 29 in Russia, nine in the United States and

TABLE 10.1 Arctic offshore oil and natural gas fields in development and production updated by 2019 (adapted from Morgunova, 2015)

	Canada	*Greenland*	*Norway*	*Russia*	*USA*	*Total*
In development stage						
by 2014	1	0	3	5	2	11
by 2019	0	0	1	2	1	4
In production						
by 2014	0	0	2	2	6	10
by 2019	0	0	4	2	7	13

zero in Greenland) (Table 10.1). (Morgunova, 2015) The selected information about all the fields in development and production stages by 2019 is available in Appendix 1 (Table 10.A1).

However, the macroeconomic situation has drastically changed, affecting exploration and production plans. Greenland's offshore development strategy was optimistic in 2010 when the oil company Cairn Energy discovered oil and natural gas for the first time and the first offshore exploration licences were granted (Ernst&Young, 2013). However, the need for tremendous investment and no discoveries of a commercial size distracted future production plans. Canada used to be a pioneer in exploring the Arctic offshore areas and Arctic Islands in the late 1960s, but currently, there is no oil and natural gas exploration or production activities in the offshore Arctic due to strong concerns about ecological safety. However, there are Newfoundland and Labrador fields, such as Hibernia, Terra Nova, White Rose and Hebron, which are operating in Arctic-like conditions. In the United States, even though the older projects continue to exist, there is no new exploration in the offshore Arctic. The new projects were delayed or abandoned due to the macroeconomic situation including a shale gas revolution, technical difficulties and regulations (e.g. the Burger prospect in the Chukchi Sea). The two countries that plan further exploitation of Arctic offshore oil and natural gas resources are Russia and Norway. Norway plans further expansion of the Barents Sea as it is its main petroleum province. In Russia, the intensive development of Arctic oil and natural gas resources offshore is one of the national strategic issues.

The majority of operating fields are located in the offshore Arctic of the United States, and long-term exploration plans are forecasted until 2050. The current number of Arctic offshore oil and natural gas fields in production has not changed dramatically, but the intensity of exploration activities decreased significantly. There were ten fields in production by 2014 (Table 10.1), and the total number increased to 13 by 2019.

Actors

For the purpose of this chapter, we identify three[1] types of actors that differ in terms of their aims and roles in the development of Arctic offshore oil and natural gas resources. The first group consists of actors such as supra-governmental, non-governmental and non-commercial organizations, which operate on a global or regional scale. Particularly prominent actors include, for example, the United Nations, the Arctic Council, the EU Parliament and Greenpeace. Countries and governments make up the second group. They mainly have particular interests in the Arctic region, mostly based on their own strategic and sovereign interests, but also connected to wider political, social and economic concerns. All the circumpolar countries have both contrary and similar goals in the region. Other non-circumpolar countries, such as China, are mainly interested in entering the Arctic to take part in resource development and benefit from the new transport and transit opportunities (Kovalenko et al., 2018). Oil and gas as well as energy companies are the third group including, for example, BP, Cairn Energy, E.ON, ExxonMobil, Gazprom, Lukoil, Lundin, Rosneft, Royal Dutch Shell, Equinor, Total and others. Those companies are the main industrial actors involved in offshore Arctic oil and gas activities. Those companies differ by size, state involvement (companies with governmental partnership or private) and their scope of operations (national and international).

In Norway, both national and international companies can gain access to the Arctic offshore oil and natural gas fields through the government's licensing rounds. The key offshore Norwegian Arctic actor is Equinor (formerly Statoil), a company founded by the Norwegian government with the formation of the Norwegian petroleum industry. Many service companies originate from Norway, and they have high competencies in working in the offshore and non-freezing Arctic. Other companies active on the Norwegian shelf are Aker, Eni, Lundin, Petoro, Suncor, Repsol, Cairn Energy and others, which have been granted production licences in the Norwegian Barents Sea (Norwegian Petroleum Directorate, 2018a). Even though the bidding is highly competitive, the largest share (in licensed square meters) is usually granted to Equinor (Marchand, 2018). Nevertheless, the latest licensing rounds showed unexpectedly high interest of energy and service companies in the Norwegian shelf in general and the Arctic shelf in particular, where 38 companies applied (Norwegian Petroleum Directorate, 2018b). Additionally, the Norwegian government stimulates a higher participation of local contractors and subcontractors (in the Snøhvit project, around 60% of the companies were local, except for two governmental Norwegian companies – Equinor and Petoro).

In Russia, the government heavily controls offshore oil and natural gas field development in the Arctic. This control is set in terms of limiting access to the offshore fields and governmental instruments of resource protectionism, such as no publicly available geological data and limited access for international companies. The only companies allowed to operate in the offshore Arctic are companies with governmental ownership, which have more than five years' experience in working offshore. There are only two companies that meet those conditions – Rosneft and Gazprom (via Gazpromneft), and they have already received nearly 80% of all offshore Arctic licences in Russia. The two other companies, privately owned, which have shown an interest in participating in the Arctic offshore development projects – Novatek and Lukoil – have limited access to offshore Arctic projects, even though both of them have experience in working in the high north and Arctic-like conditions. Novatek has only recently received an opportunity to work in the Arctic on the Gydan peninsula and Ob Bay, even though it has successfully operated projects in the Arctic (Yamal-LNG and Yurkharovskoe project) and reached a considerable level of inclusiveness of local contractors, showing better results than Rosneft (Krjukov and Krjukov, 2017). Due to the limited access to new potential oil and natural gas provinces in Russia, some companies, such as Lukoil, have chosen to switch to international projects outside Russia (Pritchin, 2018).

The Russian Arctic state-owned companies – Gazprom and Rosneft – have actively started to involve international partners in the exploration process in the Russian offshore Arctic, including ExxonMobil, Eni and Statoil, at the beginning of the 2010s. However, those initiatives were negatively influenced by sanctions imposed on the Russian oil and natural gas sector (The Council of the European Union, 2014; U.S. Department of State, n.d.). Nevertheless, there are examples of rather successful cooperation of many companies with offshore Russia in the Arctic-like climate conditions. Those are the Sakhalin I, II and III projects. The Sakhalin I project consists of Exxon Mobil and companies owned by Japan, India and Russia (Rosneft-affiliated companies). All the fields under Sakhalin I are operated by Exxon Neftegas Limited, which is a subsidiary of Exxon Mobil. The Sakhalin II project is owned and operated by Sakhalin Energy, owned by Gazprom, Royal Dutch Shell, Mitsui and Mitsubishi subsidiaries. Chevron, ExxonMobil and Rosneft operate the Sakhalin III project.

In the United States, the key actors are international companies such as Royal Dutch Shell (including its contractor Noble Energy), Exxon Mobil, BP, ConocoPhilips, Eni and Repsol. Oil and gas activities on federal lands are regulated by the US Bureau of Land Management, on state and Native lands, and in state waters – by the Alaska Oil and Gas Conservation Commission, and in federal waters – by the US Bureau of Ocean Energy Management (Allison and Mandler, 2018). There are safety and environmental regulations and restrictions in the US Arctic regulated by the government, but no other types of access limitation.

In Canada, there is currently no exploration or production in Arctic waters (Allison and Mandler, 2018), but some companies are present in the Arctic within other activities related to oil and gas. Chevron has its Arctic centre based in Canada and operates in the Arctic-like waters of Newfoundland and Labrador; ConocoPhilips holds interests in licences; Repsol has two exploration sites in Northern Canada; TransCanada is engaged in the Alaska gas pipeline and the Mackenzie Gas Project; and Husky Energy has some assets in Western Canada. (Nordea, 2017)

In Greenland, national oil companies Nunaoil and Cairn Energy were involved in exploration. There is currently no exploration or production activities offshore Greenland as between 2009 and 2010 a few unsuccessful attempts were made to discover fields of commercial size.

To summarize, the main actors in the Arctic are supra-governmental, governmental, non-governmental organizations and companies. The companies involved in the Arctic onshore and offshore oil and gas activities have not dramatically changed over time. Most of those companies entered Arctic oil and gas activities in the very beginning and continue to be present in the Arctic region, moving further offshore. Most of these actors are national companies or those with substantial governmental participation, as well as international companies with huge assets (Table 10.2), technological competencies and the ability to take high risks in long-term projects.

Technologies

By the end of the nineteenth century, the oil industry has already moved from onshore to inland waters and later further offshore. Offshore oil and gas technologies (known in the United States since the 1890s) have broadened the scope of oil and gas activities, giving rise to deep and ultra-deep offshore explorations such as those in the offshore Arctic.[2] Offshore oil production constitutes around 30% of global production (EIA, 2016). In the process of reaching one-third of global oil production, offshore technologies have expanded dramatically, from offshore barges (1950s), deep-water drillships (1956) and semisubmersible rigs (1964) (Sandrea and Sandrea, 2007) to the latest subsea automatized unmanned technologies.

The oil and natural gas value chains have no principal difference for onshore and offshore production, although offshore activities are intensified due to harsh operating conditions and much higher costs (Figure 10.2). For example, for oil, it is loaded directly from the platform to the ship for transportation, while for natural gas, the steps of processing and transportation are not linear (e.g. the Snøhvit natural gas field and Hammerfest liquefied natural gas [LNG] plant at Melkøya Island in Norway). For natural gas, the transportation and processing stages are being further optimized through floating LNG facilities (Royal Dutch Shell, 2015).

TABLE 10.2 Capitalization of international oil and gas companies present in the Arctic by 2019 (adapted by the author from "Fortune 500", 2019; PWC, 2019)

Rank global	*Company name*	*Capitalization, billion US$*
10	Exxon Mobil	316
18	Royal Dutch Shell	263
28	Chevron	218
54	BP	134
55	Total	149
–	ConocoPhillips	76
–	Noble Energy	12

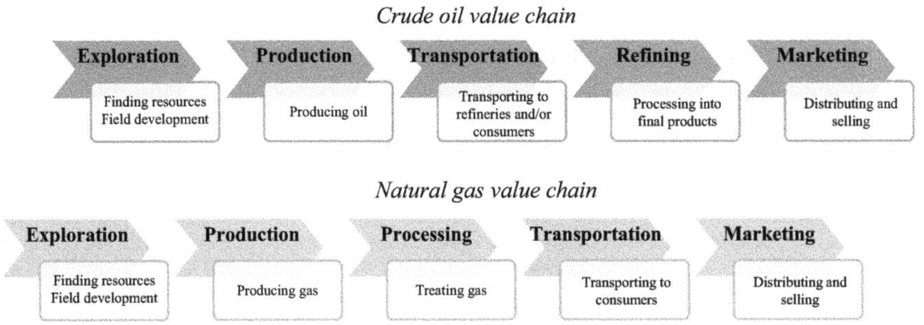

FIGURE 10.2 Global oil and natural gas value chains (adapted by the author from Tordo et al., 2011).

Technical approaches

In general, all the technologies are based on five concepts that vary depending on the surrounding environment parameters (location, water depth, climate and ice conditions) (Table 10.3).

Bottom founded structures are immovable heavy structures on the sea bottom, whereas jack-ups can be moved from site to site but also rest on the sea

TABLE 10.3 Technical approaches (adapted by the author from INTECSEA, 2012)

Concepts	*Approaches*
Bottom founded structures	• Ice island
	• Rock/gravel/sand island
	• Ballasted barge/vessel
	• Ballasted barge/vessel + berm
	• Piled barge
	• Caisson retained island
	• Concrete gravity-based structure (GBS)
	• Steel GBS
Fixed jacket/ mobile jack-up	• Mobile offshore production unit
	• Jacket
	• Monopod
Floating structures	• Floating production storage offload (FPSO) (ship-shaped vessel)
	• FSPO (round-shaped vessel)
	• Semisubmersible (SS)
	• Tension leg platform (TLP)
	• Single vertical mooring cylinder platform (SPAR)
Subsea facilities	• Flowline
	• Pipeline
	• Subsea (gloryhole)
	• Subsea protective structure
	• Subsea drill rig
Other	• Extended reach drilling

bottom. Floating structures are only anchored, and subsea facilities have no structures above the water level, with the entire production site on the sea bottom. An additional technology is extended reach drilling whereby offshore oil and natural gas resources are exploited from the shore pad by drilling long horizontal wells. These technologies also have different environmental effects on coastal and offshore ecosystems, in addition to capital and operation costs. Not all of the technological concepts and approaches are used in the offshore Arctic.

Bottom founded structures such as gravel and ice (spray) islands[3] were first used by Panarctic oil in 1973–1974 (the Hecla and Drake Point oil and gas fields in the Canadian Arctic Islands) and by Exxon Mobil in exploration drilling in 1980 (Alaska). This technology is still used in the Beaufort Sea near Alaska. Annual formation of pack ice in the Arctic seas does not allow the safe and effective use of drilling platforms and floating structures. Islands that are manufactured from gravel, concrete and iced seawater are reliable structures that are ideal for the Arctic environment because of the natural materials. It is also a relatively cheap way to explore shallow nearshore fields (Ekelund and Masterson, 1980) (Figure 10.3).

First, ice-resistant platforms, which are also bottom founded (gravity-based) structures, were developed to find Cook Inlet resources in Alaska in the late 1960s (Pratt et al., 1997). The need to withstand sea ice load, wind and currents resulted in a new generation of ice-resistant four-legged self-contained

FIGURE 10.3 Northstar field offshore island (Joint Pipeline Office, 2010) (Wikimedia Commons CC0).

platforms, for which ice resistance is also the main item of expenditure. The only currently existing bottom founded platform within the Arctic Circle is the Prirazlomnaya stationary ice-resistant platform in the Kara Sea (Russia), which started producing at the end of 2013.

Floating structures can be approximately divided into ship-shaped and platform structures, each of which serves different operational purposes, including drilling, production, storage or offloading functions. Floating ship-shaped vessels are very mobile and can safely "drop" a production line and sail away from ice hazards. Ship-shaped vessels are one of the most expensive options due to their full-pack equipment, strengthened ice protection of underwater equipment and mobility. This category of production technologies is also applicable for deep-water operations.

The most contemporary, safe and promising Arctic development concept is a subsea concept. In 2007, Statoil launched the Snøhvit gas project in the Norwegian part of the Barents Sea, the first fully subsea automated production site with no above-water facilities. This means all the operations are maintained and controlled remotely, and ice cannot damage the production system. Primarily because there is no ice hazard, subsea technologies are considered the safest. There is no theoretical limit for exploration or production in terms of water depth or the ice-free season for subsea technologies (INTECSEA, 2012). They are also considered efficient because there are no capital or operational expenses for the construction of onshore or above-water facilities.

Extended reach drilling is the most widespread development approach for partly offshore fields or the ones located close to the shore. This allows drilling wells from a shore-based pad, extending exploration with the use of the same onshore infrastructure, and therefore lowering the exploration costs. The first extended reach drilling programme of BP in the 1970s was considered a real technological breakthrough (Ghiselin, 2012). Currently, the world's record for the longest well is 15,000 meters and belongs to the Chaivo field (Sakhalin I) in the Sea of Okhotsk. Extended reach drilling became a widespread tool to access certain oil and gas reservoirs lying offshore, with a minimal environmental footprint and minimal accident probability. Extended reach drilling (or horizontal drilling) is used in combination with all the other technological development concepts.

Offshore oil and natural gas fields development in the Arctic

From 1986 to 2007, there were two main technological concepts used for the offshore Arctic – extended reach drilling and bottom founded structures. The developed fields are partly offshore fields, i.e. lying in shallow water not far from the shore. Gravel island productions in the United States were the first to be launched in the offshore Arctic, which began in 1986. The majority (seven of 13) of the Arctic fields in production is currently in the US Arctic, and five of them are operated from the gravel islands. However, Arctic offshore oil and natural gas production only started to grow in the 2000s, when investment in more technologically demanding, hard-to-reach resources increased considerably. In the 2000s, three fields in the United States (Oooguruk, Nikaitchuq and Northstar), one in Russia (Yurkharovskoye) and one in Norway (Snøhvit) were launched. The Yurkharovskoye gas field, which is only partly offshore, has significantly contributed to the total Arctic offshore production, not just because of the available resources but also because of the number of horizontal wells giving high hydrocarbon flow.

In 2007, the new subsea development concept was used in Norway on the Snøhvit natural gas and condensate field. As mentioned previously, subsea technologies are considered to have a minimal footprint on the environment and are relatively safe. However, they require huge investment and have been applied in only two fields in the Norwegian Arctic – Snøhvit and Skuld.[4] In 2014, subsea technologies contributed nearly 11% to the total Arctic offshore hydrocarbon volume and only 5.6% during the period 1986–2014, largely with Snøhvit production (Morgunova, 2015).

After 2014, the number of applied technological concepts expanded to five with the addition of floating structures and a combination of bottom founded structures and extended reach drilling. Thus, the area of Arctic offshore activity was expanded to deeper and more distant sites. However, the fields that are being exploited by floating structures do not significantly contribute to the overall Arctic offshore production during the period under review. There are also no development plans based on subsea facilities. Thus, the contribution of the technological approaches to the volume of hydrocarbons produced is not straightforward. More advanced and far-reaching technologies do not visibly extend the projected output of oil and natural gas. Technological choice is largely dictated by the remoteness of the field from the shore and the climate conditions, which have a direct influence on capital costs. According to Poltorackaja (2011), a special interest is demonstrated for reservoirs, primarily oil-bearing ones, which can be exploited with the use of horizontal wells. Most likely, the fields in place after 2020 will be developed based on climate-geographical characteristics or as satellites to fields that are already producing (for example, the Dolginskoye field, which is planned to be exploited from the Prirazlomnaya platform (RIA Novosti, 2019)).

Discussion

The Arctic is a very challenging region for industrial development due to harsh climate conditions, ecological sensitivity, long distances and remoteness. Arctic offshore areas imply even higher technical and logistical challenges for industrial activities. Such a challenging environment may be seen as a "niche" for industrial innovations and transformation. Within the multilevel perspective, the niche level represents "the micro-level where radical novelties emerge" (Geels and Schot, 2007, p. 400). The multilevel perspective builds on the idea that niches can significantly contribute to system changes by giving birth to radical innovations (Geels and Kemp, 2007).

From the geographical point of view, and due to many special natural conditions for industrial activities in the region mentioned above, which requires special technological and management solutions, the industrial activities in the Arctic are usefully viewed as a "niche". However, the overall offshore Arctic exploration and production processes have not changed significantly compared with onshore production. There are no principal differences in the oil and natural gas value chains onshore and offshore (Figure 10.2). However, due to severe exploitation conditions in the Arctic predefined by the natural environment, location (offshore) and climate, the overall process is optimized, thus shortened in many of the technological concepts presented previously (Table 10.3). The optimization of the natural gas value chain in the Arctic can be exemplified by the above-mentioned technology of the floating LNG facility (Royal Dutch Shell, 2015). Actually, the floating LNG facility could be an early move into a modified value chain for natural gas, but it has not really taken place yet (Songhurst, 2019).

Successful exploitation of Arctic offshore oil and natural gas has required a number of technological advances that have moved the oil and gas industry from onshore production to offshore and then to deeper horizons. Such technologies as horizontal drilling and automation control (remotely operated vehicles and visual control), as well as the ability to use more advanced materials, allowed firms to reach more resources located further from the shore. Nevertheless, in terms of new frontiers, oil and gas and energy companies are mainly adapting existing technologies for oil and natural gas exploitation to the new natural conditions (depth, sea ice and icebergs, currents and storm winds; Eie and Rognaas, 2014; Yang et al., 2013) – those are winterization of the technologies, a combination of technological approaches, etc. Worth mentioning, though those are incremental improvements, is that they stimulate change in the main principles of oil and natural resource development on land and less harsh conditions, for example, in terms of safety and reliability of operations (Necci et al., 2019).

Some technologies invented in the Arctic and for the Arctic cannot be entirely extended to other areas or even to more connected industries. One of those examples is the technology of iceberg towing for oil rig avoidance developed in Canada (Bruneau et al., 1978; Canada's Oil & Natural Gas Producers, n.d.). Although it can be efficiently used to tow icebergs from production sites for them not to meet production facilities such as platforms, it is not applicable for other regions of oil and natural gas exploitation, or other industries.[5]

At the same time, for other technologies outside the oil and gas industry, the Arctic technological niche creates incentives for further development and improvement of certain innovative sub-technological solutions, and even sometimes being an incubator for radical innovation pioneered in those niches (Schot, 1998). The examples are the development of floating and small-scale nuclear power stations by Russian governmental institutions (Rapier, 2019) and the application of aerostats for different purposes including equipment delivery in the Arctic region. Those have the potential to expand outside the offshore Arctic and even outside the Arctic, while also serving the oil and gas industry.

There is low industrial transformation in the Arctic offshore oil and natural gas activities from the actors' perspective because they are predominantly large international and national companies, governments of the circumpolar countries and Arctic Council observers interested in an industrial surge in the region. Only rather large actors with strong governmental support and significant assets are capable of accessing and exploiting Arctic offshore resources. The actors involved need to be able to take high risks and invest in costly long-term assets, including environmentally friendly technological solutions. Thus, there is almost no place for small (and even medium) companies. The smaller companies are predominantly subsidiaries of the larger ones.

The macroeconomic and geopolitical conditions around the Arctic are rapidly changing (Morgunova and Westphal, 2016) and affect the region's industrial development. The world economic crisis in 2008–2009 followed by a decline in oil prices resulted in a lack of necessary investment together with the delay and cancellation of some Arctic offshore projects, for example, the Goliat project in the Norwegian part and the Shtokman project in the Russian part of the Barents Sea, respectively. Further oil price volatility along with a rather low average oil price made companies abandon other exploration plans (the Shell project for the Burger area in the Chukchi Sea). At the same time, American and European sanctions on Russia, specifically on technology transfers (The Council of the European Union, 2014; US Department of State, n.d.), have dramatically undermined Arctic offshore project cooperation and have already postponed the Prinovozemelsky licence block development plans (Platts, 2014). In the Arctic, the macroeconomic and geopolitical pressures seem to be much stronger than the "pure" technological evolution in classically described niches (Geels, 2005, 2002). Nevertheless, challenging macroeconomic and geopolitical conditions stimulate co-evolution in the oil and gas industry (Morgunova and Kutcherov, 2016), for example, supporting governmental programmes and special tax regimes.

To summarize, the Arctic as a niche seems to be so far producing predominantly incremental innovations (sub-technologies) for the oil and gas industry, as well as some potential for system-level changes in the more connected industries. This does not mean though there is no place for innovations in Arctic offshore oil and natural gas exploitation, as one may conclude on a low level of industrial transformation within the Arctic niche of the oil and gas industry that those niche innovations are likely to stay within the niche.

Conclusion

The potential for oil and natural gas resources in the offshore Arctic is huge and stimulates companies and governments to look for their exploitation. However, Arctic offshore oil and natural gas resource development is far from being fundamentally new as there has been a surge in activity that can be observed historically. Arctic offshore oil and natural gas exploitation began to grow in the 2000s with ups and downs depending on the macroeconomic and geopolitical situation. This is a stepwise process of exploitation of more hard-to-access oil and natural gas resources, where companies are moving further from the shore to new undeveloped areas.

From a multilevel perspective and an analysis of industrial transformation, the exploitation of Arctic offshore oil and natural gas resources uncovers itself in questionable perspectives. First, it is a very challenging environment for oil and gas industrial activities that can be seen as a "niche", even though the size of this niche is considerable in terms of investment and assets. At the time of writing, neither does offshore Arctic oil and natural gas production significantly contribute to global production nor are there many fields being explored or increasing the scale of production.

Second, the influence of technological development is substantial for Arctic offshore oil and natural gas resources exploitation, but those technological advances are being predominantly adapted to the Arctic conditions while developed in other locations and even by other industries. Additionally, the contribution of technology to the oil and natural gas production volumes is not obvious. More advanced and far-reaching technologies do not substantially extend the output of oil and natural gas from the offshore Arctic. Technological choice can be dictated by the distance from the field to the shore, climate conditions and development costs, and the ease of access to nearshore fields and more distant fields. The historical overview has also indicated a sharp differentiation in the most used technologies between Arctic countries, which is dependent on technological availability and climate-geographical characteristics. However, there are some technological solutions born in the Arctic that have the potential of expanding from this niche, such as floating LNG facilities, aerostats for transportation and small-scale (floating) nuclear power plants.

Third, the set of companies taking part in oil and gas activities has not changed significantly. The actors are predominantly large international and national oil and gas companies, some with significant governmental participation. This is hardly surprising as the Arctic offshore business conditions with its need for long-term investments, high technological intensity and high risks constitute major entry barriers for smaller actors. There are also institutional barriers in the form of regulations that prohibit or make access to water difficult or impossible.

To conclude, Arctic offshore oil and natural gas exploitation does not seem to be going through much of an industrial transformation as it generates predominantly incremental innovations for the oil and gas industry based on the adaptation to natural conditions and intensification of production processes within the value chain, which are likely to stay within the niche.

Notes

1 The list is not limited to the three defined groups. There are also Indigenous people and organizations, professional organizations and unions, etc. involved.

2 Offshore areas where water depths exceed approximately 200 m (600 ft.) and 1500 m (4921 ft.) respectively, may vary depending on the source (Schlumberger, n.d.).
3 Ice island/floating winter ice pad/ice spray island/ice platform/floating ice.
4 The Skuld field operates as a satellite and is fixed to the Norne production vessel; subsea technologies are applied in part.
5 There are initiatives of icebergs towing to water-stressed areas though.

References

Allison, E., Mandler, B., 2018. Oil and gas in the U.S. Arctic: Managing resources in an oil-and gas-rich but harsh and fragile environment. *Am. Geosci. Inst.* 12/24, 1–4.

AMAP, 2007. *Arctic Oil and Gas 2007.* Oslo: AMAP.

Bjørnbom, E., 2013. Goliat development project. In: *Norwegian Russian Environmental Cooperation (Moscow 27.11.2013).* Eni Norge. Moscow: Norwegian Russian Environmental Cooperation. p. 22.

Bogojavlenskij, V., Bogojavlenskij, I., 2017. Arctic production: Projects and risks (Arkticheskaja dobycha: proekty i riski). *Neftegazov. Vertikal'* 5, 48–53.

Botev, R., 2008. Arctic blank map (with changes) [WWW Document]. Wikimedia Commons CC BY-SA 2.5. https://commons.wikimedia.org/wiki/File:Arctic_blank_map.png (accessed 11.9.19).

BP, 2019a. *Statistical Review of World Energy*, 68th edition. London: BP.

BP, 2019b. *BP Energy Outlook.*

Bruneau, A.A., Dempster, R.T., Peters, G.R., 1978. Iceberg towing for oil rig avoidance. In: *Iceberg Utilization: Proceedings of the First International Conference and Workshops on Iceberg Utilization for Fresh Water Production, Weather Modification and Other Applications,* held at Iowa State University, Ames, IA, October 2–6, 1977. Iowa State University Research Foundation, pp. 379–388.

Budzik, P., 2009. *Arctic Oil and Natural Gas Potential.* Washington, DC: U.S. Energy Information Administration, Office of Integrated Analysis and Forecasting Oil and Gas Division.

Canada's Oil & Natural Gas Producers, n.d. Ice management [WWW Document]. https://atlanticcanadaoffshore.ca/ice-management-newfoundland-labradors-offshore-industry/ (accessed 11.9.19).

Duhaime, G., Caron, A., Usd-ppp, M., Usd-ppp, M., 2008. The economy of the circumpolar Arctic. In: Glomsrød, S., Aslaksen, I. (Eds.), *The Economy of the North.* Oslo–Kongsvinger: Statistics Norway, pp. 17–26.

EIA, 2016. Offshore production nearly 30% of global crude oil output in 2015 [WWW Document]. *U.S. Energy Inf. Adm.* https://www.eia.gov/todayinenergy/detail.php?id=28492 (accessed 11.10.19).

Eie, R., Rognaas, G., 2014. Fixed platforms face development challenges in ice-infested waters. *Offshore Mag.* Published May 6th, 2014. https://www.offshore-mag.com/field-development/article/16757283/fixed-platforms-face-development-challenges-in-iceinfested-waters.

Ekelund, M.J., Masterson, D.M., 1980. Floating ice platforms for oil exploration in the Arctic islands. *Arct. J. Arct. Inst. North Am.* 33, 168–183.

Ernst&Young, 2013. *Arctic Oil and Gas.* EYGM Limited.

Fortune, 2019. Fortune 500 [WWW Document]. https://fortune.com/fortune500/2019 (accessed 11.10.19).

Gautier, D.L., Bird, K.J., Charpentier, R.R., Grantz, A., Houseknecht, D.W., Klett, T.R., Moore, T.E., Pitman, J.K., Schenk, C.J., Schuenemeyer, J.H., Sørensen, K.,

Tennyson, M.E., Valin, Z.C., Wandrey, C.J., 2009. Assessment of undiscovered oil and gas in the Arctic. *Science* 324, 1175–1179.
Geels, F.W., 2002. Technological transitions as evolutionary reconfiguration processes: A multi-level perspective and a case-study. *Resour. Policy* 31, 1257–1274.
Geels, F.W., 2005. The dynamics of transitions in socio-technical systems: A multi-level analysis of the transition pathway from horse-drawn carriages to automobiles (1860–1930). *Technol. Anal. Strateg. Manag.* 17, 445–476.
Geels, F.W., Kemp, R., 2007. Dynamics in socio-technical systems: Typology of change processes and contrasting case studies. *Technol. Soc.* 29, 441–455.
Geels, F.W., Schot, J., 2007. Typology of sociotechnical transition pathways. *Resour. Policy* 36, 399–417.
Ghiselin, D., 2012. Extended-reach drilling advances to meet industry need. *Offshore Mag.* Sep 1st, 2012. https://www.offshore-mag.com/business-briefs/equipment-engineering/article/16760040/extendedreach-drilling-advances-to-meet-industry-need
Glomsrød, S., Duhaime, G., Aslaksen, I., 2015. *The Economy of the North.* Oslo–Kongsvinger: Statistics Norway.
INTECSEA, 2012. Arctic development concepts (poster 2013) [WWW Document]. *Offshore Mag.* https://digital.offshore-mag.com
International Energy Agency, 2018. *Outlook for Producer Economies: What Do Changing Energy Dynamics Mean for Major Oil and Gas Exporters?* Paris: International Energy Agency.
Johnston, P.F., 2012. Arctic energy resources: Security and environmental implications. *J. Strateg. Secur.* 5, 13–32.
Joint Pipeline Office, 2010. Northstar offshore island Beaufort Sea [WWW Document]. *Wikimedia Commons CC0.* https://commons.wikimedia.org/wiki/File:Northstar_Offshore_Island_Beaufort_Sea.jpg (accessed 11.9.19).
Jungsberg, L., Turunen, E., Heleniak, T., Wang, S., Ramage, J., Roto, J., 2019. Atlas of population, society and economy in the Arctic. Nordregio Working Paper 2019: 3 doi.org/10.30689/WP2019:3.1403-2511. Stockholm, Sweden, 2019, 80 p.
Koivurova, T., 2015. Race to resources in the Arctic: Have we progressed in our understanding of what takes place in the Arctic? In: Evengård, B., Larsen, J.N., Øyvind, P. (Eds.), *The New Arctic.* Cham, Switzerland: Springer International Publishing, pp. 189–201.
Kovalenko, A.S., Morgunova, M.O., Gribkovskaia, V. V, 2018. Infrastructural synergy of the Northern Sea Route in the International context. *Jenergeticheskaya Polit.* 4, 57–67.
Krjukov, V.A., Krjukov, J. V, 2017. Как раздвинуть рамки арктических проектов (Kak razdvinut' ramki arkticheskih proektov) (In Russian). *ECO* 8, 5–32.
Larsen, J.N., Huskey, L., 2015. The Arctic economy in a global context. In: Evengård, B., Larsen, J.N., Øyvind, P. (Eds.), *The New Arctic.* Cham, Switzerland: Springer International Publishing, pp. 159–174.
Lindholt, L., Glomsrød, S., 2008. Future production of petroleum in the Arctic under alternative oil prices. In: Glomsrød, S., Aslaksen, I. (Eds.), *The Economy of the North 2008.* Oslo–Kongsvinger: Statistics Norway, pp. 69–73.
Marchand, R., 2018. *Norwegian APA 2017 Bid Round – An Indicator the Offshore Market is Opening Up?* Drillinginfo, Feb 15, 2018. https://info.drillinginfo.com/norwegian-apa-2017-bid-round-an-indicator-the-offshore-market-is-opening-up/.
Morgunova, M., 2015. *Arctic Offshore Hydrocarbon Resource Development: Past, Present and Vision of the Future.* Stockholm: KTH Royal Institute of Technology.

Morgunova, M., Kutcherov, V., 2016. Structural change in the petroleum industry. In: Blomkvist, P., Johansson, P. (Eds.), *A Dynamic Mind: Perspectives on Industrial Dynamics*. Stockholm: Universitetsservice US-AB, pp. 249–275.

Morgunova, M., Westphal, K., 2016. *Offshore Hydrocarbon Resources in the Arctic: From Cooperation to Confrontation in an Era of Geopolitical and Economic Turbulence?* Berlin: German Institute for International and Security Affairs.

Necci, A., Tarantola, S., Vamanu, B., Krausmann, E., Ponte, L., 2019. Lessons learned from offshore oil and gas incidents in the Arctic and other ice-prone seas. *Ocean Eng.* 185, 12–26.

Nordea, 2017. Analyses of key companies having business operations in the Arctic main companies from key sectors in the Arctic.

Norwegian Petroleum Directorate, 2018a. 75 new production licences in APA 2017 [WWW Document]. 16/01/2018.

Norwegian Petroleum Directorate, 2018b. 38 companies have applied for acreage in APA 2018 [WWW Document]. 07/09/2018.

Platts, 2014. *Russian Rosneft Announces Major Oil, Gas Discovery in Arctic Kara Sea*. Platts. 29 Sep 2014. https://www.platts.ru/latest-news/oil/moscow/russian-rosneft-announces-major-oil-gas-discovery-21300064

Poltorackaja, N., 2011. What directions in the development of the Arctic shelf should Russia focus on? Interview of Bogojavlenskij V.I. (Na kakih napravlenijah v osvoenii arkticheskogo shel'fa neobhodimo sosredotochit'sja Rossii? Intervju Bogojavlenskij V.I.) (In Russian) [WWW Document]. *Russ. Acad. Sci.* http://www.ras.ru/digest/showdnews.aspx?id=a4527ddc-6cb6-4058-8574-8a2a0be44eff&print=1

Pratt, J., Priest, T., Castaneda, C.J., 1997. *Offshore Pioneers: Brown & Root and the History of Offshore Oil and Gas*. Houston, TX: Gulf Publishing.

Pritchin, S., 2018. Russia's untapped Arctic potential [WWW Document]. *Chatham House*. 29 January 2018. https://www.chathamhouse.org/expert/comment/russia-s-untapped-arctic-potential (accessed 3.7.18).

PWC, 2019. Global top 100 companies by market capitalisation. https://www.pwc.com/gx/en/audit-services/publications/assets/global-top-100-companies-2019.pdf

Rapier, R., 2019. Russia's floating nuclear power plant has great potential for decarbonization trends. *Forbes*. Oct 20, 2019. https://www.forbes.com/sites/rrapier/2019/10/20/floating-nuclear-power-plants-could-save-numerous-lives/

RIA Novosti, 2019. Gazprom Neft may connect Dolginskoye field to Prirazlomnoye ("Gazprom neft" mozhet podkljuchit' Dolginskoe mestorozhdenie k Prirazlomnomu) (In Russian). *RIA Nov.* 09.04.2019. https://ria.ru/20190409/1552516831.html

Royal Dutch Shell, 2015. Floating LNG [WWW Document]. *R. Dutch Shell*. https://www.shell.com/energy-and-innovation/natural-gas/floating-lng.html (accessed 11.10.19).

Sandrea, I., Sandrea, R., 2007. GLOBAL OFFSHORE OIL-1 : Exploration trends show continued promise in world's offshore basins. *Oil Gas J.* : Mar 5th, 2007. https://www.ogj.com/drilling-production/production-operations/article/17227828/global-offshore-oil1-exploration-trends-show-continued-promise-in-worlds-offshore-basins

Schlumberger, n.d. The oilfield glossary [WWW Document]. https://glossary.oilfield.slb.com

Schot, J., 1998. The usefulness of evolutionary models for explaining innovation. The case of the Netherlands in the nineteenth century. *Hist. Technol.* 14, 173–200.

Songhurst, B., 2019. *Floating LNG Update – Liquefaction and Import Terminals*. The Oxford Institute for Energy Studies, Oxford. OIES PAPER: NG149, 29 p. DOI:

10.26889/9781784671440. https://www.oxfordenergy.org/publications/floating-lng-update-liquefaction-and-import-terminals/?v=79cba1185463

The Council of the European Union, 2014. Council decision 2014/872/CFSP, 4 December 2014.

Tordo, S., Tracy, B.S., Arfaa, N., 2011. National oil companies value creation (No. 218), *World Bank Working Paper*. Washington, DC.

US Department of State, n.d. Ukraine and Russia sanctions [WWW Document]. https://www.state.gov/ukraine-and-russia-sanctions/

USGS, 2008. Circum-Arctic resource appraisal: Estimates of undiscovered oil and gas north of the Arctic circle. U.S. Geological Survey, USGS Fact Sheet 2008-3049, U.S. Geological Survey, Mail Stop 969 345 Middlefield Road Menlo Park, CA 94025, 4 p.

Yang, M., Khan, F.I., Lye, L., Sulistiyono, H., Dolny, J., Oldford, D., 2013. Risk-based winterization for vessels operations in Arctic environments. *J. Sh. Prod. Des.* 29, 199–210.

Appendix 1

TABLE 10.A1 Some Arctic offshore fields

Country	*Field*	*Discovery*	*Development*	*Production*	*Operator company*	*Development concept*
Russia	Yurkharovskoye	1970	n/d	2003	Novatek	Extended reach drilling
	Dolginskoye	1999	2014	2031	Gazprom Neft	Bottom founded structures
	Prirazlomnoe	1989	2011	2013	Gazprom Neft	Bottom founded structures
	Kharasaveyskoye	1974	2019	2023	Gazprom	Extended reach drilling
USA	Endicott	1978	n/d	1986	BP/Hilcorp	Bottom founded structures (gravel island)
	Pt. McIntyre	1988	n/d	1993	BP	Extended reach drilling
	Badami	1990	1997	1998	BP	Extended reach drilling
	Northstar	1983	1995	2001	BP/Hilcorp	Bottom founded structures (gravel island)
	Oooguruk	2003	2006	2008	Pioneer Natural Resources	Bottom founded structures (gravel island)
	Nikaitchuq	2004	2008	2011	Eni	Bottom founded structures (gravel island)
	Liberty	1997	2014	2020	BP, Hilcorp	Bottom founded structures (gravel island) combined with extended reach drilling
	Point Thomson	1965	2012	2016	ExxonMobil	Bottom founded structures (gravel island) combined with extended reach drilling
Norway	Snøhvit	1984	2002	2007	Statoil	Subsea facilities
	Skuld	2009	2012	2013	Statoil	Subsea facilities (satellite tightened to production vessel)
	Goliat	2000	2009	2017	Eni Norge	Floating structures
	Johan Castberg	2011	2014	2022	Statoil	Floating structures
	Aasta Hansteen	1997	2012	2018	Statoil	Floating structures

11

THE INDUSTRIAL TRANSFORMATION OF THE SWEDISH HEAT PUMP SECTOR

Petter Johansson

Industrial transformations play out in long-term coevolutionary patterns (Dosi and Nelson, 1994; Nelson, 1994) and pass through different industry life cycle stages (Utterback, 1994; Klepper, 1997). The industrial transformation of the Swedish heat pump sector from the 1970s to the 2010s presents an example of such industrial dynamics.

Sweden is a leading country in both large-scale adoption and industrial manufacturing of heat pumps. More than half of all houses in Sweden – over one million – are equipped with a heat pump (The Swedish Energy Agency, 2015; SKVP, 2019) and some of Europe's largest heat pump manufacturing facilities are Swedish. However, Sweden has not always been at the forefront of heat pump technology. This chapter sets out to both describe and explain the transformation of the Swedish heat pump sector from laggard to leader. That is, the purpose of this chapter is to analyse and explain the emergence and transformation of the Swedish heat pump sector. To guide our analysis of the transformation of the Swedish heat pump sector, we use the concepts of development blocks and complementarities (Dahmén, 1950, 1991) and theories of industry life cycles (ILC) in this chapter.

Dahmén explained that industrial development happens in blocks of complementary investments and that an investment in a new venture may require complementary investments. Without these complementary investments, the potential of the original venture may never be fulfilled. In Dahmén's own words, a development block is defined as: "a sequence of complementarities that by way of a series of structural tensions, i.e. disequilibria, may end up in a balanced situation" (Dahmén, 1991, p. 139). A development block is comparable with the notion of a sociotechnical system (Bijker, Hughes and Pinch, 1987; Fridlund, 1999), insofar as it consists of technological as well as organizational and institutional structures (Geels, 2004; Jacobsson and Bergek, 2011). Similar to the notion of a "reverse salient" in a sociotechnical system – i.e. a passage that cannot be passed through, creating a backwards bulge for the advancing front (Hughes, 1983) – a structural tension between complementarities can create an impulse for innovation and promote alignment between actors, technologies and institutions, but only if the development potential of the block of complementarities is recognized as such by entrepreneurs or other actors. For example, in the first decades of the twentieth century, the Swedish company Allmänna Svenska Elektriska Aktiebolaget (ASEA – now ABB) lacked market demand for their electrical machinery products. ASEA partly solved this by promoting technological developments and investments in electricity production (upstream) and electrification of industries (downstream). After this "electrical development block" was completed, an electric power industry could develop and the demand for ASEA's products increased (Dahmén, 1950).

ILC literature has long characterized the patterns of industrial dynamics at an aggregated level as long-term industrial transformation processes (Abernathy and Utterback, 1978; Utterback, 1994; Klepper, 1997). Using ILC terminology, an industrial transformation process can be divided into distinct phases: fluid (and chaotic), transitional and specific. The first "fluid" phase involves a period with explorative activities and tensions between different technological alternatives, business models and institutional settings. The period is characterized by high-level product development and testing being made by an increasing number of entrants. The "transitional" phase is typically characterized by the increased alignment of technological, organizational and institutional complementarities and the emergence of a "dominant design" that all market actors have to relate to (Anderson and Tushman, 1990). The industry typically goes through a period of increasing consolidation, with firm exits surpassing the number of entries after a dominant design emerges. In the "specific" phase, the industry eventually ends up in a balanced and more rigid state with more focus on specialization, sustaining innovation and quality improvement than product development.

The purpose of using Dahmén's concepts with concepts from ILC literature in this chapter is to illustrate the coevolutionary mechanisms of industrial transformation – i.e. how organizational, technological and institutional complementarities align and develop interdependently – in different phases of the industrial transformation of the Swedish heat pump sector. While ILC theory illustrates the patterns of industrial dynamics, Dahmén's concepts explain the underlying foundations of these patterns.

This chapter comprises a methods section and a technology and market background section, followed by a description and discussion of four different periods of heat pump industrial transformation in Sweden. The first period comprises a description of the first formative steps towards a Swedish heat pump industry. The second period covers the long-lasting "fluid" phase of the Swedish heat pump sector with the gradual alignment of technological and organizational heat pump complementarities. The third period covers the "transitional" phase of the industry and includes how some heat pump manufacturers managed to survive the "reverse oil crisis" in the mid-1980s and outlines the breakthrough of heat pumps in Sweden in the mid-1990s followed by increasing consolidation in the sector. The fourth period covers the "specific" phase of the Swedish heat pump sector when the Swedish heat pump market had stabilized. Lessons from the Swedish heat pump case are discussed in the final part of this chapter.

Methods

This chapter is partly based on the doctoral thesis *A Silent Revolution* (Johansson, 2017). The empirical material is based on data collected from 2012 to 2017, including interviews with 18 respondents, together with contemporary and primary material from 1970 to 2015. The interviews were conducted with respondents that had been active in the Swedish heat pump sector between 1970 and 2015. The backgrounds of the respondents varied and included respondents from academia, industry, industry associations and energy companies. The interviews were in-depth and flexible with open-ended questions, and there were often follow-up interviews – sometimes several – with the respondents.

Access to Vattenfall's company archives was granted in early 2014 through the assistance of Vattenfall Cultural Heritage Committee member and Vattenfall employee Svante Färnbo. This was a particularly important source for contemporary and primary material, containing a vast library of reports, articles, notes and documented presentations regarding heat pumps from 1970 to the early 1990s. During this time period, Vattenfall was a corporate agency that was heavily involved in the development of heat pump technology and the heat pump market in Sweden. To triangulate the findings from interviews in Vattenfall's company archives and the interviews conducted for this chapter, other sources of material were used. These included: the Swedish heat pump interest organization SVEP (now SKVP), the European Heat Pump Association (EHPA), the Swedish Testing Institute (SP, afterwards RISE), books, journals and magazine articles located through the search engines of the National Library of Sweden and the Royal Institute's Library in Stockholm, the Thomson Innovation patent database, the International Energy Agency (IEA), The Swedish Energy Agency (Energimyndigheten), Folksam's insurance reports on failed heat pumps, research reports from Swedish technical universities, annual reports from heat pump manufacturers located through the National Library of Sweden and governmental reports.

The case of the industrial transformation of the Swedish heat pump sector is contingent upon historical, international and technological factors, energy commodity price developments and historical developments in Swedish industrial, political and energy system sectors. There is a temporal and geographical dimension to the Swedish heat pump case that limits its generalizability to contemporary industrial transformations. However, context dependence is the typical condition for cases of industrial transformation. Taking context-specific conditions into account, the Swedish heat pump case potentially holds lessons for contemporary technological and industrial transformations, such as the solar PV sector.

Technology and market background

A heat pump is, in principle, a reverse refrigerator – i.e. a machine that pumps heat from a relatively cold heat source (air, ground, water) to a relatively warm heat sink (typically inside of a building). The principle of the heat pump was laid out by Lord Kelvin in the mid-1800s following the theoretical work on thermodynamics by the French military scientist Nicolas Léonard Sadi Carnot. However, it would not be until the first half of the 1900s that the first heat pump manufacturing processes would start in countries like Switzerland, Austria and the United States. Advancements in compressor design needed to be made before it would be possible to develop sufficiently performing heat pumps. As with refrigerators, the compressor constitutes the heart of any modern heat pump unit. Other central components in a heat pump are the heat exchangers (condenser and evaporator), the refrigerant that circulates in the heat pump and the expansion valve and steering equipment of the heat pump cycle. See Figure 11.1 for an illustration of these components.

There are several different types of heat pumps depending on the intended type of heat source (outdoor air, exhaust air, ground and water basins) and heat sink (indoor air, hydronic heating systems and tap water heating). Air-air heat pumps are designed to heat air and are typically less costly to manufacture and install compared with heat pumps designed to heat water. Ground-source heat pumps designed for heating water are typically both more expensive and more powerful than air-air heat pumps, and as such, better suited for cold climates

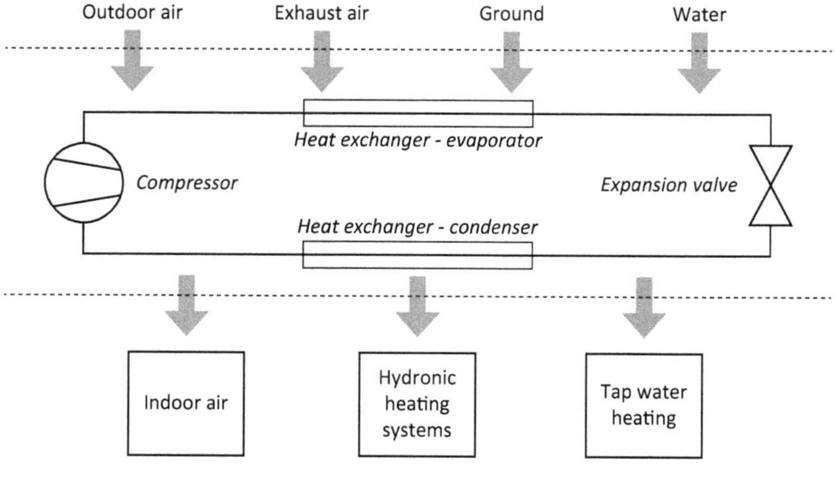

FIGURE 11.1 An illustration of a heat pump unit with different types of heat sources and heat sinks. Adapted from Johansson (2017).

(such as Sweden's). Less costly to install but also less efficient in cold winters are the outdoor air-water heat pumps.

The Swedish heat pump market grew to become Europe's largest in both relative and absolute figures after the mid-1990s, long before other European countries managed to catch up (Forsén and Nowak, 2010). This development is unusual in that ground-source heat pumps over the years have constituted a much bigger share of the total heat pump market compared with the typical low share ground-source heat pumps have held in other European markets. Many other markets in Europe have instead been dominated by air-air heat pumps (EHPA, 2014). A vast majority of the ground-source heat pumps in Sweden have been supplied by domestic manufacturers such as IVT, Thermia and NIBE. The diffusion of heat pumps in Sweden has meant the replacement of many oil boilers and electric heating systems and has been a main factor in decreased greenhouse gas emissions in the Swedish heating sector (The Swedish Energy Agency, 2015).

Given the technological nature of heat pumps as an integrated system of components, the development of heat pumps is dependent on different knowledge areas, including chemistry (refrigerants), mechanics (compressor), fluid mechanics (heat exchangers) and electronics (control and regulation). This means that in highly specialized economies, the competence necessary to develop heat pumps cannot be found in one industry but must be sourced from different industries and academic disciplines. We will see examples of this in the next part of this chapter.

The formative years of the Swedish heat pump sector during the 1970s

In October 1973, Syrian and Egyptian forces launched a surprise attack on Israel. Several Arab OPEC countries imposed an embargo on the allies of Israel following the Yom Kippur war. This created an international oil crisis where international crude oil prices doubled. Sweden was at this time highly oil-dependent and started to look for alternatives to the increasingly expensive oil.

Scholars had already pointed out the theoretical advantages of heat pumps in Sweden – with its cold climate and high oil dependence – in the 1950s (Bäckström *et al.*, 1992). The argument was that heat pumps would become an increasingly attractive alternative in the event of an oil shortage or decrease in electricity prices. However, electricity prices could not be too low, as this would make direct electric heating, with its lower investment costs, more attractive. Despite the theoretical benefits of heat pumps, as presented by its proponents, two decades later heat pumps were still a largely unknown technology. The Swedish energy policy proposals presented in the mid-1970s barely considered heat pump technology as an alternative to oil. The Swedish government's main response to the 1973 oil crisis was to intensify its efforts in nuclear power expansion, so as to make Sweden less dependent on energy imports. Another response was to invest in the research and development of alternative energy technologies that could exploit domestic energy sources (Palme and Johansson, 1975; Ullsten and Tham, 1979). Incidentally, the expansion of nuclear power during the international oil crisis underpinned the formation of a Swedish heat pump sector.

A new industry does not emerge from nowhere. Sweden's pre-existing heating equipment and refrigeration industries played central roles in the formation of the new heat pump sector. Between the 1950s and 1970s, the most common heating alternatives for Sweden's 1.5 million single-family houses were oil boilers, followed by electric heaters and bio-fuel (typically wood) furnaces (The Swedish Energy Agency, 2013; Boverket, 2014). Several Swedish heating equipment companies supplied their home market with locally manufactured heating equipment products. These companies were typically mechanical workshops, specialized in metal and sheet metalworking and machining. Over the years, advancements were made in the areas of turbines, compressors and refrigeration in Sweden, with examples such as the Ljungström Turbine and the silent and non-explosive Platen-Munters refrigerator (Bäckström *et al.*, 1992). The Swedish compressor and refrigeration industry supplied the first commercial heat pumps during the 1950s and 1960s to a niche market of customers with special cooling and heating demands, such as hospitals, malls and ice hockey arenas. These heat pumps were place-built refrigeration or air conditioning units with a heat pump add-on feature (in other words, similar to today's air-air heat pumps). They were also turn-key products, where the refrigeration company took complete responsibility for the installation, performance and reliability of the delivered solution.

While heating equipment companies possessed facilities for assembling heat pumps and had established channels into the housing market, they typically lacked knowledge concerning heat pump technology itself. Refrigeration companies considered heat pump technology to be a part of their industry and area of expertise but lacked entries into the residential heating market. Thus, neither of these industries possessed the required capabilities to commercialize heat pumps in the housing market on their own.

Back in the 1970s, the United States was the hub of air-conditioning unit development and production. In the early 1970s, several Swedish companies started to import air-air heat pumps from the established international market, typically from US brands such as Carrier and Lennox (Vattenfall, 1978). Eventually, there were Swedish companies that started to adapt and integrate imported air-air heat pumps with water heaters in order to offer air-water heat pumps for the Swedish home market. However, test results from this time showed that air-water heat pumps suffered from poor fitness to Swedish conditions, resulting in component malfunctions, sub-par energy savings and poor operational reliability. Similar problems were found for air-air heat pumps. However, there was another emerging heat pump segment that received positive judgements for their reliable performance: the ground-source heat pump segment (Vattenfall, 1978).

Ground-source heat pump development in Sweden was highly dependent on input from related and supporting industries. This is illustrated in the history of the heating equipment company Thermia, in Arvika – a pioneer of ground-source heat pumps. In the early 1970s, Geoterm – a Swedish consulting affiliate to a Danish company – sought to contract a Swedish manufacturer for its heat pump technology. They started a collaboration with Thermia that resulted in Sweden's first ground-source heat pump, with all indoor components situated in one unit. The final product was named the JBC-400. At first, Thermia had to ship every heat pump they manufactured to another city for the installation of the unit's steering equipment, since Thermia lacked this competence themselves. Thermia also solicited help from refrigeration consulting firms to develop their own heat pump test rigs. Even though the unit was large, weighed several hundred kilograms and was cumbersome to install, the JBC-400 was a ground-breaking product.

For the next version of ground-source heat pumps, Thermia relied on the expertise of Swedish academia. Eric Granryd was a researcher (and later professor) at KTH. Granryd's department had been conducting research and education concerning mechanical heating technologies since the 1910s (Bäckström *et al.*, 1992). With Granryd's help, Thermia managed to develop new, lighter heat exchangers for its next heat pump series (the DUO8 series), which allowed for much lighter heat pump units and consequently cheaper shipping and installation costs. Without access to external expertise, the DUO8 would never have been possible.

The "fluid" phase of the Swedish heat pump sector

The Iranian revolution in 1979 contributed to international crude oil prices reaching new heights in a second international oil crisis. In parallel to this second oil crisis, the Swedish heat pump sector entered a slightly chaotic period.

After 1979, heat pump technology received increased focus from new entrants, large incumbent corporations and policy makers. Important technological heat pump developments were made, such as improvements in system reliability, diffusion of reliable heat exchangers in the industry and advancements in borehole drilling. A technological standard for heat pumps had not yet emerged; diesel- and gas-driven heat pumps were seen as alternatives to electric heat pumps, absorption heat pumps were compared to gas-compression heat pumps and so on (VVS-Tekniska Föreningen, 1979). It would be the electric-driven heat pumps that would take over the residential market. The Swedish heat pump market grew from fewer than 1000 sold units in the late 1970s to over 25,000 units sold in 1984. The number of brands on the market also grew to over 100 as the number of entrants offering heat pumps rapidly increased. In industry life cycle terms, the heat pump sector was in a fluid period, with investments made mainly in product (rather than process) developments and a large number of companies offering different types of heat pumps to the market (Utterback, 1994).

Given the lack of standards, there were also many technical issues within the heat pump sector, such as leakages, noisy compressors, poor system reliability, malfunctioning compressors or other components, defrosting failures in the outdoor unit and so on. This was exacerbated by common misconceptions concerning heat pumps, for instance, that the air or ground did not contain enough heat to use for heating or that the ground would quickly freeze and result in permafrost if a ground-source heat pump was installed. These misconceptions were not only spread among potential customers but among government agencies, lending institutions and industry associations as well (Mogensen, 1979).

Government agencies played an important part in facilitating knowledge diffusion and bolstering the legitimacy of heat pump technology. Most notably, the Swedish energy corporate agency Vattenfall played an important role in this regard by administering large-scale research and development (R&D) programmes aimed towards heat pumps. To increase market demand and the transition away from oil burners, private homeowners could receive subsidized loans or direct subsidies from 1978 to 1984 (Engebeck and Zingmark, 1987). Though the monetary support was no larger than 15% of the total investment cost, it did provide positive signals regarding the legitimacy of heat pump technology. Vattenfall addressed many of the heat pump sector's issues through its research and development programme, called the "Solar Program", which ran from 1979 to 1986. This programme involved collaborations with a large number of heat pump producers, as well as educational efforts aimed at heat pump suppliers and installers. The Solar programme was a result of Vattenfall's interpretation of the government directive to "introduce into practice technology and products required to make solar energy commercially available for heating purposes" (Vattenfall, 1981, p. 16). In the 1980s, heat pump stakeholders used the favourable public view of solar energy to give heat pump technology forward momentum, while overcoming the widespread lack of knowledge concerning heat pumps. This was also the case in Vattenfall's Solar programme. While the directive for the R&D programme was to make solar energy technologies commercially available for heating purposes, Vattenfall's staff in the Solar programme redirected 80% of its resources towards heat pumps and only 20% towards technologies such as solar panels.

In the early 1980s, the Swedish government's approach to the domestic industry was to directly collaborate with industry and intervene in industrial development (Fridlund, 1999; Schön, 2012). Vattenfall's Solar programme was an example of such direct governmental intervention in industrial development. Vattenfall took on the role of a facilitator and intermediary between different heat pump manufacturers, government agencies and types of customers in the heat pump industry, increasing knowledge flow and working – together with companies and government organizations – to increase the level of competence among industry players, and particularly installers (Vattenfall, 1989a, 1989b). Another example of the close collaboration between policy makers and domestic industry was the entry of large incumbent Swedish corporations – such as ASEA and SAAB – into the heat pump sector, in what can almost be described as a consensus with the Swedish government.

Measures to define the role and responsibility of actors were introduced to control and coordinate the growth of the heat pump sector, while still supporting the technological development and marketability of heat pumps. This was done through agencies pushing for the formation of an industry association, which was the precursor to SVEP. This association initially engaged in educational activities, acted as a consultative body to the industry, developed rules for product warranties that would apply to all members and developed a database of heat pump installations (Lindholm, 2011). Vattenfall collaborated with the Swedish testing institute SP and other agencies in this programme to conduct tests on Swedish heat pump products, so as to try out new concepts and increase the lower bound of heat pump performance.

All government initiatives that increased demand for heat pumps created other structural tensions, as the industry was unable to supply the rapid increase in market demand. This created fertile soil for opportunistic actors to enter the sector. In turn, companies that manufactured quality heat pump products – such as Thermia and IVT – suffered from the poor reputation that low-quality heat pump units and installations created. Improved quality over the entire industry would benefit Thermia and IVT, and as such, though each was the other's biggest competitor, the two companies together could counteract the damage done by opportunists and improve knowledge dissemination in the industry. They did so both through lobbying activities, but also by reconfiguring their current business models and value chains.

How the heat pump value chain was reconfigured

One of the main challenges within the heat pump sector was the division of responsibilities between suppliers, manufacturers, retailers and installers. The previous division of responsibility that had worked well within the heating equipment industry, in which manufacturers took responsibility for the technological performance of their products but not for how the product was installed, now became a pressing issue. When heating equipment companies started to manufacture heat pumps, they did so within their existing business context. They manufactured some parts themselves (primarily those involving plate and steelwork) and bought other parts from their component suppliers. They then sold their finished products to wholesalers, who sold to retailers, who in turn sold the product to end users and used subcontractors for the final installation. This value chain – illustrated in Figure 11.2 – had been highly functional. However, this changed when heating equipment companies started to manufacture heat pumps.

During the 1970s and early 1980s, installers' knowledge and competence regarding heat pumps were low and lagging behind compared with that of manufacturers. Heat pump technology proved to have quite different properties from other residential heating products. The efficiency of an installed heat pump depends on how well-adapted it is to the properties of the heating system to

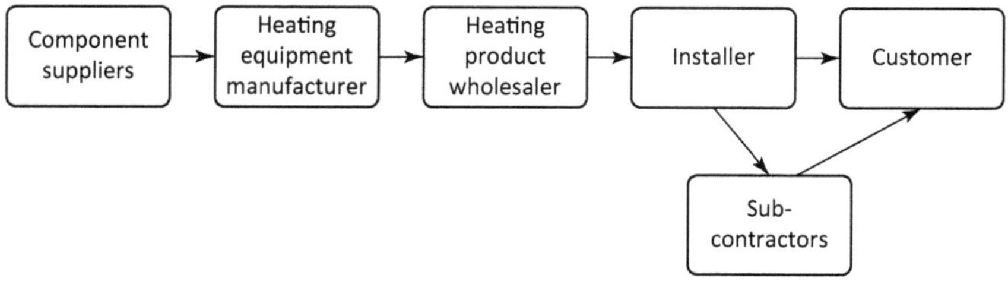

FIGURE 11.2 Heating equipment value chain in the 1970s.

which it is connected and to the properties of the heat source that it utilizes (e.g. outside air or horizontal or borehole collector). One can compare the situation to that of an oil boiler that fires up, gets hot and heats the water to the intended temperature using a shunt coupling (mixing hot water with cold water). These two technologies function in completely different ways, but many heat pump installers installed heat pumps as though they were oil boilers. Furthermore, the lack of a functional service network meant that even the most trivial malfunctions reported by customers would sometimes take weeks or months to fix.

This created a problem – or tension – for heat pump manufacturers. The tension was addressed by manufacturers such as Thermia and IVT by taking increased control over retailing and installation, integrating vertically downstream and skipping the wholesaler (see Figure 11.3). This business model innovation was influenced by the turn-key business model of the refrigeration industry. The change came at the cost of losing good relations with the industry's wholesalers. However, having a closer relationship with one's own network of installers meant being able to guarantee not only the quality of the heat pump unit but also the quality of its installation.

The expansion of large-sized heat pumps during the 1980s

At an energy systems level – where the goal was to mitigate oil dependence – heat pump technology became increasingly aligned with other complementary

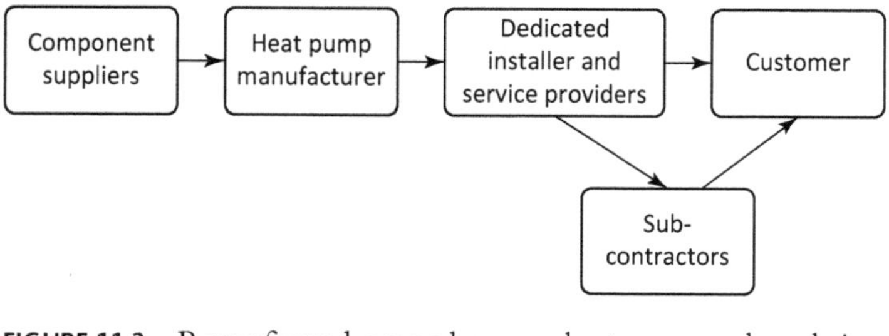

FIGURE 11.3 Reconfigured ground-source heat pump value chain within the heat pump development block.

technologies during the 1980s, including other heating technologies such as district heating and solar technology. Large-sized heat pumps installed in district heating systems had an even greater energy system impact than residential heat pumps. The economic motivation to invest in large-sized heat pumps was based on high fuel prices and affordable electricity prices. The payback time for a district heating company's investment in a large-sized heat pump dropped to as low as two to three years in the 1980s. It was, yet again, Swedish turbine and refrigeration companies that saw and exploited this opportunity.

The first installations of large-sized heat pumps in district heating facilities were actually of quite poor quality. Since Vattenfall was part supplier and part customer in these first attempts (through their "Solar Program"), Vattenfall became a mediator between suppliers and the district heating companies. This gave the suppliers time to address their early technological difficulties, improving performance for future applications.

The rapid expansion of heat pumps in district heating systems strengthened the position of both district heating technology and heat pump technology in the energy system. This meant that district heating power plants could quickly reduce a large portion of their oil dependence and/or their use of electric boilers. In the long term, however, it became increasingly difficult for district heating lobbyists to argue against the use of small heat pumps when the district heating companies themselves were using heat pumps. The use of large-sized heat pumps strengthened the overall perception of heat pumps as a functional, reliable and cost-efficient alternative to oil. The logic was that, if heat pumps were good enough to use in district heating plants, then why not use them directly in a residential house where the heat loss of the district heating distribution grid could be avoided.

By the end of the 1980s, when the expansion of place-built and large-sized heat pumps came to a halt, some of the world's largest heat pump systems had been constructed in Swedish district heating grids (Vattenfall, 1989b).

The state of the heat pump development block by the mid-1980s

When academic researcher Eric Granryd had helped Thermia to develop new lightweight heat exchangers, he had made it possible for Thermia to produce much smaller and lighter indoor heat pump units, further improving the company's competitive advantage. Fairly soon, Thermia's competitors were able to order plate heat exchangers with roughly the same properties as Granryd's heat exchanger, enabling them to catch up with Thermia. These plate heat exchangers came from the Swedish industry and were both technologically and organizationally complementary to the Swedish heat pump sector. Another important technological complement to heat pumps that received investments and underwent development in this period was borehole technology. Vattenfall had tested recharging single boreholes but realized that it was much more economical to drill longer boreholes. The companies that drilled boreholes in 1979–1985, such as water well drilling companies, had existing equipment for this task. With their complementary resources and capabilities, these companies became business partners with heat pump companies and installers. Significant advancements in borehole drilling were made during the 1980s, with a doubling of borehole drilling capacity between 1980 to 1985 (Zogg, 2008), and another doubling between 1985 and 1990 (Granryd, 2010). By 1990, the borehole technique had become so efficient that it was possible to drill up to 200 meters in just one day. This development was an important technological complement to ground-source heat pumps and was fundamental for the future development of this type of pump in Sweden.

Figure 11.4 illustrates the main actors (component suppliers, manufacturers, consultants, experts from academia, government agencies, etc.) and their interrelations in the Swedish heat pump development block in the early 1980s. While there were remaining tensions, for example, between rapidly increasing heat pump demand and the supply capacity of the industry, the Swedish development block was in a productive and developing state.

The early 1980s had been a period marked by rapid market expansion and the rapid increase of new entrants. However, in the years following 1985, the emphasis changed to a decrease in market demand and the exit of heat pump suppliers from the industry.

The "transitional" phase of the Swedish heat pump sector

The period after 1985 starts with the so-called "reverse oil crisis". This crisis was the result of a drop in international oil prices in the mid-1980s, together with the removal of heat pump subsidies and continued uncertainty regarding electricity prices. This had a significant effect on the Swedish heat pump sector. Many heat pump manufacturers had been caught off guard by the suddenly lowered price of oil. They had been concentrating on changes in electricity prices after the 1980 referendum, where it had been decided that Sweden should eventually dismantle its nuclear power plants (Energiforskningsnämnden, 1985). With the removal of subsidies, many potential customers chose to delay their planned investments in new heating systems.

The Swedish heat pump association SVEP acted as a lobbyist for the heat pump sector, lobbying for government support of heat pumps through procurement competitions. Researchers at technical universities such as KTH continued to focus on heat pumps, even as the market struggled and policy was focused elsewhere.

There were still many technological challenges for the heat pump industry to resolve. For example, steering problems with air-water heat pumps had proven much more difficult to overcome than was first expected. Varying outdoor temperatures required sophisticated steering capabilities that air-water heat pumps did not have. Customers might tolerate poor performance from cheap air-air heat pumps, but not from the more expensive air-water pumps.

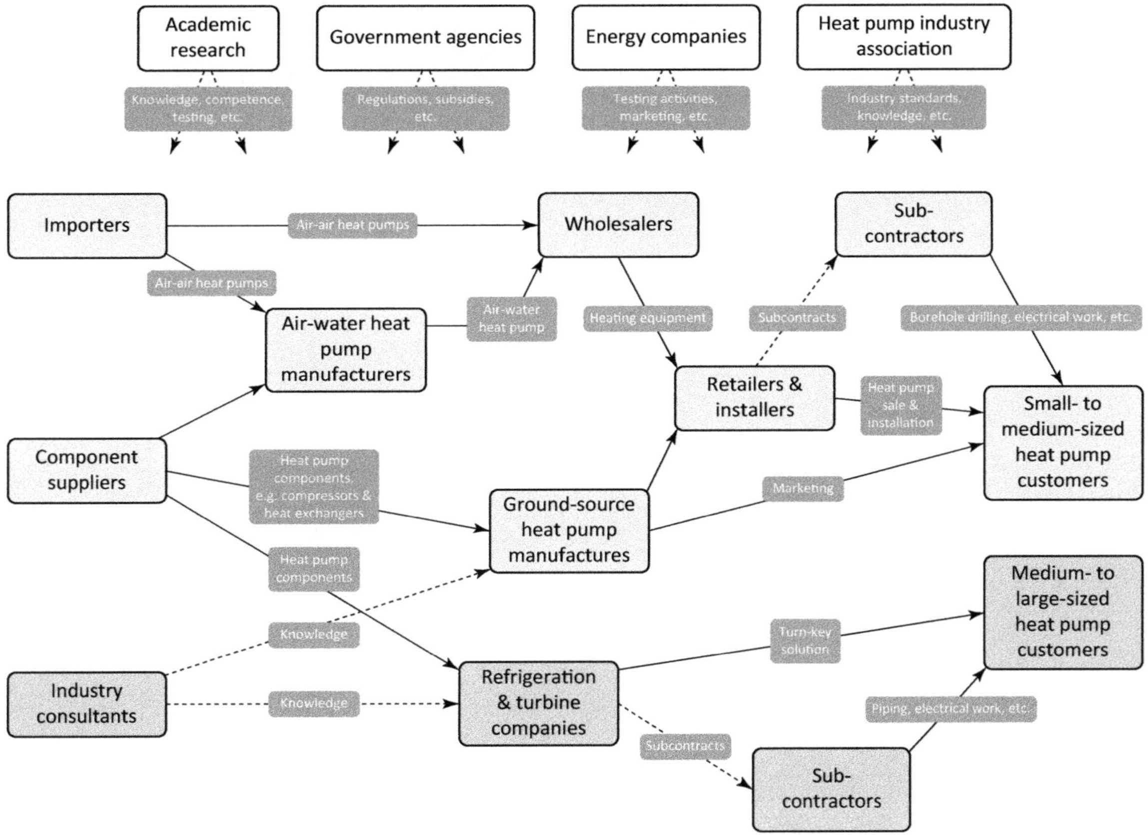

FIGURE 11.4 Illustration of value chains and interrelations between the main actors in the Swedish heat pump sector in the early 1980s. Solid arrows represent the exchange of tangibles and dotted arrows represent the exchange of intangibles. Actors that influenced the entire sector are illustrated at the top.

Consequently, the air-water heat pump segment suffered greatly, and more or less disappeared by 1987. By 1988, the ground-source heat pump market segment seemed to be going the same way. Without the perseverance of ground-source heat pump manufacturers and their networks of dedicated installers, there would not have been any ground-source heat pump companies left by the 1990s. Their survival meant that they were able to retain knowledge, competence and external networks for ground-source heat pumps that were necessary conditions for the recovery of this segment in the mid-1990s.

How some heat pump manufacturers managed to survive after 1985

Disequilibria between different heat pump market segments increased during this phase. The two market segments that made Sweden unique in Europe were large-sized heat pumps and exhaust-air heat pumps. These two market segments did not suffer from the sudden drop in oil prices in the same way that other segments did because they had formed tight couplings with stable institutional and infrastructural complementarities. The segment for large-sized heat pumps had become implicated in Vattenfall and the Swedish refrigeration/turbine industry's effort to reduce oil dependence in Sweden's large network of district heating grids. The institutional alignment of exhaust-air heat pumps was more coincidental. In 1980, the Swedish building regulation agency BFR introduced a building regulation that only passingly mentioned heat pumps, but that would have a major impact on the entire heat pump sector in Sweden. The purpose of the 1980 building regulation was to address issues resulting from increased use of electric heating. For example, a large group of homeowners that had converted from oil boilers to electric heating had suffered from unintended consequences, such as mould. The natural draft caused by their oil boilers had helped to keep house mould at bay. When an oil boiler was replaced by electric (or heat pump) heating, the natural draft often disappeared. A lack of natural draft required forced ventilation. For newly built houses, the 1980 regulation required both forced ventilation and some sort of energy recovery in the forced ventilation system. This created a niche for exhaust and supply air ventilation heat exchangers (so-called FTX systems) and exhaust-air heat pumps.

The 1980 building regulation had a long-lasting positive effect on exhaust-air heat pump technology. Because the exhaust-air heat pump segment was tightly aligned with institutional complementarities, it was not dependent on either oil prices or government subsidies and was largely untouched by the effects of the "reverse oil crisis". When the home construction market expanded in the late 1980s, the exhaust-air heat pump market also expanded – in contradistinction to other small heat pump market segments.

The exhaust-air heat pump and large-sized heat pump market segments became important complementarities to other heat pump segments in the second half of the 1980s. For example, the exhaust-air heat pump segment kept heat pump technology alive in the Swedish residential heating market and contributed to its retention in the overall Swedish energy system. The survival of heat pump manufacturers was essential for the sector's development during the 1990s. In order for ground-source heat pump companies to survive, they had to develop new capabilities and form new partnerships through changes in ownership and leadership.

Both Thermia and IVT passed through a period of regular ownership changes during the 1980s, first when large corporations invested in heat pump technology and acquired smaller manufacturers, and later when large corporations exited the industry and more speculative owners entered. Eventually, after a long period where the value of both firms decreased, Thermia and IVT enjoyed more stable ownerships, the latter under real estate owner Lars Kastengren, who acquired IVT in 1988, and the former under local industrial strongman Bengt Gustafsson, who acquired Thermia in 1992. These men were active owners that led their firms by involving themselves in production, and they were therefore more responsive to production needs and possibilities than previous owners had been. They focused on developing new product and service offerings using existing production facilities, and on finding new markets to exploit based on existing resources and competence. For example, IVT managed to become a general agent for Asian air-air heat pump manufacturer Sharp in 1990, during a period where air-air heat pump market demand was stronger than demand for ground-source heat pumps. The new leadership also increased focus on managing relations with other companies in their network, in addition to managing the companies themselves. For example, IVT, under Kastengren's leadership, tightened its relations with retailers and installers, supplied installers with improved support, started educating installers (as Thermia had done) through IVT University and put increased pressure on its network of suppliers to deliver products that were suited to IVT's needs. The new owners also had to inject capital to keep their companies afloat. In the case of IVT, Kastengren brought a large established network of contacts to IVT, which facilitated the acquisition of new financing through investors and loans. Kastengren also increased the company's amount of liquid capital by selling real estate to the local municipality and selling convertible bonds to employees.

Due to measures taken by the new owners – widening their offerings, managing their inter-organizational relations and acquiring capital – both Thermia and IVT managed to retain their existing competence regarding heat pumps. The survival of Swedish heat pump manufacturers hindered the dissolution of the heat pump development block.

The period of strong market growth starting in 1995

By the mid-1990s, some of the major tensions between complementarities in the Swedish heat pump development block had been resolved, and the development block started to gain momentum, resulting in accelerated industrial development.

Energy commodity price developments during the 1990s had a positive economic effect for homeowners looking to transition from oil or electric boilers to heat pumps. The heat pump became an increasingly standardized product and an investment that increased the value of the house in which it was installed. An increasing number of homeowners chose to replace their old oil boilers as the heat pump market grew from under 10,000 units sold in 1995 to more than 100,000 units sold annually ten years later (SKVP, 2019).

During the 1990s, the steering of heat pumps improved and heat pumps became quieter due to the use of scroll compressors instead of piston compressors, and products improved, such as rubber gaskets that did not vibrate out of place (Granryd, 2010). With improved steering technology, the operational performance and reliability of air-water heat pumps improved significantly, renewing this industry segment. Efficient plate heat exchangers available on the market allowed for smaller air-water and ground-source indoor heat pumps fitted to 60 by 60 cm casings. These were important improvements that allowed heat pumps to be installed in other parts of the house than the cellar, where the old oil boiler used to be, and where noise was of little concern. The design of indoor units stabilized after this point, and with the appearance of a dominant design came decreased uncertainty about the technology among customers and government organizations (Anderson and Tushman, 1990).

With increasingly beneficial energy prices and improved heat pump design, one of the largest remaining challenges for realizing the potential of the heat pump market was to disseminate knowledge and raise public awareness concerning the possibilities of heat pumps. In the early 1990s, the heat pump market was still a minor segment in the heating sector, and the heat pump industry was described as "weak, almost of the character of small-scale craftsmanship" (The Swedish Energy Agency, 2004). When the Swedish building research council BFR arranged a one-day seminar on heat pumps in Stockholm in 1994, no one signed up to attend and the event had to be cancelled. Ironically enough, the first presentation of the seminar had been titled "Have we forgotten about heat pumps in the energy debate?" (Plomgren, 1994). A series of procurement competitions helped to correct the low level of public awareness regarding heat pumps. Starting in 1989, three procurement competitions were held for the heat pump industry. The final one was held by the Swedish agency for industrial development (NUTEK) in 1993–1995. The competition served to both financially support heat pump manufacturers and market heat pump technology. Other stakeholders in the competition included government agencies like BFR, the governmental research and testing institute SP and Vattenfall, which participated in various ways, such as by testing the heat pumps in the competition. The Swedish government's decision to ban ozone-hazardous chlorofluorocarbons refrigerants (so-called "Freons") – prior to most other nations that had signed the Montreal Protocol – had a big impact on the Swedish heat pump industry and the NUTEK competition. Changing refrigerants was a costly procedure that required a lot of product adaptation, followed by a period of serious testing. Since the heat pump companies in the NUTEK competition were not given enough time for testing, there were large-scale technological malfunctions among many of the heat pump units sold by the two winners. This contributed to the exit of one of these winners a few years later. In 1994, several technical universities, including Eric Granryd's division at KTH, became involved in the alternative refrigerants research programme to contribute their academic expertise on the issue of substituting ozone-friendly alternatives for traditional CFC-based refrigerants. After much testing and following the development of compressors using new refrigerants outside of the Swedish heat pump sector, the issues regarding refrigerants were resolved to a sufficient degree. The support from NUTEK and other government actors helped to finance new product developments and to market heat pump technology among the public in a period when the price of fuel oil was starting to increase again. These efforts helped to complete the Swedish heat pump development block.

Both Thermia and IVT had the competence and resources to manufacture reliable and well-performing heat pumps – though not at the rapidly increasing rate that the market demanded after 1995. To avoid another period where opportunistic actors would be given a chance to enter the market, both Thermia and IVT needed to make large investments in their production capacities. However, since their treasuries were close to bare, they needed external capital to finance their investments in production complementarities. The largest investments using external capital were made by state-owned investment funds.

In the mid-1990s, as the Swedish heat pump market started to grow, there was an increasing consolidation within the heat pump sector. With filled treasuries, IVT and Thermia competed more intensely with each other, launching new products and making acquisitions to widen their product range. Both IVT and Thermia also attempted to enter the exhaust-air heat pump segment, increasing their level of competition with NIBE. IVT succeeded in its attempt by acquiring exhaust-air heat pump manufacturer Elektro Standard in 1998. Thermia, on the other hand, failed in its attempt to enter the exhaust-air heat pump market through organic growth, partly because of the high barrier to entry posed by the established network of house constructors. This horizontal consolidation of the already relatively small Swedish heat pump industry caused competition between manufacturers to become so heated that IVT was expelled from the heat pump association SVEP for having too-good offerings.

The "specific" phase and current state of the Swedish heat pump sector

The structure of the heat pump sector since the industry's specific phase is illustrated in Figure 11.5. Compared with the heat pump sector in the early 1980s (Figure 11.4), the situation was much less complex. Apart from the consolidation of different types of heat pump firms, the entire value chain that supplied large-sized heat pumps had dissolved, with only some consultancy firms remaining.

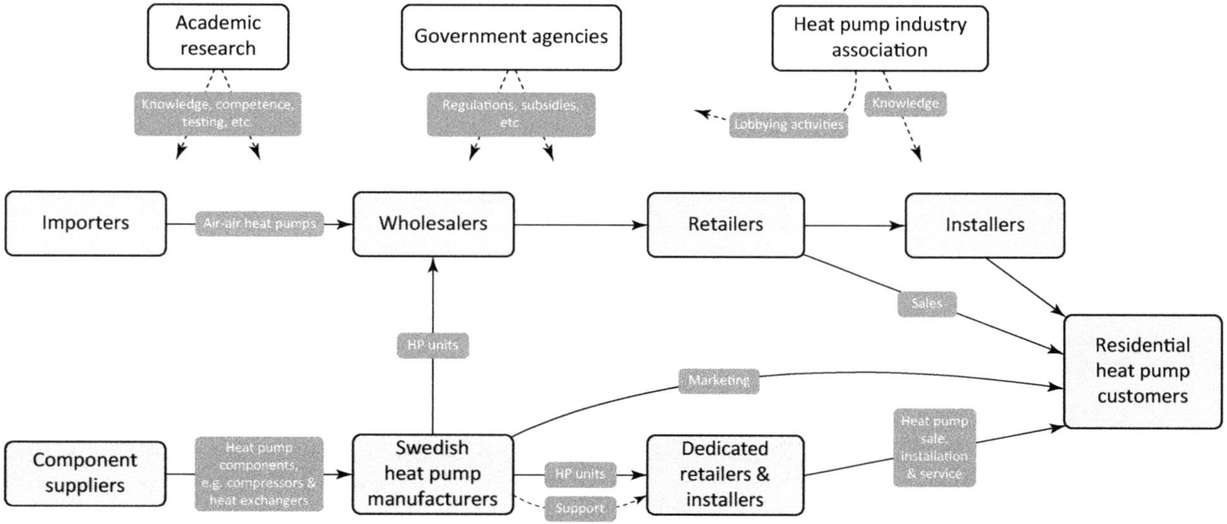

FIGURE 11.5 Illustration of value chains and interrelations between the main actors in the Swedish heat pump sector since the late 1990s. Solid arrows represent the exchange of tangibles and dotted arrows represent the exchange of intangibles. Actors that influenced the entire sector are illustrated at the top.

Retailers and installers were more specialized and less dependent on subcontractors. Energy companies were no longer active stakeholders in the sector, apart from some that acted as retailers of (mostly air-air) heat pumps. An important difference that remained after the consolidation period was that NIBE continued to supply through wholesalers while IVT and Thermia continued with their own affiliated networks of suppliers and installers.

Although the market was already growing and increasingly maturing, direct subsidies for heat pumps were introduced in 1998, lifted in 1999, reintroduced in 2001–2003, lifted in 2003 and then introduced a third time in 2006–2007 (Russell *et al.*, 2009; Boverket, 2011). These different short-term subsidies distorted home market demand for Swedish heat pumps, with no clear positive effects for long-term market growth.

The Swedish heat pump market became increasingly saturated and started to stabilize after 2005.

In the following period, Swedish heat pump companies began expanding into new markets, including foreign markets (e.g. the underdeveloped UK market) and new markets in Sweden (e.g. commercial buildings and multifamily houses). The latter contributed to increased competition between heat pumps and district heating in Sweden, marking a change from the previously synergistic relations between these solutions, as described earlier, towards more confrontational relations.

Both Thermia's and IVT's owners believed that an owner with an existing international network of suppliers would better facilitate international expansion. As such, they sold their companies: IVT to Bosch and Thermia to Danish company Danfoss. NIBE took a different route and expanded internationally through company acquisitions (instead of being acquired by an international corporation). Though increasingly internationalized, the production of heat pumps has largely remained in Sweden, where it has become increasingly concentrated. Over the last few years, the Swedish heat pump industry has made exports valued at around €100 million annually.[1] Initially, Swedish firms were able to capture half of the ground-source heat pump market in Europe, demonstrating that the Swedish heat pump development block was in a mature stage, spreading its seeds to other markets. The current status of the Swedish heat pump industry is that it is increasingly internationalized – out of the mentioned heat pump manufacturers in this chapter, only NIBE is still a Swedish owned company – but the manufacturing of heat pumps is still strong in Sweden.

Discussion and conclusions

The purpose of this chapter has been to analyse and explain the emergence and transformation of the Swedish heat pump sector. We have used ILC nomenclature to divide the industrial transformation into different phases. Using Dahmén's concepts, we have described and explained the industrial dynamics of the Swedish heat pump sector in each of these phases as the result of entrepreneurial and institutional activity, induced by tensions and the gradual alignment of technological, organizational and institutional complementarities, which altogether realized the potential of Swedish heat pump development. The transformation of the Swedish heat pump sector can be summed up as the following: after passing through a period of formation characterized by exploring, testing and learning activities, the sector underwent a period of fluidity and complexity (Figure 11.4), where tensions were addressed through exploration and testing by an increasing number of actors. The following phase was initiated by the "reverse oil crisis" and failing heat pump markets. Developments outside of the heat pump industry also contributed to the continued technological development of heat pump technology after the "reverse oil crisis". These technological developments were followed by organizational and institutional alignment, resulting in an eventual completion of the heat pump development block and accelerated growth in supply capacity together with market growth, less network structure complexity and increased competition between heat pump manufacturers (Figure 11.5). The current state of the Swedish heat pump sector is characterized by incremental innovations and international competition.

The case of the industrial transformation of the Swedish heat pump industry has been conditioned by both local and international contextual conditions. Competences and resources in local incumbent industries were prerequisites for the formation of a Swedish heat pump development block, as was the influx of knowledge from international industries such as the air-conditioning and compressor industries. The development of technological complementarities in Sweden, such as heat exchangers and borehole drilling, was important for the Swedish heat pump development block, as was the availability of compressors on the international market. The downstream part of the development block, in particular, required adaptation to local conditions, resulting in some heat pump companies integrating vertically to take greater responsibility for installations and service offerings. Other downstream complementarities that demanded adaptation involved institutional alignments, such as regulatory changes and increased public awareness regarding heat pumps.

Using Dahmén's concepts has been useful to illustrate the industrial coevolution of the Swedish heat pump sector. Industrial coevolution can be illustrated as a series of structural tensions: one structural tension calls for the development and alignment of complementarities that can affect other complementarities, creating new tensions, which calls for the development of other complementarities, etc. For example, technological and organizational tensions regarding heat pumps in the 1970s contributed to institutional alignment supporting heat pumps in the 1980s (e.g. the 1980 building regulation), which, in turn, created a niche market for heat pumps that contributed to the resolution of technological tensions in the 1990s.

Lessons for policy makers from this chapter include the need for stable institutions and the preference for long-term support rather than short-term market subsidies to complete a development block. Policy changes that contributed to the eventual completion of the Swedish heat pump development block included regulations promoting heat pumps and the taxation of fossil fuels, which increased oil prices and made heat pumps more attractive. Government agencies have also contributed to testing and learning activities, knowledge dissemination and improved public awareness through R&D programmes, procurement competitions and testing programmes – important measures for balancing the downstream portion of the development block. On the other hand, several short-term subsidies and sudden policy changes have also caused major distress to the heat pump sector over the years. Examples of such policies are lifting support during the "reverse oil crisis", the sudden changes of regulations regarding refrigerants that contributed to the malfunction of several thousand heat pump compressors after the NUTEK competition and the on-and-off subsidies that created rapid changes in market demand, which the heat pump manufacturers had trouble meeting with adequate supply capacity. This points to the industrial development benefits from policy makers focusing on long-term rather than short-term policies and being responsive to current industry conditions.

Lessons from the transformation of the Swedish heat pump sector can also be applied to other sectors. For example, emerging solar PV sectors exhibit similarities to the Swedish heat pump sector. Both sectors have highly internationalized upstream markets for core components (compressors/silicon solar cells) and require well-functioning local installation and service networks. Lessons from the heat pump transformation point to the importance of developing complementary technologies to create a complete development block. For solar PV – which functions very differently than conventional energy technologies such as gas, coal and hydropower – this means development and investments in technologies such as inverters and technologies that can balance the variable output of solar PV cells. Lessons from the heat pump transformation also point to the importance of adaptation to the local context. For solar PV this means that organizational and institutional alignment downstream will likely be important factors for the completion of a solar PV development block.

Acknowledgements

I would like to thank the Swedish Energy Agency for making the writing of this chapter possible through their funding (grant number 44638-1).

Note

1 Statistics from SCB (Swedish Statistics) using code number KN 84186100 for the period 2006–2014, and code KN 84186190 for the period 1997–2005. According to INTRASTAT KN 2013, the code KN 84186100 is defined as "Heat pumps, other than air conditioning units as per no 8415" ('Värmepumpar, andra än luftkonditioneringsapparater enligt nr 8415'), which means that reversible air-water heat pumps are not included in these figures.

References

Abernathy, W. J. and Utterback, J. M. (1978) "Patterns of Industrial Innovation", *Technology Review*, June/July, pp. 40–47.

Anderson, P. and Tushman, M. L. (1990) "Technological Discontinuities and Dominant Designs: A Cyclical Model of Technological Change", *Administrative Science Quarterly*, 35(4), pp. 604–633. doi: 10.2307/2393511.

Bäckström, B., Flyckt, U., Lindqvist, G., Löndahl, G., Olson, H., Persson, P.-O., Engblom, C., Almqvist, E., Andersson, C.-O., Aspenberg, B., Bengtssson, G., Bratt, Å., Bäckström, B., Eriksson, S., Glas, L.-O., Granryd, E., Hagberg, S., Hempel, O., Heurlin, L., Holmström, P., Isaksson, B., Jacobson, L., Jonsson, K., Kjellqvist, Å., Larsson, S., Lindborg, A., Lindqvist, G., Lundberg, A., Lundvik, B., Löndahl, G., Nilsson, T. E., Olson, H., Person, L., Persson, P.-O., Rogmark, B., Strååt, H., Tallving, B., Tegner, G., Tyllström, I. and Weister, R. (1992) *Den svenska kylteknikens historia*. Edited by B. Bäckström, U. Flyckt, G. Lindqvist, G. Löndahl, H. Olson, P.-O. Persson, and C. Engblom. Solna: Carlson Press.

Bijker, W. E., Hughes, T. P. and Pinch, T. (1987) *The Social Construction of Technological Systems*. Cambridge, MA: MIT Press.

Boverket (2011) *Utvärdering av stödet för konvertering från direktverkande elvärme i bostadshus*. Karlskrona: Boverket.

Boverket (2014) *Regionala skillnader i bostadssektorn. Rapport 2014:2*. Karlskrona: Boverket.

Dahmén, E. (1950) *Svensk industriell företagarverksamhet : kausalanalys av den industriella utvecklingen 1919-1939, Bd 1*. Uppsala: Almqvist & Wiksells Boktryckeri AB.

Dahmén, E. (1991) *Development Blocks and Industrial Transformation. The Dahménian Approach to Economic Development*. Edited by B. Carlsson and R. G. H. Henriksson. Stockholm: Industrial Institute for Economic and Social Research.

Dosi, G. and Nelson, R. R. (1994) "An Introduction to Evolutionary Theories in Economics", *Journal of Evolutionary Economics*, 4, pp. 153–172.

EHPA (2014) *European Heat Pump Market and Statistics Report 2014: Executive Summary*. Available at: https://www.ehpa.org/fileadmin/red/07._Market_Data/2014/EHPA_European_Heat_Pump_Market_and_Statistics_Report_2015_-_executive_Summary.pdf.

Energiforskningsnämnden (1985) *Solvärme och värmepumpar. Efn-rapport nr 13*. Stockholm: Liber.

Engebeck, L. and Zingmark, A. (1987) *Utvärdering av investeringsprogrammet värmepumpar*. Gävle: Statens institut för byggnadsforskning.

Forsén, M. and Nowak, T. (2010) *Outlook 2010 - European Heat Pump Statistics*. Brussels: European Heat Pump Association EEIG (EHPA).

Fridlund, M. (1999) *Den gemensamma utvecklingen. Staten, storföretaget och samarbetet kring den svenska elkrafttekniken*. Stockholm: KTH Royal Institute of Technology.

Geels, F. W. (2004) "From Sectoral Systems of Innovation to Socio-Technical Systems", *Research Policy*, 33(6–7), pp. 897–920. doi: 10.1016/j.respol.2004.01.015.

Granryd, E. (2010) "Värmepumpens Historia", *VVS Forum. September 2010. Tema Värmepumpar*, September. Available at: http://www.e-magin.se/v5/viewer/files/viewer_s.aspx?gKey=p10v0g2r&gInitPage=21.

Hughes, T. P. (1983) *Networks of Power - Electrification in Western Society, 1880–1930*. Softshell. Baltimore, MD: Johns Hopkins University Press.

Jacobsson, S. and Bergek, A. (2011) "Innovation System Analyses and Sustainability Transitions: Contributions and Suggestions for Research", *Environmental Innovation and Societal Transitions*, 1(1), pp. 41–57. doi: 10.1016/j.eist.2011.04.006.

Johansson, P. (2017) *A Silent Revolution. The Swedish Transition towards Heat Pumps, 1970–2015.* KTH Royal Institute of Technology. Available at: https://kth.diva-portal.org/smash/get/diva2:1151181/FULLTEXT01.pdf.

Klepper, S. (1997) "Industry Life Cycles", *Industrial and Corporate Change*, 6(1), pp. 145–182. doi: 10.1093/icc/6.1.145.

Lindholm, H. (2011) *Svenska Värmepumpföreningen 30 år.* Katrineholm: SVEP Svenska Värmepumpföreningen.

Mogensen, P. (1979) "Experiences from Earth Heat Pumps in Sweden", in *Nordic Symposium on Earth Heat Pump Systems.* Göteborg: Earth Heat Pump Group CTH.

Nelson, R. R. (1994) "The Co-evolution of Technology, Industrial Structure, and Supporting Institutions", *Industrial and Corporate Change*, 3(1), pp. 47–63. doi: 10.1093/icc/3.1.47.

Palme, O. and Johansson, R. B. (1975) *Regeringens Proposition nr 30 år 1975.* Sweden: Sveriges Riksdag.

Plomgren, B. (1994) "Vattenfall vill värma svala intresset för värmepumpar", *EnergiTeknik*, December.

Russell, S., Rummeni, J., Kancheva, M., Kaniadakis, A., Larsson, A., Müller, U., Nordman, R., Russell, S., Stewart, J., Thonon, B., Tonev, T., Tyrberg, M. and Winkel, T. (2009) *Ground Source Heat Pumps - Preliminary Analysis of Industry Structures, Policies, Support Mechanisms and Promotion Campaigns in the ProHeatPump Partner Countries.* EIE/06/072.

Schön, L. (2012) *En modern svensk ekonomisk historia.* 3rd ed. Stockholm: SNS Förlag.

SKVP (2019) *Värmepumpsförsäljning.* Available at: https://skvp.se/aktuellt-o-opinion/statistik/varmepumpsforsaljning (Accessed: January 2, 2020).

The Swedish Energy Agency (2004) *Uppföljning av Teknikupphandling. Projektnamn: Värmepumpar. Diarienummer: 803576.* Eskilstuna: Swedish Energy Agency.

The Swedish Energy Agency (2013) *Energistatistik för småhus 2012. ES 2013:05.* Eskilstuna: Swedish Energy Agency.

The Swedish Energy Agency (2015) *Energy in Sweden 2015.* Eskilstuna: Swedish Energy Agency. Available at: http://www.energimyndigheten.se/globalassets/statistik/overgripande-rapporter/energy-in-sweden-till-webben.pdf.

Ullsten, O. and Tham, C. (1979) *Regeringens Proposition 1978/9:115.* Sweden: Sveriges Riksdag.

Utterback, J. M. (1994) *Mastering the Dynamics of Innovation.* Boston, MA: Harvard Business School Press.

Vattenfall (1978) *Lägesrapport från Vattenfalls värmepumpprogram.* Vällingby: Statens Vattenfallsverk.

Vattenfall (1981) *Forskning Utveckling Demonstration; 5-årsplan 1981.* Vällingby: Statens Vattenfallsverk.

Vattenfall (1989a) *Små Värmepumpar - Erfarenheter från Vattenfalls FUD-insatser 1979–1987.* Vällingby: Statens Vattenfallsverk.

Vattenfall (1989b) *Stora Värmepumpar - Erfarenheter från Vattenfalls FUD-insatser 1979–1987.* Vällingby: Statens Vattenfallsverk.

VVS-Tekniska Föreningen (1979) "VVS-Specialnummer värmepumpar", *Värmepumpar*, January.

Zogg, M. (2008) "History of Heat Pumps - Swiss Contributions and International Milestones", in *9th International IEA Heat Pump Conference*, Berne.

12

CONCLUSIONS

Magnus Holmén and Vicky Long

General remarks

This chapter addresses how to understand and conceptualize the phenomenon of industrial transformation by discussing lessons from this book. The chapter first provides some general remarks on industrial transformation, followed by a discussion of the relationship between technology and the control of purposive activities by means of organization and digitalization. The chapter concludes by drawing on the seminal work of Allyn Young (1928) to explain how demand changes, digitalization and industrial transformation coevolve cumulatively.

This book has explored and explained industrial transformation, paying attention to the role of technological change and the role of digitalization while highlighting the importance of environmental sustainability as a driver and outcome of industrial transformation. While much of the digitalization literature may be categorized as supply push and the sustainability literature may be categorized as demand pull, industrial transformation is viewed across this book's chapters as consisting of different types of changes in the structure of industrial activities. Individual chapters have analysed the mechanisms or determinants of industrial transformation such as innovative activities and the creation, diffusion and use of knowledge.

More precisely, this book views industrial transformation as consisting of qualitative changes in the *structure of inter-firm activities and relations* when they create, produce and deliver value in terms of products or services for customers or users. This means that industrial transformation consists of changes in the structure of relations between firms, with other types of organizations or with customers. These changes are constituted as changes in the system of activities on the meso level, and consequently, the creation, renewal or termination of organizationally and technologically useful capabilities. One typical aspect of industrial transformation relates to changes in the Youngian division of labour between firms, with new types of specialization emerging, enabled by increases in the size of the market. Other important aspects of industrial transformation include downstream firms' downstream movements, diversification into related markets and technological and industrial convergence.

Viewed in this manner, industrial transformation is important on the macro level because of its impact on society and the economy, not to mention labour markets and individuals. In addition, industrial transformation is important for the micro level because firm managers may need to initiate and respond to industrial transformation. None of these are industrial transformation per se, however. Instead, the goal of the book is to contribute to a better understanding and explanation of the processes of industrial transformation in relation to digitalization and sustainability rather than the magnitude and effects of industrial transformation for society and firms. In so doing, this book combines a nomothetic ambition in the sense of aiming to find general patterns and an idiographic approach in that it analyses contingent, case-specific aspects. An obvious aspect of the latter is stressing the importance of identifying and understanding the actors themselves as they engage, react to and drive industrial transformation.

Given this, it is not surprising that the book chapters draw on rich bodies of literature that analyse and explain industrial transformation. Broadly speaking, the literature includes evolutionary economics, institutional economics and development economics, economic history and history of technology, industrial dynamics studies, innovation systems, (sustainability) transition literature, ecosystems, industry life cycles, industrial networks and organizational and management studies (see Chapter 2). It covers fields like neo-Schumpeterian studies and concepts such as increasing returns, cumulative causation and development blocks. Publications in these bodies of literature have demonstrated the shortcomings of how mainstream or neo-Walrasian economics characterize changes in the economy pertinent to the meso level (for critiques, see Nelson and Winter, 1982, 2002; Mirowski, 1989; Beinhocker, 2006; Loasby, 2001). In fact, such critiques are so rich and well understood that the book bypasses this issue and instead focuses on the lessons for analysing industrial transformation per se.

The terminology *industrial transformation* may invoke the idea that it refers to changes in a well-defined industry, and perhaps most commonly a manufacturing sector such as the automotive industry. This view is not erroneous, but our understanding of industrial transformation is broader. The term industry in this book is not limited to a population of manufacturing firms, or an ex ante well-defined population of firms creating, producing and disseminating similar products or services for adjacent markets. Our focus is on the meso level, where several transacting, innovating, competing and collaborating actors create, realize and capture value. These activities may lead to ongoing fluctuations and changes of firm and industrial boundaries, which means that industrial transformation is open ended. In other words, economic growth and development – and the extent of the entry and exit – can be described at the macro level but they cannot be explained at that level.

The book covers sectors beyond manufacturing goods that are useful to outline the variety and similarity of sectors. For example, the home care sector (see Chapter 4) shares many characteristics with other service sectors, exemplified by the simultaneity of supply and consumption. However, there is a peculiarity in that the adoption and adaptation of new technologies are slow and cumbersome in the home care sector – and the healthcare sector in general – because of ethical considerations and a high degree of regulation. Another peculiarity lies in reimbursement, where consumers (patients) in many countries do not directly pay for healthcare services, as much of this is handled by government or insurance companies. Such aspects have large implications in terms of who should make decisions, who will do the job, and consequently, the speed of change.

Industrial transformation may refer to one or several relational changes along a value stream of adjacent industries, upstream and downstream movements of firms and changes in the locus of innovation and appropriability. For example, the rise of online and mobile gaming has changed the types of products and services established game developers and publishers provide, and in part, it has broken up the industrial structure by changing the relationships and importance of publishers and retailers in the value chain. Typically, the old type of actors such as the bricks-and-mortar distributors are disappearing and publishers are taking new roles.

At times, other actors than firms, such as public organizations, non-governmental organizations, universities, customers and users, can become main actors of industrial transformation. The rich plethora of variants of industrial transformation is, of course, an explanation of why studies of industrial transformation are informed by many bodies of literature, and why it hardly can or should be analysed or explained from only one perspective.

Industrial transformation study as specified in this book fits in the tradition of industrial dynamics initiated by the Danish Research Unit for Industrial Dynamics (DRUID) in 1996, as both address the causes of industrial development including the dynamics of industries and the role of entrepreneurship, knowledge, technological change and public policy in the development process (Carlsson and Lundvall, 1998; Carlsson, 2016). There are differences, however. One difference between industrial dynamics and industrial transformation is how to understand, analyse and explain changes. While industrial dynamics addresses competition and collaboration at the firm level (e.g. firm boundaries), in this book, we argue that a transformation study often needs to move down to the value chain level to analyse and explain transformation. The value-chain and value-creation literatures are traditionally approached by (business model) strategy scholars (see Teece, 1986; Pisano and Teece, 2007). Another difference is that industrial transformation studies focus on the historical process of the transformation and looks at the determinants and consequences of each step of changes from diverse perspectives. In other words, the latter is prone to a causal mechanism approach, to peer into the box of causality to identify the intermediate factors explaining the effect.

We stress that industrial transformation consists of and needs to be understood as *qualitative* state changes in the relations and interactions among firms. One example of a pervasive change in inter-firm or inter-organizational relations is the shift from serially organized value chains to platform-based ecosystems and multisided markets that allow for direct interaction between customers and (formerly) upstream actors.

Of course, for a transformation to be economically significant, the qualitative changes need to correspond to quantitative changes in, for example, the evolving number of actors (entry/exit), industry turnover, R&D and innovation intensity, total cost, marginal or unit cost or the number of staff or professions. However, industrial transformation cannot and should not be reduced to mere quantitative changes (see Potts, 2000). This implies that industrial transformation processes refer to endogenous activities and qualitative changes, such as innovation, learning, collaboration and competition. Indeed, while industrial transformation refers to state changes in the structure of the relations and activities of the actors, each of the book chapters emphasizes the importance of the *dynamics* of industrial transformation.

Dynamics may be interpreted as exogenous changes only, in line with the interpretation in the field ontologies in many scientific or engineering disciplines. In contrast, processes of industrial transformation need to be understood largely, but not only as endogenous, uncertain, open-ended and non-teleological. By endogenous, we mean that the motivations, cognitive framing, activities and capabilities of the actors are the main aspects that initiate, shape and terminate industrial transformation. This stands in stark contrast to focusing on the role of government or institutions, which are normally positioned outside a sector. Examples of endogenous changes include how firms may recognize and act upon innovative or entrepreneurial opportunities, or by participating in a Red Queen race, where they need to innovate to sustain their competitive position. Such recognition is often based on an actor interpreting changes and events that are external to the industry. Thus, we do not deny the crucial importance of exogenous changes, say changes in institutions, in scientific breakthroughs, natural disasters or pandemics such as Covid-19, or changes in demand, which trigger and guide the processes of industrial transformation. In other words, actors sometimes make exogenous changes endogenous to the industry, which then shapes the direction and rate of transformation.

By uncertainty, we mean that for transformation processes it is difficult or impossible for actors to ascertain when to attempt to change behaviour, how to do it and what the outcome of a potential transformation of an industry will be. Many concepts outline specific aspects of the inability to predict, such as bounded rationality, which states that while humans are rational, they will not be able to capture all information, or the fallibility of induction or black swan events, which states there can always be a novelty not encompassed within an explanation derived from data. Indeed, Knightian uncertainty specifies that there are and will always be limits to knowledge. This means that in the general case, transformation processes do not result in a predetermined end-state. For example, processes of product, process, application and market diversification may allow for new uses of technologies. Ex ante, it is impossible to list all the new uses that a genius, average Joe or Jane or madman may find in the future of a technology, especially when combined with other technologies, or what new ideas they will identify based on previously ignored or poorly understood traits of the technology (exaptation).

Moreover, user and other types of feedback shape and guide progress, but this guidance is neither fully predictive nor completely erratic. This means that precisely which activities will transform an industry and how that process will unfold can only be found ex post. Industrial transformation, just like the outcome of any evolutionary processes, is not determined ex ante, but rather is shaped by Knightian (true) uncertainty and where change begets change and knowledge begets knowledge (see, for example, Hanusch and Pyke, 2007). Thus, novelties within the industry may lead to new novelties, at times combined with external novelties. The fact that change is not predictable with full certainty does not mean that all is lost, however. There will be patterns in the transformation that much of the time will allow actors to adapt their behaviour reasonably well.

Transformation may be argued as an outcome of a combination of reactive and proactive approaches. Being reactive here may be broadly understood as a problem-solving approach. The transformation of the pulp-and-paper industry, such as Stora Enso's shift from newspaper-centred production to bio-composite (e.g. recyclable plastics) and bio-refinery (e.g. viscose for clothes) production, for example, is an outcome of being reactive to the downturn of newspaper demand (due to the rise of digital news), and of being proactive to the sustainability agenda. The actual shift – to a concrete production line – is a process of trial and error, which is impossible to foresee, at least in detail.

Industrial transformation is open ended, meaning that precisely which actors influence the meso level such as a well-defined industry or value stream (chain) is likely to vary over time. A mechanism is that boundedly rational actors search for novelties that may renew the industry in a path-dependent and/or path-creating manner. Their search is based on their experiences, aspirations and capabilities. The heterogeneity of actors and changes in their relations in turn may itself be an important endogenous source of novelty. Well-known examples include the entry of new firms where former outsiders influence an industry, or when incumbents change behaviour because they form new alliances or networks or exploit weak ties.

Technology and digitalization

To understand the role that technology and technological change plays in industrial transformation better, we briefly recapitulate how technological changes affect industrial transformation. The focus is on digitization, which converts analogue information into a digital format, and digitalization, how actors explore and exploit ICT to change their products or services, processes, business models, customer communication and interaction.

All industries are affected by digitalization. This is not surprising given that ICT may radically change what a firm or an individual consumer can find, analyse, use or know. We briefly recapitulate the changing role of ICT. First, while advances in computing technologies continue to be impressive, ICT should not only be thought of as cumulative improvements based on chip design and manufacturing, as in Moore's law, or in the growth of created and used software programs, such as mobile applications (apps), but also as facilitating the explosion of sensors (e.g. cameras, the IoT) that automatically or manually (voluntarily) dramatically expand data accessibility for a range of applications, user situations and users. Examples of more recent types of common sensors include phone cameras, surveillance cameras or radio frequency identification. These sensors and actuators are just as important as the ongoing proliferation of computing devices, such as computers, mobiles or tablets. Thus, digitalization needs to be understood as partly driven by the coevolution of computer hardware, software applications, sensors and data captured by sensors or humans. This can be illustrated by the rapid growth of the development and use of ML, where complementary improvements in data collection and access, and faster hardware form a basis for rapid diffusion of ML (see Chapter 7).

Second, and partly because of the first point, digitalization has moved beyond the focus on improving technology per se to deal with how to apply and use ICT from an individual, organizational and industrial perspective. For example, digitalization may lower barriers to industrial entry and allow for early stage experimentation leading to changes in skills, expectations and knowledge development for firms and organizations or utility for consumers. Recent examples include additive manufacturing or 3D printing, which lowers the cost and difficulty of becoming a producer, or digital distribution for online games such as Steam or the Apple Apps Store, which lowers the entry barrier for small indie developers.

Therefore, it is hardly surprising that views on how to improve the usefulness of ICT have changed dramatically over the years, moving away from a focus on hardware to software-related problems, and more recently into to the realms of networking and of platform, communication and applied data analytics, which stresses the relationship of ICT with users. Several book chapters have analysed how digitalization affects what individuals or organizations can do in the sense that they can do more now than was previously possible, without needing to master the knowledge required for performing those tasks. This may lead to exponentially improved abilities to search, which may change the Smithian or Youngian divisions of labour (i.e. the division of labour within an organization or between firms). Specifically, digitalization is shaped by the emergence of new roundabout or indirect methods of production (Young, 1928), in which new capital goods are created and used across a range of activities and sectors. Examples include new software tools or platforms that may be used for a number of activities, or R&D equipment, such as computer-based simulations or analyses of wind tunnel experiments, which is used as a complement to or even substitute for real-life experiments while developing aeroplanes or cars. In short, digitalization has changed what a firm can control in terms of its activities and relations, and how it controls them.

Digitalization and the control revolution

By drawing on the lessons from the individual chapters, we now discuss the relationship between technology, control and industrial transformation. Digitalization plays a key role in the transformation of industries, for example, in terms of changes in the Youngian division of labour, i.e. changes in the specializations of firms and changes in user–producer relations such as the rise of cocreation. Increasing returns from production and adoption provide a key explanation for why digitalization is such a powerful mechanism of industrial transformation.

Increasing returns come in many forms. For the sake of simplicity, we may say that increasing returns from production may consist of economies of scale and scope of production and distribution. Three aspects of increasing returns are (a) a larger scale of operation at a given time leading to lower unit costs; (b) experience curves, which means that costs are lower given the accumulation of production over time; and (c) network effects, which increase the likelihood and value of entering a specific standard the greater the number of users the particular standard already has.

Increasing returns from production and adoption may both freeze and unfreeze the structure and activities of industries by determining the basic costs and usefulness of adopting a technology. On the one hand, over time, economies of scale and scope of production and distribution, learning curves and network effects may lead to a lock-in of industrial leadership, but on the other hand, entries of new firms, innovations or new sources of increasing returns may break up leading positions.

The extent and nature of how increasing returns act as a powerful driver of industrial transformation are in part determined by their coevolution with uncertainty. Uncertainty is here understood as some fundamental ignorance and when some events are unpredictable in advance. This means that uncertainty stands in contrast to risk, which refers to a quantity susceptible to measurement such as the statistical likelihood of a specific outcome (Knight, 1921).

Uncertainty imposes a limit on increasing returns, where, for example, economies of scale are limited by the scale of operations that are technologically and economically feasible given, say, the ability of technology to scale and function, or irregular fluctuations in demand. For example, as the scale of operation increases, there will be a time of crisis of control, where the current organization and technologies are unable to deal with the larger scale of activities.

Fortunately, even if uncertainty can never be fully eliminated, many types of uncertainty can be managed or reduced by increasing *control*. Control may be defined as "purposive influence toward a predetermined goal", which involves ongoing comparisons between future goals and current states (Beniger, 1986, p. 6). Control may be imposed by changes in organization, technology or institutions, such as legislation or instituted industrial patterns (Chandler, 1990). Beniger (1986) argues that the emergence of the information society is critically dependent on its ability to increase control of the uncertainty involving the evolution of industrialization. However, qualitative changes such as product or market innovations, or quantitative changes in the scale and scope of the operation of firms, industry or any meso-level activities, put pressure on the existing means of control and may lead to a crisis of control (Beniger, 1986; Björkdahl and Holmén, 2019). To manage a crisis of control, a situation where uncertainty and complexity grow beyond the ability of managers to adapt, managers need to reorganize and implement new routines or adopt or adapt new control technologies.

Problems related to control become a managerial focusing device to reimpose control (Hughes, 1983). The successive advances in means of control were described by Beniger (1986) as the control revolution, and these can include ICT advances (Davies, 1996; Nightingale et al., 2003). An important consequence of the digitalization-driven control revolution is that firms may move downstream because of the need to change business models to profit from their innovations (Björkdahl and Holmén, 2019) or move towards new positions in an ecosystem because changes in control affect industrial barriers in terms of needs of resources or complementary assets (cf. Teece, 1986). This means that digitalization is a powerful mechanism driving the control revolution, and consequently, industrial transformation.

We can illustrate this by discussing industrial transformation by drawing on the lessons of the book. A simple way to characterize industrial activities is to distinguish between research, design and development (RD&D) and production and distribution. RD&D consists of engineered and artistic ways of creating novelty in products, processes and services. For example, Chapter 6 studied the Icelandic film industry over 40 years, focusing on the composition, performance and recording of movies and film music. The chapter showed that there have been large shifts in uncertainty barriers because of digitization and digitalization, meaning that the boundaries of innovative and routine work were changed. An example is that key decisions often become centralized and postponed until late in the process because digital technologies allow designers to control larger numbers of activities (data). At the same time, work was increasingly distributed in space.

Chapter 5, which analysed the transformation of the division of innovative labour in software creation, demonstrated these findings more generally. The chapter showed that the nature of development per se is changing because the technology of software creation has changed into an infrastructure, allowing for the abstraction of hardware, application domains, database architectures and billions of messy details. This means that software developers can focus on working on specific aspects while ignoring most others, often without even being aware they exist. Of course, abstractions are not all-powerful, as increased complexity and ignoring potential issues may lead to poorly functioning systems. Indeed, over the years, there have been multiple crises of control in software creation, such as the rise of bugs, the proliferation of viruses, single points of failure and budget overruns. Nonetheless, over time, the control by new modes of organization, such as open source or agile programming, and technological improvements in automated testing and higher-level languages have allowed for increased control over galaxies of abstraction.

As Chapter 7 showed, an overlapping and related change is the use of new tools and techniques for data analysis, such as ML. Such technologies allow for analysing large quantities of data in terms of size, variety and frequency and finding new, hitherto unknown relations in the data. More precisely, shifts in the locus of bottlenecks, illustrated by AI or ML, which allow for better control of the analysis of large quantities of data, may prevent or at least postpone the crisis in control of receiving too much information. Thus, ML and other, presumably less disruptive, technologies should enable industrial transformation.

Of course, changes are characterized by much turbulence because of technological, managerial, organizational, relational, institutional and/or policy failures, but still, during the last decades, shifts towards a larger scope have taken place. The Janus face of doing more by knowing less (of the whole) and increasing control have thus characterized how digitalization affects and drives industrial transformation.

Digitalization has, of course, changed production and distribution too. A key example is how industries have emerged and been transformed by the rise of physical and digital extra-organizational platforms. A platform refers to a set of components, which is a part of a larger system of modules or applications (Baldwin, 2008). The platform is of low variability, while modules provide the opportunities to customise and flexibly alter the functions of a platform-based offer. The automotive sector has reaped economies of scale and scope by creating and exploiting platforms internal to particular firms, but they have also made these platforms available to suppliers. More recently (see Chapters 3 and 8), platforms have allowed for changing from value streams to digital business ecosystems, where the platform is controlled by a company (or a set of companies). Platforms have allowed for unbundling value propositions in time and space. For example, online retailing allows customers to purchase products anywhere at any time, and not at the convenience of retailers or wholesalers.

Platform ecosystems have many specific features of control. They allow for the cocreation of users and producers, where much interaction is mediated and controlled by the platform and the platform owners. Upstream actors may move downstream, interact and transact with consumers and firms with customers or firms previously outside their reach. An intended side-effect is that platform owners ultimately control what is permissible on their platforms. In many sectors, competition is increasingly between platforms, as firms use platforms to compete and collaborate with complementors.

Technology is an important factor in industrial transformation. While Chapter 6 illustrated that many technologies simply reinforce old behaviour, Chapter 4 (Welfare) showed that quite small technological changes may fundamentally alter who the actors are, what they do, their responsibilities and their roles. For example, allowing elderly people with mental illnesses freedom to go out may be ethically and physically wise, but it also invites accidents and, at times, life-threatening situations because of weather or traffic. Increasing control by means of GPS devices, allowing for locating such people, may solve many of the potential issues, but it also requires entirely new routines for relationships among healthcare providers and family, none of which may be easy to solve.

In some ways, the distinction between RD&D and production and distribution is flawed. Film production may be characterized as belonging to changes in RD&D (design), but production is also changing from the physical domain into an increasingly digital domain, where design and production may be difficult to separate. The same holds true for production and distribution, as digitalization may change both. For much creative work, the distribution of production can be understood as the division and integration of innovative labour, and it must now allow for production across the globe.

Changes in control do not depend solely on digitalization. Chapter 11 analysed changes in system boundaries, where increased control due to institutional changes such as the emergence of independent testing has verified that products fulfil standards and quality requirements. This has allowed for the sector to recover from a poor reputation and grow by regaining customer and supplier confidence. Institutions and technological innovations are also crucial in other sectors (see Chapter 10), as they are the foundation for what can be extracted and whether a well can be found and exploited profitably. Technological innovations have strengthened the existing structure, and they allow for oil and gas exploration in increasingly challenging situations and regions, such as offshore searches for deposits or the Arctic. While improved technological control by means of ICT may not transform the industry as such, arguably, improved technology is necessary for the exploration and exploitation to take place, or at the very least, to be cost competitive. However, we stress that technology by itself does not cause digital transformation; at times, it reinforces routines and firm specializations.

Digitalization and the process of industrial transformation

In our view, Young's (1928) seminal work on increasing returns and economic progress, which connects growth of demand, changes in the division of labour between firms and productivity improvement, is an excellent starting point for understanding how digitalization shapes industrial transformation. Digitalization may lead to increasing returns. For example, due to the learning effects of digitalization, the more users or producers use or produce a product, the better they tend to perform. More precisely, Young (1928) argued that the growth of the final market increases the potential for reorganizing the division of labour between firms. In turn, new specializations in firms may improve productivity, because they may allow for increased learning by specialization, better alignment between motivation, capabilities and resources and job tasks, and reductions in costs when switching activities. A specific case is the increased affordability of roundabout (indirect) methods of production, understood as longer chains of activities, each of which may allow automation, such as machine tools, sensor-based monitoring or software development tools. This, in turn, induces opportunities for innovation.

A related phenomenon is technological convergence, which is a specific mechanism that increases the size of the market (Rosenberg, 1969). Technological convergence is when problem-solving skills and technology become used in a new context (industry). Spin-offs or entrants may create a new upstream division of labour consisting of a supplier industry servicing a downstream market. Technological convergence increases the size of the market and allows for exploiting economies of scale and scope.

Over time, a positive feedback loop (virtuous cycle) of increased demand may lead to an increased or changed specialization that improves productivity, lowers costs and generates financial resources that can be invested to expand the market further. This may create a positive feedback cycle between demand and supply, which may increase the market.

It should be noted that while Young was trying to explain economic progress rather than the progress of a specific industry, his explanation around the organization of the industry in terms of new divisions of labour among firms is a meso-level phenomenon. The same can be said about the size of the final market. He did not, however, provide much help for better analysing and explaining the meso-level phenomena, such as value chains or value streams, industrial networks or business or innovation ecosystems, which can be used to outline the structure of innovation, production, distribution and use more forcefully. Here, we do this by briefly comparing the Youngian explanation with the role of digitalization across the book's chapters, which cover RD&D, manufacturing and distribution.

Undoubtedly, there have been increases in the size of the market for the analysed industries, such as in the energy sector (heat pumps, oil and gas extraction), housing and retailing, and the same also holds true for the markets for software and data analytics tools and services. For several of the industries, we can observe an increased Youngian division of labour, which has been followed by a consolidation of the main actors, such as software tools, film, retailing or heat pumps. Other aspects seem not to have consolidated into fewer actors, even though multinational firms are forcefully moving into the area of ML and welfare. At the same time, new specializations have emerged for each of the areas, consisting of, for example, specialized digital tools and resources.

Technological convergence is very strong in terms of digitalization, but also in terms of other technologies. Obvious points are the increased use of software and both digital and physical platforms for all the analysed industries. Software creation, and its associated tools and skills, are used in both upstream and downstream industries. In the same manner, technological convergence is driven by platforms that coordinate distribution, transportation and transactions across a whole range of industries. The tools and the platforms control the interaction with the hardware and the realm of possible interaction with other individuals or firms but leave other aspects open. Thus, the control is predetermined and specific but also flexible.

An interesting difference between different industries may be inferred from the chapters, however, in terms of cumulative causation. For the technological areas of software creation and ML, there is an ongoing and expected positive feedback between demand, innovation and production. For oil and gas, and the well-established industries of book publishing, retailing and logistics, these processes have been going on for a long time, and they are partly driven by digitalization and the rise of digital platforms. There seems to be a different story for welfare and housing. Here, regulation constrains the market and limits the use of digital technologies, which limits innovation and experimentation. Here, progress is much slower, despite the efforts of multinational firms to enter these areas.

References

Baldwin, C. (2008) Where Do Transactions Come From? Modularity, Transactions, and the Boundaries of Firms, *Industrial and Corporate Change*, 17(1), 155–195.

Beinhocker, E. D. (2006) *Origin of Wealth: Evolution, Complexity, and the Radical Remaking of Economics*. Harvard Business Review Press, Boston, MA.

Beniger, J. R. (1986) *The Control Revolution. Technological and Economic Origins of the Information Society*. Harvard University Press, Cambridge, MA.

Björkdahl, J., and Holmén, M. (2019) Exploiting the Control Revolution by Means of Digitalization: Value Creation, Value Capture and Downstream Movements, *Industrial and Corporate Change*, 28(3), 423–426. doi: 10.1093/icc/dty022

Carlsson, B. (2016) Industrial Dynamics: A Review of the Literature 1990–2009, *Industry and Innovation*, 23(1), 1–61. doi: 10.1080/13662716.2015.1120658

Carlsson, B., and Lundvall, B.-Å. (1998) Industrial Dynamics Revisited: What Have We Learned? *Paper presented at the DRUID Conference on "Competencies, Governance and Entrepreneurship"*, Bornholm, Denmark, June 9–11.

Chandler, A. (1990) *Scale and Scope: The Dynamics of Industrial Capitalism*. Harvard University Press, Cambridge, MA.

Davies, A. (1996) Innovation in Large Technical Systems: The Case of Telecommunications, *Industrial and Corporate Change*, 5(4), 1143–1180.

Hanusch, H., and Pyke, A. (eds.) (2007) *Elgar Companion to Neo-Schumpeterian Economics*. Edvard Elgar, Cheltenham.

Hughes, T. P. (1983) *Networks of Power: Electrification in Western Society, 1880–1939.* John Hopkins University Press, Baltimore, MD.
Knight, F. (1921) *Risk, Uncertainty and Profit.* Hart, Schaffner & Marx; Houghton Mifflin Co., Boston, MA.
Loasby, B. (2001) Time, Knowledge and Evolutionary Dynamics: Why Connections Matter, *Journal of Evolutionary Economics*, 11, 393–412.
Mirowski, P. (1989) *More Heat than Light: Economics as Social Physics, Physics as Nature's Economics.* Cambridge University Press, Cambridge.
Nelson, R., and Winter, S. G. (1982) *An Evolutionary Theory of Economic Change.* The Belknap Press of Harvard University Press, Cambridge, MA.
Nelson, R., and Winter, S. J. (2002) Evolutionary Theorizing in Economics, *Journal of Economic Perspectives*, 16(2), 23–46.
Nightingale, P., Brady, T., Davies, A., and Hall, J. (2003) Capacity Utilization Revisited: Software, Control and the Growth of Large Technical Systems, *Industrial and Corporate Change*, 12(3), 477–517.
Pisano, G. P., and Teece, D. J. (2007) How to Capture Value from Innovation: Shaping Intellectual Property and Industry Architecture, *California Management Review*, 50(1), 278–296.
Potts, J. (2000) *The New Evolutionary Microeconomics: Complexity, Competence and Adaptive Behaviour.* Edvard Elgar, Cheltenham.
Rosenberg, N. (1969) The Direction of Technological Change: Inducement Mechanisms and Focusing Devices, *Economic Development and Cultural Change*, 18(1) Part 1, 1–24.
Teece, D. (1986) Profiting from Technological Innovation, *Research Policy*, 15(6), 285–305.
Young, A. (1928) Increasing Returns and Economic Progress, *The Economic Journal*, 38(152), 527–547.

INDEX

**Page numbers in bold reference tables.
**Page numbers in italics reference figures.

For Product Safety Concerns and Information please contact our EU
representative GPSR@taylorandfrancis.com
Taylor & Francis Verlag GmbH, Kaufingerstraße 24, 80331 München, Germany

www.ingramcontent.com/pod-product-compliance
Ingram Content Group UK Ltd.
Pitfield, Milton Keynes, MK11 3LW, UK
UKHW020148200926
475702UK00016B/2606
* 9 7 8 1 1 3 8 3 9 0 0 3 4 *